THE WRITINGS OF
WILL ROGERS
III-4

SPONSORED BY

The Will Rogers Memorial Commission
and Oklahoma State University

THE WRITINGS OF WILL ROGERS

SERIES   I: *Books of Will Rogers*
        1 *Ether and Me, or "Just Relax"*
        2 *There's Not a Bathing Suit in Russia & Other Bare Facts*
        3 *The Illiterate Digest*
        4 *The Cowboy Philosopher on The Peace Conference*
        5 *The Cowboy Philosopher on Prohibition*
        6 *Letters of a Self-Made Diplomat to His President*

SERIES II: *Convention Articles of Will Rogers*
        (in one volume)

SERIES III: *Daily Telegrams of Will Rogers*
        1 *Coolidge Years 1926-1929*
        2 *Hoover Years 1929-1931*
        3 *Hoover Years 1931-1933*
        4 **Roosevelt Years 1933-1935**

SERIES IV: *Weekly Articles of Will Rogers*
        (in four volumes)

SERIES V: *The Worst Story I've Heard Today*
        (in one volume)

OTHER VOLUMES TO BE ANNOUNCED

WILL ROGERS MEMORIAL COMMISSION

James C. Leake, *Chairman*
Roy G. Cartwright
Edward L. Byrd
Irving Fisher
Harry Hoagland
David R. Milsten
Will Rogers, Jr.

Governor George Nigh, *ex-officio*

MEMORIAL STAFF

Reba Neighbors Collins,
Curator
Delmar Collins,
Manager

SPECIAL CREDIT

The late Paula McSpadden Love
Curator, 1938-73

OSU ADVISORY COMMITTEE

George A. Gries, *Chairman*
W. David Baird
Howard R. Jarrell
Edward P. Pharr
Roscoe Rouse
William A. Sibley

President Lawrence L. Boger, *ex-officio*

EDITORIAL CONSULTANTS

Ray B. Browne, *Bowling Green State University*
LeRoy H. Fischer, *Oklahoma State University*
Wilbur R. Jacobs, *University of California, Santa Barbara*
Howard L. Lamar, *Yale University*
Russel B. Nye, *Michigan State University*

Will Rogers'
DAILY TELEGRAMS

JAMES M. SMALLWOOD, *EDITOR*

Steven K. Gragert, *Assistant Editor*

Volume 4
THE ROOSEVELT YEARS: 1933-1935

OKLAHOMA STATE UNIVERSITY PRESS
Stillwater, Oklahoma
1979

© 1979 Oklahoma State University Press

Printed in the United States of America
Library of Congress Catalog Card Number 77-91791
International Standard Book Number 0-914956-13-2

CONTENTS

INTRODUCTION   xiii

Daily Telegrams 1933   1

Daily Telegrams 1934   123

Daily Telegrams 1935   259

NOTES   349

INDEX   445

Illustrations courtesy
Will Rogers Memorial
Claremore, Oklahoma

INTRODUCTION

In this volume, the fourth and last in Series III of *The Writings of Will Rogers,* the Daily Telegrams of the famed humorist, cowboy-philosopher are continued. The first volume of Rogers' widely syndicated daily newspaper column, which appeared from 1926 until his death in 1935, spanned the latter years of the presidency of Calvin Coolidge. The second volume covered the first two years of the administration of Herbert C. Hoover. The third release spanned the latter half of Hoover's presidency. Herein are found the telegrams published during the administration of Franklin D. Roosevelt (until the death of Will Rogers on August 15, 1935).

The origins of Rogers' columns and a discussion of his methods of preparing them are found in the introduction to this series in Volume I. Similarly, therein the editors described their general guidelines, objectives, and procedures for endnote annotations. There were few editorial innovations in the second or third volumes and few in this, the fourth release. The editors once again have reproduced Rogers' telegrams as they appeared in original, syndicated form.

Rogers' telegrams were accepted by most newspaper editors with little revision of the original drafts. Yet, a selected textual analysis reveals that slight variations appeared. When some editors saw certain phrases of which they disapproved, they deleted them; others edited references to political personalities; still others "blue-penciled" lines simply for brevity. Because Rogers' work was in some cases slightly altered, our editorial task in Volume IV remains difficult—few original copies of the telegrams survive. Consequently, in this release we have continued to follow the guidelines established in Volume I. We have chosen the best available source for presentation. In most cases we have followed the *New York Times,* the newspaper which ran most of the articles and which is the most convenient for the use of future researchers. Other newspapers were consulted, however. When textual differences appeared, we attempted to show at least one major variation, selected from among the *Los Angeles Times,* the *Boston Daily Globe,* and the *Kansas City Times,* other newspapers which carried most of the telegrams.

Much of Rogers' humor was of a topical nature, geared to the happenings of his day. He sometimes referred to events which are not common knowledge to the present generation. He also referred to individuals who need identification. Consequently, endnotes have been used to identify people or explain events which would no longer be widely known. The editors, together with the editorial board and advisory committee of the Will Rogers Project, have decided to delete footnote numbers in the text to avoid needless distractions to the reader. Endnotes to the volume are "keyed" to the number of the telegrams and to the dates of their appearance.

The publication of *The Writings of Will Rogers* continues to require considerable effort on the part of many people. As always, since the inception of the Will Rogers Research Project, Will Rogers, Jr., and Reba Neighbors Collins, Curator of the Will Rogers Memorial, read the manuscript carefully and offered valuable advice for the endnotes. Glenn D. Shirley's editorial advice and designs for the books are greatly appreciated. Oklahoma State University President Lawrence L. Boger and Dean George A. Gries have provided encouragement. Special appreciation also is expressed for the continued support of the Will Rogers Memorial Commission, the Regents, administration, and advisory committee of Oklahoma State University, the Oklahoma Historical Society, the Oklahoma State Regents for Higher Education, and the Oklahoma Legislature. Earlier in this project the Kerr-McGee Foundation, the Phillips Petroleum Corporation, Mr. and Mrs. Robert W. Love, Mrs. T. S. Loffland, and Mr. Sylvan N. Goldman provided assistance. The editors also wish to acknowledge the assistance provided by Patty F. Nelson, secretary for the Will Rogers Project who typed the manuscript.

James M. Smallwood
Steven K. Gragert

DAILY TELEGRAMS
1933-1935

DAILY TELEGRAMS — 1933

2054   WILL ROGERS SEES THE NATION UNITED AND EVEN HAPPY AGAIN

SANTA MONICA, Cal., March 5.—America hasn't been as happy in three years as they are today.

No money, no banks, no work, no nothing, but they know they got a man in there who is wise to Congress, wise to our big bankers and wise to our so-called big men.

The whole country is with him. Even if what he does is wrong they are with him. Just so he does something. If he burned down the Capitol we would cheer and say, "Well, we at least got a fire started anyhow." We have had years of "Don't rock the boat," go on and sink it if you want to, we just as well be swimming as like we are.

Yours,
Will Rogers.

2055   MR. ROGERS HAILS THE ADVENT OF A SUBSTITUTE FOR MONEY

BEVERLY HILLS, Cal., March 6. — Everybody is all excited over "scrip." We are all for it. The way it sounds all you need is a fountain pen and a prescription blank. That's what we been looking for for years, a substitute for money.

Say this Roosevelt is a fast worker. Even on Sunday when all a President is supposed to do is put on a silk hat and have his picture taken coming out of church, why this President closed all the banks and called Congress in extra session, and that's not all he is going to call 'em either if they don't get something done.

Yours,
Will Rogers.

P. S. — So come on with your scrip. The psychology of the stuff not being actual money is going to make everybody want to buy something.

2056   WILL ROGERS WRITES EPITAPHS FOR TWO GREAT AMERICANS

BEVERLY HILLS, Cal., March 7. — "I am glad it was me instead of you, Mr. President."

I hope they use that. No tombstone in America could carry a finer tribute. His courage, his fighting spirit were great, but most of all his devotion to his family during his battle for life endeared Mayor Cermak to his adopted country.

On another train returning home forever goes Tom Walsh to Montana. His epitaph might read "Fairness lost a friend, crookedness lost an enemy."

But it's only the inspiration of those who die that make those who live realize what constitutes a useful life.

Yours,
Will Rogers.

2057   MR. ROGERS NEVER SAW A NATION SO TICKLED WITH ITS POVERTY

BEVERLY HILLS, Cal., March 8. — It's surprising how little money we can get along on. Let the banks never open. Let scrip never come. Just everybody keep on trusting everybody else.

Why it's such a novelty to find that somebody will trust you that it's changed our whole feeling toward human nature. Why never was our country so united, never was a country so tickled with their poverty.

For three years we have had nothing but "America is fundamentally sound." It should have been "America is fundamentally cuckoo."

The worse off we get the louder we laugh, which is a great thing. And every American international banker ought to have printed on his office door "Alive today by the grace of a nation that has a sense of humor."

Yours,
Will Rogers.

2058   MR. ROGERS IS A BIT CRITICAL OF THE WAY THINGS ARE DONE

SANTA MONICA, Cal., March 9. — Say, while you are giving credit for all this bank holiday, remember it was an old ex-cow-puncher, Governor Balzar of Nevada, that started it away last Summer, and if everybody would have done it then the banks would have had a whole lot more to divide up than they will have now.

But that is one thing you would have never got a Republican administration to do, voluntarily close a bank. Their theory was leave 'em open till they shut.

We can think of the most things that would benefit the patient, but we never think of 'em till we see the hearse going by.

Yours,
Will Rogers.

2059   WILL ROGERS REMARKS

BEVERLY HILLS, Cal., March 10. — Say, didn't the Rockefellers (through their hired man, Mr. Aldrich) throw a custard pie right in the face of the Morgan banking outfit. Why if the Chase National turns "square" and removes itself from security companies, (that's the bank's roulette wheel) it will be a death blow to modern banking. Imagine a bank just having to live on interest alone. Removing their security or holding companies is like taking the loaded dice away from a crap shooter.

Yours,
Will Rogers.

2060   MR. ROGERS VIEWS THE QUAKE
            FROM A PHILOSOPHIC ANGLE

SANTA MONICA, Cal., March 12. — Bless Arthur Brisbane's loyal heart, he tried to say it wasn't an earthquake. He said the buildings were non-union construction and the people were killed through a sudden stroke of old age.

But he didn't know that our California papers had turned frank and just said:

"We had an earthquake. It was no fire, no tidal wave, no act of the Democratic party, it was just an old fashioned earthquake."

You see the Lord in his justice works everything on a handicap basis. California having the best of everything else must take a slice of the calamities. Even my native Oklahoma (the Garden of Eden of the West) has a cyclone. Kansas, while blessed with its grasshoppers, must endure its politicians. New York with its splendors has its Wall Street, and Washington, the world's most beautiful city, has a lobbyist crawling out to attack you from every manhole. Even J. P. Morgan is not sitting as pretty as he was.

So every human and every place is equal after all.

Yours,
Will Rogers.

2061   WILL ROGERS CLAPS HANDS FOR THE PRESIDENT'S SPEECH

SANTA MONICA, Cal., March 13. — Mr. Roosevelt stepped to the microphone last night and knocked another home run.

His message was not only a great comfort to the people, but it pointed a lesson to all radio announcers and public speakers what to do with a big vocabulary, leave it at home in the dictionary.

Some people spend a lifetime juggling with words, with not an idea in a carload.

Our President took such a dry subject as banking, (and when I say "dry" I mean dry, for if it had been liquid he wouldn't have had to speak on it at all).

Well he made everybody understand it, even the bankers.

Yours,
Will Rogers.

2062   WILL ROGERS IS READY TO GO THE WHOLE ROUTE, REGARDLESS

SANTA MONICA, Cal., March 14. — I don't know what additional authority Roosevelt may ask, but give it to him, even if it's to drown all the boy babies, for the way the grown up ones have acted, he will be perfectly justified in drowning any new ones.

So, viva Roosevelt, and, banzai everything.

It just shows you what a country can do when you take their affairs out of the hands of Congress.

Yours,
Will Rogers.

2063   WILL ROGERS FINDS IT HELPS TO DWELL ON OUR OWN WOES

BEVERLY HILLS, Cal., March 15. — My bank opened today. Instead of being there to draw my little dab out, I didn't even go to town. Shows you I heard Roosevelt on the radio.

Bankers should have over their desks this motto, "God bless Roosevelt, God bless radio, and then, P. S. God bless interest."

But I am telling you that Roosevelt should come ahead of interest. All in the world it took to do these things was to forget about war debts, disarmament, China's plight, Germany's plight, and just concentrate one week on "America's plight."

America can carry herself and get along in pretty fair shape, but when she stops and picks up the whole world and puts it on her shoulders she just can't "get it done."

               Yours,
               Will Rogers.

2064   WILL ROGERS LOOKS AT THINGS WITH AN AIR OF SATISFACTION

BEVERLY HILLS, Cal., March 16. — The millinium (whatever that is) has arrived.

On a Senate vote on economy only thirteen Senators voted that they could run the country better than the President, among 'em Huey Long and Champ Clark.

California passed the racing bill. Maybe Texas, the greatest horse-raising State in the Union, will allow one to run for his oats.

Beer is coming back, wine is coming back, Greta Garbo is coming back, Sister Aimee is coming back.

Senators' salaries cut 15 per cent, that's fair, movie salaries cut 50 per cent (not so hot), newspaper columnists' salaries cut (that's a crime), stage comedians' salaries cut (that ain't fair), but if Roosevelt says it is, why it's O. K.

               Yours,
               Will Rogers.

2065   WILL ROGERS FINDS THINGS 'NEVER WAS LOOKING BETTER'

SANTA MONICA, Cal., March 17. — I tell you things never was looking better. And Congress! I want to go on record as giving those rascals a world of credit. They have reformed and they look like they are sorry for what they have done for years.

Nowadays Mr. Roosevelt just makes out a little list of things every morning that he wants them to do (kinder like a housewife's menu list), and for the first time in their lives they are acting like United States citizens and not like United States Senators or Congressmen.

There has never been anything radically wrong with our lawmakers only they thought they were thinking. Now we got a man to do their thinking for 'em, and the whole country is better off.

Yours,
Will Rogers.

2066 MR. ROGERS SEES A NATION
OF ARITHMETICAL TIPPLERS

SANTA MONICA, Cal., March 19. — If the beer is three and a fraction per cent alcoholic and you want to get 100 percent drunk, why all you're going to have to do is drink thirty-three and a third glasses; 50 per cent drunk, sixteen and a half glasses . . .

We will be the only country in the world where you can just regulate your intoxication by arithmetic. You say to some friends "Let's go out and have a 10 per cent good time." So you get out your pencils and find that's only three glasses so you all decide to raise it to a 20 per cent party. A wife will bawl out "John, you have had 12½ per cent too much now."

From the looks of it the Treasury is going to get a bigger kick out of it than the drinkers.

Yours,
Will Rogers.

2067 WILL ROGERS HAILS A MOVE
LAUNCHED BY A FLORIDA CITY

BEVERLY HILLS, Cal., March 20. — There is no end to the blessings that this fellow Roosevelt has indirectly brought about.

Orlando, Florida, has saw (or has seen) the light and has suspended six civic (eating) clubs and one Chamber of Commerce for sixty days.

Now there is an injunction that should be made permanent. This country just civic luncheoned itself into depression. If they will all go home and eat with their own families, they will not only get their first good lunch in years, but will be surprised how much more intelligently their own wife can talk than the "speaker of the day."

God bless Orlando, Florida.

Yours,
Will Rogers.

2068   WILL ROGERS IS IN FAVOR
OF A WIDER INCOME TAX

BEVERLY HILLS, Cal., March 21. — Here is a heartbreaking thing for an income-tax payer to relate.

Did you notice in this the worst year in history that the receipts from the income tax doubled over last year? Well, that kinder knocks into a cock hat the idea that if you taxed incomes too much there wouldn't be any.

That is a lot of hooey. Folks that can earn money will earn it, no matter what percentage they themselves get out of it, but you must always remember the government has left one loophole open for those with money, and that is the tax-exempt bonds.

So our financial ills will never be settled till you fix it so every man will pay an income tax on what he earns, be it a farm, grocery store or municipal or government bonds.

Yours,
Will Rogers.

2069   MR. ROGERS GIVES A FORMULA
FOR AVOIDANCE OF BAD NEWS

BEVERLY HILLS, Cal., March 22. — Here is a suggestion that will help you all out of a lot of anxiety and anguish in case your town or district should be hit by some disaster.

Run quick and turn off the radio, otherwise you will hear where your own home has been swept away by the flood, you have been lost in the fire and your husband kidnapped.

We had an earthquake here. That's all we had (which was plenty) but that wasn't enough news for the radio. They added "oil wells overflowing and on fire, a city burning to the ground" and as a P.S. "a tidal wave coming in from the ocean."

So, in case of disaster, run (don't walk) to the nearest radio and turn it off, for they take delight in killing you, whether you have been killed or not.

Yours,
Will Rogers.

2070   MR. ROGERS GIVES DEMOCRATS
        CREDIT FOR KILLING TWO FADS

BEVERLY HILLS, Cal., March 23. — These Democrats are going so fast they are relieving the same man twice before they know it. The House passed the farm relief bill and now are starting on an unemployment relief bill.

Well, the farm relief bill relieves the unemployed, it gives everybody that isn't working a job to watch the farmer and see that he don't put in any more rows of potatoes than he did in 1921. It should be called the "Sherlock Holmes bill." It creates 5,000,000 Democratic detectives.

But anyhow, the Democrats have justified their existence, for there are two words we haven't heard uttered in three weeks. One is "Republican" and the other is "Technocrat."

Did you ever see two fads pass out as quick?

Yours,
Will Rogers.

2071   WILL ROGERS IS IMPRESSED
        BY ONE GEORGE BERNARD SHAW

BEVERLY HILLS, Cal., March 24. — Bernard Shaw, you let me come to your home in London, talk to you for a long time. I always said I never met a man I didn't like. You would all like Shaw if you met him, that is everybody that is fair and honest with themselves.

You won't be able to figure him out, and that makes the smart fellows sore. He is one crossword puzzle that has never been worked. Writers' animosity to Shaw is that they didn't think of saying what he had already said. He is away ahead of 'em. England in all these years don't know if he's for 'em or against 'em, and a fellow Irishman knows more about him than a Zulu.

Now when a guy can do all that and put it over, give him credit. He does no harm.

Sir James Barrie told me that he was a very charitable, human man. He does much good, amuses and instructs multitudes, so as "wisecracking" is our national pastime and we have a foreigner come here who can make a sucker out of us doing it, why let's be good sports and admit it. For, as far as knowing the "real" Bernard Shaw, we haven't got a man in America that can see past his whiskers.

So, viva Bernard, look us over, and don't let our hospitality stand in the way of you telling us about what cage in the zoo we belong. It's bound to do us some good.

Yours,
Will Rogers.

2072   Mr. Rogers Strays To Arizona
        And Picks Up A Few Personals

NOGALES, Ariz., March 26. — Nogales, Arizona, it's what Western towns used to be but it still is.

Had a fine visit with General Pershing at Tucson. Am mighty glad to relate to you that he is looking fine and feeling much better. It's an education to talk to him on Europe. Who have we got that should know more?

Saw Mrs. Greenway, Arizona's Mother Superior, who will perhaps and should be, Arizona's new Congresswoman.

Arizona has a fine old character for its new Governor. He is a country doctor, brought ten thousand babies into the world and when they got to voting age he ran for office.

Arizona's Legislature passed its bills and adjourned, then somebody accidentally read 'em and they was all unconstitutional and cockeyed so they want another session. But the old Doc says "No, they are liable to get 'em worse than that the next time."

There is a man that not only knows maternity but knows State Congressmen.

Yours,
Will Rogers.

2073   WILL ROGERS HAS THE OFFER
OF A NEW JOB, HE REPORTS

BEVERLY HILLS, Cal., March 27. — Papers all state Hitler is trying to copy Mussolini. Looks to me like it's the Ku Klux that he is copying. He don't want to be Emperor, he wants to be Kleagle.

But ain't it a relief to have a government over here that is going to let 'em solve their own troubles over there?

I see where he is kinder toning down on his racial and religious hatreds. If he does, that guy is liable to come through at that.

You know nobody thought the Democrats could do anything either when our old form of government was overthrown last fall. But the Democrats surprised not only the world but themselves, and now every country is trying to borrow a good Democrat to come and put 'em on their feet.

Mexico has already made me an offer.

Yours,
Will Rogers.

2074   MR. ROGERS FINDS THE SLUMP
HAS PRODUCED REAL PATRIOTS

BEVERLY HILLS, Cal., March 28. — Our country may be short of work, short of ready cash, but by golly depression has bred real patriots.

Right here in Beverly Hills (the heart of art) in the exclusive Beverly Wilshire Hotel, some friend of the common people sneaked in and stole six saxophones, four clarinets, a bull fiddle and base drum.

Our town constable is looking for him to prosecute him. The people are looking for him to reward him.

Pardon me for bragging too quick. Just yesterday I said "Hurrah for the U. S. She is spending her time solving her own problems." I wake up today finding we are trying to get into the World Court. My error.

Yours,
Will Rogers.

2075   Mr. Rogers Is Getting Worried
About This Beer Business

SANTA MONICA, Cal., March 29. — Beer is supposed to be coming. From what I can read from all the States, nobody knows who is going to sell it, where you are supposed to get it, what it will cost, or what it will taste like.

The whole thing came up so quick that the boys can't hardly arrange how the graft will be distributed, all but New York. Tammany Hall, of course, got the privilege there.

I tell you what I will lay you a little bet on. I bet they mess this thing up so that it will do away with the passing of the real prohibition amendment.

The whole country is buying a blind horse. Suppose this stuff don't taste like we think it will.

                      Yours,
                         Will Rogers.

2076   Will Rogers Sees The Need
For More Forested Areas

BEVERLY HILLS, Cal., March 30. — Glad to see that reforestration and employment bill pass. We got to have a lot more forests and trees, otherwise these cigarette smokers won't have anything to burn up.

Say, here is something that for the good of the Internal Revenue collectors ought to be made straight. We all kinder smile and the papers headline it any time that somebody gets a refund on their income tax. That's given wide publicity. But here is something that everybody don't know, because they are not allowed to publicize it. They collect in lots more back disputed taxes than they pay out.

It's news if you can get anything out of the government, but if the government gets anything out of you, that ain't news, that's just a habit.

But Uncle Sam has no more faithful, or fair servants.

                      Yours,
                         Will Rogers.

2077   MR. ROGERS IS SURPRISED AGAIN
        BY OUR VERSATILE PRESIDENT

BEVERLY HILLS, Cal., March 31. — This fellow Roosevelt never gets through surprising us. We just find out now that he speaks French fluently.

That's the second linguistic surprise he has handed us. The other was the night the banks closed. We knew he could speak English, but we didn't know he could talk "American" till that night.

In fact, he has got three speaking accomplishments. He is the only guy who can talk "turkey" to the Senate.

Every man gets an opportunity once in a lifetime. That little country banker in New York named Morgan has his now. If he just steps up to the Senate witness stand and can show the boys where he has a business and not a racket, why he can step down a hero; but if he can't, the boat sails Wednesday.

Yours,
Will Rogers.

2078   WILL ROGERS AND LIPPMANN
        CAN NOW SEE GREEN LIGHTS

SANTA MONICA, Cal., April 2. — Walter Lippmann. You all read him. If you don't you ought to. He was a Democrat before the deluge to Democracy. But his writings were so fair and impartial that Republicans used to sneak off around behind the house and read 'em. But being Republicans they never profited by his sage advice. But now they read him and weep.

Well he was out to our igloo and broke cornbread and chili with us the other day. He thinks the green lights are with us, and the only thing can stop us again is prosperity. (There is nothing that sets a nation back as far in civilization as prosperity.)

He is proud of all parties uniting during this pilgrimage of "back from ga-ga." He thinks that America will not only remain on the gold, but will remain on its feet, which is more important.

Yours,
Will Rogers.

2079   WILL ROGERS FAVORS A JOB
        FOR MRS. RUTH BRYAN OWEN

BEVERLY HILLS, Cal., April 3. — Ruth Bryan Owen is going as Ambassadoress to Denmark, or Sweden or Norway, or one of those.

(Americans will never become civilized enough to tell a Swede from a Dane, or a Norwegian from a Swede. I know the difference means a lot to them, but it just means another tall blonde to us.) Well anyhow, Roosevelt is trading Ruth to that part of the country for Greta Garbo and it's the only bad trade he has made since he got in. Ruth's got it on her any way you jump. Those three countries we have always thought a lot of (even if we don't know 'em apart). They built up our great Northwest, and when we sent the talented daughter of our Great Commoner we are giving 'em the best we got.

Yours,
Will Rogers.

2080   WILL ROGERS KNOWS ONE MAN
             WHO DESERVES A RISE IN PAY

BEVERLY HILLS, Cal., April 4. — This is a bad time to suggest a rise in salary for anybody, but there is one job that Roosevelt has created and the fellow who is doing it is underpaid, no matter what they pay him. That's the fellow that carries the messages from the White House to Congress.

There is a guy that Roosevelt is running ragged, and when he sends a message to Congress it "stays sent."

Well, beer will be here Friday with the politician replacing the bootlegger.

Yours,
Will Rogers.

2081   WILL ROGERS PAYS TRIBUTE
             TO ADMIRAL MOFFET'S CAREER

BEVERLY HILLS, Cal., April 5. — Loving aviation like I do and believing in it like I do, this loss was a terrible jolt. My main friend among them was Admiral Moffett. We had been to two disarmament conferences together. I could always go to him and get a little inside news what the conference was trying to do. He was a grand soul. Moffett was the "propeller" of naval aviation.

Now don't fly off and say "that aviation is not safe or not practical." There is certain things nature can do to you, whether its an earthquake in California, a flood in Mississippi, a tornado in Ohio, or a drouth in Arkansas. When nature enters into it, don't criticize.

Yours,
Will Rogers.

2082   WILL ROGERS READY TO BUY
        BEER FOR ALL CONGRESSMEN

BEVERLY HILLS, Cal., April 6. — Well it don't make much difference what we write tonight for you folks to read tomorrow (Friday) for you won't be able to read anyhow. Nobody has any idea what this low-voltage beer will taste like, but I bet it will be mighty potent, for this guy Roosevelt hasn't pulled a bad one yet.

Another thing, too. You take those Congressmen and Senators, the fine way they been acting in this Congress they deserve a little nip. The boys have been mighty fine. We haven't heard the word Republican or Democrat in a month. They are in there really trying to help out the country. So if you are in reach of any of 'em tomorrow buy 'em a drink and send me the bill.

P. S. — This holds good up to one beer.

Yours,
Will Rogers.

2083   WILL ROGERS SEES THE RIGHT
        TO DRINK, NOT LIQUOR, WANTED

BEVERLY HILLS, Cal., April 7. — Well I can't speak with any authority on the condition of the country today, for here it is late in the afternoon and I haven't sampled a single glass of the "spirit of rejuvenated America." I have always claimed America didn't want a drink as bad as they wanted the right to take a drink if they did happen to want one.

And say, did you see what the Senate voted for yesterday, that a week's work was to consist of thirty hours, six hours a day for five days? I doubt very much if the people working will agree on an increase in time of work like that. We stick to the old American principle of only working when the boss is looking.

Yours,
Will Rogers.

2084   MR. ROGERS REPORTS HOARDING
        ENDED OUT WEST ON FRIDAY

SANTA MONICA, Cal., April 9. — This Roosevelt knows his human nature.

People had been pleaded with not to hoard. Laws had been passed to stop it. But when Roosevelt said "Let 'em buy beer" the money come out of hoarding in a high lope.

Why out here the first few thousand cases of beer sold was paid for with silver dollars worn so thin they was pasted together like a dollar bill.

Every town of course run out of beer Friday. But Beverly Hills (always unique and extraordinary), they were the first town to run out of pretzels.

Very little intoxication over the country, and what there was was caused by people using gin as a chaser.

Yours,
Will Rogers.

2085   MR. ROGERS FINDS A REASON
        FOR THE QUIET WEEK-END

BEVERLY HILLS, Cal., April 10. — Beer brought on one of the most quiet week-ends we ever had, less accidents and everything. People just got full of beer and layed down and took a good nap.

I was playing polo, went to sleep, woke up and found I had been beaten. But it was all right. I did it for Roosevelt. There ain't nothing we can do too much for Roosevelt nowadays.

I tell you we never was living in a better time. We got a smart man doing our thinking for us. You see what put this country on the bum was dumb people thinking for themselves.

Yours,
Will Rogers.

2086   WILL ROGERS FINDS REASON
        FOR A LITTLE HANDCLAPPING

BEVERLY HILLS, Cal., April 11. — Some sort of handclapping is due the Republican Newspapers for their generous support of the administration, for nothing is as bull-headed as a party newspaper, be it Republican or Democratic. People are the first to forget party lines; newspapers are the last. This is a lesson in generosity to Democratic papers.

And, talking about newspapers. Return of beer must have given some new advertising men a job, for never was there as attractive and intelligent ads in the papers as these new beer ads.

Finally we are seeing something as an ad besides a pretty girl smoking a cigarette.

Yours,
Will Rogers.

2087   WILL ROGERS FEELS A PANG
        OF SYMPATHY FOR CHICAGO

SANTA MONICA, Cal., April 12. — Poor Chicago. The teachers are trying to get their salaries; the beer bootleggers claim they have been discriminated against, that America overnight wiped out an industry, and right in the midst of all their troubles they are hit by a world's fair.

But I believe they will come out of it. In years to come Chicago will be the biggest city in the world. Soon as Capone gets out and gets back, you will see a big difference.

Bernard Shaw lectured on "America." That's about like me lecturing on the atmospheric conditions over the South Pole.

He left by police escort for his boat.

Yours,
Will Rogers.

2088   WILL ROGERS IS LIQUIDATING
        ON THAT FREE DRINK PROMISE

BEVERLY HILLS, Cal., April 13. — Say, my beer offer the other day to buy the Senators or Congressmen a nip in return for their unlooked for public good has brought me a lot of bills. Here is one from a man in New Hampshire:

"You didn't say anything about ex-Senators, but knowing your personal regard for ex-Senator Moses, thought it would be O. K., so bought him one. The beer didn't suit him. Said he couldn't get back onto it, so had to give him something better. So enclosed bill, to one drink for Senator Moses, 50 cents, discount 40 cents, which I took care of myself, which leaves a balance due 10 cents. Moses seemed mighty satisfied with this arrangement."

That's O. K. with me. An ex-Republican Senator is worth a dime anywhere. Will do the same for Jim Watson of Indiana.

Yours,
Will Rogers.

2089   ROGERS LAUDS MRS. ROOSEVELT
        FOR USING HORSE AND PLANE

BEVERLY HILLS, Cal., April 14. — Hurrah for the First Lady of the land. I am strong for her, she uses a horse and an airplane, the plane for business and the horse for pleasure.

You talk about beer and a lot of things coming back, say the old horse is just headed back in a high lope. Why for young folks not to be able to ride nowadays is almost as bad as not "seeing your dentist twice a year." Hundreds of riding academys where there used to be none, and this dude ranching thing is one of the healthiest and finest vacations in the world. Think of anybody being able to be a rancher and not having to stand the loss and pay the taxes.

Mrs. Roosevelt good naturedly admitted she fell off in a mudhole. Say, if we could ever see a mudhole once more in California, we would all purposely fall off in it and wallow.

Yours,
Will Rogers.

2090   MR. ROGERS NEARLY RUNS OUT
         OF SOMETHING TO TALK ABOUT

SANTA MONICA, Cal., April 16. — Since the whole country is all agreed that we are headed toward the feed trough, and since the members of Congress have been so fine and decent and the Senators have taken out United States citizenship papers and swore allegiance to our land, and since the bankers have finally seen the errors of their ways and started banking instead of gambling, there just ain't much left a poor writer to pick on.

Course, there is always Huey Long, the Japanese and the French, but the French are repenting, the Japanese have captured more than they can hold and the old "kingfish" of the Louisiana cane brakes has not been convicted by court of law.

You must always remember that in "that great fraternity, the mystic nights of the politics," there is some crookedness going on on both sides.

Yours,
Will Rogers.

2091   WILL ROGERS IS THANKFUL
         FOR ONE FREEDOM WE HAVE

BEVERLY HILLS, Cal., April 17. — Every day just shows us what a lucky country we are.

We got lots of fleas on us, and everybody is scratching to get 'em off, but there is one insect that bothers most of the world that we are at least free from and that is a newspaper press that is not free.

Everybody wants to know if the Englishmen in Russia are guilty or framed. Everybody would love to know the very facts of what is going on in Germany.

But over here you can write whatever you want to. The only trouble is getting somebody that will read it.

Yours,
Will Rogers.

2092   WILL ROGERS FINDS A MEETING
IN KANSAS THAT INTERESTS HIM

WICHITA, Kan., April 18. — Fly at night, the air is smoother, it's cooler and the lights are wonderful. Flew from the West Coast last night over the American Airways.

The International Society for Crippled Children are in convention in this hustling little Western city. If there could be a greater organization it hasn't been invented yet. In the olden days history records they killed their cripples. And even though we don't think so sometimes, civilization has advanced.

This society has proved that all can be helped and over half can be cured. Kansas and Ohio have kinder led the field in this. If your State is not affiliated then it is not doing all that it can to help the most sympathetic invalid we have, the crippled child.

Incidentally their statistics show that they are brighter and more cheerful than their unafflicted mates. There is gameness for you.

Yours,
Will Rogers.

2093   MR. ROGERS FLIES MIGHTY HIGH
TO DODGE THOSE TEXAS STEERS

AMARILLO, Tex., April 19. — Just flew in here, headed west.

We had to come in mighty high to dodge all the farms and ranches that were blowing around down on the lower strata. It ain't anything to be hit in the eye with a cow that is blowing with the dust from one ranch to another, but with all her dust and all her drought she is a pretty country.

Will Rogers as a country doctor in Doctor Bull, *the motion picture based on James Cozzens' novel,* The Last Adam (Fox Film Corporation, 1933).

This fellow Clarence Young, the head of commercial aviation, has done more for it than anybody since the Wright brothers. I don't know anything about his going to be removed for Democratic purposes, but it will take twelve Democrats to take his place.

Yours,
Will Rogers.

2094   MR. ROGERS WENT OFF GOLD
       IN 1902, SO HE'S NOT EXCITED

WINSLOW, Ariz., April 20. — All I know is just what I read in the Albuquerque (N.M.) papers. They say we are off the gold.

Well, I am flying over Arizona and New Mexico as I write this and you could take a parachute and jump out any place.

The best way to tell when each one of us went off the gold is to figure back how many years it was since we had any. Well, that's when we went off.

The last I remember getting my clutches on was in Johannesburg, South Africa; some five-dollar English gold pieces that we carried in a belt around our waist. I used the last one to pay a third-class passage to Australia, so I went off the gold in 1902.

So this move strikes me as no great novelty or calamity.

Yours,
Will Rogers.

2095   WILL ROGERS REMEMBERS
       ONE CAMPAIGN PROMISE

BEVERLY HILLS, Cal., April 21. — Well, there just ain't much to write about today but gold and there ain't much gold to write about.

There is one good thing about this whole economic move, a dumb man knows just as much about it as a smart one does. For I bet you there is not a man in America could tell you exactly what it will lead to. For after all a printing press can make you awful rich (for a little while).

Here is something you might have forgot, in the campaign last fall the Republicans said if the Democrats got in they would inflate money, and the Democrats swore they wouldn't. But who can remember a campaign promise?

I don't know how I ever happened to remember that one. But let 'er go, we are all on a drunk for the time being anyhow and the durn thing might accidentally work permanently.

Yours,
Will Rogers.

2096   Mr. Rogers Was Only Confused
               By This Inflation Business

LOS ANGELES, Cal., April 23. — My old friend Arthur Brisbane accused me good-naturedly of being worried over this "inflation."

I wasn't worried. I was just "confused." There is quite a difference. When you are worried you know what you are worried about, but when you are "confused" it's when you don't know enough about a thing to be worried.

But Arthur, even my confusion is all over now. Everybody that I meet has explained this whole "inflation" thing so clearly that now I am going around explaining it myself.

You see medical science has developed two ways of actually tracing insanity. One is if the patient cuts out paper dolls or works a jig-saw puzzle, and the other is if the patient says "I will tell you what this economic business really means."

Yours,
Will Rogers.

2097   Will Rogers Is Prepared
               For Any Monetary Shift

BEVERLY HILLS, Cal., April 24. — I don't know whether this going off the gold is official or not.

The French have vetoed it. They claim we have no right to go off the gold and leave them high and dry on it.

It seems like if you are on the gold every nation in the world is out to get you. They all say "What's the idea of that big bum having gold? Say we will figure out a way to bump him off."

But this is a time when you got to be ready for anything. I have got some old Cherokee Indian beads, or wampum. Suppose we go off the silver, suppose we go off the paper, well, look where I will be setting with my wampum.

Yours,
Will Rogers.

2098   WILL ROGERS REMARKS

BEVERLY HILLS, Cal., April 25. — Every paper just keeps saying how Mr. Roosevelt and Mr. MacDonald are "in accord," and how Mr. Herriot and Mr. Roosevelt are "in accord." Now that all sounds mighty chummy and docile. But knowing Europe like we ought to know 'em, there is just a little too much "in accord." There is one awful good time to watch those babies from over there and that is when they are "in accord." But I imagine we can trust Mr. Roosevelt, while this is his first poker game with Europe, he has played with Tammany, so he is not exactly what you would call an amateur. He has seen guys pull 'em out of their sleeve before. But he has got to watch that "in accord" stuff.

                                 Yours,
                                 Will Rogers.

2099   MR. ROGERS APPROVES HEARTILY
             OF ONE OF THE 'NEW DEALERS'

BEVERLY HILLS, Cal., April 26. — This labor woman Perkins looks like she is not only going to do something for labor, but is going to be a real contribution to women in politics. She has put common sense ahead of lip rouge and the petticoat.

See there is a newspaper convention in New York. (They are always holding a convention of some sort some place. Lord only knows when they ever have time to write or read anything.) Well, the rascals, regardless of politics, all were unanimous in saying there was a "better feeling."

Well, a better feeling is all you want. If you feel better you are not going to die.

                                 Yours,
                                 Will Rogers.

2100   MR. ROGERS HAS FIGURED OUT
            WHAT WORRIES THE NATIONS

BEVERLY HILLS, Cal., April 27. — Governments are having the same trouble now that individuals have been having for three years, that is, trying to find out the actual value of what they have.

You don't know the value of your land, your stocks, your house, or anything. Now England and America and France have met to find out what the dollar is worth, what the pound sterling is worth, what silver is worth.

Everything is jumping up and down like an international banker at a Senatorial investigation. Nations are like a lot of women with their babies. Each thinks that theirs is the best.

Yours,
Will Rogers.

2101   WILL ROGERS FLYING EAST
            COMMENTS ON SPEED MANIA

DES MOINES, Iowa, April 28. — Now this aviation is getting somewhere. Traveling east to do a broadcast on a Democratic President on President's Day evening. Am on one of the new Boeing ships, two-motored (not three), ten-passenger. And it really has speed for a big ship, cruises 180.

You see all our advancement in speed has been made with small single-motored ships. But now they are all out to cut down the flying time at least a third.

And by the way, the old railroad could grab off many a new customer if they would knock a third off their schedules, which they could do.

There never was such a demand for speed, for less reason. There is not a one of us that couldn't walk where we are going and then get there earlier than we have any business.

Yours,
Will Rogers.

2102   WILL ROGERS GOT A BIG KICK
            OUT OF THE GRIDIRON DINNER

NEW YORK, N. Y., April 30. — Did you ever go to a dinner and have to stand up, and not even get any dinner?

Well, I did last night, at the Gridiron dinner to President Roosevelt. It was sure worth it. Those Washington newspaper men are the cleverest ones we have. They have the cleverest skits and take-offs on our public men. This one was a great show.

It's a pity they don't arrange to do 'em before a regular audience, for Lord, those prominent men there miss many a gag. I know a regular audience would be twice as keen and appreciative.

I think it's because each man in Washington is so engrossed in his own sphere that he is not well up on all topics as the average reader. And these sketches cover everything. Ogden Mills and the President both made good speeches.

I think those things do a lot of good to help keep those old big boys' feet on the ground.

But say, I would stand on my head to see another one.

Yours,
Will Rogers.

2103   WILL ROGERS REPORTS FINDING
          EVERY ONE IN NEW YORK HAPPY

NEW YORK, N. Y., May 1. — Everybody is happy here in New York tonight. The market went up today. Spirits here just go up or down according to that day's market. They think the whole United States just depends on what pocket the little white ball rolled into on the Exchange roulette table that day.

But, our country has got so that each one of us have to live by a "racket" of some kind and none of us must be too critical of the other fellow's "racket."

When you figure it right down none of us are in a really essential business but the farmer, and he raises so much that even his business is partly non-essential.

But we got to be tolerant, for these New Yorkers are likable rascals even when they are skinning you.

Yours,
Will Rogers.

2104   MR. ROGERS WILL SPEND TODAY
          IN THE QUEST OF KNOWLEDGE

NEW YORK, N. Y., May 2. —Well, let's see what scandal the evening papers have here that will bear repeating tomorrow.

The House of Representatives is going to limit debate on inflation to five hours tomorrow. I wish to goodness there was a way to limit individuals that try to explain it to you to five hours.

We thought technocracy was a tough bird to get the low-down on, but it's only a first reader compared to hearing a guy explain "inflation."

I am going down to Washington tomorrow and hear the Congressmen bite into it.

There is one thing about it. It's made every man's intelligence equal.

Yours,
Will Rogers.

2105   MR. ROGERS IS UNABLE TO LEARN
        A GREAT DEAL IN THE CAPITAL

WASHINGTON, D. C., May 3. — Seemed good to get in here today. See old friends.

Mr. Vice President turned over his office to me to hold conferences in. He is the same Garner he was even before he was Speaker. Had a long chat with Speaker Rainey. Saw Congress pass the inflation bill, the biggest bill ever to pass any Legislature in the history of the world.

Invited right into our new Treasurer's office, Mr. Woodin, while the Federal Reserve Board was in session. He says, "Maby you can give us a laugh; we can't get anybody to give us any money." They seemed cheerful, and they are the ones who has to dig it up.

Then over to Lew Douglas, the old Arizona cowpuncher, head of the budget, who says, "You are just in time. All I need to balance the books today is six billion."

What a tough job that guy's got, but he is able.

I had lunch with Senator Joe Robinson of Arkansas and Senator Connally of Texas, and not a one of all these men knew what inflation was.

Yours,
Will Rogers.

2106   MR. ROGERS FINALLY REVEALS
        HIS REAL MISSION AT CAPITAL

WASHINGTON, D. C., May 4. — Foreign delegations coming in here to join Mr. Roosevelt's bread line. Italy's and Oklahoma's got in the same day.

Man named Jung sent by Dictator Mussolini to see what "Lady Bountiful" held in store for Italy.

Man named Rogers was sent by Dictator Alfalfa Bill Murray to pick up any loose crumbs that might fall locally.

Congress disgraced themselves something terrible today. There was three solid hours they didn't pass a single bill, not even an appropriation bill, then they realized how slow they were going and woke up and practically passed a little dinky thing appropriating only one hundred million for the insurance companies. Hardly worth monkeying with.

Going to hear the President lecture the U. S. Chamber of Commerce. Was going to broadcast it but that was called off. Looks like one of those affairs for men only.

Yours,
Will Rogers.

2107   WILL ROGERS NOTES SLOGANS
       'GOT,' 'WE GOT' AND 'FORGOT'

NEW YORK, N. Y., May 5. — Big United States Chamber of Commerce dinner in Washington was fine. The humorous part of it was that all the big manufacturers and producers in there had been all their lives hollering "Keep the government out of business."

Well, my companion was Jesse Jones of the Reconstruction Finance Corporation, who held a mortgage on every full dress suit in the house. There is not a business that the government hasn't been asked to join. Nothing makes a man broad-minded like adversity.

Mr. Roosevelt told us the new international slogan was "got." Well, MacDonald agreed with him, says "we got." He didn't say how much. Then they searched for the word for "got" in French, and that was it, "forgot."

Yours,
Will Rogers.

2108   MR. ROGERS OFFERS HIS ADVICE
       ON A MATTER OF SOME MOMENT

NEW YORK, N. Y., May 7. — Now our President has been going along mighty nice and our Congress, both Democratic and Republican, have been decent beyond all expectations.

They have given him every power from mayhem to manslaughter, but if he starts asking for the sole and exclusive right to deal with this debt thing he is going to ride his horse under the first limb he has hit.

These debts have become embedded into the people's minds like religion has and any time you come out on either side (just like arguing religion) you are going to lose and change nobody's opinion.

Yours,
Will Rogers.

2109   MR. ROGERS ADDS TO THE PRAISE
       OF THE PRESIDENT'S SPEECH

NEW YORK, N. Y., May 8. — Mr. Roosevelt made us a mighty fine speech over the radio Sunday night.

He spoke our language, "not ballyhoo the nation to prosperity," "nation in a tailspin," "can't make a hit every time we come to bat."

And in addition to all this he has the best radio voice in America.

Course, he just read the minutes of the last meeting, but he did it so nice that we didn't hardly notice that he forgot to mention what might be in his mind for the future.

Yours,
Will Rogers.

2110   WILL ROGERS FINDS A LOT
       OF CONVERTS IN THE CAPITAL

WASHINGTON, D. C., May 9. — The Senate's not in session today, so the country got a break.

Everybody down here feeling mighty fine since the President's speech. Talked to a lot of what used to be old time Republicans. Why they are the most rabid Democrats we got now.

You know I don't believe there is a thing that this man Roosevelt couldn't put over if he was a mind to.

He is so strong with the people, and so convincing over the radio, that if he ever got in a fight with Congress, all he would have to do is to take it to the people, via the air, and he would lick any of 'em.

Yours,
Will Rogers.

2111   'RUBE' ROGERS TAKES A PEEK
             AT THE GREAT CHICAGO FAIR

CHICAGO, Ill., May 10. — I've been looking at the great Chicago World's Fair which opens two weeks from Saturday. I am the first "rube" to visit it.

I know you will say, what's it all about and why don't they pay their teachers? Well, I am just like you about the teachers, but this fair is just an association and it's not the city itself doing it. I do think it would be a generous thing if it did make any money and the teachers hadn't been paid by then to cut them in on it.

This fair is a tremendous thing. It would take me a week to tell you about it. It's exactly what everybody needs. People have been sitting at home grouching at each other for three years.

Now, don't think we have outgrown the "fair" stage. In the days when we were a great nation we enjoyed 'em.

Now you can see the whole thing for fifty cents and the way this Roosevelt is going, by then we will have the fifty cents.

Yours,
Will Rogers.

2112   MR. ROGERS FEELS THE THRILL
             OF SPRING ON HIS OLD RANGE

CHELSEA, Okla., May 11. — Oklahoma never looked prettier.

Haven't seen a tractor working all day. The country has gone sane and got back to horses. Farmers all look worse, but they feel better.

One of the very next things Mr. Roosevelt is going to do, so I was told in Washington on the best authority, was to appoint an oil "czar." No industry needs a warden worse.

Spring has come. Rockefeller and Brisbane are drifting north from Florida. These two fellers are a surer sign than the geese used to be.

Yours,
Will Rogers.

2113   WILL ROGERS SENDS REPORT
             FROM THE OKLAHOMA FRONT

TULSA, Okla., May 12. — Well, here we are, flying out of Tulsa, the first town in America to become a city. This is one of the best and busiest airports in our country. Oklahoma wants to vote on the beer thing, but they have no money to pay for the election, so Missouri offers to pay for Oklahoma's election provided Oklahoma will guarantee to vote dry and let them have the sales privilege as they do now.

Corn is forty and fifty cents a bushel, but no farmer has any. He sold last fall and winter at fifteen cents. They thought Roosevelt was just another President.

Yours,
Will Rogers.

2114   WILL ROGERS SEES A MORAL
IN THE ROW OVER THE MURAL

SANTA MONICA, Cal., May 14. — I am hereby entering this argument between young Rockefeller and the Mexican artist, for there is two things that a dumb guy knows as much about as a smart one, and that's art and inflation.

I string with Rockefeller. This artist was selling some art and sneaking in some propaganda. Rockefeller had ordered a plain ham sandwich, but the cook put some onions on it. Rockefeller says "I will pay you for it, but I won't eat the onions."

Now the above is said in no disparagement of the Mexican artist, for he is the best in the world, but you should never try to fool a Rockefeller in oils.

Yours,
Will Rogers.

2115   WILL ROGERS PROPOSES SMITH
FOR A NEW AND IMPORTANT JOB

BEVERLY HILLS, Cal., May 15. — Is this a good tip, or ain't it?

No business in the United States is as cockeyed as the oil business (and many States depend on it for their prosperity). If ever a business needed a dictator it is them. It would be the biggest job held by a single man outside the President.

It must not be an oil man, for he is already linked with one side or the other. It's got to be a man that the whole oil industry knew is on the level, fearless, fair, seeking nothing but justice to thousands that produce oil and millions that use it.

Well, if there is a man in America that will fill this position any better than Al Smith I defy you to think of him.

Yours,
Will Rogers.

2116   WILL ROGERS IS NOT SURPRISED
AT THE RATTLING OF SABERS

BEVERLY HILLS, Cal., May 16. — Well, lots of war news in the papers today. I knew it was coming when I saw that we had cut down on our army and navy.

If you want to know when a war is coming just watch the United States and see when they start cutting down on their defense. It's the surest barometer in the world.

The Democrats have one great failing (that I was in hopes they had lived down) and that is they just want to fix the affairs of the world.

Now it's big hearted and it's mighty generous, but it's just not possible for me (3,000 miles away) to tell you what caliber gun to have in your house. You know your neighbors better than I do.

Yours,
Will Rogers.

2117   MR. ROGERS MARVELS AT WAY
THAT EVENTS ARE BEING TURNED

BEVERLY HILLS, Cal., May 17. — Say, this man Roosevelt not only makes Congress roll over and play dead but, by golly he made this tough guy Hitler promise to bring sticks out of the water. Is there no end to this man's cleverness?

Course there is one thing about Europe. You can never believe 'em the first time. They will agree to anything till it comes time to sign up.

This might be just the ideal time to stop a war, for nobody has anything to fight one with. Like disarmament, it's not done for humanitarian reasons, it's only done for economic reasons.

The whole thing seems too good to be true, but the whole world is changing, so maybe they are going to turn human.

Yours,
Will Rogers.

2118 Will Rogers Is In The Race
   For A Loan From The R. F. C.

SKY HARBOR, Tenn., May 18. — Dinner in Hollywood, breakfast in Fort Worth, lunch in Little Rock, dinner in Cincinnati and breakfast (as you read this) in Rooseveltville, D. C. (Depression Concluded).

I'm going as a delegation of one from the American Comedian's Association to get some aid from the Reconstruction Finance. No industry has been hit worse than professional humor. There is too much unconscious amateur talent.

We hope to pay off the R. F. C. (like the bankers and everybody else does) in laughs.

Yours,
Will Rogers.

2119 Rogers Extols Roosevelt's
   Handling Of Bonus Parade

WASHINGTON, D. C., May 19. — Wish you could see the way this fellow Roosevelt handles bonus armies, feeds 'em, talks to 'em, does everything but march with 'em. They had the most orderly quiet parade today. This fellow is uncanny in knowing what to do and say under any given condition.

Carter Glass, who knows more about money than any man in America, talked in the Senate today on his new bank bill. It protects deposits and makes bankers responsible to each other. In other words he wants to set a banker to watch a banker, instead of leaving it to the depositor to try. He also stops banks from racketeering in trusts and holding companies. It really sounds too good to pass.

Yours,
Will Rogers.

2120   WILL ROGERS SPENDS THE DAY
         SEEING THINGS IN THE CAPITAL

WASHINGTON, D. C., May 21. — That fellow Hitler kinder prides himself on his oratory. Say, if he could have heard Rabbi Wise of New York at a great Jewish convention here today Hitler would have been speechless. Wise had everything.

Also saw beautiful ceremony by Gold Star Mothers at Unknown Soldier's Grave. This is the most beautiful city in the world.

Roosevelt is just about through with Congress, so you can look for 'em back home pretty soon. This is one time that a Senator can come home without a police escort for protection. They will all be saying, "Well, I told Franklin if he would do this we would be out of it."

Yours,
Will Rogers.

2121   MR. ROGERS THINKS THE BIG TEST
         FOR THE PRESIDENT IS AT HAND

NEW YORK, N. Y., May 22. — The phenomenal popularity of the Roosevelt administration now meets its severest test.

They are starting to decide where all this money they have been appropriating will come from.

Now if he can extract this money and still receive the plaudits, then there can be no doubt of his being a messiah.

For taxpayers cheer, not from the heart, but from the pocketbook.

Yours,
Will Rogers.

2122   MR. ROGERS THINKS WE WILL GET
         ALL OF THESE PROPOSED TAXES

NEW YORK, N. Y., May 23. — Lew Douglas, the very efficient director of our family grouch bag (budget to you) proposed four different schemes of raising money.

Congress adopted the first one of the four yesterday and will go right along in rotation till they use all four of the plans, finally getting to the sales tax which is the best of the bunch.

When Japan gets all of China captured, then is when the laugh will be on Japan, for China will say, "You catch um China, now what you do with 'em now you got him? One timee Mongolian he takee China too, where he Mongolian now, ha, ha."
Yours,
Will Rogers.

2123   MR. ROGERS IS AT THE RINGSIDE
       OF THE BIG BOUT IN THE CAPITAL

WASHINGTON, D. C., May 24. — Back in here to see the "Morgan Follies."

You know he has made himself a mighty pleasant and agreeable witness.

This "preferred list" that they read today, everybody that's not on it is knocking it. Some think the whole trial won't do much good, but any time one half learn how the other half live why it does us all good:

You see there is a lot of things these old boys have done that are within the law, but it's so near the edge that you couldn't slip a safety razor blade between their acts and a prosecution.
Yours,
Will Rogers.

2124   MR. ROGERS EXPECTS MORGAN
       TO GET SOME NEW BUSINESS

NEW YORK, N. Y., May 25. — Just flew in from Washington, from the Morgan investigation.

I have always said I never met a man I didn't like. Well, I liked this Morgan. You would like him. You couldn't help it.

I am not speaking of his "racket." I am speaking of the man.

These Senators will be banking with him before this thing ends. When I met him I started to hand him what little I had, right there.

Now these Senators started out to prosecute him. I want to save him. I can see the makings in him of a regular guy. He has the money, he has the brains and above all he has the personality.

If he will devote (we will say just the afternoons) of his life to public service, or philanthropy of some sort, he will die happy and loved.

Yours,
Will Rogers.

2125 WILL ROGERS NOW DISCOVERS
    IT WAS REALLY A 'SUCKER LIST'

NEW YORK, N. Y., May 26. — Funny thing about this so-called preferred list that the Morgan Company put out. All of 'em held the stock too long and it died on their hands, so it was really a "sucker list."

New York City collected a million dollars yesterday just for beer licenses alone. A State to remain dry nowadays not only has to have some will power, but it has to find some mysterious way of getting in some dough. Maby a State sales tax on everybody, will keep it off the beer drinkers.

Flying to Chicago tonight to see if this fair looks as big to me as the other one did as a kid. At midnight when you are asleep there is eighty airplanes in the air in this country, forty of 'em carrying passengers.

Yours,
Will Rogers.

2126 MR. ROGERS GETS INTO THE FAIR
    AND GIVES IT HIS APPROVAL

CHICAGO, Ill., May 28. — Well, the big Chicago Fair opened on time.

It had to open on time to give everybody making those long speeches a chance to get 'em over before it closed. Even the preacher who was supposed to ask the blessing stuck long enough to continue it into the doxology.

But it was worth all the praying and talking for. Only thing they had thousands of policemen to block you off at every street to see that you didn't get into it. At that there was 40,000 got by the police and got in.

My old friend Brisbane couldn't get in till he used Walter Winchell's card. I sneaked in inside Amon Carter's silk hat. Me and twelve other mice.

If there is anywhere in the world you want to go in a crowd, get an old silk hat (the mangier the better). Policemen and ushers have more respect for it than a gold engraved card from President Roosevelt.

But it's a great fair, don't miss it.

Yours,
Will Rogers.

2127   MR. ROGERS, ON A FLYING VISIT,
       FINDS THE OLD HOME THIRSTY

CLAREMORE, Okla., May 29. — Took a train out of Chicago last night to catch a plane out of Kansas City this morning.

The train was late, "engine trouble and forced landing," so missed my plane. So flew down here and out of Fort Worth tonight for night flight to the Coast.

In Kansas City this morning, where the girl was kidnapped. If I live a thousand years I will never know what would keep any State from making that punishable by death.

Nobody here in Oklahoma. They are all driving to Missouri to get their beer. In that way the State retains its morals and its appetite, too.

Yours,
Will Rogers.

2128   MR. ROGERS GIVES HIS IDEA
       OF SOMETHING WORTH WHILE

SANTA MONICA, Cal., May 30. — There is nothing any more gratifying than to have been away and get back and get ahold of some home town paper. It's like meeting an old friend having a glass of three times two with him.

Knowing I had been to the Morgan investigation everybody asked me on the way out "What's it going to lead to and will it do any good?"

Yes, it's going to be very educational, not only the Morgan investigation but of all big business. It's going to show us just how "big business" got big.

It got big according to law. But not according to Hoyle.

Yours,
Will Rogers.

2129   MR: ROGERS NOTES A HARD TASK
        ACCOMPLISHED BY ROOSEVELT

BEVERLY HILLS, Cal., May 31. — Mr. Roosevelt has been for six weeks trying to find a Republican. He wanted to put him on the Economic Conference and send him to London.

Well, he finally located one, Senator Jim Couzens of Detroit, and he only admitted to being one just to get the trip.

I tell you, it takes bribery to get a fellow to write Republican after his name nowadays.

Well, they are leaving with high hopes, and it would be wonderful if they could do something besides just seeing the King when he delivers his address.

Yours,
Will Rogers.

2130   MR. ROGERS OFFERS A CANDIDATE
        FOR THE PRESIDENCY IN 1936

BEVERLY HILLS, Cal., June 1. — "Farm prices have advanced 17 per cent in the last month."

Now, that's better news than a speech on "good relations" by Mussolini and Hitler combined.

Our new ambassador to England got so elated over the Prince of Wales introducing him that he turned over America to England to be used as they saw fit. It takes a strong man to remember what country he is representing when the wine and the flattery start flowing.

If the Republicans ever decide to enter another Presidential candidate they better hire this little Pecora to run for 'em. He is the best bet I see right now.

Yours,
Will Rogers.

2131   Mr. Rogers Suggests A Way
To End That Inquiry Happily

BEVERLY HILLS, Cal., June 2. — Well, I am glad to see the midgets get a break. In all my experience around show business, they are a mighty fine little breed of folks.

We have had "bank relief," "big business relief," and now we get "midget relief."

Mr. Morgan acted mighty human. He just picked up that little midget and played with it as though it was the Federal Reserve or the United States Chamber of Commerce.

I'll tell you how Mr. Morgan can square this whole thing, and you will never hear another word against him. That's by simply putting everybody on the preferred list that wasn't on it already. I haven't heard a kick, only by those that were overlooked.

                        Yours,
                        Will Rogers.

2132   Will Rogers Would End
Tax Exemptions In Bonds

SANTA MONICA, Cal., June 4. — Now we went off gold. That is you had a government bond, and it said they would pay you in gold, now they won't. Well you can alibi the situation, but that is repudiation. But they claim it was necessary, and we needed the money.

Now if they can do that in an emergency why can't they pass another one to do away with the exemption on all tax-exempt bonds? There would be more justice in that, for everybody bought 'em just to evade the tax. In other words, we knew we were buying a stolen car when we bought it. But that's why we bought it.

When you repudiate all tax-exempt bonds you only beat 'em out 3 or 4 per cent, but when you repudiated the gold it will take years to find out what you beat him out of.

                        Yours,
                        Will Rogers.

2133   Will Rogers Sees Congress
Two Weeks Too Long On Job

BEVERLY HILLS, Cal., June 5. — Things been just going along fine and it looked like we was going to have some real recovery with Mr. Roosevelt piloting. But I guess it's about over. I see where Congress is starting taking themselves serious again. That means he will have to go on the radio some night and put those gentlemen right back in their place. He made the mistake of keeping 'em there two weeks too long.

I see where the government ruled that beer couldn't be sold on an Indian reservation. They don't want to take 'em off whiskey too quick.

Yours,
Will Rogers.

2134   WILL ROGERS URGES PECORA
TO EXPLAIN OVER THE RADIO

BEVERLY HILLS, Cal., June 6. — Attorney Pecora is liable to have to do like Roosevelt, go on the radio and tell his troubles. That old radio is the greatest club ever invented for a quick appeal. It's worth fifty vetoes. Pecora can make those Senators say "uncle" for him if he tells it to the people.

This is a great country. You never know where our heroes will come from. This Mattern was a trap drummer in a jazz orchestra. That, I think, is the greatest reformation in history.

Yours,
Will Rogers.

2135   MR. ROGERS LISTS FIRST LADY
AS NEW HEROINE IN AVIATION

BEVERLY HILLS, Cal., June 7. — Aviation developed another Lindbergh, Jimmie Mattern and Amelia Earhart last night when Mrs. Franklin D. Roosevelt finished a transcontinental flight. There is a real boost for aviation.

But here is what she really takes the medal for, out at every stop, day or night, standing for photographs by the hour, being interviewed, talking over radio, no sleep. And yet they say she never showed one sign of weariness or annoyance of any kind. No maid, no secretary, just the First Lady of the land on a paid ticket on a regular passenger plane.

If some of our female screen stars had made that trip they would have had one plane for secretaries, one for maids, one for chefs and chauffers and a trailer for "business representatives" and "press agents."

Yours,
Will Rogers.

2136   WILL ROGERS SEES WAR DEBTS
BEING IGNORED ON ALL SIDES

BEVERLY HILLS, Cal., June 8. — All I know is just what I read in the papers. I see where they are not going to discuss the war debts on account of it being rather embarrassing to discuss 'em on the day they are due. They are just going to make out like nobody is paying any attention to 'em and Europe won't be.

They talked about how fast Roosevelt got things done. Congress is going to make a snail out of him. They are going to undo in ten days what it took him ten weeks to do. Excuse me, I got to listen to the fight.

Yours,
Will Rogers.

2137   WILL ROGERS SEES CONGRESS
AS THE 'UNWELCOME GUEST'

BEVERLY HILLS, Cal., June 9. — The Baers are going strong. "Bugs" Baer is the champion humorist, and "Max" the champion boxer. This fellow Schmeling, however, deserves a lot of credit. He has from the start here conducted himself both in and out of the ring in a mighty commendable way that has brought nothing but credit on his country.

Roosevelt is trying to get rid of Congress by tomorrow night. He has tried everything he knows. He has hinted, handed 'em their hat and almost insulted 'em. No more unwelcome guest has ever been invented than Congress. "One-Eyed" Connelly is a sweetheart in comparison.

Yours,
Will Rogers.

2138   WILL ROGERS NOTES ONE ITEM
        OF NEWS THAT IS 'BAD NEWS'

BEVERLY HILLS, Cal., June 11. — Well, there is bad news for the country this morning. There is no earthquake anywhere, no new war, no flood, no pestilence, no new inflation, no new budget that's not balanced, no new Morgan preferred list. It's not any of those terrible things you might think it is, it's worse. It's worse than all of those combined. Aw, gee, I just hate to tell you. I know it will break your heart, but I am going to tell it if it kills us all. Congress didn't adjourn.

Yours,
Will Rogers.

2139   WILL ROGERS WANTS TIME
        STABILIZED BY CONFERENCE

BEVERLY HILLS, Cal., June 12. — The King spoke over the radio this morning. It was 5 o'clock out here. (I was just going to work.) Why don't this world's conference fix it so that whenever anybody does anything it will be the same hour all over.

You will say, "Silly, they can't do that." They can just as easy as they can agree on anything else. Different nations have different problems, just like different nations have the sun shine on 'em at different times. So when they fix how many guns each one is to have, how much foreign goods each one shall consume, and how much each one's money is worth, why at that same time fix it so it's 5 o'clock in the morning everywhere at once.

Yours,
Will Rogers.

2140   ROGERS EXPLAINS RAISING
        OF DEBT ISSUE AT LONDON

BEVERLY HILLS, Cal., June 13. — Even Prime Ministers don't get so "big" that they can overlook what they consider an old insult. When Ramsey McDonald was on the ocean coming over (apparently with all the advantages of a cheap money) why we went off the gold, and he liked to have jumped in the ocean.

40

(l to r) *Will Rogers, Eleanor Roosevelt and Amon G. Carter, Texas publisher, on arrival by plane in Los Angeles, June, 1933.*

Well that stuck in his craw, and when we are all ready to be welcomed to the conference (and it was understood before hand that debts were not to be mentioned), he said "Ha, ha, my revenge," and remarked as follows, "Debts are not to be mentioned here, and I am not going to mention 'em, outside of just casually hinting that they won't be paid. But outside of that I want you to know that I am not going to say a word about 'em."

Yours,
Will Rogers.

2141   ROGERS SEES THE PRESIDENT
           SPARING CONGRESS A SHOCK

BEVERLY HILLS, Cal., June 14. — President has been breaking his neck to get Congress "off the Potomac" before Thursday (the day the debts were due.) He was afraid to have 'em there when the bad news arrived. He was afraid they would commit suicide.

See where some American heiress gave as her reasons for marrying one of this mess of Mdivanis that he was "smart, cute, amusing, interesting, and hangs around all the time." Sounds almost like the recommendation of a good setter pup.

Everyone at London says "something must be done," and it looks like it will be us.

Yours,
Will Rogers.

2142   ROGERS DECIDES TO LEAVE
           DEBT ISSUE TO ROOSEVELT

BEVERLY HILLS, Cal., June 15. — Well, I had a tough time communicating with you all today. I first wrote a piece demanding the other 90 per cent of the debts. Then I got to thinking that maybe we better grab the 10 per cent before they changed their minds. So I just finally decided that Roosevelt would just have to handle it alone. I refuse to enter into it. A debt is just like a religious one—it's a mighty good thing to stay out of. Everybody's mind is made up already.

When that little New England Yankee, Calvin Coolidge said "they hired the money, didn't they?" he covered all the ground.

Yours,
Will Rogers.

2143   WILL ROGERS PAYS TRIBUTE
TO A NATION THAT PAID 100%

BEVERLY HILLS, Cal., June 16. — Give a big hand to little Finland, the only one to pay all she was supposed to. So in picking up hitch hikers along the road, give preference to any one of Finnish descent. The slogan is, "Haul nothing but Finns all the way." Englishman a tenth of the way, but a Frenchman, a Pole, a Czechoslovakian, or a Belgian, let 'em take a bus.

Yours,
Will Rogers.

2144   WILL ROGERS IS NOT CONVINCED
THAT FATHER DESERVES A DAY

SANTA MONICA, Cal., June 18. — So father had a day today did he? Where? But you figure it out and he didn't deserve any more a day than he got.

There is a lot of hooey about poor father being imposed on. Dear old father gets away with quite a bit of murder just because he is father. If he was some outsider and pulled the junk he does they would chuck him in the alley. There is nothing outside of an economist that's been any more overestimated than a father. He is a necessity and that about lets him out.

Yours,
Will Rogers.

2145   WILL ROGERS TELLS ONE WAY
TO DISCOVER A REAL PRINCE

BEVERLY HILLS, Cal., June 19. — There ain't but one way for these foreign Princes (or so-called titled birds) to prove it to Americans, and that is for one of 'em to marry a poor girl. Then we will know he is a Prince. For in all our storybook reading the prince always married the poor girl.

Mr. Roosevelt went out on what he hoped would be a quiet private cruise. All that followed him was a battleship, three Coast Guard cutters, three shiploads of newspaper men and two of camera men. Talk about a gossipy old woman wanting to see and hear everything. American newspapers make an amateur out of her for hanging on the back fence and peeping in the keyhole. If I was him I would make a parachute jump some time and see if I couldn't get a few seconds of privacy.

Yours,
Will Rogers.

2146   Mr. Rogers Discovers Why Conference Met

BEVERLY HILLS, Cal., June 20. — When the economic conference first met in London there was a great deal of doubt as to just what were its hopes and aims. Well, after ten days we are no longer in doubt. They had three reasons for meeting. The first was to cancel the debt to America. The second was to cancel the debt to America. And the third was to cancel the debt to America.

From then on they could take up any little loose odds and ends such as lowering American tariffs, stabilizing American money above the price of their own.

With these accomplished they could all go home and if things didn't pick up in their own countries, think up something else to blame America for, then meet and have another conference.

Yours,
Will Rogers.

2147   Rogers Sees Harvest For Needy Democrats

BEVERLY HILLS, Cal., June 21. — Did you read this in the paper this morning, there are 800 people (get that eight hundred) at work in the Library of Congress. Didn't know there was anybody there but a watchman. Why, that's a librarian to each book. Well the Democrats have found that there is only 40 of these that are Democrats. The total salary in there is $773,360, so the Democrats figure there is about $750,000 of this is a total waste to the country, unless they can get Democrats in there to help read the books for the Congressmen.

The American dollar is down to 75 cents abroad. Be a good time to go over and buy some, for they are still worth $1.60 over here.

Yours,
Will Rogers.

2148   WILL ROGERS EXPOSES
            ONE OLD LINE OF BUNK

BEVERLY HILLS, Cal., June 2. — There is one line of bunk that this country falls for, and always has, "We are looking to America for leadership during the conference, she has a great moral responsibility." And we like a big simp just eat it up. Our delegates swell out their chests and really believe that the world is just hanging by a thread and the American delegates control that thread.

Why they didn't discover us till 1492. And the world had 1492 wars, 1492 peace and economic conferences, all before we was ever heard of. England controls all the oceans, half the land, over half the world's international commerce. France is no babe in arms, Japan and Russia are of age, yet it's America they kid into thinking she is the whole cheese.

Yours,
Will Rogers.

2149   ROGERS NOTES TWO ITEMS
            OF INTEREST IN THE NEWS

BEVERLY HILLS, Cal., June 23. — Harvard decorated Al Smith. Glad to see 'em recognizing achievement instead of just vocabulary.

Champion flyers from all over the world are gathering in here. The Olympic Games of the air start here July first to fourth. You will see every known land plane record broken. This is the National Air Races, the one official meet of the year.

There is a German coming that can do more crazy things in the air than Hitler can on the ground. Then Mussolini is sending his crack flyers. Remember it's one international gathering that gets somewhere.

Yours,
Will Rogers.

2150   WILL ROGERS REMARKS

SANTA MONICA, Cal., June 25. — You talk about an earthquake hitting California. That was kindergarten stuff compared to the news that some nut sent over the cables that Sister Aimee has had a baby. It looked like a case of maternity by remote control. Science is so marvelous it is being confused with miracles, and it looked like birth control by electrical transcription. But now that the facts are all in, we find the visit to the hospital was to beautify the present generation, and not to perpetuate the future.

Yours,
Will Rogers.

2151   ROGERS LIKES THE PLAN
        JOHNSON IS PROPOSING

SANTA MONICA, Cal., June 26. — Did you read this fellow Hugh Johnson's statement in today's papers? He is the dictator of this new "Recovery Act." It sounded awful good and it made sense. Instead of letting a big concern take all the money they make and build a bigger factory, why just give the workers a little more, the stockholders a little more and just keep the factory you have.

I have heard a lot of this fellow Johnson. Barney Baruch thinks he is one of our most able men. He must be on the right track, I see where some of the "big industrialists" are kicking on him already. Well, the President couldn't have appointed a wet nurse for any more needy group of people than the "big ones."

Yours,
Will Rogers.

2152   MR. ROGERS DISCUSSES
        FLIERS AND PARACHUTES

BEVERLY HILLS, Cal., June 27. — Had lunch today at the studio with Udet, the greatest living German ace, with sixty-three planes to his credit, a marvelous stunt flyer, and Lieutenant Falconi, Mussolini's crack acrobatic ace flyer, a young fellow just 25. Both speak English. A couple of fine young fellows. On Saturday we see these babies do their stuff, along with all our crack boys.

During the war we wouldn't let our boys have parachutes for somebody "decided they wasn't safe." The latter part of the war Germany had chutes, and Udet had had his only eleven days when his plane was shot down. Had there been no chute there would have been no Udet today.

46

It makes you sick when you think of the boys we might have saved. But they was afraid maybe one of the chutes wouldn't open.

Yours,
Will Rogers.

2153   WILL ROGERS EXPLAINS
       WHY REPUBLICANS LOST

BEVERLY HILLS, Cal., June 28. — California went so wet Tuesday that they arrested a guy today for bathing in water instead of native wine. West Virginia, which by geography, breeding, dialect and stills, should be Southern, but politically has never been anything, well it reached for a cocktail instead of a coke.

It's not a question of sentiment any more. It's just a question of "where can I get ahold of a ballot, and where is a box to put it in?"

No wonder the Republicans appeared so dumb in there. Anybody that couldn't judge public opinion any better than they did on this question, it's little wonder they are unemployed.

Yours,
Will Rogers.

2154   MILLIONS MADE IN WHEAT
       INTEREST WILL ROGERS

BEVERLY HILLS, Cal., June 29. — That Economic Conference ought to be starting now over in London. The American delegation arrived there Wednesday.

There has been millions and millions of dollars made out of wheat in the last month, but not a cent made by anybody that ever raised any, or anybody that ever really owned any. No wonder the people in so many States voted for legal betting on horse racing. The State does get a per cent of that.

Those who demanded their pound of flesh finally received their satisfaction. "Fatty" Arbuckle accommodated 'em by dying, and from a broken heart. He brought much happiness to many, and never knowingly wronged a soul. The Lord will pass on his innocence or guilt now, and not the reformers.

Yours,
Will Rogers.

2155   Rogers Sees The Dollar
                Fluctuate Like A Wife

BEVERLY HILLS, Cal., June 30. — With all the rest of us using silver, copper, buttons, pins, checkers, wampum and watermelons for money, France can't see any advantage in using real money, so they are liable to dive off the gold standard any day now.

Europe is disgusted with America because she won't say exactly what her dollar is worth. We say our dollar is like a wife, they are worth whatever they are worth to you. They may go to ten cents abroad but they are still worth a dollar to us.

                        Yours,
                        Will Rogers.

2156   Mr. Rogers Gets Thrill
                At Air Races On Coast

SANTA MONICA, Cal., July 2. — Did you ever see real air races by the world's greatest fliers? They are breakfasting in New York and flying in here for lunch.

Mussolini has a flier here who can stay upside down longer than the American delegation in London.

There is the cutest little German war ace who cuts out his engine and does everything in the air with a dead engine, loops, spins, rolls, climbs, and then lands, all this with no more power than Congress had the last session.

Our army, navy and marine exhibition was real thrills. My wife whispered "When I see that it makes me feel that all of our tax money hasn't been wasted."

Aviation is just started.

                        Yours,
                        Will Rogers.

2157   Will Rogers Suggests
                Permanent Delegation

BEVERLY HILLS, Cal., July 3. — This London conference, I read everything I can find about it, but I can't make sense out of what they are driving at. Each nation has its own plan and the minute it's turned down by the others, why you got another anarchist on your hands. Some nation suggested they adjourn but the others won't do it, for it wasn't originally their proposal.

If they do adjourn till January we ought to just leave our troops over there. It would be cheaper than bringing 'em home and then sending 'em back. Why not have a permanent commission, appointed by the year and they just go from one to another of the conferences.

Get men that love to travel and don't take international affairs too serious. Just go for the trip and the laughs. I'll consider heading that delegation.

Yours,
Will Rogers.

2158   WILL ROGERS REMARKS
THAT IT IS OUR DOLLAR

PRESCOTT, Ariz., July 4. — Well, here we are in Prescott, Ariz., the real Western town a mile high and a 100 miles wide. I would rather have Arizona's record as a State than New York with her numbers, Massachusetts with her intellect, or California with her modesty. Arizona prolongs the life of the afflicted as well as makes perpetual the lives of the well.

By the way I see in The Arizona Republic that the London Conference was knocked cuckoo when Roosevelt told them it was our dollar and we could arrange the price of it.

Yours,
Will Rogers.

2159   MR. ROGERS HAS AN IDEA
HOW CONFERENCES END

BEVERLY HILLS, Cal., July 5. — Now Europe is saying that they didn't get so sore at what Mr. Roosevelt said as they did the way he said it. You see diplomats have a thing they call diplomatic language. It's just lots of words, and when they are all added up, they don't mean anything. Well, on account of the President having something to say, and wanting to say it, there is no diplomatic language for that. A diplomat has a hundred ways of saying nothing, but **no** way of saying something, because he has never had anything to say. That's why they call 'em diplomats.

I have always said that a conference was held for one reason only, to give everybody a chance to get sore at everybody else. Sometimes it takes two or three conferences to scare up a war, but generally one will do it. I'll bet there was never a war between two nations that had never conferred first.

Yours,
Will Rogers.

2160   WILL ROGERS ANALYZES
        THE FRENCH SITUATION

BEVERLY HILLS, Cal., July 6. — The morning papers said the London conference blew up, the afternoon ones say it's blown back in again. They ought to put that thing on the stock market and let people make bets on what it will do next.

Well, the boys got to see the King, and that was about all the trip ever was for anyhow.

The whole thing don't seem to be worrying Roosevelt. He has gained eight pounds since it started. I'll bet France has perspired away twenty-five pounds per diplomat in the same time.

They are going to yank her off that gold, just as she yanked England and America off. One wolf can't be in pack and have a bone all to himself.

Yours,
Will Rogers.

2161   MR. ROGERS FINDS WE WIN
        AT GOLF, NOT AT PARLEYS

BEVERLY HILLS, Cal., July 7. — I always did feel that Jimmy Mattern would come through.

This fellow Crawford beat Vines playing tennis in Australia, so why the surprise?

We won the golf championship of England, and run second in the economic conference. (It's on again today.)

John D. Rockefeller is 94 years old. He set the rich a great example by giving away hundreds of millions. The others just as well have done it, they lost it anyhow.

Harvard, Yale and Cornell are rowing out here tomorrow. That's the furthest they ever rowed away from home. If they lose they are going to make 'em row back through the canal.

Yours,
Will Rogers.

2162   MR. ROGERS SUGGESTS
                A SWITCH IN DIET

SANTA MONICA, Cal., July 9. — I thought wheat tax wasn't to be applied only in case wheat prices were below the cost of production. You better switch to eating corn bread. It's better anyhow.

Mr. Hull issued a statement at the conference. I believe what makes Switzerland a great, independent, prosperous and highly educated little country is that I have never read where they "issued a statement."

Fifteen hundred Americans who have been living in Paris for years have decided to come home on account of the price of our money. There is a bunch of folks will be an awful big help to us.

Yours,
Will Rogers.

2163   MR. ROGERS DISCOVERS
                A PARLEY TO EMULATE

SANTA MONICA, Cal., July 10. — It is certainly gratifying to read about one conference that got somewhere.

The Navajo Indians held a conference and decided that they could get along without the services of about twenty-five white officeholders that had been appointed to help look after them. The Indians said they were doing it to save the white man money. Who said the Indian didn't have any humor.

The London conference votes today to see if they meet tomorrow. If they meet tomorrow it will be to find a reason to split up, to keep from meeting the next day.

Then we send white people to take care of the Navajos.

Yours,
Will Rogers.

2164   WILL ROGERS REMARKS

BEVERLY HILLS, Cal, July 11.. — Frank Phillips, of oil fame was out the other day, said he was going to Washington. The oil men were going to draw up a code of ethics. Everybody present had to laugh. If he had said the gangsters of America were drawing up a code of ethics, it wouldn't have sounded near as impossible.

Mary McCormic, the opera singer was at the studio yesterday. She was just "washing up" one of those gold rush M'divani brothers. He had asked her if she couldn't use him any longer, could she kindly recommend him to some wealthy American girl, so Mary and I are going to dig him up one, and we will work on a commission basis.

Yours,
Will Rogers.

2165   MR. ROGERS IS WATCHING OKLAHOMA AND LONDON

BEVERLY HILLS, Cal., July 12. — I see by the papers where my old Governor friend, Bill Murray of Oklahoma, called out the National Guard to keep the folks from voting for beer. Now he will have to call out the United States Army to keep the folks from celebrating the voting of beer.

The London conference has decided to hold on for two more weeks in order for the hotels to kinder play even on the thing and give the American delegation a little golf against the Prince of Wales.

There is nothing as sad, forlorn and forgotten in the world as a delegation returning from a conference. We have forgot now who we sent over.

Yours,
Will Rogers.

2166   MR. ROGERS THINKS THINGS HAVE GONE FAR ENOUGH

BEVERLY HILLS, Cal., July 13. — This fellow Roosevelt can close the banks, he can tell industry how much to pay and how many hours to work, he can hold back the sun, he can evaporate the water, but when he demands that a postmaster has to be able to read, that's carrying dictatorship too far.

When he takes the postmasters out of politics he is monkeying with the very fundamentals of American political parties. How is the army going to fight if they don't get any of the loot?

I tell you this suggestion of his is bordering on treason. The idea of a postmaster being able to read. It looks like an undemocratic move to favor the college man. I tell you he will ruin the Democratic party. We mustn't let him get away with it.

Yours,
Will Rogers.

2167   MR. ROGERS FINDS NOTHING
        IMPORTANT A MONTH LATER

BEVERLY HILLS, Cal., July 14. — Do you remember some of the statements before the London Conference started? The world was to stop revolving, air was to lose its oxygen if the conference failed. Herriot of France said: "America and France look with a like purpose on economic problems. The conference must succeed." Cordell Hull really waxed dramatic. "The failure of the conference will mean the failure of statesmanship, selfishness must be banished from all minds." Well, the thing has flopped and we are getting along better than ever. It just shows that nothing is important a month later.

The funny part about it is that all those statesmen really thought they were going to "make history." Well, history makes itself and the statesmen just drag along.

Yours,
Will Rogers.

2168   MR. ROGERS KEEPS TABS
        ON THE BUSY FLIERS

SANTA MONICA, Cal., July 16. — It's a good thing those Italians landed in seaplanes. If they had landed on the ground they wouldn't have had room to land for Italians.

Well, they have great cause to rejoice. You know where the idea come from don't you? Teddy Roosevelt, when he sent the fleet around the world. There was a lot of Mussolini in that old boy.

I will bet you that this Wiley Post makes it around the world and breaks his own record. I would have liked to have been in there with Post instead of the robot. And I could have if I had known as much as it does.

Well the unemployed will be coming in pretty soon from the London conference.

Yours,
Will Rogers.

2169   MR. ROGERS IS WORKING
         ON CODES AND CALVES

SANTA MONICA Cal., July 17. — Will Hayes was out to see me yesterday. Between working on a movie "code" and roping calves (Bill doing fine on the calves) we had a hard day.

Jack Dempsey getting married in Nevada today. There is an idea for Nevada. If they could build up their marriage industry like their divorces, what would be the matter with guaranteeing everybody a wife, or husband, after six weeks' residence?

Much interested in Wiley Post's trip from Koenigsberg, Germany, to Moscow. Eight years ago I made it with a Russian pilot. He kept pulling the blinds down so I couldn't see anything. I didn't care, I was asleep anyhow.

Yours,
Will Rogers.

2170   MR. ROGERS SEES NEED
         FOR A BIT OF CAUTION

SANTA MONICA, Cal., July 18. — Mr. Roosevelt, most of your plans are working.

Recovery is slow but is fairly sure in most lines. But one gang beat the barrier. It recovered entirely and is now re-recovering on its late recovery.

I don't think I need remind you what "industry" this is. I think a signal sign saying "slow" on a street called Wall (placed there by you personally in order to let 500 essential industries catch

(l to r) Will Rogers, Irvin S. Cobb, Mrs. Cobb, O. O. McIntyre and Will Hays at Santa Monica Ranch.

up to them) would be appreciated by all other traffic headed for recovery.

It wouldn't be so bad, but these are the same traffic violators who got too far ahead and gummed up our last parade.

Yours,
Will Rogers.

2171   MR. ROGERS DEVOTES
        HIS DAY TO GUESSING

BEVERLY HILLS, Cal., July 19. — I guess Dempsey's got a cheerful little earful. I guess Balbo (the only young man that ever looked well in whiskers) is flying somewhere.

I guess the photographers to the London conference are breaking up all the plates they exposed there.

I guess Alabama and Arkansaw voted to show their natives that there was bourbon as well as corn, that all whiskey was not white.

I guess our great little Oklahoma flier is ahead of his record.

I guess California (as usual to be the biggest) passed the highest sales tax rate of the whole forty-eight.

I say I guess all these things for they are not in any of the papers out here. Nothing can get in a paper here when sister Aimee is in, so we are all practically isolated from the world for the next couple of weeks.

Yours,
Will Rogers.

2172   MR. ROGERS WOULD LET
        DRINKERS FEED THE POOR

BEVERLY HILLS, Cal., July 20. — The nearest thing we have to a "non-kick tax," so far, has been the gasoline tax, because they knew the money was going for roads.

Now that repeal is assured, they better get in early and have it understood what the revenue will go to.

What would be the matter with using every cent just for charity and unemployed relief. And make the tax very high, even as high as 50 per cent. If it was a 50 per cent tax, and it went to charity, you couldn't drink alone. Some poor family would be drinking with you.

Five cents a glass beer would cost you a dime. You get the beer, somebody gets a loaf of bread. Anybody give a big champagne party and spend hundreds of dollars, not even a Communist could kick on it for the needy get half of it.

Even at double the price it wouldn't be as high as the country has been paying. Nobody could kick on a person drinking if he gave an equal amount to somebody that was hungry.

That would come nearer being a painless tax than any I know of.

Yours,
Will Rogers.

2173   MR. ROGERS ANALYZES
TENNESSEE DRY VOTE

SALINAS, Cal., July 21. — Say, I got kinder mixed up on my per cent in the paper this morning. I said liquor tax should be 50 per cent. Well, I am going to have to raise you another 50. I meant 100 per cent. You don't mind that little raise do you?

Say, those old moonshiners in Tennessee come pretty near protecting their industry in yesterday's election didn't they?

What did I tell you about that little one-eyed Oklahoma boy. He is a hawk, ain't he? He holds the doubles and singles championship now. If he ever decided to make up a foursome to go round I will take out a ticket with him.

This is Salinas' big day, the king of California rodeos. Here is where you see the old California boys with the long rawhide riatas.

Beautiful flight here by the Seaboard Air Line, and saw all the beautiful ranches.

Yours,
Will Rogers.

2174   ROGERS SEES TREE CROP
FOR REPUBLICANS TO CUT

TRUCKEE, Cal., July 23. — Well last night at midnight we met all the Governors at the line. Fired a nineteen-gun salute (Governors' salute used to be 17, but Mr. Roosevelt on account of being a Governor himself raised 'em 2 guns). Took quite awhile because we only had one cannon, we were able to wake everybody up but Governor Parks of Missouri.

Today they all planted a tree at Lake Tahoe so we at least got 'em working for the first time since they been in office. It's the first reforestation camp for Governors.

It will just about be the Democrats' luck to plant trees all over the country and about the time they are big enough to harvest the Republicans will be back in. Or is that too early?

Yours,
Will Rogers.

2175   MR. ROGERS IS BUSY
            HERDING GOVERNORS·

OAKLAND, Cal., July 24. — Well, I am still herding Governors. Got to go by air to keep up with some of 'em. I'm in Roscoe Turner's Lockheed headed for Oakland, where I will file this.

With Roscoe is Fred Balzar, the flying Governor of Nevada, and Governor Greene of Rhode Island, who has just flown all around Central America.

Governor White of Ohio and family flew from Columbus yesterday. Governor Miller of Wyoming flew from Cheyenne.

This herding Governors ain't near as bad as I thought it would be. Just give 'em plenty to eat and let 'em speak and they don't give you any bother.

Governor Greene of Rhode Island and Governor Cross of Connecticut are awful highly educated and speak different from these western and southern Governors. So my job is really an interpreter for Greene and Cross.

I am carrying a proxy from Bill Murray and Ma Ferguson both, so I got a lot of voting strength in the convention.

Yours,
Will Rogers.

2176   MR. ROGERS IS STILL BUSY
            WITH THOSE GOVERNORS

BEVERLY HILLS, Cal., July 25. — Coming from Frisco to Los Angeles with Roscoe Turner is no more of a trip than going from the observation car to the diner.

I found a lot of good grass, feed and water, and I turned my Governors out for a few days to give their feet and voices a rest. I rushed down here to try and settle the movie strike before they get here as all of 'em want to see the "gals" working.

Here is the best one I have seen yet. A Hollywood film extra, suing her husband for divorce, claimed it on the grounds that "her husband accused her of being the cause of all the depression."

That will certainly be welcome news to Mr. Hoover to know there is somebody blamed for all the world's depression besides him.

Yours,
Will Rogers.

2177   MR. ROGERS WILL FORGIVE
POST FOR MOST ANYTHING

BEVERLY HILLS, Cal., July 26. — Wiley Post said "I have an offer on the stage, and I hope no one will criticise me if I take it." Say, after what that little guy went through with, nobody would criticise him even if he turned banker or took a seat on the stock exchange.

By the way, Mr. Roosevelt has cut the stock market down to three hours a day. They say they did it themselves. Yeah? He just told 'em "now you be good boys. I will give you three hours a day to work on these suckers, and the other twenty-one hours they are under the protection of the fish and game laws."

Yours,
Will Rogers.

2178   MR. ROGERS'S OPINION
OF THE LONDON AFFAIR

BEVERLY HILLS, Cal., July 27. — Well, the London conference closed today.

It just disbanded today, but it ended the day it started.

You will hear a lot of 'em say that it didn't accomplish anything, but it did. They stayed in session till every nation got thoroughly disgusted with each other.

There is no place in the world like a conference to find out the shortcomings of each other.

Now every delegation goes home and tells tales on the others. Of course we leave as the principal villian. We were supposed to bring the pie that they were to cut. When we didn't bring it the banquet was a total loss.

Where is the next conference? We just love to confer.

Yours,
Will Rogers.

2179   WILL ROGERS UPHOLDS
                      NEW KIDNAPPING CODE

SANTA MONICA, Cal., July 28. — Everybody and every industry is getting new codes but this code that the State of Missouri has adopted for kidnapping seems to be the most popular one adopted during this code era.

Well, the Governors are down with us today, looking over the studios, and such. It's one conference that broke up in good humor, and an exchange of ideas no doubt helped each to assist 'em how to run their own State. Mighty pleasant and fine bunch of fellows, tried to sell 'em a lot, but there wasn't a sucker in the bunch.

They are getting out of the State just in time, 'cause Sister Aimee is coming in, and when she comes even Roosevelt has to take to the back pages.

Yours,
Will Rogers.

2180   WILL ROGERS SUBMITS
                      A CHILD-RAISING CODE

SANTA MONICA, Cal., July 30. — Roger Babson who savvies a lot about things before they happen, says people are going back to the old-fashioned investments, that they are starting in to raise children, figuring on the children raising them in their older years. It was becoming a kind of lost art.

Babson figures that if we will just deprive ourselves and furnish the children gas now, that they will do the same for us in our old days.

That's about all there is to supporting anybody nowadays. You never hear, "Who will board me, who will room me?" It's always, "Who will furnish the gas?"

If we could get the State to furnish the gas instead of the school and the teacher we could really put on a child-raising campaign.

Yours,
Will Rogers.

2181   MR. ROGERS OF OKLAHOMA
             HEARS A CALL TO ARMS

BEVERLY HILLS, Cal., July 31. — War Lord Bill Murray has called us Oklahomans to arms again.

Most States use their National Guard for parading purposes, but Bill will call his out just like you ring for ice water.

There is a river between Oklahoma and Texas. Bill owns half of it and Ma Ferguson owns half. If they want to build a bridge let 'em build to the middle and turn around and go back. If they want a dam, let 'em dam their half and let our half alone.

So I guess the next time you hear of me I will be standing in water up to my ankles, right in the middle of Red River, with an old squirrel rifle aimed at that giant octopus Texas, and if Bill says shoot I will shoot.

We will show 'em they can't monkey with our half of the river.

Yours,
Will Rogers.

2182   MR. ROGERS IS IMPRESSED
             BY THAT SALE OF BONDS

BEVERLY HILLS, Cal., Aug. 1. — Yesterday before breakfast the United States Treasury offered $850,000,000 worth of bonds and before the ham and eggs were reached they were all sold.

That means sold and paid for, and salted away, not part paid for and the rest on margins till you sold 'em over the ticker to somebody else.

If industry could interest some permanent buyers, like Roosevelt can in his business, then they could truly call themselves industrialists.

As it is now, they are just manufacturing dice for Wall Street to shoot craps with. Nobody is buying a pair to keep.
                                    Yours,
                                        Will Rogers.

2183   Mr. Rogers, Californian,
                Offers His Sympathy

SANTA BARBARA, Cal., Aug. 2. — If it's as hot back East as the California papers say it is, there is no use me writing you. I should just send flowers to the funerals.

(Excuse me while I put some wood on this fireplace here in the room. Looks like we will never have any Summer.)

This is fiesta week in Santa Barbara. The most colorful event in California. The home of yellow horses and silver saddles.
                                    Yours,
                                        Will Rogers.

2184   Mr. Rogers Reports Rift
                In The California Lute

BEVERLY HILLS, Cal., Aug. 3. — California is pawing the ground over a proposed State income tax. The kicks would carry more weight if we could get somebody to kick that didn't have to pay it.

Some of our patriotic citizens have offered to leave the State if it passes and the State may take 'em up on it.

So, if you see a drove of Rolls-Royces, Lincolns and Cadillacs going East through your town, feed 'em and take care of 'em. They are awful nice folks. They ain't got a thing in the world the matter with 'em only they are millionaires.

You can't legitimately kick on taxes when the money has been made; it's taxes on farms, ranches and business property that has lost money for years. Those folks have the holler coming.

Now excuse me while I hide before some of my good friends shoot me.
                                    Yours,
                                        Will Rogers.

2185   Mr. Rogers Comments
On The Wall St. News

BEVERLY HILLS, Cal., Aug. 4. — Say, that old boy with one shot of teargas on the New York Exchange did more than Roosevelt. He closed it.

It must have been quite a novelty to see the brokers crying instead of the customers.

I been looking since yesterday into this income-tax payment. Now, I can't find a single group to shoulder that tax either. There just don't seem to be any volunteer taxpayers.

I see now what makes a Congressman so unpopular. He just will not fix it so that tax falls on nobody.

                      Yours,
                      Will Rogers.

2186   Mr. Rogers Applauds
The 'No Strikes' Move

SANTA MONICA, Cal., Aug. 6. — Every week or so another fine plan comes from the administration.

This last one of "no strikes during these times and it's to be settled fairly by the government," is one of the best yet.

Unions are fine things, for they are in every line of business. Bankers have their association for mutual benefit. Governors have theirs. All big industries are banded together in some way. But a strike should be the very last means for it is like war. It always falls on those who had nothing to do with calling it.

So viva this last move.

                      Yours,
                      Will Rogers.

2187   Mr. Rogers Gets Back
To The Day's News

BEVERLY HILLS, Cal., Aug. 7. — Cordell Hull, a mighty able man, arrived and told Roosevelt what the London conference had done. That took the first five minutes. Then he told Roosevelt what could have been done if the nations had really wanted to do something. That took hours.

Mr. Roosevelt and Mr. Moley are trying to discourage the kidnappers. When Missouri hangs that one that they sentenced, it's going to be terrible discouragement to one of 'em.

This Oklahoma boy Johnson that is running this NRA, you better not monkey with him. He is hard-boiled and is liable to make you do what you are supposed to do.

Yours,
Will Rogers.

2188   Mr. Rogers Sees In Cuba
             Another Lesson For Us

BEVERLY HILLS, Cal., Aug. 8. — It takes a long time to find out how wrong you are sometimes.

In 1898 we was all in beaded perspiration trying to fix it so Cuba would have liberty and all the accompanying benefits. Now Cuba is having one of the best civil wars that's been produced in years. They got rid of the Spaniards, now they can have a real fight.

Around 1917 we also decided that the world ought to have a mess of democracy, so we went a long ways from home to fix it up for 'em. Well, you can kinder get a rough idea of how we fixed it.

So the moral of the whole thing seems to be stay home, build a big army and navy. They can't come here to lick us, we are not going there to lick them, so how you going to have a war?

Yours,
Will Rogers.

2189   Mr. Rogers Issues
            A Warning On Cuba

SANTA MONICA, Cal., Aug. 9. — Now look out Democratic administration; you are about to revert to the old Republican type. You are telling some Latin American country who can be President and who can't.

There is no doubt that Cuba is run "cockeyed," but what country ain't?

Now, we get our sugar from Cuba, and anything we do in Cuba is going to be misunderstood.

So about the best thing we can do in Cuba is to let Cuba take care of Cuba.

I don't care how little your country is, you got a right to run it like you want to.

When the big nations quit meddling then the world will have peace.

Yours,
Will Rogers.

2190   Mr. Rogers Is Critical
Of Our Policy In Cuba

SANTA MONICA, Cal., Aug. 10. — Everybody knows Mr. Roosevelt don't want any armed trouble with Cuba or anybody else, but when you start telling somebody what they "must do," why you got to back it up with something. You can't tell the bully to quit picking on the boy unless you are prepared to do something to him in case he don't quit picking on him.

The trouble is we never did set Cuba plum free. We kept a clause in the contract where we were to remain the guardian.

Take the sugar out of Cuba and the sugar out of the Philippines and our altruistic feelings would kinder cool off.

Yours,
Will Rogers.

2191   Mr. Rogers, In A Fight,
Craves Real Backing

BEVERLY HILLS, Cal., Aug. 11. — All I know is just what I read in the papers.

I see where United States Congressman Hamilton Fish, whose father made a mighty fine record with the Rough Riders in Cuba, has offered our President the support of the entire Republican party in case of invasion of Cuba. That's great.

Hamilton Fish is a mighty fine patriotic citizen, but I would sure hate to go into Cuba (or even the littlest country on earth) with nothing behind me but the Republican party.

Suppose they shot 'em both, where would you be?

Yours,
Will Rogers.

2192   MR. ROGERS TELLS WHAT
         IS BACK OF THE NEWS

BEVERLY HILLS, Cal., Aug. 13. — Balbo finished a great trip and Mussolini and all Italy kissed him feverently on both cheeks. Now we know why he was growing that beard.

If you see a strange man hiding in the bushes around your place, it's more than apt to be an ex-President of Cuba.

I see by the papers that during this kidnapping epidemic a well-known machine gun company has patriotically agreed to not sell any to gangsters till they have used up the ones they have.

Yours,
Will Rogers.

2193   MR. ROGERS SEES OPENING
         FOR A NEW ENTERPRISE

SANTA MONICA, Cal., Aug. 14. — Course I could talk about "our warships going to Cuba," "our foreign trade picking up," "sixteen nations bought more," "President of France knocked down by a bicycle." That's not as bad as me the night I landed in Yokohama, Japan, and got run over by a rickshaw. But the real bit of news was some ingenious Swiss from Switzerland who wanted to smuggle some Swiss watches into Spain. So this old "yodeler" drove a bunch of geese afoot from Switzerland clear across France to Spain and he had the watches tied under the geese's wings.

Think what a fellow could bring into this country if he had himself a good bunch of trained whales.

Yours,
Will Rogers.

2194   MR. ROGERS TAKES ONE
         OF THOSE LITTLE JAUNTS

BEVERLY HILLS, Cal., Aug. 15. — Well, I was just sitting around here late this afternoon and happened to have a day off tomorrow (Wednesday) and the West is playing the East polo in Chicago tomorrow.

I think of leaving here late this evening, flying to Chicago, see the game and get back Wednesday night.

Over Boulder Dam about 9 tonight, Salt Lake at midnight, see the sun rise in Cheyenne, breakfast in Omaha, lunch in Chicago, all on a passenger line.

And by the way the old airplane came in pretty handy getting the ex-Presidents out of Cuba. There is nothing that will drive you to flying quicker than to have somebody after you.

If this NRA works out (and it certainly looks like it will) it will just show you, you don't have to have war to make folks patriotic.

Yours,
Will Rogers.

2195   MR. ROGERS IS BOUND UP
        IN POLO AT THE MOMENT

LAKE FOREST, Ill., Aug. 16. — Well, the old Western polo boys got licked today. It now stands one game each and the finals Sunday.

It was anybody's game for a long time, then our old cowpuncher Rube Williams got hurt. We got to try and get Eric Pedley, a crack player from the Coast, to come back here.

Well, all you hear back here is codes, "How do you think NRA is going?" and it's wonderful the way every one seems to enter into it.

Yours,
Will Rogers.

2196   MR. ROGERS, IN CAPITAL,
        SEES WHEELS GO ROUND

WASHINGTON, D. C., Aug. 17. — Well, I flew in here this afternoon from Chicago. Come to the old fountain of rumors to watch the hired boys work under perspiration.

The town has got "coditis." Every time you come to Washington somebody is headlined. All the interest is centered here. Last time I was here they were featuring J. P. Morgan, once the R. F. C., but this time all briefcases can be followed and they lead to the Hoover building (the Department of Commerce Building, covering the lower end of the District of Columbia and the entire northeastern part of Virginia).

Well, this old Oklahoma Johnson is in there and he is papa in Washington now. You bring your code to him. He uncodes it, recodes you another one, you sign it, get you a bluebird and go back in business again.

Yours,
Will Rogers.

2197   ROGERS BARS POLITICIANS
FROM COMEDIANS' CODE

WASHINGTON, D. C., Aug. 18. — I been working day and night since almost yesterday with this fellow Johnson on a code for comedians. He claims that Senators and Congressmen come under our code. I claim theirs is a separate union, that they are professionals and in a class by themselves and that us amateur comedians should not be classed with 'em.

I hate to defy this NRA, but I am going to carry my fight to the country, because, according to his code, it would give work to more Senators and Congressmen, and I claim that's the only thing we don't want any more of. So it looks like I am really the first one to lock horns with this tough guy Johnson. But I believe I got the people with me.

Yours,
Will Rogers.

2198   MR. ROGERS FINDS PACE
IN CAPITAL TOO SWIFT

CHICAGO, Ill., Aug. 20. — My friend Johnson, the code man, was going too fast for me so I left him. His code for himself and staff is 35 hours, not a week, but a day. If he ever goes to sleep he won't wake up till Xmas.

Here is the best one happened in Washington. All the big oil men of course were there and that of course meant a big poker game. Any time two oil men meet they don't open a filling station; they open a poker game. Then an oil man never travels without his big lawyer. Then in another room the lawyers have a crap game.

In the poker game for the first time it was all cash on the table, no checks. They didn't trust each other. That's their new code.

The lawyers used their same old code, of cash. They had never trusted each other.

Yours,
Will Rogers.

P. S. — Now for the big polo game to watch the West take the East like Huey Long took Louisiana.

2199   Mr. Rogers Gloats A Bit
             Over The Polo Result

CHICAGO, Ill., Aug. 21. — Well, the "hill billies" beat the "dudes" and took the polo championship of the world right out of the drawing rooms and into the bunk house.

She won't go East in years, for the West always thought you had to have a birth certificate to play it. Now every cowpuncher is herding in the heifers with a corn-plaster saddle and even the "hay-heavers" have changed a pitchfork into a polo mallet.

Twenty thousand Chicagoans witnessed Sunday's social massacre. Nineteen thousand of 'em had never seen a horse, much less a polo game.

So from now on west of the Mississippi "Old Dobbin" plows in the field only till 4 o'clock, when he will be washed, scrubbed and his teeth polished and he goes out on the lawn to cavort in what used to be known as strictly a social recreation.

Poor old society, they got nothing exclusive left. The movie folks outmarried and outdivorced 'em, the common folks took their cocktails, "near" society took to bridge. Now polo has gone to the buckwheat belt, so poor old society hasn't even been left a code.

Yours,
Will Rogers.

2200   Mr. Rogers Discusses
             A Few Farm Problems

LAS VEGAS, Nev., Aug. 22. — I'm going to drop this off here at Hoover Dam.

Hope they don't irrigate more land so they can raise more things that they can't sell and have to plow up more rows, kill more pigs to keep 'em from becoming hogs.

Looks like this whole hog-destroying scheme of Mr. Wallace's is a direct slap against my old friend and companion "Blue Boy."

What Wallace is trying to do is to teach the farmer corn acreage control and the hogs birth control, and one is just as hard to make understand it as the other.

Yours,
Will Rogers.

2201   MR. ROGERS TAKES A POLL
ON THIS NRA BUSINESS

BEVERLY HILLS, Cal., Aug. 23. — As I look at this NRA after having a long chat with the President about it, and Hugh Johnson, the chief executioner, Secretary of Labor Miss Perkins, Senators, well informed Washington writers, airplane pilots, taxi drivers, bell hops, steel men, oil men and one lone optimistic bootlegger (who still believed this country would soon see the error of its ways and return him back his stolen profession).

Now as I say I have asked all about it. (For once in my life I kept still and let them do the talking.)

Now, the doubt about the scheme is in proportion to the extra money each particular party would be asked to put in the scheme, and even each disagreer hoped that it would work, but would prefer having it work without affecting him.

Still many a big man was for it heart and soul.

Yours,
Will Rogers.

2202   MR. ROGERS HAS A MAN
HE WOULD LIKE TO PLACE

BEVERLY HILLS, Cal., Aug. 24. — As usual, Al Smith made the best speech made on the NRA, the most sensible and clear reasoning in support of it.

I hope in all this readjustment that some real important place can be found where we can utilize that fellow's good common sense.

And talking about what people said, this McCormick of Chicago, who has just returned from Germany, editor of the great Chicago

Tribune (no, I don't write for it) says very astonishingly, but no doubt truthfully:

"Along with the youth of Germany in this war spirit is the women. When bigger wars are made, women will make 'em, as always."

Yours,
Will Rogers.

2203   MR. ROGERS IS ABSORBED
IN HIS HOME TOWN NEWS

BEVERLY HILLS, Cal., Aug. 25. — California has a murder trial going on out here now (some professor is supposed to have killed his wife,) so you all know when your hometown papers can scare up a good murder trial, why, that's just like striking pay dirt, so I don't know what Hugh Johnson is doing with the auto code, how Secretary Wallace of Agriculture is making out trying to keep pigs from growing up, what Cordell Hull is doing toward making international conferences useful as well as decorative, what Secretary of Labor Miss Perkins is doing to see that everything in the N.R.A. is not unionized, or is unionized, or whatever they decide to do with it. As I say, we got a murder trial, and we don't know a thing in the world that is happening outside of that, so pardon my ignorance.

Yours,
Will Rogers.

2204   MR. ROGERS GUESSED RIGHT
ON THE TEXAS ELECTION

SANTA MONICA, Cal., Aug. 27. — Helen Wills Moody, congratulations.

I don't believe the Armistice got as much publicity. And poor Texas, they would be unfortunate enough to have their prohibition election on the same day Helen was losing her championship.

So it will be Tuesday or Wednesday before we hear what happened down there. Voted like they drink, I guess, just for a change.

President Roosevelt yesterday made a speech to his rich Dutchess County neighbors, none of whom voted for him (smart bunch of lads?).

I would like to see the "code" he makes out for them.

Yours,
Will Rogers.

2205   MR. ROGERS ON THE EXIT
OF A 'BRAIN TRUSTER'

SANTA MONICA, Cal., Aug. 28. — I believe that Mr. Moley, chief of the "brain trusters," getting out is about the starting of the end of college professors in government.

A professor gets all of his out of a book, but the politician, as bad as he is, does have an understanding of human nature and the mob.

So we just as well become reconciled to the fact that the old politician is with us, "even unto death."

Theories are great, they sound great, but the minute you are asked to prove one in actual life, why the thing blows up.

So professors back to the classroom, idealists back to the drawing room, Communists back to the soap box (and use some of it), but old Congressman "Hokum" and old Senator "Hooey" are still the Mussolinis of our country.

                       Yours,
                       Will Rogers.

2206   MR. ROGERS SUGGESTS
A NEW KIND OF 'WEEK'

BEVERLY HILLS, Cal., Aug. 29. — So Germany has barred Schumann-Heink. Say, if my own wife barred Schumann-Heink from anything I would be with Schumann. A grand liberal-minded soul.

Some fellow on Long Island, N. Y., in a dress suit pounced on my old friend Huey Long. Huey didn't recognize him in the disguise. Dress suits are used only in Louisiana to encase dead politicians.

By the way, did anybody ever see a United States Senator in his home State after the night he is elected? I have met 'em all over the world when Congress was not in session, but never saw one at home. They are always making speeches about "my fine people back home," but they never want to see 'em.

So I hereby start a movement to create another week. Like apple week, prune week, it's "meet your own Senator week" and make him come home no matter what happens to him.

                       Yours,
                       Will Rogers.

2207   MR. ROGERS HAS NEW IDEA
        FOR LONG ISLAND PARTIES

BEVERLY HILLS, Cal., Aug. 30. — See picture in the papers of an old boy eating fifty-four ears of corn as an appetizer, and a woman 71 years old stored away forty-five.

Since we give 'em the vote there just is no end to women's cleverness. Men just can't hardly beat 'em at anything.

If Secretary of Agriculture Wallace will get busy and promote a lot of these corn-eating contests (there is no reason why it can't be made as popular as bridge; it has much more to recommend it).

Well, with a lot of these contests they won't have to be plowing up every third row of corn.

Long Island better have this kind of parties, then they can't throw anything at the Senators but the cobs.

Yours,
Will Rogers.

2208   MR. ROGERS SEES AN IDEA
        OF HIS FLOP WITH A THUD

SANTA MONICA, Cal., Aug. 31. — Well, like a lot of my big ideas, they don't seem to work out. There must be a bit of college professor in me somewhere.

You remember a couple of days ago I wanted to have the home folks meet their Senator. Now that sounded practical but you would be surprised at the amount of resentment that has come to my roll-top desk. Why, my idea was as "wet" as the State of Washington.

They all claim they don't want to see their Senator. That's why they elected him, was to get rid of him. If they had wanted him at home they would have kept him at home.

So there goes another big Rogers idea in the ash can.

Yours,
Will Rogers.

2209   WILL ROGERS IS PUZZLED
        OVER ALL THIS INFLATION

BEVERLY HILLS, Cal., Sept. 1. — We got a little shot of inflation coming along now in a few weeks, and a lot of us dumb ones are trying to find out just what it is, just where it attacks you, and how.

All you can learn about it is "money will be cheaper." Cheaper than what? If a dollar is worth only 10 cents how are you going to get your clutches on it any easier than now. Unless they give it away, I can't see where its going to be any big help to everybody.

Now I am only asking these questions, I don't want 'em answered.

Had a chat yesterday with Mr. Raskob, a wealthy man that was a Democrat before it was fashionable, in fact he was ostracised from the other rich for years. He is in favor of inflation (rather unique for a millionaire). Well even he had a little trouble explaining what it was so I certainly don't want to have to listen to any of you amateurs in the money business.

Yours,
Will Rogers.

2210   MR. ROGERS OFFERS A BIT
       OF ADVICE TO THE NRA

SANTA MONICA, Cal., Sept. 3. — Now like any good cause, it's naturally going to have a little gossip and whisperings about it.

So, you Democrats that are handing out the jobs in Washington on all this National Recovery program don't discriminate against the old Republican. This is a national thing and I doubt if any country, regardless of politics, ever in peace time entered into a thing any more wholeheartedly.

Somebody good naturedly started the definition of NRA, "no Republicans allowed." You want to keep that a joke.

This thing is on a much higher plane than handing out the old postoffices.

Yours,
Will Rogers.

2211   MR. ROGERS IS IN SEARCH
       OF A TIRELESS HOLIDAY

SANTA MONICA, Cal., Sept. 4. — Every holiday ought to be named "Labor Day." If we could ever get vacations down to where you wasn't any more tired on the day one was over than on our regular work day it would be wonderful.

The President caught Vincent Astor not watching him close and sneaked off his yacht and went on a whaler. From what I can hear about yachting the tough part is getting somebody to ride with you. One rough day and you lose half your crew and all your guests.

By the way, a good stiff sales tax on hamburgers today would have paid our national debt. Give an American a one-piece bathing suit, a hamburger and five gallons of gas and they are just as tickled as a movie star with a new divorce.

Yours,
Will Rogers.

2212 MR. ROGERS IS NOT UPSET
BY THE FORD IMPASSE

BEVERLY HILLS, Cal., Sept. 5. — See some of the papers are kinder excited over "what will Henry Ford do?"

Well, that's the least thing we got to worry about nowadays. He will do better by labor than anybody else. So that's good enough.

There is only one drawback to this "buying in September." Women with charge accounts and sending stuff on approval, they will do a lot of September buying, but Lord help October when they start to returning the clothes because they didn't look good at the party.

They say there is a hurricane down in Texas and Florida. Think I saw a little squib about it in some California paper.

Yours,
Will Rogers.

2213 MR. ROGERS REMAINS COOL
DESPITE THE CUBAN NEWS

SANTA MONICA, Cal., Sept. 6. — Even experts don't know what the weather will do. Even millionaires don't know what Wall Street will do.

There is millions of things that nobody knows anything about in advance, but the dumbest guy in the world knows that the minute a Latin American country has a revolution that it is just the opening game of a series of 'em.

You know we got the wrong impression of a revolution. They was raised on 'em down there. They love 'em. It's their only relaxation. Sure people get killed sometimes. If it's a first-class Grade A revolution, they may lose about as many as we lose over our weekends by trying to pass somebody on a turn.

There is one thing about a Latin American country. No matter who is running it, they are always run the same.

Yours,
Will Rogers.

2214   WILL ROGERS REMARKS

BEVERLY HILLS, Cal., Sept. 7. — Most of us had the impression that the late big war was started all at once by Germany deciding it would be a good time to go through Belgium. Well do you know this fellow that died yesterday, the Englishman, Viscount Grey, who at that time was Britain's Foreign Secretary? Well, according to all official records that have been published they had had dozens of conferences and communications among all these nations for weeks (also read Col. House's books.) So according to all the dope, this fellow Grey had quite a time arranging the war. It looked for a while like he wasn't going to be able to put it on. Now I see where Lloyd George's book says the same thing. It's awful hard to get into a war without a diplomat.

Yours,
Will Rogers.

2215   ROGERS SEES A PARADE
                   OF PRESIDENTS IN CUBA

BEVERLY HILLS, Cal., Sept. 8. — Must seem like the old Republican days to the marines to be loading on a boat and be going to somebody else's country to help 'em run it.

I see where some time today they are supposed to pick out Cuba's next week's President.

Our Secretary of the Navy has gone abroad to review the American fleet. Cuba don't care so much for a new President as they do just to see how quick the last one can leave town.

If these last few Presidents Cuba throws out have got as big a family as Machado had, Cuba will wake up some morning with no population.

      Yours,
      Will Rogers.

2216   Mr. Rogers Sympathizes
     With The Little Nation

SANTA MONICA, Cal., Sept. 10. — Well, I guess I am all wet as usual, but a headline in all the papers like this don't particularly add to my patriotism:

"Cuba picks new president as battleship Mississippi steams into port."

Any more than the following one would: "United States of America having internal trouble and his Majesty King George has dispatched his dreadnaughts to stand by in New York harbor to protect British investments in America and to see that the right man is elected."

But that couldn't happen for they are both big nations, and would mean war. But when one nation is big and one is little, why the little nation's port is just like a public regatta. Everybody can come in that's got a boat.

The whole thing as I see it all over the world today is that the little nations has got no business being little.

      Yours,
      Will Rogers.

2217   Mr. Rogers Has New Idea
     Of What NRA Really Is

BEVERLY HILLS, Cal., Sept. 11. — I was talking to Oscar Lawler yesterday, California's most capable and common sense lawyer.

He says that the NRA is nothing but a code of fair ethics of people doing business with each other, and thinks it was rather a slam against a nation that we have to be forced by government control and patriotic persuasion to do what's right.

I never had thought of it in that light, but that's all it is.

It looks like they are trying to get a little more conscience on the market and a little less preferred stock.

It's just decency by government control.

Yours,
Will Rogers.

2218   Mr. Rogers Again Offers
            Some Advice On Cuba

BEVERLY HILLS, Cal., Sept. 12. — Did you see in the paper this afternoon where Cuba is liable to have another change of government?

Well, the other day I told you (or was you listening?) that revolutions run in packs, like hounds or bananas. One revolution is just like one cocktail. It gets you organized to get ready for the next.

Now they are just having more fun down there than they have had in years, if old "Mother Superior" America wasn't trying to horn in on all of it.

It's their country. It's their sugar. Take the sugar out of Cuba and we would no more be interested in their troubles than we would a revolution among the Zulus.

Yours,
Will Rogers.

2219   Mr. Rogers Recommends
            A New Anti-Crime Move

BEVERLY HILLS, Cal., Sept. 13. — Say Los Angeles come through with something yesterday that looks like one of the best measures to help offset this crime racket.

It looks like every time a man commits a crime and is caught his prison record reads like he had been a tourist inmate of every prison worth attending. There hasn't been an amateur crook caught in years.

Well, Los Angeles makes every visiting ex-criminal register. Course you will say, "Yes, but he won't register." Well that's the catch. If he don't he is liable to six months' imprisonment for not complying with the law.

Certain state paroled ones are exempt to save injustice to ones who are doing right. But it's mainly to catch the visiting gentleman. It might be worth you other towns looking into.

Yours,
Will Rogers.

2220   Mr. Rogers Bares Secret
Of 'Cockeyed' Oil Wells

BEVERLY HILLS, Cal., Sept. 14. — Say, they are having a time out here in California in the courts over something I bet a lot of you didn't know anything about.

They drill an oil well down straight for quite a little ways, then they got a gadget that turns it off to one side and they head it out towards where they know some oil is.

Mr. Roosevelt owns what's in the ocean, but these old boys are diving down, turning to the left and robbing the poor Democrats.

It's a great thing for these States that have no oil. All you do is drill a few "cockeyed" wells near the line and go over and get it from "Ma" Ferguson or "Alfalfa Bill" Murray.

By the way, where do you get one of those tools?

Yours,
Will Rogers.

2221   Mr. Rogers Philosophizes
On Big And Little Things

BEVERLY HILLS, Cal., Sept. 15. — Cuba, you better hurry and get a dictator, a President, a keeper, or something. For one more week is all you got to stay on the front page. When the Giants have won two games, Washington two, and the Notre Dame back field starts percolating. Cuba just as well be Tasmania as far as the papers are concerned.

And that's what makes us a great nation. We take the little things serious, and the big ones as a joke.

Many, many people out of work, some even in actual want, yet carrying on in confidence, and in hope. When the little fellow, that is actually in want, can have faith in his government, by golly the big ones should certainly carry on, for they have never missed a meal so far.

Yours,
Will Rogers.

2222   MR. ROGERS CONFESSES
                TO FAILURE AS CRUSADER

SANTA MONICA, Cal., Sept. 17. — Looks like the days of these "sob sisters" moaning around over everyone on trial is over. Juries have started in giving the deceased or injured party a break.

Looks like my single-handed crusade to keep us out of Cuba hasn't been very successful. Now we got to go in to protect Americans who would have needed no protection had we had no diplomacy or battleships to get us in wrong in the first place.

We are just getting ready to trade lives for sugar. It would be better if we all learned to drink it black.

                              Yours,
                                 Will Rogers.

2223   MR. ROGERS IS CONVINCED
               THE OIL MEN ARE HARD UP

BEVERLY HILLS, Cal., Sept. 18. — Hope the oil business gets straightened out for it is tough.

Just today in a movie I was making I had a scene where I met an Indian. During our conversation I found out that he was an Osage. That's the rich tribe that lives by us down in Oklahoma. Why when oil was going good, an Osage wouldn't have even spoken to a poor Cherokee. They used Rolls Royces for trailers.

See now where the French are about to go off the gold. If we get as much enjoyment out of them going off as they did us, we ought to feel great all winter.

                              Yours,
                                 Will Rogers.

2224   MR. ROGERS CONFESSES
               TO A LOT OF GUESSING

BEVERLY HILLS, Cal., Sept. 19. — "Mr. Hoover meets reporter, but won't discuss national topics."

The rest of us discuss 'em morning, night and noon and I don't suppose there ever was a time when everybody knew as little about what they were talking about as they do today.

Actual knowledge of the future was never lower but hope was never higher.

Confidence will beat predictions any time.

       Yours,
       Will Rogers.

2225   Mr. Rogers Goes Highbrow
     On The Inflation Question

BEVERLY HILLS, Cal., Sept. 20. — To inflate or not to inflate, that is the Democratic question. Whether it's nobler in the minds to suffer the slings and arrows of southern politicians or to take up inflation against a sea of economists, and by opposing, end them.

To expand, to inflate, to inflate perchance to dream. Aye there's the rub.

For in that sleep of inflation, what dreams may come, puzzle the will and make us doubtful whether to bear those ills we have or fly to others we know not of.

       Yours,
       Will Rogers.

2226   Will Rogers Remarks

BEVERLY HILLS, Cal., Sept. 21. — Put a tax on the New York Stock Exchange, so they say they are going to move to New Jersey. There is no industry that could move easier. All they have to do is change their telephone number, pick up the blackboard and tell the loafers where to meet tomorrow. But those old Jersey politicians are not far behind the Tammany one. The minute they see what an easy "racket" it is they will be there with the tax too. Wouldn't it be wonderful if a man could move his farm or house when the tax comes?

       Yours,
       Will Rogers.

2227   ROGERS CALLS THE ROLL
                 ON REGIMENT OF INITIALS

    BEVERLY HILLS, Cal., Sept. 22. — The President just created the F. E. R. A. (Federal Emergency Relief Association) and the A. A. A. (Agricultural Adjustment Administration) and the P. W. A. (Public Works Administration), so the F. E. R. A., and the A. A. A. and the P. W. A. are to work in conjunction with the N. R. A. with the financial help of the R. F. C., who will pay the C. O. D.s of the C. C. C. (Citizens Conservation Camps) and take in return for all money loaned out to all these initials, I.O.U.s.

    Never was a country in the throes of more capital letters than the old U. S. A. But we still haven't sent out the S. O. S.

                              Yours,
                              Will Rogers.

2228   MR. ROGERS SEES STRIKES
                 VERY UNPOPULAR TODAY

    SANTA MONICA, Cal., Sept. 24. — "The Iowa Farmers Holiday Association will strike if the President don't guarantee passage of the Frazier Mortgage Refinancing Bill." How in the world can Mr. Roosevelt guarantee what Congress will do? There is not even a fortune teller would dare predict. They will meet and from then on we just got to put our trust in the Lord.

    I am not trying to advise the "holiday farmers," for I don't know what a holiday farmer is, but it's a tough time for any one group to start making demands, for I think you will find this fellow feels he owes allegiance to the eater as well as the raiser. The farmer deserves a profit, but the guy that's not eating deserves a meal more. The stockholder deserves his dividend, but the unemployed deserves his job more.

    I can think of nothing more unpopular than a strike, a strike of anything.

                              Yours,
                              Will Rogers.

2229   MR. ROGERS THINKS MCKEE
                 MAY NOW KNOW BETTER

    BEVERLY HILLS, Cal., Sept. 25. — This President of Cuba has been in now two weeks. One more week and he will be retired by the Cuban Constitution for "long service to his country." He hasn't got many votes with him but he has some of the best marksmen in

Cuba. We have messed around now till we don't know whether to go in or have our folks come out.

Talk of opening seven thousand closed banks. That will put over a half-million vice presidents back on the payroll.

This fellow McKee that was Mayor of N. Y. and was discharged for efficiency, I see they are going to give him another chance. Maybe he will know enough to just be a N. Y. Mayor the next time.

Yours,
Will Rogers.

2230   MR. ROGERS SEES RAILROADS
             NOW FINALLY WAKING UP

BEVERLY HILLS, Cal., Sept. 26. — Roscoe Turner crossed the country in ten hours. That's bringing towns too close together. Railroads are finally waking up. They are building a new train now that wasn't modeled in the Nineties.

But we have to take the bad news with the good. Ring Lardner died. You can always get better planes, better trains, but we can't get another Ring Lardner. What a privilege to have known him since those good old days when he wrote sketches for Mr. Ziegfeld's Follies.

In years to come, when libraries put just books in one wing and literature in the other, you are mighty liable to find Lardner's writings right in with the literature.

Yours,
Will Rogers.

2231   WILL ROGERS SUGGESTS
             CARE IN BROADCASTING

BEVERLY HILLS Cal., Sept. 27. — While some of these radio commissions are telling how many kilowatts and how many detours stations can have, why don't they limit them to how many rumors they can broadcast without any single iota of facts.

I am getting tired of being used as the object of some catastrophe, and I suppose lots of others have the same thing happen to 'em all over the country. Let 'em lose some lawsuits, and they will start investigating before they start broadcasting.

Well, I see where the New York Stock Exchange bluffed Tammany out of the tax. They are going to put it on the street car and subway travelers.

Yours,
Will Rogers.

2232   ROGERS SEES TAXPAYER
TURNING ON POLITICIAN

BEVERLY HILLS, Cal., Sept. 28. — With a white rat rising up and knocking the ears down on six rattlesnakes, it may be the turning of a new era. A taxpayer is liable to become aroused and bump off about half the political payroll. Then when kidnappers admit where 75,000 bucks are buried, and it was really there and had been for several months, why that shows we have somebody in the country that can live off their income and not have to dig up their principal.

But when it costs the government $66,000 to hire a steamship company to carry one pound of picture postcards across the water, when it would be cheaper to cable at government expense.

Yours,
Will Rogers.

2233   ROGERS SUGGESTS WAR
OF KENTUCKY COLONELS

BEVERLY HILLS, Cal., Sept. 29. — There is so many boni-fide Colonels of Kentucky that they have formed an association and have been split up into zones. Irvin Cobb (who can't return to Paducah) has been commander in chief of the Colonels east of the Mississippi River. And I have been appointed to direct all Kentucky Colonels west of the river.

A war of extermination of Kentucky Colonels may be just what the country needs, so nothing would please me better than to meet Irv, and his fat, gouty, worn out Negro-dialect old Colonels, with my bunch of young, agile, alert boys that reside on the progressive side of the river.

Our men are Colonels through achievement and not just through appetite.

Yours,
Will Rogers.

Will Rogers in scenes from the motion picture Mr. Skitch, *based on Ann Cameron's novel,* Green Dice (Fox Film Corporation, 1933).

2234   WILL ROGERS EXTOLS MEN
WHO PIONEER IN THE AIR

SANTA MONICA, Cal., Oct. 1. — Roscoe Turner who just broke the West-East record, already holding the East-West was just out. Men like Turner, Hawkes, Doolittle, Post, Mattern and others promote the money, risk their lives then do things that today are considered a stunt, but tomorrow are an everyday affair.

We used to think the Japanese couldn't fly but I saw a weekly where it looked like there was millions doing it. Lindbergh says Russia has a plane for every beard, so we got to speed up. Railroads, airlines, kidnapping jury convictions and everything. Whatever is going to happen to us let it happen quick, and get it over with.

Yours,
Will Rogers.

2235   ROGERS PRAISES ROOSEVELT
FOR HIS ADDRESS TO LEGION

BEVERLY HILLS, Cal., Oct. 2. — You know the thing you got to admire about Roosevelt when he is in some argument with somebody he goes right before 'em personally and lays his reason right before 'em.

Politicians said it would be suicide to cut any pensions. Politicians said he shouldn't go to the American Legion convention. He did both.

Sending an emissary or a message has ruined many a big man. Everybody likes to hear it straight from the boss, even if you are going to get fired, and the Legion loved him for it.

Yours,
Will Rogers.

2236   MR. ROGERS GETS AN IDEA
FOR RADIO IMPROVEMENT

BEVERLY HILLS, Cal., Oct. 3. — These announcers of the World Series in both the radio systems did a great job.

I got a radio in my stable. Well, they made it seem so real that half a dozen times I started into a box stall to buy a hot dog and a bottle of beer.

I like the way they announced where the batter come from, his home town, his weight, age, batting average and who he had been keeping company with.

And that's what should be done with radio singers.

"This crooner is from Adenoid, N. J. He sings left handed, weighs 118 pounds without his tonsils, he sang 335 songs last year, with nothing to remember 'em by but his manuscript. He was first with Claremore, Okla., in the O. K. League. Divorced three times, and is looking for a break."

      Yours,
      Will Rogers.

2237   MR. ROGERS CASTS AN EYE
     OVER THE LATEST NEWS

BEVERLY HILLS, Cal., Oct. 4. — Mr. Roosevelt's reforestation program will pay for itself if they do nothing but teach young men what to do in a forest fire. Our catastrophe out here will be a lesson to politicians as to who to put in charge of men.

I had known Young Bill Stribling, the prize fighter, and his family for years. Gee, he was a fine young man, a credit to any profession.

The savior of Austria, a little fellow standing three feet six on stilts, was shot, but fortunately no damage, and a nation was saved by physique.

      Yours,
      Will Rogers.

2238   MR. ROGERS SENDS ALONG
     A PICTURE FANCY WEAVES

BEVERLY HILLS, Cal., Oct. 5. — For days I have heard on the radio these baseball announcers say, "I will now give you the picture of the World's Series. Washington versus New York at Washington. New York at bat. Ninth inning."

Well, they got me doing it. I will now give you the picture. It's the U. S. versus depression. The score is three to two in favor of depression. It's the last half of the ninth inning. U. S. at bat. Two men are out and the bases are loaded.

Unemployment is on third, NRA is on second, Farm Relief on first and Roosevelt at bat. He has already had two hits during the game.

There is three balls and two strikes on the batter. Depression's team has gathered around its pitcher. The batter is all confident. He rubs his hands in dirt, he smiles; here it comes. Bang!

It's a hit. It's a hit. Unemployment crosses the plate. NRA comes home with the winning run.

Boy, oh boy! What a game!

Yours,
Will Rogers.

2239 MR. ROGERS HAILS LEGION
FOR SANE CHICAGO STAND

BEVERLY HILLS, Cal., Oct. 6. — Just been reading over the resolutions that were passed in Chicago by the American Legion this week. They were as level-headed and broad-minded as ever passed by any organization, and here was an astonishing thing, they come out unanimous for a sound dollar.

Now that showed they wasn't taking the easy way out. And there was a body of men representing the cross section of our country if ever one did. You would be surprised at the amount of people that don't care how much anything else jumps up and down every day, but they want to know what that old dollar is worth asleep or awake.

But enough of this. For the one way to detect a feeble-minded man is to get one arguing on economics.

Yours,
Will Rogers.

2240 MR. ROGERS GETS A LAUGH
OUT OF A GOOD-WILL TRIP

SANTA MONICA, Cal., Oct. 8. — When you really figure it out, there is no individual that is as funny as a nation (any nation; not just these).

An Argentine President visited Brazil (the first time in generations). He went there in an Argentine battleship, was met by Brazilian cruisers and seventy-five fighting planes (now all this mind you is on a good-will trip).

Imagine individuals doing that. I go to visit you and take along a Winchester and belt full of cartridges. You meet me at your gate with your best polished machine gun and two Colt's .45s.

But at the banquet that night there is wonderful speeches of good-will. Then next morning both of 'em start building more guns. Viva diplomacy, nobody is fooled, nobody is hurt. Viva hooey.
     Yours,
      Will Rogers.

2241   Mr. Rogers Puts Britain
     On The Preferred List

BEVERLY HILLS, Cal., Oct. 9. — The British are over here now talking to us about debts. That's one thing you got to say for them, they were the first to pay us anything, and even if they are not going to pay us any more, they at least come over and talk it over with us.

And, if ever a different settlement is made they certainly deserve the first break.

We dislike their tea, we kid their poor English dialect and we think they are snobbish, but by golly, we know that their honor all over the world is recognized.
     Yours,
      Will Rogers.

2242   Mr. Rogers Turns To Sports
     In A Digest Of The News

BEVERLY HILLS, Cal., Oct. 10. — Poor Mr. Roosevelt. He no more than gets one national thing straightened out than along comes something else. Just getting the codes out of the way when along comes Kansas and almost beats Notre Dame. Now he has to drop everything till he gets Notre Dame straightened out.

Manager Terry of the Giants was sentenced to five years in New York. Looks like Cronin was really the winner. He was only sentenced to three years in Washington. He is young yet and will be when he gets out.

Say, did you know our popular Governor Jimmy Rolph, who has worn boots all his life is not well? Some crazy doctor made him put on shoes.
     Yours,
      Will Rogers.

2243   MR. ROGERS HAS SIGHTED
         SOME FORGOTTEN MEN

BEVERLY HILLS, Cal., Oct. 11. — Various groups have arisen to sorter gnaw at the old Democratic party's heels.

Now I don't want to cause undue worry at a time like this, but I do want to call your attention to another cloud in the sky. Since autumn weather has set in and the leaves have begun to fall you can see quite a few Republicans that have been hiding in the trees, a few more than last year.

On the banks of the Wabash the other day Jim Watson climbed right out on a sycamore limb in plain view (brazenly mind you) and started chirping. I discovered Ambassador Edge out here yesterday traveling under his own name, for the first time in a year.

All this is not a good omen and I think the uprising should be put down immediately. You know how anxious ignorant people are about joining some fad.

                                        Yours,
                                        Will Rogers.

2244   MR. ROGERS IS OF OPINION
         COLUMBUS WAS ALL RIGHT

BEVERLY HILLS, Cal., Oct. 12. — We are celebrating Columbus Day here, and he never even saw California, (Chamber of Commerce fell down again).

Old "Eric the Red" from Garboland already had a home in America where he spent his summers, but this Columbus was quite a fellow. He is the only man then, or since, who ever had a Queen pawning jewels. Columbus was an Italian, but he made Spain pay his fare over.

The other night up to Charley Chaplin's house I met Emil Ludwig, the world's greatest biographer, who has written more things about big men than Walter Winchell has about little ones.

Well, Ludwig tells me that Napoleon was an Italian, too, that was just operating under the auspices of France. Lafayette saved the U. S. Pershing and some Englishmen saved France. I can't find where any local boy ever made good at home.

I got to get with this Ludwig and go into history deeper when Chaplin ain't clowning around.

                            Yours in search of facts,
                                        Will Rogers.

2245   Mr. Rogers Tells Labor
                 How To Serve The Nation

BEVERLY HILLS, Cal., Oct. 13. — It must be terribly discouraging to Mr. Roosevelt after eight months of hard work to try to get people a job to have 'em strike the minute they get it.

It looks like if all these dissatisfied groups instead of striking would keep on working and lay their complaints before the government with the proviso that if it's settled in their favor they get the extra back pay.

Labor has seen enough of Roosevelt to know he is in sympathy with 'em, and that in a government arbitration they will get a square deal.

Help your company to start making some money, and when they do Roosevelt will see that you get a fair part of it. If American labor would work while their case is being arbitrated, instead of striking, they would have the gratitude of our President and the sympathy of everybody.

                         Yours,
                         Will Rogers.

2246   Mr. Rogers Sheds A Tear
                 For The Troubled League

SANTA MONICA, Cal., Oct. 15. — So Germany left the League. Well, we can't criticize. We never even went in.

The poor old League never had a chance, for it had no power. It tried to keep everybody good by having 'em sign a pledge (but there was nothing they could do to you if you broke the pledge).

They didn't need guns to make the League a real success. An economic boycott against any nation by all the others would have done the trick. Let the world quit trading with Japan and China will have Manchuria back by breakfast time.

Nations will give up their lives (even cheer about it). They will give up their money in order to give up their lives, but to ask one to give up their trade to prevent a war, well, that has never been done.

                         Yours,
                         Will Rogers.

2247   Mr. Rogers Notes A Gain
　　　　　　　　　　In The Conference Game

BEVERLY HILLS, Cal., Oct. 16. — The best omen of international good-will is that conferences are getting shorter. Now if they will do away with 'em entirely there will be no war.

The biggest one ever held was at Versailles after the war, and all the others held since then was to fix something that was done wrong at that one.

The biggest disarmament conference was at Washington in 1922, and all the other disarmament ones have been held to try and fix what was done wrong at that one.

So the ideal thing is, don't hold the original conference, then you won't have to hold any more to fix anything.

The same bunch of delegates go to all of 'em anyhow, so just put 'em on a government pension, let 'em put on their high hats, take movies of 'em and let 'em play like they was at a conference.

　　　　　　　　　　　　　　　　Yours,
　　　　　　　　　　　　　　　　Will Rogers.

2248   Mr. Rogers Offers A Tip
　　　　　　　　　　On How To Keep Posted

BEVERLY HILLS, Cal., Oct. 17. — In order to see what little information I can pick up during these "loco" days, I talk and ask questions of every one I meet.

Yesterday I ran onto a fellow who had hitch-hiked his way out here from New York. Rather dignified looking old bird but kinder down at the heels. He give me about the most information I have had.

He hopes they won't inflate. In fact, he hopes they announce they will soon go back on gold, then everybody will know what their money is worth. Had optimistic hopes of our future. Thought too many people, both large and small, looked too much to the government to fix their troubles, and do nothing themselves. He wasn't sore at the world, and had a good word for everybody.

As I let him out of my car to catch a ride with some one else, I asked his name. Said his name was Baruch, Bernard Baruch.

So pick up all old men you meet, some of 'em are mightly smart.

　　　　　　　　　　　　　　　　Yours,
　　　　　　　　　　　　　　　　Will Rogers.

2249   MR. ROGERS ISN'T WORRIED
         ABOUT THE NATION'S FATE

SANTA MONICA, Cal., Oct. 18. — Nothing really disastrous to this country can ever happen, for right in the middle of serious troubles will come up some fool thing.

"The world is about to go to war." "Farm mortgages are selling for fifty cents a bushel." "The American dollar is bouncing like a rubber check."

But in the midst of all this Washington is excited and about to declare a special session of Congress over Baby Leroy's and Jackie Cooper's salaries.

If the government starts regulating everybody's salaries, you are going to have this country clogged up with dollar a year men again.

Thousands pay voluntarily to see Baby Leroy, but before they can get the Senate gallery full (free of admission) they have to advertise that two Senators will probably kill each other.

That's what makes us a great country. The little things are serious and the big ones are not.

                            Yours,
                              Will Rogers.

2250   ROGERS BOBS UP AGAIN
         AT A DEMOCRATIC SHINDIG

FORT WORTH, Tex., Oct. 19. — Vice President Garner, Postmaster General Farley, all the Democrats in Washington that amount to anything, Governor Ferguson and everybody was in Fort Worth at the opening of racing today and to attend Amon Carter's dinner.

Twenty or thirty thousand people at a beautiful race track in a State where the horse was responsible for making it what it is, a lovely sight.

Texas is full of Democrats, full of resources and full of confidence.

                            Yours,
                              Will Rogers.

2251   SAN ANTONIO AIR FIELDS
         IMPRESS WILL ROGERS

SAN ANTONIO, Tex., Oct. 20. — Flew in here this morning with Vice President Garner and Mr. Farley. There is something that you ought to come all the way to San Antonio to see, that's Randolph Flying Field, the finest flying field in the world and the prettiest laid out thing in America. Then there's Kelly Field. Our salvation in the next war comes out of this unique little city.

Flying on down to Garner's home at Uvalde, where for thirty years he represented them in Congress, and the prairie dogs all voted for him.

Where other Vice Presidents have done nothing but make speeches, Garner just fishes. If all politicians fished instead of speaking publicly we would be at peace with the world.

Yours,
Will Rogers.

2252   MR. ROGERS IN A FLYING BED
             TAKES LONG-DISTANCE NAP

SANTA MONICA, Cal., Oct. 22. — Left Fort Worth, Texas, last night at 9; in Los Angeles at 7:30 A.M., regular American Airways passenger line.

The co-pilot made our seats down into a regular bed and all the passengers slept through the landings and the taking on of gas at El Paso, Douglas, Tucson and Phoenix.

There is your success of passenger aviation. Fix it so everybody can lay down and have a good sleep. The air is much better at night.

Been on a tour with this fellow Farley for three days. Thousands turned out to see him everywhere. Lots of 'em looking for a postoffice. When he finished talking to 'em they all felt satisfied even if they hadn't received as much as a postcard.

Quite a President maker that lad. Presidents become great, but they have to be made Presidents first.

Yours,
Will Rogers.

2253   MR. ROGERS PUTS A FINGER
             ON CAUSE OF FARM REVOLT

BEVERLY HILLS, Cal., Oct. 23. — Farmers are having a tough time but they had no idea that they were so bad off till they joined an organization and had some paid leaders tell 'em how poor they were.

Vice President John Nance Garner and Will Rogers (far right) at political rally in 1933.

If ever an industry was having a field day, it's the industry of paid leaders in every line, who are explaining to their followers "what the government owes them."

I haven't seen a copy of the Constitution in years (I guess they are out of print), but I don't remember in there anything about what it was to do if you raised too much, or if you manufactured too much, or if you went in debt too much, or if you drove your automobile too much, or if you bathed in one of your bathrooms too much.

In fact, if I remember right we owed more to the Constitution than it did to us.

Yours,
Will Rogers.

2254   WILL ROGERS DIAGNOSES
THE CONDITION OF WALL ST.

SANTA MONICA, Cal., Oct. 24. — Mr. Roosevelt is the only man who can raise the stock market without putting up any money.

The market not only operates on O. P. M. (other people's money) but O. P. R. (other people's rumors).

A war in Europe would mean nothing to the stock market (provided it actually happened) but let a rumor get out that Mr. Ford was building a six-door sedan or that the present government was going to recognize Tammany Hall, or that Bernard Baruch was growing a beard—any of these rumors and wheat would jump 10 points, American Can 8, American T. and T. 9.

So the only thing can break the stock market is a fact.

Yours,
Will Rogers.

2255   WILL ROGERS PREPARES
TO MARKET SOME GOLD

BEVERLY HILLS, Cal., Oct. 25. — Jesse Jones of Texas starts in buying gold for the government today, so get your old wedding rings ready. It's going to be a great thing for a lot of these Hollywood females. They got buckets full of 'em. If gold gets to forty dollars an ounce, I got some old teeth fillings that will go.

I would love to see the loot that Jesse gathers in. There will be many a one of these old hunting gold watch cases. Gold-headed canes is another commodity that will be resurrected.

If we had just thought of all this five years ago, when every paper headlined the daily millions and millions that was going out. We have some great ideas, but most of 'em come too late to do us any good.

                        Yours,
                            Will Rogers.

2256   MR. ROGERS FINDS THE WEST
                 IS TAX-HARRIED, ALSO

BEVERLY HILLS, Cal., Oct. 26. — All the Western States held a convention here in Los Angeles the other day on taxation to see what the running of the various States was costing 'em.

Well, they found it was costing 'em so much that they are talking now about letting Mexico have them back.

It's taken since, I believe it was 1812, for us to realize Mexico won that war.

But, like all conventions, it did nothing but hold a business meeting and pass some resolutions, then hold a banquet and the waiters passed some cocktails.

Then they all went home and got ready to vote for the same politicians that put the last tax raise on 'em.

But a good time was had by all.

Please pass the gravy.

                        Yours,
                            Will Rogers.

2257   ROGERS'S INTEREST IN PRICE
                 OF GOLD ONLY ACADEMIC

BEVERLY HILLS, Cal., Oct. 27. — Papers every day in big headlines tell what gold sells for. Just as well tell what radium sells for. Who has any of either?

Nevada has a great law. When they vote on a bond issue, or any money to be spent, they have two ballots. One is for property owners and one is for non-property owners, and to pass, it has to be a majority of both.

Nevada will take your wife away from you with representation, but they won't let anybody who pays no taxes take your property away from you.

Yours,
Will Rogers.

2258   MR. ROGERS FINDS NRA
        HAS A TASK ON GRIDIRON

SANTA MONICA, Cal., Oct. 29. — What's the RFC farm relief and sportsmanship going to do about this?

Oregon has a football team, and Washington has one, that has played all year with the same eleven men and beaten or tied everything on the Coast.

The rules say everybody that has a uniform is eligible; that in case a player has a phone call he can excuse himself for a few minutes and come back again. Then if he has a luncheon engagement can take time out for that, even if he sees on old friend in the stands, can send in a substitute while he chats with him. Then of course in case of slight fatigue, he can come out and sleep a bit.

But I don't want to criticize. They may be operating under the NRA. They are giving shorter hours and more work to more men.

Yours,
Will Rogers.

2259   MR. ROGERS DOESN'T GET
        ALL THIS GOLD STUFF

BEVERLY HILLS, Cal., Oct. 30. — Going to buy gold on the world market now. What we been buying has been just "home-talent" gold.

They claim the more you buy and the more you pay, the cheaper your dollar will get. Well, you will have no trouble on foreign support in this scheme. It will be no hardship for them to charge you even fifty dollars an ounce.

Now here is what us dumb ones don't get: When we had practically half the world's gold our dollar was still higher than a flagpole sitter.

But this is no place for the ignorant, for there are two people you can't argue with. One is a professor, for he has specs, and the other is an economist, for he has a title.

Yours,
Will Rogers.

2260   Mr. Rogers Offers Advice
To A Couple Of Kings

BEVERLY HILLS, Cal., Oct. 31. — News today says "United States and England agree on gold control." But it didn't say nothing about France, who has all the gold. It's always good to take it up with the teacher before a couple of students decide when school will be out.

King Bor-us of Bulgaria and King Carol of Rumania met yesterday to decide ways to improve relations between the two countries. It was suggested Carol take Bor-us's sister to wife.

Nations have got a funny sense of humor, ain't they? English royalty waited 'till they had all married Germans, then they went to war with 'em. Germans all married Russians, then fought.

Bor-us, you better pan that sister off to some local guy.

Yours,
Will Rogers.

2261   Will Rogers, Farmer,
Is A Little Mystified

BEVERLY HILLS, Cal., Nov. 1. — Up in Dingville, Iowa, named for the great cartoonist Ding and sometimes called Des Moines, the farmers and the Governors are in convention.

It don't take a convention to tell that the farmers are in a bad plight.

The speeches were all made by farm leaders. Now what is a farm leader? I was raised on a farm. We had farm hands, farm hired girls, farm horses, farm mortgages (not many) but I never saw a farm that raised farm leaders.

This leader thing is a type of growth that has sprung up since everybody started joining organizations, not only in farming but in everything.

In the old days if you was smart enough to be in a business, you was smart enough to tend to your own business without listening to a leader make a speech.

Yours for less leaders and less followers of leaders.

Yours,
Will Rogers.

2262   Mr. Rogers Is Watching
       Our Gold Experiment

BEVERLY HILLS, Cal., Nov. 2. — Well, I see today my old friend from Buffalo Bayou, Texas, Jesse Jones, went right out in the wide open market and announced to the cockeyed world (including ourselves) that we wanted to buy gold.

Price was no object; the folks we bought it from was no object, Eskimos, Russians, Hindus, Zulus, bootleggers or anything.

The only thing we hadn't thought about, we got to give gold to get gold. Jesse couldn't start out with some of our paper money and buy a thimble full of gold between now and the big argument.

What do I mean, the big argument? Why, when Congress meets.

Yours,
Will Rogers.

2263   Rogers Finds One Thing
       Permanent In Our Lives

BEVERLY HILLS, Cal., Nov. 3. — We are awful glad those two strong-minded men, Ford and Johnson, arbitrated and made up. Your RFC can buy the gold crown off King George's head, your dollar can go to a dime, your Republican can come dragging, cut and bleeding, back to his old party; you can take the rouge from the female lips, the cigarettes from the raised hands, the hot dog from the tourists's greasy paw, but when you start jerking the Fords out from under the traveling public, you are monkeying with the very fundamentals of American life.

Yours,
Will Rogers.

2264   Mr. Rogers Is Impressed
By White House 'Yeahs?'

BEVERLY HILLS, Cal., Nov. 5 — Say you don't rush this Roosevelt into everything that is pulled on him.

Saturday was refusal day with him (he must have collected a bad stamp). To the farmers' resolution from their convention telling him what to do, he just said "yeah?" Swope had a plan, and he just said "yeah?" England's debt commission goes home with nothing but "yeah?" Wall Street said the dollar must be stabilized. He just said, "yeah?" They even told him the big bad wolf, Congress, was coming in eight weeks, and he just said "yeah?"

It looked like the "yeahs" had it. It takes a lot of "yeahs" to keep you from being a "yes" man.

                        Yours,
                        Will Rogers.

2265   Mr. Rogers Doffs His Hat
To The Old Brown Derby

SANTA MONICA, Cal., Nov. 6. — As you read this it will be election day. Six States are repealing prohibition and New York City is repealing its Mayor.

It's taken Al Smith twelve years of his life (and a defeat for nomination, a defeat for the Presidency) and just about every other type of bad break that a man that is in the right could get so when you newspapers write your editorials tomorrow (Wednesday) telling how it all come about, kindly remember there was something under the brown derby besides a New York dialect.

And P. S.: There is quite a few other things that this same gentleman has been ahead of his time on. Smith's obituary should read "He thought too fast for the mob."

                        Yours,
                        Will Rogers.

2266   Mr. Rogers Interprets
The Situation In Italy

BEVERLY HILLS, Cal., Nov. 7. — Every time some country gets to thinking it has a dictator why along comes the old master dictator of all and shows 'em really how to dictate.

They applauded too loud for Mr. Balbo on his arrival in Italy and Mussolini couldn't help but hear it, so now Mussolini is head of the aviation himself.

Next year at Chicago's second Century of Progress why Italy will send a hundred planes and Mussolini will grow a beard and ride in the front plane.

Gold went up 17 cents yesterday but they can't get anything to go up with it. Trouble with us is we can't get anything to go up without the government buying it.

Yours,
Will Rogers.

2267   MR. ROGERS MOVED TO SONG
             BY THE NEW YORK ELECTION

BEVERLY HILLS, Cal., Nov. 8. — Tammanee, Tammanee, big chief got to get out of his tepee to make room for the Italian LaGuardee. Tammanee, Tammanee, swampum, swampum, voters got no wampum, out goes Tammanee.

I have known this little LaGuardia for years. He is not only quite an Italian but he is quite an American. He used to be considered a radical, but a radical of those days is a long-haired, hard-shelled die-hard in these times.

See where North Carolina went dry just through devilment, and not through preference.

Yours,
Will Rogers.

2268   MR. ROGERS SEES PROGRESS
             IN TUESDAY'S ELECTIONS

BEVERLY HILLS, Cal., Nov. 9. — This country is coming back.

The best indication was old Kentucky. She disposed of sixteen at Tuesday's elections. That's a mighty good showing on what's called an off election year, and when you consider that they needn't have voted at all, for prohibition had already been repealed by thirty-six States.

102

Old Kentucky has a law which gives the doctors the benefit of the doubt. They won't count votes or bodies till the next day.

Clubs were wielded and heads were disorganized in New York, too. This is all a good omen. It shows we are getting out of our effeminate period of voting where you do nothing but vote.

Led by the spirit of old Kentucky we are returning to American principles. All but the Carolinas.

Yours,
Will Rogers.

2269   Mr. Rogers Fails To Find
        Any Cheap Dollars Here

BEVERLY HILLS, Cal., Nov. 10. — Well, we got a lot of excitement out here in Los Angeles. Five United States Senators arrived here to investigate and the fan dancer from the Chicago fair arrived to be investigated. It looks like a worth-while session.

The dollar was lower yesterday in Europe than it has ever been before. What a tough break for the Americans that go to see Europe and have never been further away from home in their own country than the garage.

The dollar may have been cheap in London, but there certainly wasn't any laying around for nothing in our country. And after all, it is a home talent commodity.

Yours,
Will Rogers.

2270   Mr. Rogers Would Guard
        The Educated Investor

BEVERLY HILLS, Cal., Nov. 12. — Just been talking today out here to all the Senators investigating these stock swindles and overcapitalizations. There has been millions and hundreds of millions lost.

There ought to be some form of guardianship for people that buy all this junk. Get Chambers of Commerce, clubs, priests and preachers. Don't get school teachers for they say they are the biggest suckers.

Educations won't do it for they say that only 5 per cent of these sales are made to people who can't read or write. It's the ones we have educated up till they are just smart enough to fall for everything that comes along.

      Yours,
      Will Rogers.

2271   MR. ROGERS NOTES SLUMP
      IN STANDING OF SILK HATS

BEVERLY HILLS, Cal., Nov. 13. — Germany had an election to see if they approved leaving the League of Nations. There was one fellow voted against it, but they are on the track of him.

Poor old League. Always felt on account of her having no policemen nobody was going to pay much attention to it.

We just seem to be living in an era when good ideas don't get over. Everybody is out to protect themselves in the clinch. They are not depending on the referee helping 'em out much.

Look at little Switzerland. Always gone along minding their own business, now they got them going out buying a gun.

The world has just lost faith in a bunch of guys with silk hats.

      Yours,
      Will Rogers.

2272   WILL ROGERS HAILS NEWS
      OF A GAIN IN A LONG WAR

BEVERLY HILLS, Cal., Nov. 14. — An international authority on the subject claims that they are in sight of a remedy for tuberculosis.

Well, if that's true that beats all the price of gold, all the disarmament, even the stopping of wars. For you bring war on yourself, but tuberculosis is brought unto you.

It looks like the day is finally arriving when medical scientists will receive the glory that we used to bestow entirely on our big financiers, industrialists and statesmen (hic).

Well, anyhow, the world is certainly praying for this fellow to be right.

      Yours,
      Will Rogers.

2273   MR. ROGERS TAKES A STAND
        ON NEW EUROPEAN DISPUTE

BEVERLY HILLS, Cal., Nov. 15. — Those two friendly gentlemen are at it again.

Germany voted confidence in their man. France had no election billed, but they got up in the middle of the night to vote confidence in theirs.

Germany wants to talk it over. France says not without the League being present.

Germany says she will arm. France says she shouldn't; that they will keep the peace for her.

Now for once in our lives, if we just let those two old tomcats whose tails are tied over the fence alone and try to cure the scratches we got from the last time we tried to untie 'em.

Yours,
Will Rogers.

2274   MR. ROGERS HEARS RUMOR
        OF NEW LINE-UP SHIFT

BEVERLY HILLS, Cal., Nov. 16. — Well, in one of the papers I read today, it had an awful lot of information, if true.

It said Al Smith, No. 99, was to go to the Senate, replacing Dr. Copeland, No. 86. Copeland to go to France as Ambassador, replacing Jesse Straus, No. 63. Postmaster Farley, No. 77, to go in as next Democratic Governor of New York, replacing Lehman, No. 66. Raskob, No. 55, to replace as U. S. Treasurer, Mr. Woodin, No. 44.

Even if this is just a rumor it makes good reading, and if it's a fact it makes Democratic history. It means the shock troops are going in.

Yours,
Will Rogers.

2275   WILL ROGERS LOOKS INTO
        SENATE INVESTIGATIONS

BEVERLY HILLS, Cal., Nov. 17. — The Senate went out investigating, some went East, some went West and some went over the cuckoo's nest. New Orleans, the home of the Sazerack cocktail, and the best food in America but they won't stand investigation. My good friend Senator Connally of Texas was among 'em, and the committee

have been making their entrances into the court room by sliding down the flag pole and retiring through a trap door.

The Washington bunch with Pecora (the last word in digging up devilment on the evil doer) and the California committee, who were looking into receiverships, and fake stock sales schemes (which are one and the same) they found out Californians will buy anything in the way of stock if its phoney enough.

Yours,
Will Rogers.

2276   Mr. Rogers Reports Slump
      In A California Industry

SANTA MONICA, Cal., Nov. 19. — Been so warm and nice out here that it's knocked a lot of people out of work. Leaves Californians with nothing to do. They can't lie about the weather.

Germany has got everybody all excited now. It sure seems good to have all the ills of the world blamed on somebody besides us.

This country is gradually getting democratic, at that. See where J. P. Morgan had tea for the first time in the White House. Of course he took his own tea, but it was nice of him to drop into the old farm hut at that. I tell you big men are changing.

Yours,
Will Rogers.

2277   Mr. Rogers Is Impressed
      By Two Names In News

BEVERLY HILLS, Cal., Nov. 20. — Well the name of the new Russian Ambassador appeared in the papers today and it just about took up all the paper. It's Alexanderovich Antonovich Trovanovsky. That's an alphabetic rhapsody in vowels and consonants.

But they don't put much over on Mr. Roosevelt. He sent 'em a guy named Bullitt. That was just a kind of subtle hint.

Mr. Roosevelt was rather undecided exactly what to do on the stabilization of the dollar till the U. S. Chamber of Commerce come out and told him what to do. Then he knew exactly what to do, do what the chamber said not to do.

Mr. Roosevelt knows he is right now, before he was in doubt.

Yours,
Will Rogers.

2278   Will Rogers Is Cheered
By A Talk With Baruch

SANTA MONICA, Cal., Nov. 21. — After reading Mr. Barney Baruch's non-inflation article in a little Philadelphia periodical run by Benjamin Franklin and Horace Lorimer, I was talking last night on the phone to Mr. Baruch in New York and here is a very interesting thing he said:

"This fellow down in Washington is not going to be stampeded by the U. S. Chamber of Commerce, or any the rest of us non-inflationists or by the inflationists, either. He listens to all of us and then, regardless of professors, pedagogues, economists or financiers, he makes up his mind himself, and he is going mighty easy and I think will handle this money situation in a way that is beneficial to the majority, if not to a small minority."

That sounded mighty hopeful coming from a man like Baruch.

Yours,
Will Rogers.

2279   Will Rogers Marvels
At Zeal Of Scientists

BEVERLY HILLS, Cal., Nov. 22. — These breeds of scientists they risk their lives, receive no money, all to find out something.

But they are awful queer to us dumb ones. They fly over the Poles when there is no pole. They go eleven miles straight up to see something, when there is nothing to see but air.

Now air is a mighty fine thing (when not oozing from a public speaker), but to take your life in your hands to go eleven miles up just to see it, when there is nothing more uninteresting to look at than air!

Yours,
Will Rogers.

2280   Mr. Rogers Finds Slump
In Incentive To Do Right

BEVERLY HILLS, Cal., Nov. 23. — The Cubans sent a big delegation to Montevideo, South America, to attend a peace conference. That leaves 'em kinder short handed in their war at home till these get back.

There certainly is not much incentive for anything to be done right nowadays. A U. S. stamp printer made a mistake on one little batch of 24-cent air mail stamps (had it turned crosswise) and they brought $12,000. If he had had it plum upside down it would have brought $100,000.

We get another illustration of an "expert." This fellow Sprague that left the Treasury in such a huff has been all this time finding out Mr. Roosevelt had already inflated.

Yours,
Will Rogers.

2281   WILL ROGERS REMEMBERS
              RECENT SERVICE TO BANKS

BEVERLY HILLS, Cal., Nov. 24. — Big headlines in today's papers say that the big bankers, to show Roosevelt his financial scheme don't suit them, they are unloading government bonds and securities by the bushel. He won't play their way so they are going to sell their ball and bat and get out.

I can't just recall, but as well as I remember, wasn't they the fellows that the government was helping so much not long ago? They ought to pray every night, "God bless mama and papa, and all my family, and interests, and Roosevelt."

Yours,
Will Rogers.

P. S. — I want to apologize to the President for putting interest ahead of him, but interest has been helping 'em out longer than he has.

2282   MR. ROGERS GETS A THRILL
              AS WORTHY FOES CLASH

SANTA MONICA, Cal., Nov. 26. — Just when it looked like Al was going to have his gold argument go by default, why up comes an old country boy from out of the wheat shocks of Idaho and he takes up what I suppose would be known as the negative side of the dispute. He says "If your gold is so hot, how did we get in the shape **we are in?**"

Well, it's going to require a little thought to answer that one.

The gentleman I am about to introduce you to needs no introduction. It's William E. Borah, and if a man searched the United States over he couldn't find a more worthy foe to enter into combat with.

Al, I know you didn't mean to, but you choosed a tough baby.
Yours,
Will Rogers.

2283   MR. ROGERS PICKS A TEAM
             FOR ROSE BOWL GAME

BEVERLY HILLS, Cal., Nov. 27. — All the Californians I met are going around proud today.

Had a visit from young Senator La Follette, for whom I have great admiration. Any man smart enough to know that both political parties are wrong deserves careful consideration. He is thought mighty well of by all those elderly Senators.

He thinks (and no doubt correct) that the NRA should have been backed up by a revokable license, and not by just singing a pledge. He don't think that we have reached the moral stage where a parade and a promise will make people do the right thing.
Yours,
Will Rogers.

P. S. — Send the Army out here for the New Year's football game. If it was left to a vote of everybody, ten to one would vote for them over any other school.

Stanford vs. the U. S. Army.

2284   WILL ROGERS UNWORRIED
             BY MONEY CONTROVERSY

BEVERLY HILLS, Cal., Nov. 28. — You can watch it from telling jokes about it. Every once in so often America "goes serious," gets all excited and mad at each other.

One of these times is just before election, anything that's said the other side takes offense. Yet all our last Presidents have been elected by millions, showing that all that heat and perspiration was wasted. Then after election is over, you can call the other side a yellow dog, and they just laugh, for they have their sense of humor back.

Now, we are going into another one of those serious tail spins over this money racket. And it's just like the election. Nothing you can do, nothing you can say, will change a person's opinion. It will all work itself out, without any personal lather from any of us. And in a few months we will regain our humor and balance.

It's just a serious spree that we have ever so often to get it out of our system.

Yours,
Will Rogers.

2285   MR. ROGERS FEELS HIS WAY
             OVER GOLD BATTLEFIELD

SANTA MONICA, Cal., Nov. 29. — Today would be an awful good day to not get in bad with either side on this gold. What I mean by that is not to mention it at all.

I have always heard the old expression, "Where there is a lot of smoke there must be fire." Well, I don't believe that holds good, for there is certainly a terrible lot of gold arguments where there is not an ounce of gold.

Now the above don't offend either side does it? Or does it offend both sides?

Yours,
Will Rogers.

2286   WILL ROGERS REPORTS
             ON HIS TURKEY DAY

BEVERLY HILLS, Cal., Nov. 30. — Didn't want to get too enthusiastic about Thanksgiving till I saw how it turned out.

My old friend W. S. (Bill) Hart showed up at my igloo with a "gobbler" that he had shot with two guns. Now if you bring everything, I defy anybody to give you a nicer party than I will.

Homer Croy, the writer of "They Had to See Paris," as hungry as an author can be. Mrs. Florenz Ziegfeld, looking exactly twenty-five years old, and not reducing.

Then an outlaw dropped in, but he was only the Crown Prince's son and the Kaiser's grandson, Prince Ferdinand. While he got no white meat as in his early childhood, he seemed mighty cheerful and a fine young chap and was satisfied with the wings.

None of us had any gold, so we were in a receptive mood.

Yours,
Will Rogers.

2287   ROGERS FINDS SOLO ROLE
        IN GOLD VERY DIFFICULT

BEVERLY HILLS, Cal., Dec. 1. — This staying on gold is a tough job, unless everybody is on it. If you are on gold, and the rest of the boys are not, why you change your money into theirs, then demand it in gold.

Now France is on the gold and are cuckoo. She reads every morning how many millions in gold was shipped out the day before (just like we used to do before we went off gold) and it's gradually driving them "nuts."

So it looks like everybody has either got to be on it, or off of it. You can't play solo.

Yours,
Will Rogers.

2288   WILL ROGERS MOURNS
        LOSS OF A REAL FRIEND

SANTA MONICA, Cal., Dec. 3. — I can't get my mind on what's in the papers today.

Maby the "better element" are going to lynch my good old friend Governor Rolph for speaking from his heart instead of from diplomacy.

Maby another old friend, Ethel Barrymore, is hanging from a limb for telling about 90 per cent of the truth about modern society.

Maby the world is in mortal turmoil, but I just can't get interested in it today for our pet dog was killed by a truck.

So, darn everything. O. O. McIntyre will know how we feel.

I love a dog, he does nothing for political reasons.

Yours,
Will Rogers.

2289   MR. ROGERS SEES REPEAL
FREEING THE FILIPINOS

BEVERLY HILLS, Cal., Dec. 4. — Talked to the Philippine delegation going through here on their way to Washington. Missed seeing Manual Quezon, their very able leader.

They will be a unique delegation in Washington and one that I believe the President will welcome for they are asking for liberty and not money. A thing like that is unheard of.

Why can't we set the Philippines free now? We kept 'em for years just on account of their sugar. When they take you off liquor, you crave sugar and sweets. Well, today we got back on a liquor diet, so they can take us off sugar.

That automatically sets the Philippines free.

Yours,
Will Rogers.

2290   MR. ROGERS SEES START
OF THE REAL EXPERIMENT

BEVERLY HILLS, Cal., Dec. 5. — Talk about the "noble experiment." "The noble experiment" is just starting. Every State is in doubt as to how their liquor will be handled.

Say, it's not how the State will handle its liquor, it's how the folks will handle theirs.

States are going to have scandal over the sale of it, and politicians will fight over the taxes of it. But anyhow, the first week will be the hardest.

Yours,
Will Rogers.

2291   MR. ROGERS IS GRATIFIED
BY OUR SELF-CONTROL

BEVERLY HILLS, Cal., Dec. 6. — Well sir, from what I can read and hear today folks stood the shock of getting a drink (without giving their name) in mighty good shape.

Course the ones that are clear "out" we won't hear of for days. But it looked like everything went off better than expected.

You see the whole problem is getting people from bad drinks back onto good drinks. You take a good bucking horse rider. He would rather ride a bad horse than a nice gentle one.

So it's going to take time to get 'em to having a sociable drink without watching the door.
                    Yours,
                        Will Rogers.

2292   Mr. Rogers Awards Palm
            For Radio Speechmaking

BEVERLY HILLS, Cal., Dec. 7. — Guess you all heard Mr. Roosevelt on the radio Wednesday night.

These old big boys can all get up before their little audiences and yell for stabilization, amortization, gold standard or platinum finish. The President can come to the microphone with that convincing manner of his and the rest of 'em might just as well wash up their little speeches and go home.

Say, I guess there must be another conference on somewhere. I see where the United States is accused of connivery by noon and the conference only opened at 11 A.M.

What would a conference be without the "goat"?
                    Yours,
                        Will Rogers.

2293   Will Rogers Discusses
            Vital Football Crises

BEVERLY HILLS, Cal., Dec. 8. — United States Cabinet members can change, but when Notre Dame changes coaches you are getting into real news. Anderson just run into bad breaks. I bet he will go somewhere else and turn out a great team, and Elmer Layden will come there and do great, for he won't be following Rockne.

There just didn't happen to be anybody living that could follow Rockne.

And while we are on football and off the gold, this Columbia College that's coming here New Year's, being New Yorkers they never was away from home so naturally they are not known out here, but

113

we have heard of Nicholas Murray Butler, so we want 'em to bring "Nicholas" with 'em. We will hear a good speech even if the game is bad.

>   Yours,
>   *Will Rogers.*

2294   WILL ROGERS SIMPLIFIES
         THE STATUS OF THE DOLLAR

SANTA MONICA, Cal., Dec. 10. — Many a thing in our Sunday papers today that showed a great picking up of things, and it was not ballyhoo and not all government paid works either.

This thing of "we can't go ahead till we know exactly what our dollar is worth" is hooey.

Your bankers and your financiers marry with no gold clause. The preacher just guarantees you she is a wife. How long you can keep her and what she is worth to you is all up to you.

Roosevelt, like the preacher, says "here is a dollar, it can always be used for a dollar."

>   Yours,
>   *Will Rogers.*

2295   MR. ROGERS HAS A PLAN
         OF RELIEF FOR DRINKERS

BEVERLY HILLS, Cal., Dec. 11. — From the prices they are charging for drinks all over the country I guess there never was as much temperance as now.

Unless the government makes the drinkers some kind of a loan, they just can't carry on.

Let the government do like they do in other Federal projects, match you dollar for dollar, or in this case drink for drink. You buy one, the government buys the next. (Better let the government buy the first one.)

>   Yours,
>   *Will Rogers.*

2296   MR. ROGERS TAKES NOTICE
         OF SOME SMART HOMBRES

BEVERLY HILLS, Cal., Dec. 12. — The best writer on the Pacific Coast, Harry Carr, making a world tour and seeing all of the governments in action, says England is over the hump first and going great.

Now that's the country that was held up to us as a horrible example because they were giving aid to unemployed. We adopted it two years later than we should.

England lowered the price of their money just about to what ours is and it must have helped them.

Pretty smart "hombres," those Englishmen.

Yours,
Will Rogers.

2297   MR. ROGERS NOTES A LULL
         IN THE GOLD ARGUMENTS

BEVERLY HILLS, Cal., Dec. 13. — Say, these gold dollar arguments are dying down. Used to pick up a paper and all you could see was what Mr. "Got His" had to say about money, but no you don't hear a peep.

Everybody seems to be trying to get ahold of any kind. This would be an awful good time to pass off some Confederate money.

They are holding a big peace conference in South America, just a drive and two niblick shots away from the war. Every time there is a big conference they always have a war to go with it.

I was in Geneva a couple of years ago at a conference when Japanese recruiting officers come in and drafted their delegation to go help take Manchuria.

Yours,
Will Rogers.

2298   MR. ROGERS FINDS IT HARD
         TO DIG UP A WISECRACK

PHOENIX, Ariz., Dec. 14. — Roscoe Turner and I just breezed in here — 2 hours, 400 miles — to do a little stage acting at a benefit.

Roscoe's jokes better be good, for with the Democrats doing all that can be done and the Republicans keeping still, why it don't leave me much to work on. So my little riddles are not so hot.

France handed us their yearly laugh. We told 'em it was debt-paying time, and they just said "yeah?" They have even borrowed our English language.

Say, with Jesse Jones offering $35 an ounce for new gold, every man, woman or child that could get a burro and a pick have gone to the hills. This country has gone "nugget minded."

And if they do what they ought to do and make silver a money instead of just a thing to shoot craps with, why this whole West will boom and we will have the king coming over with a pick and shovel.

Yours,
Will Rogers.

2299   MR. ROGERS PHILOSOPHIZES
          ON BANKERS AND STEERS

BEVERLY HILLS, Cal., Dec. 15. — Well, I see where the boss says things are going along as well as Roosevelt expected and that he is not going to stabilize the dollar.

Now that will do just as much good as if he had said that he would, maby more. For a funny thing about the big men and financiers, after they have realized and got it set in their head that they are not going to have their own way, why like an old steer, they sulk a little bit and then join the herd.

Everybody likes to make a dollar his way, but if he finds he is not allowed to make it his way, why he is not going to overlook the chance of making it your way.

Yours,
Will Rogers.

2300   WILL ROGERS DISCOVERS
          A NEW FEDERAL CHARITY

SANTA MONICA, Cal., Dec. 17. — You sure got to give it to this administration for trying to do something for the down and out.

Over in Phoenix, Ariz., the other day I run onto something that I had not read about, but I understand there is quite a few in Southwestern States. It's called a government transient camp.

I went out to see 'em. There was about 700 men and boys (lots of 'em very young) and they kept 'em there and fed 'em and gave 'em clothes. They received no money, good food, good cots and blankets. All had to work. Lot of 'em were making wooden toys for the children in Phoenix for Christmas.

A taxpayer can't kick on his money being spent if it's on food.

Yours,
Will Rogers.

2301   WILL ROGERS REMARKS

BEVERLY HILLS, Cal., Dec. 18. — I see where Jesse Jones and his R.F.C. (Redistribution Finance Corporation) are not satisfied with the way the banks are just sitting counting their money. So to make the banks ashamed of themselves the R.F.C. is going to make loans to industries. The banks will about be so humiliated that they will be the first ones to borrow all that Jesse has. Jesse, you been a banker yourself, you ought to know you can't shame a banker, especially a big one.

Yours,
Will Rogers.

2302   MR. ROGERS PASSES ALONG
ENGLAND'S OPINION OF US

BEVERLY HILLS, Cal., Dec. 19. — Just had a long talk with a mighty well-informed man, Mr. Hutchinson, the Fox Film Company's man in London.

He said the English just stocked up on our securities during all these low prices. There is a real weather vane. There is nothing with his feet on the ground (and as much of 'em) as an old conservative Englishman. He sees further than our rich men. That's why they are coming out of their mess ahead of us.

Another thing, too, the fellow sitting off looking at you can tell better how you are doing and what your prospects are than you can yourself.

Hutchinson says England looks on us as a bad boy who has been out on a toot but will sober up, change some of his ways and be a better boy for it.

Yours,
Will Rogers.

2303   Mr. Rogers Points Out
                     Some Real Dictating

BEVERLY HILLS, Cal., Dec. 20. — That Mussolini is a "darb."

Yesterday he interviewed ninety-two mothers with a gross total of 1,288 children, which divides out to about fourteen head per each. While our great slogan for the perpetuation of civilization was "a car in every garage," Mussolini's was "a baby in every arm, and more if you can carry 'em."

He knows no nation ever become great on garages. You can't win a war in a Ford sedan, or repel an invasion in a Chevrolet coupe.

These other dictators think they are doing some "dictating" when they announce a budget quota. But when you start laying out a maternity quota for the women then you are really in the dictating business.

That makes these other dictators look like amateurs.

                                           Yours,
                                           Will Rogers.

2304   Will Rogers Tells How
                     To Get A Drink Out West

BEVERLY HILLS, Cal., Dec. 21. — California had a new ruling this morning on the sale of liquor in hotels.

The latest one is you buy it in the lobby of the hotel at the news stand, then take it in the dining room and drink it.

"Give me a quart of gin, the Morning Times, a pint of French Vermouth, an American Mercury, some Angastora bitters, a Physical Culture magazine and a box of Baer's aspirin."

See where they captured an American spy in France. He must have been working on his own, for we already know all we want to know about 'em.

                                           Yours,
                                           Will Rogers.

2305   Will Rogers Says Bryan
                     Was 37 Years Too Early

BEVERLY HILLS, Cal., Dec. 22. — There is really not much new under the sun. Thirty-seven years ago a long-haired young man came riding a day coach out of the West and said something about,

"You can't crucify us on a cross of gold. We want the wreath on our brow to be studded with about sixteen silver ducats to one gold dubloon." In the meantime silver was used as the sole medium of exchange by over three-quarters of the earth's population. With us it was a money, but never official, it just had a slot machine value. So lying under Arlington's hallowed soil tonight must be a satisfied smile. For it's something to be thirty-seven years ahead of your government.

Yours,
Will Rogers.

2306 WILL ROGERS SEES A GAIN
IN CHEER THIS CHRISTMAS

SANTA MONICA, Cal., Dec. 24. — Well, there is lots more good cheer this Christmas than last (or the last three) and it's not all out of bottles either. It's in the heart, in the confidence and in the renewed hope of everybody.

Course there is an awful lot of folks that are not working. But they have never been the ones that's complained. Fear has never come from the fellow with no job or no food. He has stood it wonderful. I doubt if a parallel will be found where millions hung on with such continued hope and patience as in this country.

But I believe even the most down and out while he might not see a turkey Xmas Day, he can see one in the future.

Yours,
Will Rogers.

2307 WILL ROGERS IS MOVED
BY THE FRENCH DISASTER

SANTA MONICA, Cal., Dec. 25. — Between looking at our Xmas necktie and new sox, it don't give us men much chance to read the Xmas day papers.

There is something about a terrible accident or calamity that draws even nations close together. Now France, we cuss 'em (for looking out for France better than we look for ourselves), but when we read of this terrible train wreck, all debts are forgotten, all overcharges to us when we were tourists there are bygones.

We just think of 'em as folks like us, who have about the same problems to face, wooden coaches on railroads.

Yours,
Will Rogers.

P. S. — This P. S. is put in here to save all R. R. presidents from sending good natured or indignant wires. We know that you are all doing away with the wooden ones as fast as you can. How's that, Mr. Stotesbury?

2308   MR. ROGERS CITES A CASE
          OF JAPAN'S SUPERIORITY

BEVERLY HILLS, Cal., Dec. 26. — I got my berries mixed up this morning. I mentioned Stotesbury, when I meant Atterbury. Now I don't know which one to apologize to.

They say Japan imitates us in everything, but they certainly didn't get this idea from us.

"In appointing an Ambassador to the U. S. at this important time, with the 1936 crisis ahead, such consideration as dignity, past career and sentiment must be discarded and a man of ability appointed."

Then they wonder why that country is going ahead.

They appointed a fellow named Saito, who hadn't contributed a cent to the last campaign.

That's political treason.

Yours,
Will Rogers.

2309   WILL ROGERS REVIEWS
          THE OPERA FIRST NIGHTS

SANTA MONICA, Cal., Dec. 27. — This is a day and time when everybody gives opinions on something they know nothing about. So today I discuss opera, grand opera.

The Chicago Opera House opened for the first time in two years. It was never a success because it was constructed wrong. It was built so everybody could see the stage, but nobody could see each other. So now it's been remodeled so you can't see the stage but can see the price mark on every dress in the house. And it's doing fine.

New York opened its season with an American opera for the first time in history. American music has always been considered by the opera goers as fit for nothing but the ear. It never looked good through a lorgnette from a box.

That's about all the opera news that's fit to print.

Yours,
Will Rogers.

2310   Mr. Rogers Is Satisfied
         With The Latest Parley

BEVERLY HILLS, Cal., Dec. 28. — The big Pan-American Conference in Uruguay adjourned. While it did nothing it did it so well that they all left friends, which is more than any conference in years has accomplished.

You can't hope to gain ground at a conference. You only try to remedy the damage done at the last one.

Our Mr. Cordell Hull must have done a very creditable job for us for I see he is able to visit Argentine, Chile, Peru and other countries under his own name.

Generally our delegates arrive at a conference with a band and leave incognito.

Yours,
Will Rogers.

P. S. You may have to look that incognito up. I did.

2311   Rogers Says Roosevelt
         Makes Friends By Radio

BEVERLY HILLS, Cal., Dec. 29. — Roosevelt is the most consistently good radio man there is. Just when you would think there is nothing of importance to be said that hadn't been said, he comes on Thursday night and gained over a 100,000,000 new friends outside of the U. S. and perhaps that many here, by announcing that the U. S. was not going to mess around in any South or Central American country with a gun. It was his best speech of all.

He should have gone a little further and said, "We not only won't interfere, but we won't have any battleships peeping in the window while you are having your party."

While we didn't land troops in Cuba, we were close enough that they all could have waded ashore.

> Yours,
> *Will Rogers.*

2312   WILL ROGERS GIVES '33 BENEFIT OF THE DOUBT

SANTA MONICA, Cal., Dec. 31. — A few hours from the time I am penning you these lines the old year will be going out and it looks like she is going out without a single mourner.

And at that it hasn't been a bad old year (as years have been going lately); in fact in years to come when all these professors switch from economists to historians, they are liable to label 1933 as the historical year, the year of the big switch, from worse to better.

So, so long '33, panics come every twenty years, so we will be seeing you in '53.

> Yours,
> *Will Rogers.*

DAILY TELEGRAMS — 1934

2313   WILL ROGERS FINDS OUT
                 CALIFORNIA HAS RIVERS

BEVERLY HILLS, Cal., Jan. 1. — Everybody comes to California. They see a lot of great wide rocky sandy creek and river beds with not a hot water bottle full of water in 'em, and they are a big joke. They wonder what they are for.

Well, yesterday they showed what they were there for. Us old settlers (that have been here five or ten years) never saw anything like it. We are so tickled to see rain out here that we put on a big parade in honor of it.

I am writing this before I go to the big game today. I am about half mad because Nicholas Murray Butler didn't come out here with his team. Somebody ought to have told him it was a Republican convention. That's his principal relaxation.

                 Yours,
                 Will Rogers.

2314   WILL ROGERS EXPLAINS
                 DEFEAT OF STANFORD

BEVERLY HILLS, Cal., Jan. 2. — The big Columbia-Stanford football game. Mr. Hoover was there, looked fine and got a big reception. He was the main old grad from Stanford. I was the main old grad from Columbia. I took a correspondence course from there one time in tenor singing.

Just the make of the skin that covers the ball beat Stanford. If, instead of pig skin, the ball has been covered with porcupine hide (with quills on) maybe Stanford could have held onto it.

But the game was in keeping with everything else that happened in sports, government and economics the past year. The experts were wrong again.

                 Yours,
                 Will Rogers.

2315   WILL ROGERS COMMENTS
                 ON DOINGS AT THE CAPITOL

BEVERLY HILLS, Cal., Jan. 3. — Roosevelt handled that Congress this morning just like a mother would a fretting baby.

But when any other mother would have told it to hush and be a good baby and not cry, he didn't tell 'em a single thing to do. Just slipped 'em all a piece of candy (the little black Republican babies along with the white ones) and he left 'em feeling that mother had confidence in 'em. And they were all just tickled to death, rolling on the floor with their toes in their mouth and goo-gooing at each other.
Yours,
Will Rogers.

2316   MR. ROGERS SEES HURDLE
             FOR SOME BUSINESS MEN

BEVERLY HILLS, Cal., Jan. 4. — Mr. Roosevelt proposed in his speech that the NRA and a lot of these other government-regulated business ethics would be made permanent.

Well, that was a terrible blow to some business men. They had figured they would only be required to be honest by the government till the emergency was over.

The papers today tell of a little country in the Pyrenees Mountains that has six army officers and only six plain soldiers.

Well, that strikes us as being mighty comical. Yet we got 120,000,000 people and 60,000,000 hold government jobs.
Yours,
Will Rogers.

2317   ROGERS SEES COMPLIMENT
             IN THE 10 BILLION BUDGET

BEVERLY HILLS, Cal., Jan. 5. — This country runs to the figure ten. There has been many who has had to say, "Mr., can you spare a dime?" but President Roosevelt is the first man in the history of the world who looked a nation right in the face and said, "Mister, can you spare ten billion dollars?"

Well, Congress and the American people considered it such a compliment to be asked for that much that they really liked it.
Yours,
Will Rogers.

2318   WILL ROGERS IS GLAD
                WE ARE NOT AMBITIOUS

BEVERLY HILLS, Cal., Jan. 7. — Poor old France and Japan are about in the same fix.

France don't know whether it would be better to jump on Germany and lick 'em now while they can or "will I set here and wait till they are ready to pounce on me?"

Japan is on the same spot. They feel they can lick Russia now. Or, will she wait till Russia is able to come pounce on them?

This thing of living in an ambitious nation is not what it's cracked up to be. We are certainly glad Mr. Roosevelt announced that we had about all the country we wanted. In fact, he suggested that if we could get a decent offer he would let some of it go.

                          Yours,
                            Will Rogers.

2319   WILL ROGERS REMARKS

RIVERSIDE, Cal., Jan. 8. — Among the society notes of Rochester, Minn., I see where Dr. Cary Grayson of Washington, D. C., arrived at Mayo's roadhouse. Admiral Grayson was President Wilson's private physician. Scare him Charley, but don't hurt him, for he is the best liked man in Washington, the best storyteller, raises good horses and is personal physician to Senator Carter Glass' fighting roosters. President Wilson used his sense of humor when he made Doc an admiral. Doc had never been on any water bigger than Culpepper Creek, and he forded it horseback on a possum hunt. You Mayo boys get Doc to tell you about when he and Jesse Jones of the R.F.C. got into Buckingham Palace with President Wilson and Jesse took off his shoes in the reception hall and was warming his feet by the king's fireside.

                          Yours,
                            Will Rogers.

2320   MR. ROGERS OFFERS A REPLY
              TO A REPUBLICAN VOLLEY

RIVERSIDE, Cal., Jan. 9. — The Republican National Committee come out strongly yesterday against Roosevelt's economic policy.

Just two days before the deficit of the Republican National Committee had been published. It was the biggest on record.

California's Supreme Court ruled yesterday that if male students of a State university took all the advantages of free education, that a little military training would not be asking too much of them.

If you are going to let out conscientious objectors, nobody would take anything but football, swimming, theatricals and saxophone playing (all of which the States provide).

Yours,
Will Rogers.

2321 MR. ROGERS FINDS THRILL
IN AN OLD-TIME SPORT

RIVERSIDE, Cal., Jan. 10. — Did you ever drive one of these "sulkys" in a trotting horse race? Well, they got old David Harum sitting straddle of a horse's tail out here on the Riverside track, and if you think that hasn't got it on all auto driving you are wrong.

I am getting just about old enough and crabbed enough to take up the Grand Circuit. So look out Goshen and Lexington, young Pop Geers is coming East.

We have our radios, autos, golf, bridge and a million contraptions, but all of it don't pay for the thrill missed in stepping out in the red wheel buggy and high stepper.

You could be a pretty poor type of lover, but the horse made up for it. That's how a lot of us was able to go out of our class and get the wives we did.

Yours,
Will Rogers.

2322 MR. ROGERS SEEKS LIGHT
ON FINLAND'S EYE-OPENER

RIVERSIDE, Cal., Jan. 11. — The Senate passed a bill yesterday that we only buy drinks from those who pay us.

That had everybody rushing to the statistics this morning to see how Scotland stood.

I don't know what Finland's national drink is, but we better be getting used to it, for they are the only ones that have really paid in full. Whatever it is, you can certainly run on it. I guess it's a "Nurmi punch."

Well, I bet this scheme goes just like all the rest have. They have tried everything in the world to bring France to time. France is a nation that don't shame easy.

Yours,
Will Rogers.

2323   ROGERS KNOWS ONE TAIL
        THAT DOESN'T WAG THE DOG

SANTA MONICA, Cal., Jan. 12. — Yesterday's immortal lines that I penned to you is today null and void. I told you the Senate was to buy no liquor from nations that wouldn't pay. Well, that was what they had passed, but it seemed to have been their own idea. When the President saw it, he give 'em an eraser and says you boys go back and rub that out.

So hereafter any news that I bring you in regard to what the Senate has done, why, it's subject to cancellation. This is one session of Congress where the tail is not wagging the dog.

Yours,
Will Rogers.

2324   MR. ROGERS LOOKS BACK
        TO THE OLD WET DAYS

BEVERLY HILLS, Cal., Jan. 14. — Trouble with us is we had the tax on liquor at the wrong time. We should have had it on from 1919 to 1933, when people were drinking.

A prospector in the heart of Death Valley is not as lonesome looking as a salesman in a liquor store.

That Japanese Admiral that declared war on America got a lot of publicity but no war. In fact all the writers and predictors haven't been able to produce a war as readily as they promised.

Every nation thinks they are getting ready for it quicker than the other, and if they each know that the other is ready there will be none.

Yours,
Will Rogers.

2325   Mr. Rogers Is Converted
              To Game New To West

BEVERLY HILLS, Cal., Jan. 15. — I never thought the time would come when I thought I would be able to advise colleges how to run their business, but in California Sunday we saw our first real professional football played, and 25,000 come away raving about it. Especially the rules under which they play, where you can pass from anywhere, any time.

Now as football is not only the backbone but the gravy of college existence, you fellows better open up your game, for this pro game was just made for an audience. No penalty every minute to keep an audience sore, nobody getting hurt every play, referees not in the way of the players.

Colleges have developed the yelling, but the pros have developed the game. Now you colleges wake up. I don't want to see you have to close up your doors.

Yours,
Will Rogers.

2326   Mr. Rogers Is Too Busy
              To Talk Of The Dollar

SANTA MONICA, Cal., Jan. 16. — Papers are all excited today over the dollar being sixty cents.

Well, it's been sixty cents for months, but we just love to have something new to get excited over.

Worst thing about the whole mess is we are going to have to listen to all the same old arguments all over again.

It's a good argument for us dumb ones to stay out of. So, sic 'em, Tige, may the loudest man win.

I am going to get onto some news. Did you know that Greta Garbo is prowling around in the Arizona desert under the name of Jones, with some "furriner" going by the name of Brown?

I got to get that settled before I can take up this gold business.

Yours,
Will Rogers.

2327   Mr. Rogers Is Astounded
              At News From Vermont

BEVERLY HILLS, Cal., Jan. 17. — I want to stay off any reference to this sixty-cent dollar until I have seen one.

So I started searching the paper mighty thoroughly, and what do you think I found away down in one corner like one of those denials that a paper is sometimes forced to make? It stated, "Republican elected to Congress in Vermont."

That's a mighty serious rumor, in case it proves to be true, and I have no doubt that Congress will be asked to pass a law preventing it happening again.

Course the thing come up so sudden like, they didn't think there was one in million miles.

Yours,
Will Rogers.

2328   MR. ROGERS IS SATISFIED
WITH THE NEW DOLLAR

BEVERLY HILLS, Cal., Jan. 18. — I am still trying to stay off writing about the sixty-cent dollar. It looks like the argument is pretty well taken care of without any expert aid from me. We got France scared, so the experience has already paid for itself.

Cuba kinder nosed in on the front page again today, with a new President, but it's getting so that's not news. So about two more Presidents and they will be back with the want ads news.

Tammany Hall had the biggest quake it's had in years. A Mr. Flynn, a very able man and friend of our President who heretofore only had one district, has taken over the whole thing. Tammany deaths, however, are always temporary.

Yours,
Will Rogers.

2329   WILL ROGERS COMMENTS
ON DULL BUDGET OF NEWS

BEVERLY HILLS, Cal., Jan. 19. — Plenty of headlines today, but not much news. "Congress votes on the sixty-cent dollar Saturday." Wonder if they will have one in there as an exhibit. "Government undecided about what they can do with Japanese taking pictures of fortification." Make 'em agree to send us some of the pictures if they turn out O.K. "Cuba hails new president." Hails him with what? "The man that found the 726-carat diamond in Africa, received $350,000 for it and wants to buy a farm and silk hat." Well, I can understand a man perhaps being eccentric enough to want to own a silk hat.

       Yours,
       Will Rogers.

2330   Mr. Rogers Has His Eye
     On The 60-Cent Dollar

  SANTA MONICA, Cal., Jan. 21. — Well, the sixty-cent dollar passed the House by nine to one.
  Where did that one come from? Can it be the President's power is waning?
  The Senate will talk against it, but vote for it.
  This leaves Mr. Roosevelt in sole charge of the money. It's the first time the banker has lost control of it since interest was invented.
  Japan hasn't got much humor. They say we don't recognize Manchukuo. We do recognize it; we recognize it as a part of Japan.
  I tell you there is matrimonial hope for any man. I see where a radio announcer got married. Good luck, Graham.

       Yours,
       Will Rogers.

2331   Mr. Rogers Approves
     Of The New Diplomacy

  SANTA MONICA, Cal., Jan. 22. — Our able and amiable Secretary of State, Cordell Hull, returned from a conference and entered through the front door. Our delegates generally climb over the back fence in the dead of night when they get back.
  If this administration never did another thing, the new deal toward all our neighbors to the south has gained us many friends, and the best friend any one can have is their neighbors.
  Give the Philippines their freedom and take that godfather clause out of our Cuban treaty, and first thing you know we would be called "brother" and not "big brother."

       Yours,
       Will (Bing) Rogers.

2332   Mr. Rogers Is Cheered
By The Japanese News

BEVERLY HILLS, Cal., Jan. 23. — Good deal of Japanese news last day or so.

One day our eyes are turned to Europe (to see if the boys have any token payment.) The next day it's Japan that draws our attention. We are going to have a crooked neck from trying to look both ways at once.

That old hostile baby over in Japan that was Secretary of War, why he has resigned, and their Foreign Minister Koki Hirota, why he seems to be about half peaceable.

He seems to kinder favor licking Russia first, then take care of us later. But this boy that resigned, he was for a doubleheader the same day.

Yours,
Will Rogers.

2333   Mr. Rogers Gets Word
That Kansas Is Satisfied

BEVERLY HILLS, Cal., Jan. 24. — As a rule folks don't like war headlines, but here was one that was in the papers that hit the spot, "Roosevelt Declares War on Civil Works Grafters."

We recognized the new President in Cuba. I hope he stays in long enough to get acquainted with.

Just had a nice visit from Senator Henry Allen of Kansas. He said Kansas was feeling fine. Now, when Kansas ain't kicking things have got to be running about perfect.

Yours,
Will Rogers.

2334   Mr. Rogers's Homeland
Still Has Bootleggers

CLAREMORE, Okla., Jan. 25. — The old homing pigeon flew back to its nest today. Crossed Arizona, New Mexico and Texas last night. Slept all the way. Fort Worth for breakfast.

Amon Carter meets all planes and sells tickets for the Big Roosevelt ball Tuesday night. I bet Fort Worth raises more money for that splendid cause than any city five times its size.

Bill Murray has taken good care of the old State since I been gone.

In California we had forgotten there was such a thing left as a bootlegger, but back in these States, Oklahoma, Texas and Arkansas, they are thicker than CWA workers.

Yours,
Will Rogers.

2335   ROGERS FLIES TO CAPITAL
TO ATTEND THE BIG SHOW

COLUMBUS, Ohio, Jan. 26. — As I got to the field in Tulsa this morning "Jypsy" Smith, the great English evangelist, came out to the airport, and we had a fine chat. He talks to 10,000 people a night there, a very earnest, fine man, who advertises no particular route to salvation. I asked him, in saving Oklahoma for the Lord, to save Alfalfa Bill Murray, him and Jim Ferguson of Texas, for there ain't any more like those two, and I just kinder like 'em.

Missouri, Indiana and Ohio all passed under us in order. Three great old States, whose statesmen have made history. Will make Washington by lighted airways by 11 o'clock tonight. Then tomorrow to the big show and see the actors, maby see 'em vote on the most momentous question outside of war.

Yours,
Will Rogers.

2336   MR. ROGERS FINDS SENATE
'FINE BUNCH OF FELLOWS'

NEW YORK, N. Y., Jan. 28. — Well, visited the Senate Saturday and renewed many pleasant acquaintances.

They are a fine bunch of fellows when you take into consideration the amount of things the people lay onto 'em. They rant at each other in there, then come out and are good friends.

Had the pleasure of sitting by Mrs. Alice Longworth in the

Senate gallery when the gold bill was passed. Alice, due to the Roosevelt tradition, took it right on the chin and smiled.

She sincerely believes that no President ever carried the faith of as many people as this distant relative.

Yours,
Will Rogers.

2337   MR. ROGERS IS IN THE THICK
             OF THINGS AT THE CAPITOL

WASHINGTON, D. C., Jan. 29. — The Senate layed off today on account of Huey Long going to speak tomorrow. They give 'em a day off to get rested up.

Huey give me a dose of my own medicine. I generally talk everybody to death, but he got a hold of me and rehearsed his speech on me. He was trying it out on the dog. I can remember it myself in case anything happens to him.

Since the big money stabilization bill passed Saturday everybody here is in fine cheer and great optimism.

The Senators all practicing dancing for the big ball. Our President is going to have a wonderful birthday, but many a lady's feet is going to suffer for their loyalty.

Yours,
Will Rogers.

2338   MR. ROGERS ENLIGHTENS
             A 'LADY CONGRESSMAN'

WASHINGTON, D. C., Jan. 30. — The Vice President and Mrs. Garner's party to the President was one of the finest and most enjoyed affairs you ever saw. They were marvelous hosts and the President did enjoy himself. Mr. Roosevelt couldn't get over Mr. Garner staying up till 12 o'clock.

Been visiting and listening to speeches in both ends of the Capitol all day. Debating on the big navy bill in the House.

Was talking to a lady Congressman and she said to me, "Why do all those men say that a big navy will bring peace?"

I told her, well, even if it don't bring peace it will come in mighty handy.

Yours,
Will Rogers.

2339   WILL ROGERS CONSIDERS
                 MILLS'S SPEECH ILL-TIMED

NEW YORK, N. Y., Jan. 31. — Everything is based on psychology and I believe that Ogden Mills, as clever and as able as he is, picked a bad day to explain to the country that they were prostrate under a tax which they couldn't possibly be able to pay.

Why in 6,000 cities people had on that very day to lay aside Ogden's speech in order to dress in silks and plush and enter expensive limousines to get to the ball.

No, Ogden, there was too many silk hats showed up that night to make a tax collector be misled by the cry of poverty. That speech just didn't harmonize with ermine and champagne.

                             Yours,
                                 Will Rogers.

2340   MR. ROGERS CAN'T TAKE IT;
                   HURRIES TO CALIFORNIA

WASHINGTON, D. C., Feb. 1. — Say the snow is knee deep tonight and still a-falling. California, here I come.

The aeroplanes are awful fine, but the old trains come in mighty handy and they are getting their rates down now where lots of folks are riding on the trains.

In the Senate this afternoon was the St. Lawrence River Canal Bill. It will be the first Presidential measure that may meet defeat. It will be mighty close.

Was in the Vice President's office when he was visited by the Russian Ambasador, he and his wife. He seemed an awful nice fellow. I asked him about war with Japan. He said it had been delayed indefinitely on account of bad weather.

                             Yours,
                                 Will Rogers.

2341   ROGERS SAYS CRIMINALS
                   GET TOO MUCH PUBLICITY

CHICAGO, Ill., Feb. 2. — Watched Congress open in Washington around noon today, then I realized I couldn't do anything about it. So I left. Into Chicago at four thirty, Salt Lake by midnight, and Los Angeles for breakfast. That's rambling. Got a lot of blind flying by radio beams on account of the snow. I don't know what the ground hog saw, but we didn't even see the ground all day.

Have read all the papers in all the cities along the route, and all have had the same front page, big pictures of Sankey and Dillinger (generally both). We don't give our criminals much punishment, but we sure give 'em plenty of publicity.

Yours,
Will Rogers.

2342   MR. ROGERS GIVES ADVICE
TO THE MONEY EXPERTS

BEVERLY HILLS, Cal., Feb. 4. — Now that the principal thing to gamble in is money you watch the Chinamen entering into your brokerage offices.

No people in the world can gamble on money exchange like a Chinaman. The quickest figurers in their heads of anybody. That money market in Shanghai makes the New York stock market look like a wake. And not a pencil in the house.

I here and now suggest to Mr. Morgenthau, our Treasurer, don't monkey with the Princeton or Harvard professor when he starts out with that two billion to stabilize with. Can all those professors and get a Chinaman.

Yours,
Will Rogers.

2343   MR. ROGERS IS RESIGNED
TO A LOT OF TAXATION

BEVERLY HILLS, Cal., Feb. 5. — Well, all I know is what I see by the papers and I see where the manufacturers' sales tax comes up in Congress this week. They been needing that for a long time and I imagine it will pass.

But it's not going to do what a lot of 'em want it to, replace the income tax. And there is no reason why it should. You are going to need sales taxes, both Federal and State, income tax and a lot of other kinds.

It's a great country but you can't live in it for nothing.

Yours,
Will Rogers.

2344   Mr. Rogers Joins Army
                Of Government Workers

BEVERLY HILLS, Cal., Feb. 6. — You know a couple of days ago I said that what our treasurer Mr. Morganthau needed when he went out with this two billion to gamble with these money exchange "jips" was not a pack of professors but a Chinaman.

Well this morning I got a mighty nice wire from Mr. Morganthau and he agreed with me and appointed me a committee of one to dig up the Chinaman.

So I am in the market now for a keen-minded Chinaman, kind of a cross between Confuscious, Alexander Hamilton and Barney Baruch.

So if you see me dashing into laundries and chop suey joints you will know I am working for the government.

                            Yours,
                            Will Rogers.

2345   Mr. Rogers Sees Bankers
                Caught In A Cross-Fire

SANTA MONICA, Cal., Feb. 7. — Say did you read what Jesse Jones, head of the Reconstruction Finance, told the New York Bankers' Convention?

Jesse told 'em, "You boys will either start in loaning business and industry some money to operate on or the government will do it."

Course the bankers just got four years of good cussing by everybody for loaning too much money. Well, they got some awful nice buildings. So when a banker fails, he fails in splendor, so that's something.

                            Yours,
                            Will Rogers.

2346   Will Rogers Discusses
                Riots Here And Abroad

SANTA MONICA, Cal., Feb. 8. — All we read in the papers today out here is riots in Paris and taxicab riots in New York.

We know what they are fighting over in New York. They are fighting over a nickel, but nobody (even in France) knows exactly what they are fighting over.

France has got more different political parties than any nation on earth. There is over thirty different parties represented in the House of Deputies. Now in a fight on the street there is not that many different kind of badges to wear.

Well it's good to see France sore at somebody besides us.

Yours,
Will Rogers.

2347   WILL ROGERS SAYS FRANCE
GOT JUST THE RIGHT ADVICE

BEVERLY HILLS, Cal., Feb. 9. — In England statistics show that over 50 per cent of criminals commit suicide before being caught, knowing what will happen to 'em when they are captured. Can you imagine ours doing that? Look at the publicity they would miss. But are our courts and judges changing, for didn't this Sankey commit suicide in jail? Maybe this is liable to start a fad.

Monday France wanted communism. Tuesday they wanted a king. Wednesday an old man told 'em to go home and have a good drink of wine, take a nap and forget it. Just about what will satisfy any mob.

Yours,
Will Rogers.

2348   MR. ROGERS IS UNHAPPY
OVER THE AIR MAIL AFFAIR

SANTA MONICA, Cal., Feb. 11. — What's all the hundreds of airplane pilots and the thousands of people who make an honest living in the airplane business going to do? It's like finding a crooked railroad president, then stopping all the trains.

You are going to lose some fine boys in these army flyers who are marvelously trained in their line but not in night cross-country flying, in rain and snow.

I trust an air line, for I know that that pilot has flown that course hundreds of times. He knows it in the dark. Neither could the mail pilots do the army flyer's stunts and his close-formation flying.

I do wish they would prosecute the crook but not make a great growing industry (where 99 per cent are hard working and honest) suffer.

I hope they don't stop every industry where they find crookedness at the top.

Yours,
Will Rogers.

2349   WILL ROGERS VISUALIZES
LINCOLN IN THESE DAYS

BEVERLY HILLS, Cal., Feb. 12. — Papers today say, "What would Lincoln do today?"

Well, in the first place, he wouldn't chop any wood. He would trade his axe in on a Ford. Being a Republican he would vote the Democratic ticket. Being in sympathy for the underdog he would be classed as a radical progressive. Having a sense of humor he would be called eccentric.

And it's Alice's birthday, too. Alice Longworth has for the last thirty years, and I hope thirty more, had a reserved seat at the biggest show on earth.

Yours,
Will Rogers.

P. S. — In this aeroplane mess I don't own one cent of stock. I don't own one cent of stock in anything. (I have some lots in Beverly Hills I would like to talk to you about.) I love to fly. I pay my way and do it. Now there must have been some monkey business higher up, or Mr. Roosevelt wouldn't do what he has. And I would like to sit on the jury and help convict 'em, for they have brought injury to a great industry.

2350   MR. ROGERS SEES NO NEED
TO WORRY ABOUT THINGS

SANTA BARBARA, Cal., Feb. 13. — Funny thing just when I was reading about our great ship the Leviathan being tied up and rotting, why who drops in to my igloo to see me but my old friend Captain Hartley who was the skipper of that ship during all its great years.

He says that the excuse is that it is too big to operate, yet England and France both are building ones bigger. Then Germany is waiting to see what they do then she will build one still bigger. But ours is laid up because it's too big.

Well, anyhow what is there to worry over? Greta Garbo is not married, so cheer up, everything is fine again.

What does it matter who carries the mail? There hasn't been an important letter written in years.

Yours,
Will Rogers.

2351   Mr. Rogers Hopes We Do
                   Our Fighting At Home

SANTA MONICA, Cal., Feb. 14. — Austria? Say isn't that down there about in shooting distance of where the other war broke out?

England has told Germany to "lay off." Now what if Germany don't "choose" to lay off?

The boys are looking around now, kinder choosing up sides again. Russia would like to look down that way. But she can't take her eyes off Japan long enough. Mussolini is waiting for the best offer. France has got every propeller aspinning.

Now is one of the best times in the world for us to fight among ourselves. It will at least keep us out of some bigger devilment.

                         Yours,
                         Will Rogers.

2352   Will Rogers Proposes
                     A Policy Of Isolation

BEVERLY HILLS, Cal., Feb. 15. — Lotsa headlines today.

"Mussolini's Troops Camped on the Austrian Border." "Hitler Says Nothing," which means that he is too busy moving troops. "England Lends Moral Support." Yes, and two battleships. "France Backs Austrian Government" and sends a few hundred planes over to deliver the message. "Japan almost on verge of prostration in fear Russia won't get into this European war."

Mr. Franklin D., shut your front door to all foreign ambassadors running to you with news. Just send 'em these words:

"Boys, it's your cats that's fighting, you pull 'em apart."

                         Yours,
                         Will Rogers.

2353   Will Rogers Analyzes
                    Contents Of Air Mail

SANTA BARBARA, Cal., Feb. 16. — All this argument over who will carry the mail, and if you tore a sack open here is what you would find:

Twenty per cent would be chain letters. "Mail this to ten others, it will bring you good luck." And we spend a half billion a year on education.

Forty percent will be asking somebody for an autograph, as I said before we spend a half billion on education.

Ten per cent will be Congressional records (and there is not a house that can't pick up their own kindling).

Ten per cent is pamphlets of somebody's scheme of how to solve something.

Ten per cent is bills which won't be paid, so they just as well not send 'em.

Ten per cent is newspapers being sent to a place where there is a better paper printed.

And that's what a boy risks his life with over the mountains every night.

Yours,
Will Rogers.

2354 WILL ROGERS COMMENTS ON BELGIUM'S TRAGEDY

SANTA MONICA, Cal., Feb. 18. — Well, wasn't that too bad about the King of Belgium. I think he had always appealed to us as a fine human man with great love and concern for his people.

Well, England has great love for their King George, too. And Italy, too. Mussolini runs everything, but their little King stands mighty high with 'em and Mussolini is smart enough to just handle it right.

Say did you hear that little fellow Dollfus talking on the radio from away over in Austria? He must be a pretty keen little "hombre."

Yours,
Will Rogers.

2355 WILL ROGERS FINDS FLYING IN THE WEST TOUGH, TOO

GRAND ISLAND, Neb., Feb. 19. — Glad they didn't start the army fliers out on this route till morning, for it's a tough night.

Been talking to army pilots all the way across today, and, gee, they are just kids. I preached and pled with 'em if it got tough to turn around and go back, or set her down in an emergency field. Don't try to show how brave you are. Show how sensible you are. There is not a letter being written that's one-tenth as valuable as one of you kids' lives.

But they are just so keen to make good, well it kinder scares you. Mr. Roosevelt, I believe it would do great good if you would warn 'em that you don't expect the service the level-headed old experienced regulars delivered.

Col. Arnold, an old friend of mine, in charge of all of 'em in the West, told me in Salt Lake today that he had been preaching that to 'em.

I know you will like the way the regular mail pilots take it, (and most of them are ex-sore heads) they are men of fine judgment.

Yours,
Will Rogers.

2356   WILL ROGERS IS WAFTED
        INTO TOWN ON THE GALE

NEW YORK, N. Y., Feb. 20. — After flying all night, got in here at 8 o'clock this morning right in the wildest of what even California would call unusual weather. The plane stuck in the snow after it landed.

An army flier came breezing in, in an open cockpit, who had made the same run from Cleveland, these being the only two planes to land in Newark all day.

So give a big hand to Lieutenant Wackwitz of the U. S. Army, not forgetting (just because he is used to doing such things after years of service) Mr. Maurice Mars, pilot of the United passenger plane I was on.

It was so cold today that for one hour this morning they didn't roll the dice on the New York Stock Exchange. When those crap shooters hands can't roll 'em it's cold.

Yours,
Will Rogers.

2357   MR. ROGERS FINDS SNOW
        AND LOBBYISTS IN CAPITAL

WASHINGTON, D. C., Feb. 21. — Flew in this afternoon to see what the boys who live by the aid of the ballot box are doing. Busy as usual passing appropriation bills like hot biscuits at a country farm house.

Saw the Senate vote full pay back to government employees, so the old government is not so tough to work for at that. Many another fellow would like to be able to get what he used to.

Went into the air mail investigation. Mr. Black had been asking Mr. Brown questions since early Monday morning. That's about the longest any man has ever had to think up answers, but they was both doing it so friendly and nice you would think they room together.

Snowed here, but you can't see the ground for the lobbyists.

Nighttime is when you find out the news, so I will know more by tomorrow.

      Yours,
      Will Rogers.

2358   Mr. Rogers Recalls Chase
      Of Sandino By Plane

WASHINGTON, D. C., Feb. 22. — Reading today of Sandino's death in Nicaragua.

There is one thing that he and I always agreed on and that was that American armed forces had no right down there. As to whether he was a George Washington or a Jesse James, that's for his own people to judge.

And while the nation's mind at the present seems to be on aviation, I want to tell you that some of the greatest flying ever done by army, navy or commercial was done by the marine aviators in their flights through those mountains after this same Sandino.

I spent a week with the marines in temporary camp, arriving just three days after the Managua earthquake, and I flew with them over the Sandino country, dropping supplies to marine camps hundreds of miles up in the mountains.

I am glad we didn't find him that week.

      Yours,
      Will Rogers.

2359   Will Rogers Discovers
      Investigations On Sugar

NEW YORK, N. Y., Feb. 23. — Just flew up from Washington late this evening. Senate or the House neither one was operating today. Shows you what giving 'em a raise does.

But they was awful busy investigatin'. Run into my old friends Pat Harrison and Bob La Follette and they was investigating sugar. We have more arguments over sugar than we do over all the things combined that sugar goes on, or in. Pat was kinder protecting Mississippi. They got a kind of kaffir corn that renders out a thing they think is sorter sweet.

In another room they was investigating Wall Street. That was a real sugar investigation. Corporations loaned 20 billions to Wall Street in '29, so Mr. Roosevelt didn't invent the word billion.

Yours,
Will Rogers.

2360   WILL ROGERS REPORTS
                   ON THE DOINGS HERE

NEW YORK, N. Y., Feb. 25. — Say, these New York weather fellows deliver the goods. They advertised in all the papers yesterday that they had another storm in rehearsal, that they would be ready to produce one that would be a bigger production than the last one, and by gosh I believe it looks tonight like the boys are going to make good.

Clark Gable is back here appearing on the stage and I am here trying to help keep the women off him.

The big brokers of Wall Street are all moving down to Washington, for all their big clients are on the stand there all the time. They are putting tickers in the investigating rooms now.

Yours,
Will Rogers.

2361   WILL ROGERS GOES SOFT
                   AND CAN'T STAND SNOW

NEW YORK, N. Y., Feb. 26. — Hurry up planes and start leaving here. I can't walk in these snowshoes. Been run over by two sleighs today. Taxicabs are being pulled by dog teams and the weather man says there will be a blizzard tonight.

And to add to the gloom of this city is the death of John McGraw. New York owes much to him. He was responsible for bringing more people to New York to see his Giants in World Series and league games than any man New York ever had. Typified the spirit of his day and time and was a sweet character and a fine friend.

Yours,
Will Rogers.

2362   Mr. Rogers Visits Capital
            And Digs Up Some News

WASHINGTON, D. C., Feb. 27. — Flew in here today. You got to fly back here to get over the tops of these snow drifts. And brother, you got to have altitude.

My friend General Johnson opened up his complaint division of the NRA today. House was sold out before it opened.

And I saw something today with my own eyes that you wouldn't believe could happen. The Senate voted not to take the raise in salary. Thank Senator Borah for that, I say YOU thank him. I doubt if many of the Senators will thank him. But they did it, so give 'em a hand. The return of the 15 per cent in salary is only to apply up to six thousand dollar salaries.

I tell you a lot of folks got these Senators wrong. They are a fine bunch.

That fellow they sent to jail just got out yesterday.

Yours,
Will Rogers.

2363   Mr. Rogers Reconsiders
            And Is Back In Our Midst

NEW YORK, N. Y., Feb. 28. — Landing in Newark from Washington today, the pilot put us in the back end of the plane, so it would keep her tail down when the wheels hit the deep snow.

Give you an idea how many thousand men clearing the streets in New York, they have misplaced 51 thousand and can't find 'em.

Seven below zero in Washington this morning and snow a foot deep. Lobbyists standing frozen to death outside of Congressmen's homes. A lobbyist has nothing to keep him warm but his brief case.

The hotels of Washington should erect a monument to General Hugh Johnson. They been coming on pilgrimages by the thousands since last July to make a code, change a code or cuss a code. Washington, D. C. (Dam Code).

Yours,
Will Rogers.

2364   Will Rogers Is In Favor
            Of Leaving Panama Flat

NEW YORK, N. Y., March 1. — The first person to really question us on the worth of our 59-cent dollar is Panama.

We are supposed to pay 'em 250 thousand a year for killing all their mosquitoes and putting an irrigation ditch from one ocean to the other through their property. They say we are to pay in gold. Be a good joke on 'em if we just picked up our canal and come home.

Japan coronated the new emperor of Manchuria. They would have had the coronation earlier, but they didn't have any car to haul him to the festivities in.

Washington got liquor today. Must have been a big novelty, about like a baby being continued on milk.

Yours,
Will Rogers.

2365   WILL ROGERS FINDS ARMY
DOING WELL ON AIR MAIL

OMAHA, Neb., March 2. — The army is handling the mail very sensibly now. I left New York at 2 a.m., arrived Chicago at 6 a.m. Weather in and around Chicago was bad. They held us there until noon. No mail in or out. You see both army and commercial are very careful.

Talked to General Westover, in charge of all army fliers, and Colonel Hickam of Chicago area. They said they were taking no chances. (Some banker may lose a day's interest on his checks, but that's the worst can happen.)

And what about the fliers, and the old buck privates, some of which draw only 21 dollars a month, and have been moved away off up here from their posts? They want some money. They are eating and sleeping on credit and living off the generosity of the towns they are in.

So hurry up and get busy, Congress, and straighten the whole thing out. All of you say you want to. Well, then do it.

Salt Lake at midnight, Beverly for breakfast.

Yours,
Will Rogers.

2366   WILL ROGERS IS AMUSED
BY NEWS FROM HSINGKING

SANTA MONICA, Cal., March 4. — Funniest thing I ever read about a coronation was that one over in Manchuria. It seems that they would have had it sooner but Japan had to wait till they could get an armoured carriage to haul him there. That shows what you call being Emperor by popular demand.

Did you know that we got 10 dry states, 11 part dry, and the other 27 can have anything they want, the same as these 21 do?

Chile is selling nitrates. Europe is fertilizing again.

Yours,
Will Rogers.

2367   MR. ROGERS FAILS TO READ
        HIS PAPER AND IS SORRY

BEVERLY HILLS, Cal., March 5. — Missed President Roosevelt's speech this morning. (It was at 8 o'clock here.)

Yes, I was up in time, but here is the joke on me. I hadn't read it in the papers. Now I will have to read it.

But there is a great difference between him talking, and then you just reading it. He is the king of the air. Course he has the advantage of the rest of us. He don't come on the air till he has something to say and the rest of us, we have to come on when we have nothing to say.

Not changing the subject too soon, but I feel kinder sorry for that woman Sheriff in Indiana. She thought she was surrounded by men.

Yours,
Will Rogers.

2368   MR. ROGERS IS IMPRESSED
        BY PRESIDENT'S SPEECH

BEVERLY HILLS, Cal., March 6. — Statistics is about the poorest form of reading that we hate to listen to but I believe these that President Roosevelt used ought to be drummed into our heads.

"Ninety per cent of our people live on salary or wages, ten per cent on profits alone. People in this country whose income is less than two thousand a year buy more than two thirds of all the goods sold."

His talk come at a mighty opportune time, for lots of folks had figured, "Ah, well, the NRA has died out, why have to abide by it."

This will put new life in it and incidentally throw a scare into some of the boys.

Yours,
Will Rogers.

2369   Mr. Rogers Has Solution
Of The Wall St. Problem

SANTA MONICA, Cal., March 7. — See where they caught two of the guards that got out of the jail with Dillinger.

They had him surrounded in Chicago but he robbed a bank in South Dakota that day, so they was right on his trail. Just three States behind.

They can't seem to agree on the Wall Street Control Bill (Fletcher-Rayburn bill). What they ought to do with Wall Street is like with the farmers, say, "How much gambling did you do last year?"

"Your Honor, I bet a hundred thousand dollars."

"Well, this year we want you to cut it down to seventy-five thousand and we will pay you thirty thousand for not betting the other twenty-five."

                      Yours,
                      Will Rogers.

2370   Mr. Rogers Is Interested
In Mail Pilots And A Turk

BEVERLY HILLS, Cal., March 8. — Lots of news today.

Mr. Roosevelt gives a very clear statement of what they are doing to straighten out the air mail. And, you remember days ago I wrote you that the army men (especially the privates whose army salary is very small) who had to leave their home barracks and pay for food, rooms and everything, that the government hasn't given 'em any extra money. Well, it's still like it was then, only they are more broke than they was then.

An old boy whose picture appears before me, Zara Agha, don't mean anything, does it? Well, ladies, you better wake up, for Zara is on the loose looking for his 14th wife. Zara is 160 years old and a Turk. Zara is coming to Hollywood.

                      Yours,
                      Will Rogers.

2371   Mr. Rogers Pays Tribute
To A Fine Air Mail Flier

BEVERLY HILLS, Cal., March 9. — It's hard for me to keep these Notre Dame names clear in my mind, but just from memory I believe this army flier killed, named Wienecke, is the same lad I wrote you about three weeks ago that flew into Newark in the blizzard with the mail. He was a fine flier.

The more we read about that jail-breaking the funnier it gets. (That is if we didn't know that there was going to be a lot of people killed as a result of it.) Now we find one of the guards was 84 years old. All they have to do now to make the whole thing perfect is to find that Baby Leroy was the turnkey.

Yours,
Will Rogers.

2372   MR. ROGERS AGAIN GIVES
        HIS VIEWS ON THE AIR MAIL

SANTA MONICA, Cal., March 11. — Everybody cheers the President's air mail move. It was a big thing to do. His next popular move would be to say to his legal department, "We said there was fraud. There was fraud. We'll get busy and try somebody and, if guilty, convict 'em. That's all today, gentlemen."

Most criticism of the army flier is going to be very unjust. He is taught to fight in the air. When he fails at that, then criticize him. He didn't hire out as a postman. In fact, in modern warfare, they don't correspond with each other.

Our air mail pilots are the best in the world. That's why we have two departments in Washington, one for war and one for mail. Both very efficient, but not at each other's jobs.

Yours,
Will Rogers.

P. S. Eddie Rickenbacker did mighty well for us in the last war, and he had never delivered a letter in his life.

2373   WILL ROGERS NOTES STEP
        FORWARD BY RAILROADS

BEVERLY HILLS, Cal., March 12. — Well, just as the air mail stopped that famous new streamlined train pulled into our village. It looks like more than an ad. It looks like a fact.

Railroads are waking up now. They are speeding up and giving great service, and getting their rates down, finally competing with the bus and truck now instead of just cussing 'em.

Will Rogers in scenes from the motion picture David Harum, *based on the novel by Edward Noyes Westcott* (Fox Film Corporation, 1934).

Trouble with American transportation is that you can get somewhere quicker than you can think of a reason for going there. What we need now is a new excuse to go somewhere.

Yours,
Will Rogers.

2374 MR. ROGERS SAYS WE ALL
WILL TRY ANYTHING ONCE

BEVERLY HILLS, Cal., March 13. — Sure the army said they could fly the mails, be a fine army that would say, "No sir, Mr. President, we can't fly 'em."

If my movie company says "We are producing Shakespeare, how about it?" Yes sir. I can't do it like the Barrymores, but I will give it an awful tussle. The Romeo part may ground loop me, but I will take old Hamlet over the mountains on the darkest night.

And tomorrow if the President calls in the navy and says, "Can you relieve the farmer?" an admiral will say, "Yes sir, the ships will be ready at 12 o'clock to take him off the farm."

Yours,
Will Rogers.

2375 MR. ROGERS GETS AROUND
A BIT IN HIS NEWS VIEWS

SANTA MONICA, Cal., March 14. — A Russian plane had a forced landing while flying over that new independent country of Manchukuo and when they landed they were captured by Japanese. Guess the Japanese had had a forced landing there just ahead of 'em?

Little Dolfuss (Austria's demitasse Premier), Premier Gumbo of Hungary and Mussolini of Italy (the sire of all the dictators) are holding a conference in Rome to see who should start the war, and why, but before the conference got well under way, little Dolfuss had sold Mussolini 12 million bushels of wheat.

That's the only practical thing I ever heard come out of an international conference.

Yours,
Will Rogers.

2376   Mr. Rogers Understands
The St. Lawrence Defeat

HOLLYWOOD, Cal., March 15. — I was just thinking, if it really is religion with these nudist colonies they sure must turn atheists in the Winter time.

Well, the St. Lawrence Canal which Canada and U. S. were to build together was defeated in the Senate. I always thought that sounded like a pretty good thing. There is nobody we would rather be partners with in something than Canada. In fact both political parties thought it was so good that it's in both platforms (which of course don't mean anything.)

Every Senator voted against it if it didn't run by his house. The whole South was against it. But wait till they want to deepen the Mississippi, then these other babies will get back at 'em.

Yours,
Will Rogers.

2377   Rogers Doubts We Want
Insull Back Very Much

HOLLYWOOD, Cal., March 16. — Mr. Insull was trying to get out of Greece on boat, and Greece caught him with their navy. Well, I don't know whether we really want the old fellow as bad as we let on. I can't imagine any punishment worse than not being able to return to your own country, no matter what the country is.

Monday the House of Representatives votes on the silver question. I wonder what effect it would have made on present-day affairs if Bryan had had his in '96. I reckon we would have been just as broke. You can't legislate intelligence and common sense into people. We was riding for the fall. Would have gotten it anyhow.

Yours,
Will Rogers.

2378   Will Rogers Is Tiring
Of The Air Mail Fuss

SANTA MONICA, Cal., March 18. — This air mail thing—wish they would get them all kinder calmed down over it.

Everybody is so heated up over it till they can't see the other fellow's side, or any other side, but theirs.

No use talking about what the government shouldn't have done. It's done done. No use saying "The government can't do this, and they can't do that." Say, you would be surprised at the things the government can do.

The army may not be the one to carry the mails. I don't think so, but I am not going to go to blows with anybody over it. After all, it's the government's mail and the government's army. They can do what they want to with it.

This thing is not going to be settled according to any one man's wishes, so they'd just as well cool off and start compromising now.

Yours,
Will Rogers.

2379   MR. ROGERS IS INCLINED
       TOWARD A 60-YEAR PLAN

HOLLYWOOD, Cal., March 19. — Talk about Russia with her Five-Year Plan. Mussolini just saw their five and raised 'em fifty-five. Italy is now with a sixty-year plan.

Smart guy, that Mussolini. He laid out a plan where if it proved at the end that it wouldn't work, they couldn't find him.

Here are a few things even we could do with a sixty-year plan. Everybody could get their code signed up; Louisiana could catch up with Huey Long; get the air mail straightened out; get the bonus settled; vote on remonetizing silver, and send a delegation to the disarmament conference.

Yours,
Will Rogers.

2380   WILL ROGERS SETS FORTH
       SOME FACTS AND FIGURES

HOLLYWOOD, Cal., March 20. — Just like to show you what our cousins are doing in the way of toting the mail:

"London, March 16. The British postoffice showed a profit at the end of this fiscal year of seventy million dollars. Last year $57,000,000 postoffice profits were applied to the reduction of taxes."

We lost 150 million a year. Who's looney now?

They also run the telephone and telegraph, so when you say, "a government can't run a business," you mean our government can't run it.

So don't forget to always put that word "our" in there.

Jim, this is no reflection on you and your P. O. gang. It's on our lawmakers who won't charge for a letter, paper or crate of eggs what it costs to carry it, be it by plane, boat, train or mule, and charge accordingly.

Yours,
Will Rogers.

2381   MR. ROGERS IS FOR ARGUING
             BUT WOULD KEEP WORKING

HOLLYWOOD, Cal., March 21. — Well the country woke up mighty relieved this morning when they found the President had been able to stall off those strikes.

Don't it look like in case of a wage dispute it would be compulsory that you keep on working, but you send say two men, the owners two men and the government two. Now if they were months settling this and labor won, their increase in pay would go back to the time when the first protest was made or if it was a shortening of hours and labor won, they would also be paid for back hours.

Looks like nobody would be hurt much and the labor leaders and the owners could cuss each other in a room, the same as they do now in the newspapers, yet nobody would have to be idle listening to 'em.

Yours,
Will Rogers.

2382   MR. ROGERS PAYS TRIBUTE
             TO AN OLD WESTERN FRIEND

HOLLYWOOD, Cal., March 22. — Well, there ain't many Republicans left and the good ones of them are dying off.

Lost a good one, and a fine friend, yesterday, Fred Balzar, cowpuncher, railroader and miner, a real two-fisted Governor of the most independent State in our Union, Nevada.

He drove out to see me when down here a few weeks ago and brought me a quirt. I knew it was his last trip, and he did too, but he never flinched.

You would love Nevada. It's the West without dressing up to look the part. A herd of cows and a hole in the ground made it a unique State, and a long riata and a pick keep it a unique State.

Yours,
Will Rogers.

2383   WILL ROGERS DISCOVERS
A NEW TRAFFIC PROBLEM

HOLLYWOOD, Cal., March 23. — Those old Wall Street boys are putting up an awful fight to keep the government from putting a cop on their corner.

You don't hear as much of Senator Bill Borah as you used to. With all the new-fangled things they have for breakfast nowadays, you don't hear much of ham and eggs as you used to either, but it's still mighty good eating.

Mr. Borah says, "When you cut down your wheat production 43,000,000 acres, where are the farmers and people that farmed those 43,000,000 acres going?" Then it's proposed to send 2,000,000 from the crowded cities to the country. How are these two going to pass going and coming?

Those professors in the Agriculture Department are going to have a tough time answering that traffic problem.

Yours,
Will Rogers.

2384   MR. ROGERS SEES NO CAUSE
FOR ANY ONE FIGHTING NOW

SANTA MONICA, Cal., March 25. — Been reading all the Sunday articles by world known writers and they all talk war.

Well, if there is any excuse for anybody fighting at this time, it's beyond me. The consensus of opinion is that, "so and so has to fight so and so sooner or later." Well I believe if I had to fight a man "sooner or later" I would fight him later, the later the better.

The only legitimate reason I can see why Germany and France must fight is they haven't fought in sixteen years, and the only reason I can see why us and Japan has to fight is because we haven't fought before.

                Yours,
                Will Rogers.

2385   Mr. Rogers Is Gratified
             By The Turn Of Affairs

BEVERLY HILLS, Cal., March 26. — Say, that stopping that strike was the best bit of luck that's happened to us in a long time, for it looks like the basis of stopping all of them if the participants will all be as liberal as these were.

There was one new thing they brought out in the agreement that seemed pretty fair. That was that no matter what union, or group, or if none at all, that in any settlement you was to have representation in proportion to the number of workers in your group.

That's been one of the big troubles before. Supposed leaders who didn't represent anybody were in there talking for 'em.

So it looks like the President has earned his vacation, even if he is going on Astor's yacht.

                Yours,
                Will Rogers.

2386   Will Rogers Rounds Up
             Highlights Of The News

HOLLYWOOD, Cal., March 27. — Mr. Wrigley, the chewing wax man, did a thing today that will eventually become universal. He set aside a sum of money for unemployment insurance. He put by a million dollars.

On April first steel will raise wages 10 per cent. No April fool's joke out of that.

Funniest thing in this controversy over a bill to regulate Wall Street. Wall Street now wants to write their own bill. They are pleading guilty, but want the privilege of pronouncing their own sentence.

Wonder who the brain truster was that wanted us to go to Moscow?

                Yours,
                Will Rogers.

2387 Mr. Rogers Says Congress
    Should Have Gone Fishing

  HOLLYWOOD, Cal., March 28. — Well, Congress thought they knew more about how to run the country than the President so the President decided to go fishing. The trouble is the wrong one went fishing.

  Say, if they bring each one of the brain trusters up to ask 'em questions, and them being all college men, those Congressmen that ask 'em the questions will have to do it through an interpreter.

  We will see now how those Florida fish bite for a Democrat. Mr. Hoover went down there one time and they wouldn't come to the polls at all.

         Yours,
         Will Rogers.

2388 Mr. Rogers Finds News
    Of Real Importance

  PASADENA, Cal., March 29. — They say the air mail will be flying commercially soon.

  They say Congress votes on greenbacks for bonus money soon.

  They say Dillinger is headed West (but I bet you not to Tucson, Ariz.).

  They say the President is going to appoint a warden for Wall Street.

  All these don't mean a thing in the papers today. But when Rabbit Maranville breaks a leg right at the opening of the season that constitutes America's greatest crisis.

  The office seeker and the humorists naturally look to Washington for news, but the youth of America look to Rabbit and Babe.

  And, if anybody reading this has to ask who Rabbit is then you should be made to show your citizenship papers.

         Yours,
         Will Rogers.

2389 Rogers Tells Of Heroism
    Of Two Boys In The West

  PASADENA, Cal., March 30. — Here is something I think will bear repeating. Two kid brothers, one 14, the other 12, were hiking in the mountains out here. The young kid bit by a rattlesnake. The 14-

year-old one cut the wound all up with a knife and they took turns sucking the poisoned blood out. The younger one finally fainted, the other carried him up the mountain two miles on his back and he has saved him.

We are not so bad off. These kids are Daniel Boones and Davey Crocketts in any age.

Yours,
Will Rogers.

2390 WILL ROGERS SUGGESTS
A HAVEN FOR OUR FLEET

SANTA MONICA, Cal., April 1. — Not much news the last couple of days from Astor's fishing smack. Pretty nice of England to let our President fish in their ocean.

Speaking of oceans, our grand fleet of 110 ships have to leave this coast this week. Japan says they have been in their ocean long enough. We are about the only nation that has a fleet but no ocean to put it on.

The thing we ought to do is dig a canal right smack dab across the United States from East to West. Then, when there is objections from the proprietors of the Atlantic and Pacific, we could cruise in our own waters, something we can't do now.

Yours,
Will Rogers.

2391 WILL ROGERS PAYS TRIBUTE
TO A NOTED HORSEWOMAN

HOLLYWOOD, Cal., April 2. — You can't pass a park without seeing a statue of some old codger on a horse. It must be to his bravery, you can tell it's not to his horsemanship.

Women are twice as brave as men, yet they never seem to have reached the statue stage. But one is due now.

Horsemanship through the history of all nations has been considered one of the highest of accomplishments. Well, courage, horsemanship, sportsmanship and great paternal love was all embodied in one frail little white-haired woman, 67 years old. Mrs. Thomas Hitchcock, godmother, mother and patron saint of American polo, and lover of a horse.

Yours,
Will Rogers.

2392   WILL ROGERS PREDICTS
              DULL DAYS FOR ROOSEVELT

BEVERLY HILLS, Cal., April 3. — See where the President is prolonging his fishing trip. Going to stay away from Congress till they get about a dozen bills, then come back and veto 'em all at once.

It's going to be pretty tame for him when he gets back. He has been used to fishing for real game fish like the broadbill and the swordfish, then he will come home and have to bait his hook with some little postoffice worms and fish for mudcat Congressmen and eel Senators.

                      Yours,
                          Will Rogers.

2393   MR. ROGERS INCLUDES A BIT
              OF SARCASM IN HIS NOTES

BEVERLY HILLS, Cal., April 4. — Well, they had a big moving picture opening in Hollywood last night. Dillinger was there. I suppose he was. He is everywhere else where anything of importance takes place.

Looks like the only way we ever going to catch him is to wait till he hires a yacht and starts through Turkey.

If I was Insull I wouldn't mind coming back here and facing an investigation, if nothing more happens than at all the other investigations that start out so sensationally and peter out so quietly.

Investigations are held just for photographers.

                      Yours,
                          Will Rogers.

2394   MR. ROGERS RUNS ACROSS
              A SCOUT FOR OLD ELI

HOLLYWOOD, Cal., April 5. — Out to the studio here where we are working night and day on a picture came Dr. Professor Angell of Yale. I had always thought that a fellow from Santa Barbara named Harkness was the angel of Yale.

This was an awful nice fellow, and a very pleasant charming wife. He wanted me to help him on a couple of things. Wants to get

Yale made a CCC camp and have education put on the basic industry list. He is looking for five men for the line and three back-field men. He is on his way to Honolulu where he has heard of a quarterback.

Yale is doing all she can to get back among the 400 of football teams. He is doing all he can to get Yale graduates to take up some other work than "braintrusting." He thinks it's a business that won't last.

Yours,
Will Rogers.

2395   WILL ROGERS TELLS HOW
             TO MAKE TAXES POPULAR

HOLLYWOOD, Cal., April 6. — Can't bring Insull back yet. I see by the papers today where he hasn't finished his memoirs.

New York Stock Exchange is having their own investigation. They are investigating fourteen different stocks that have been acting so funny that Wall Street itself didn't know what they were doing. In other words you can fool the public, but you mustn't fool the members of the lodge.

The high income tax come pretty near passing Thursday in the Senate. Only lacked about six votes. So it won't be long now. Well, there is millions and millions that are not making it, that would be glad to give up 99 per cent if you would let 'em earn a hundred thousand or more.

Yours,
Will Rogers.

2396   WILL ROGERS DISCUSSES
             PRESIDENTS AND FISHING

SANTA MONICA, Cal., April 8. — We haven't heard of our President now in days. We haven't heard of Dillinger in days. You don't reckon he could be on there with 'em?

I will say one thing about a Democratic President fishing. Maybe he hasn't caught anything, but we won't have to look at pictures in the papers of him dragging some poor little trained perch in. The Republicans would get a cameraman before they did their bait.

One Summer here one poor little fish got so he would get his picture taken, then take the hook out of his own mouth and go back and wait for the President the next day with a new photographer.

Yours.
Will Rogers.

2397   MR. ROGERS OFFERS A PLAN
FOR ANCHORING OUR FLEET

HOLLYWOOD, Cal., April 9. — The whole American fleet left the Pacific today. It had to in order to be away around on the Atlantic side by the time war broke out in Japan and Russia.

Eastern seacoast Congressmen demand the sailors spend some wages in their towns. Western ones want the same. The government ought to let each town (East and West) figure out how much the navy spends there, then let the government pay it.

But let it be done with the understanding that politicians and chambers of commerce have no hold on the fleet and that it can be placed wherever it's needed.

Yours,
Will Rogers.

2398   MR. ROGERS IS WITNESS
TO A DISPLAY OF FAITH

SANTA MONICA, Cal., April 10. — In these days of everybody waiting to see how much they can get out of some government appropriation, it's gratifying to find a big man who is willing to spend a terrific wad of his own money.

I just saw the laying of the cornerstone of a new Los Angeles Times Building. I don't suppose Mr. Chandler absolutely had to build a new building, and if he had been like lots of our wealthy he would have said, "Well, I will just wait and see how things turn out."

He evidently don't believe that in a year's time we will all be calling each other "comrade."

Yours,
Will Rogers.

2399   Mr. Rogers Gets A Report
Of Import On Business

SANTA MONICA, Cal., April 11. — We got the moving picture theatre owners out here on a big convention. They all report business much better all over. Now what better barometer can you get than them?

Their convention informed the producers that about everything in the way of sex had been produced, and that the audience didn't care to see it over again. They suggested that for a change they thought the audience would like to see just an old fashioned movie.

And they also want to eliminate the sensational and suggestive advertising used for pictures. You can't make a picture as bad as the ads lead you to believe it is.

Yours,
Will Rogers.

2400   'Honest Taxpayer' Calls
For A Real Investigation

BEVERLY HILLS, Cal., April 12. — Well, Mr. Roosevelt gets back tomorrow and suppose his fishing trip will be followed by an investigation, for the Democrats claim he caught some fish and the Republicans are equally insistent that he didn't.

It's like all the investigations. It's absolutely necessary. It's going to have a big bearing on the future of this country.

If there is men in this country that claim they caught a fish when they didn't catch one, it should be known by the people of this country (no matter how high up the investigation has to reach).

So appoint your committee, three Democrats and two Republicans, so we can have a fair investigation and see if this country is going Russian and catching fish for caviar purposes.

Honest Taxpayer

2401   Rogers Sees No Exodus
Despite The High Taxes

BEVERLY HILLS, Cal., April 13. — I don't know what the President caught, but that Senate just by howling "yea," caught five hundred million (that will bear a second reading, 500,000,000) extra out of a gentleman called "Old Man Taxpayer."

They were just about to put on their hats to go home when they happened to think of the last 116 million. The way they got it now when you get all through with your taxes, you add an extra 10 per cent. That's the "cover charge."

But they can't do all these things they are doing without paying for 'em. As high priced as it is to live in, I don't see anybody leaving the country.

Yours,
Will Rogers.

2402   WILL ROGERS REMARKS

SANTA MONICA, Cal., April 15. — On this Sabbath day with a newspaper hid behind my song book, I saw where the Republic of Ireland was about to do away with their Senate. Now ordinarily that looks like a popular move in any country. But this being Sunday, and having a generous feeling toward all mankind (no matter how unfortunate his position) let's ask our Redeemer to not let us act too hastily in following Ireland's example. Thou Almighty, who seeist all things, must know that as disciples there is not a Saint Peter in the Senate, and as for prophets, there is not a Moses in a carload. They seeist not, but neither do the ones who sent 'em there see, so let's be charitable. But oh Gracious One, if Ireland should be right, help us to see the light immediately.

Amen,
Will.

2403   MR. ROGERS TAKES NOTICE
                     OF A NEW BONUS MARCH

SANTA MONICA, Cal., April 16. — Woman died at Savannah, Ga., age 123.

She had smoked a pipe for 112 years, while cigarette smokers figure they are passing out daily at the ripe old age of 30 and 40.

I think it's the fatigue from tapping 'em on the cigarette case that wears 'em down so early.

Saw a picture of the Congressmen in their march to meet the President at the depot in Washington.

It was a bonus march, for today they asked him for one and a half billion more to be spent by the government in their respective districts, especially the ones where they come up for re-election this Fall.

       Yours,
       Will Rogers.

2404   Mr. Rogers Gets A Thrill As The Bats Crack Again

SANTA MONICA, Cal., April 17. — With the baseball season opened and Washington headed for another pennant, boy, Congress better be good from now on!

Baseball is in for a great year. It's our national game and will always be our national game. We become a great nation under baseball and commenced to flop the minute we started to take up a lot of other poor substitutes.

Golf is played for conversational purposes. Polo is played by us lazy ones, because the horse does all the work and we love to just go for the ride.

But you have to play baseball for itself alone, for there is no clubhouse to talk it over in after the game.

From an old first baseman of the Oolagah (Okla.) Giants.

       Yours,
       Will Rogers.

2405   Mr. Rogers Sees A Lesson In That Wirt Dinner

SANTA MONICA, Cal., April 18. — The famous "Wirt Dinner" proved one thing. That is, these highbrows can't remember what happened at their dinners any more than us dumb ones can remember what happens at ours.

What difference does it make what was said at a dinner anyhow? If it's a real dinner and everybody is going good, there won't be anything sensible said anyhow.

You know there is two places where what a person says should not be held against 'em in a court of law. One is at a dinner and the other on the witness stand of a Washington investigation. Both affairs are purely social and should be covered only by the society editor.

       Yours,
       Will Rogers.

2406   WILL ROGERS ANSWERS
THE LEXINGTON PATRIOTS

SANTA MONICA, Cal., April 19. — In opposite columns appear these two different items:

"Lexington, Mass., citizens march to Washington as in revolutionary days to protest the government having anything to do with business."

"Washington, D. C., Secretary Perkins reports 2,750,000 employed in past year, employment in March was 80 per cent of what it was during peak of 1923-25 average. Weekly payrolls increased $70,000,000 in twelve months, since last March."

So it looks like the boys from Lexington will find quite a few along the line of March to Washington that will be too busy to join 'em. I imagine it would be awful hard to ruin a country by paying wages.

Yours,
Will Rogers.

2407   ROGERS ASKS A QUESTION
ABOUT THAT WIRT AFFAIR

SANTA MONICA, Cal., April 20. — See where all the brain trusters are saying the whole Wirt affair was a joke on him. In other words they framed up to make a joke out of him. Now are we right sure that they ain't making a joke out of the taxpayer too?

Japan last week announced they had taken over the supervision of China in person, and that American, British, French, or German would kindly take notice. But see by today's papers they claim they were a little too ambitious, and that other nations can go into China, but will have to have all passports "visa," (or is that "viza?") by Tokyo.

Yours,
Will Rogers.

2408   MR. ROGERS GIVES ADVICE
TO CLASSES AT HARVARD

SANTA MONICA, Cal., April 22. — Well, we just got over "Be Kind to Animals Week." So, now you can start again writing to your Congressman.

Saturday President Roosevelt had at the White House his graduating class of Harvard, 1904. There was over 300 of 'em, and all Republicans. I think he was just quietly rubbing it in on 'em, for the press couldn't name a one of 'em that anybody had ever heard of.

I think F. D., with his usual sense of humor, was just in a subtle way impressing on the boys, "If there hadn't been a Democrat in the class, youse guys would never have got to even see the inside of the White House."

It only illustrates that every Harvard class should have one Democrat to rescue it from oblivion.

Yours,
Will Rogers.

2409   Rogers Thinks Dillinger Will Get Shot Some Day

BEVERLY HILLS, Cal., April 23. — Well they had Dillinger surrounded and was all ready to shoot him when he come out. But another bunch of folks come out ahead, so they just shot them instead.

Dillinger is going to accidentally get with some innocent bystanders some time. Then he will get shot.

Here is the usual daily A. P. dispatch from Indiana:

"Michigan City, Ind., April 23. — Four prisoners, three serving life terms, escaped from the prison today."

An Indiana sentence from a judge reads: "You are sentenced to prison as long as it's made comfortable for you and you desire to remain. In checking out, kindly let the warden know, so he will know how many will be there for supper."

Yours,
Will Rogers.

2410   Mr. Rogers Is Puzzled By The Dillinger Case

HOLLYWOOD, Cal., April 24. — Headline in papers today said, "Dillinger hunters ordered to shoot to kill."

Would be interesting to know what their instructions had been up to now. They keep catching his women though, but he always is able to keep at least two women ahead of 'em.

Speaking about capturing renegades, I see President Roosevelt has captured Congress again. They escaped there for a few weeks, but he whittled him a wooden gun while in Florida and he has 'em right back marching in lock step again.

All but one, and Mrs. Roosevelt is taking care of him personally.

Yours,
Will Rogers.

2411   WILL ROGERS ADMIRES
MR. TUGWELL'S 'DOGMAS'

BEVERLY HILLS, Cal., April 25. — Most of the news in today's papers concern Dillinger and Tugwell.

Mr. Tugwell is just one of the nicest and most pleasant fellows you ever met in your life. All of those brain trust fellows are.

But don't let 'em start explaining something to you. They get you down with theorys and then stomp on you with phrases. You start to raise up and they will hit you in the face with a thing called "dogma."

Mr. Tugwell knocked a pretty smart bunch over lately with a pair of "dogmas" called "modernized process" and "experimental approach."

Einstein couldn't have had 'em as mentally goofy.

Yours,
Will Rogers.

2412   MR. ROGERS CITES ASSET
JAPAN DOESN'T POSSESS

SANTA MONICA, Cal., April 26. — Japan. You got to admire 'em. They are so ambitious, and they just got everything that all the other nations have but a sense of humor.

Their papers took great satisfaction and glee and screamed it in headlines, "The American Fleet Can't Get Through Panama Canal in 24 Hours." They never figured that the size of the fleet might have something to do with it.

Twenty-nine new ships have been authorized, so when the fleet comes back through there, and it can't get through in a day and a half, that will be a scream to Japan.

The Republicans coming out pretty strong now against the administration. Looks like if the Democrats don't get Dillinger, they may lose this Fall's election.

       Yours,
        Will Rogers.

2413   ROGERS PUTS IN A BOOST
      FOR HIS CALIFORNIA WINE

FRESNO, Cal., April 27. — This is Fresno, Calif., a beautiful little city of 80,000. You might ask, "Well, what about it? What's that to us?" Well, you go home tonight and have a nice glass of native wine with your meal. Fresno gives it to you.

Grapes grow here like lobbyists in Washington. Forty wineries here and a Rotary convention. All forty-one are going strong, night and day.

The Bulwinkle Congressional committee, investigator of the famous Wirt dinner (where nothing but applesauce was served), exonerated everybody connected with it including the cook, but advised the doctor the next time he dined out to take a dictaphone with him.

       Yours,
        Will Rogers.

P. S. No news from Dillinger today, so the papers are all half-size.

2414   MR. ROGERS RECALLS A DAY
      WHEN HE TALKED TOO LONG

GILROY, Cal., April 29. — Mrs. Rogers and I driving along from Fresno to San Francisco seeing all the ranches run in at Willie Tevis ranch (the champion endurance rider) and there at a barbecue was the Sultan of Jahore the biggest game hunter of all the Indian royal pack and tremendously popular over there and a regular guy.

Well, I got to tell you how I talked myself out of seeing his place and stable and horses. He is just out of Singapore. I had come in on a boat from Hong Kong and was going to take the plane the next morning for London so was going to drive to his estate that afternoon.

But, I talked at the Rotary Club luncheon, and did I talk? I must have blathered for hours, bored the whole of Singapore and missed the Palace of Jahore.

That's one case in history where a long-winded speaker suffered in the long run more than his listeners.

Yours,
Will Rogers.

2415   M<small>R</small>. R<small>OGERS</small> R<small>EDISCOVERS</small>
            A C<small>ITY</small> T<small>HAT</small> I<small>S</small> A C<small>ITY</small>

SAN FRANCISCO, Cal., April 30. — Well, San Francisco.

I bet that San Francisco was a city from the very first time it had a dozen settlers.

Cities are like gentlemen, they are born, not made. You are either a city, or you are not. Size has nothing to do with it. New York is "yokel" but San Francisco is "city" at heart.

Boats coming from the East Coast through the canal are crowded with people that didn't know that a boat went anywhere but Europe. The old Bret Hart and Mark Twain gold mining districts are opening up again. Men are trading in their golf clubs for a pick and shovel and burro.

Yours,
Will Rogers.

2416   M<small>R</small>. R<small>OGERS</small> I<small>S</small> P<small>REPARED</small>
            F<small>OR</small> A P<small>OSSIBLE</small> S<small>URPRISE</small>

SAN FRANCISCO, Cal., May 1. — I see by the papers today that there is some talk of Russia paying (and that's on a debt this Russian Government didn't contract). They owe $700,000,000 and we may get $200,000,000.

Be a good joke on everybody if the Communists turned out to be the only ones you could trust.

The Philippines are voting on whether they want freedom or not. They were in favor of it till they sent a commission over here and saw what it was. Now they are in doubt.

Yours,
Will Rogers.

2417   Mr. Rogers Makes Public
                A Little Inside Stuff

SAN FRANCISCO, Cal., May 2. — See where the U. S. Chamber of Commerce are gathered in Washington again. It's the caviar of big business.

Last time they met I happened to be in Washington and was the guest of Jesse Jones (head of the Reconstruction Finance) at their dinner.

Now the whole constitution, bylaws and secret ritual of that Orchid Club is to "keep the government out of business."

Well, that's all right, for every organization must have a purpose, but here was the joke:

They introduced all the big financiers—the head of this, that and the other. As each stood up Jesse would write on the back of the menu card just what he had loaned him from the R. F. C. (got that menu card yet).

Yet, they said "keep the government out of business."
                              Yours,
                          Will Rogers.

2418   Mr. Rogers Arises To Ask
                Silas Just One Question

SAN FRANCISCO, Cal., May 3. — Headline in papers today says, "Silas Says We Are Drifting."

I had to do a little research work to find out who Silas was and see if he had any idea where we were drifting.

I found out he is an attorney from Chicago and was delivering a speech in Washington before the United States Chamber of Commerce. Silas had the whole thing in brief-case form, excepting the destination.

It was like some big Federal officer arising at a banquet and saying "Dillinger is drifting," and you couldn't very well dispute him unless you happen to ask him "Where?"
                              Yours,
                          Will Rogers.

2419   Mr. Rogers Notices A Ray
                Of Hope For The Weary

SAN FRANCISCO, Cal., May 4. — At the U. S. Chamber of Commerce meeting last time Mr. Roosevelt appeared (in person) and delivered a lovely talk. This time he just sent the boys a note and told 'em to quit hollering "Wolf" and go to work.

"Private business can and must take up the slack. The people will be impatient of those who complain."

So the chamber looked at each other, scratched their heads and went back to "passing resolutions."

But the President did hand 'em out one bright hope. He said Congress was about through.

Yours,
Will Rogers.

2420   MR. ROGERS IS A BIT SHY
             OF UNCLE SAM'S ADVISERS

SAN FRANCISCO, Cal., May 6. — From all I can read in the papers dated from some foreign capital, the ambition of their lives seems to be to get us and Japan into a war.

Now, if any nation on earth can give any excuse why we should fight Japan any more than they should, they ought to get a prize for thinking of it.

Naturally, everybody feels sorry for China, but there seems to be a concerted plan among the others to get us to feel so much sorrier for 'em than they do that we will do all the fighting for 'em.

Besides, we couldn't go to war with 'em now, for we just sent our fleet around on the East Coast in case we would have trouble with Portugal or Spain.

Yours,
Will Rogers.

2421   MR. ROGERS VOTES TO LET
             THE OTHER FELLOW WORRY

SALINAS, Cal., May 7. — This is Salinas, the home of the Wild West Rodeo. It takes place in July. They let everybody in free that comes horseback, and they come by the hundreds. The horse, all over the country, is not coming back. He is back.

Fred Stone and I spent all day Sunday, went four or five hundred miles, just driving through these old California ranches that were land grants from Spain and seeing the old missions.

Good horses, fat cattle, plenty to eat and plenty of mortgages but, lord, every branch of businesses have them.

There is a change coming over the country anyhow. People have just got to get more used to debt. Let's all let the fellow we owe do the worrying and the U. S. will be the happiest land on earth.

Yours,
Will Rogers.

2422 MR. ROGERS IS IN A TOWN
WHERE THE DOLLAR CLINKS

SAN FRANCISCO, Cal., May 8. — The big news in the papers this week is Insull and silver. Before he went away it would have been Insull and gold.

They say it would be "inflation" to make silver a money. Well, maby, it would be, but it wouldn't be exactly like taking a perfect stranger into the family. You would be surprised at the things it will buy now.

This is a silver town. Everything under $5 is all silver. That's how they can tell a "dude," they will ask for dollar bills.

Arguing the money question sounds learned, but it's never made anybody any money yet.

Yours,
Will Rogers.

2423 MR. ROGERS NOTES REVIVAL
OF TWO POLITICAL PARTIES

SAN FRANCISCO, Cal., May 9. — In California's primary race for Governor there is the largest entry of different parties that ever went to the post—Democrats, Progressive, Socialists, Prohibition, Liberty, Torys and Republicans. These last two are revivals of old-time parties that have been out of existence for years.

On our darkest days there is a ray of hope somewhere in the papers. "A gigolo committed suicide." It may be the starting of a fad.

Twenty-five scheming, designing American mothers pulled every political rope possible to get their daughters to see the King this week in London. He asked to have a look at Sophie Tucker.

Yours,
Will Rogers.

2424   MR. ROGERS SEES A WAY
OUT OF THIS DEBT JAM

SAN FRANCISCO, Cal., May 10. — See where President Roosevelt figures on having a free hand in the foreign debt settlement thing personally. That's fine.

Congress sent 'em a bill for the full amount, the Senate threatened to sue 'em, the American taxpayers tried to shame 'em into paying, so let's turn it over to Mr. Roosevelt and give him a commission on what he can get.

Either that, or have the J. P. Morgan Company foreclose on all of 'em. They are more afraid of him than they are of us.

The thing has dragged along so far now, that it looks like we will have to loan some of 'em some money in order to get 'em to even agree to cancel.

                                            Yours,
                                            Will Rogers.

2425   ROGERS FINDS 'ELEMENTS'
MAKES SUCKER OF EXPERT

SAN FRANCISCO, Cal., May 11. — These old boys with a pair of specs and a tablet and pencil can sit and figure out how much wheat, corn and oats can be raised each year in order to sell each bushel of it at a profit. Then along comes a guy called "Elements." This bird "Elements" never went to college, he has never been called an "expert" and he has been laying pretty low for quite awhile, but when this guy "Elements" breaks out he can make a sucker out of more experts than anybody.

                                            Yours,
                                            Will Rogers.

2426   MR. ROGERS JOINS RANKS
OF DISGRUNTLED FATHERS

SANTA MONICA, Cal., May 13. — Mothers had their day today but they will be back where they belong tomorrow. Don't want to spoil 'em. If you brag on 'em too much they will get as swellheaded as father and children.

Senate passed the bill to regulate Wall Street. The government is going to put traffic lights on it. It's always been a hit and run street.

The red light tells you you better stop and wait before buying, the green light tells you that you are a sucker anyhow and you might just as well go ahead. The yellow light means, put up no more margins, let 'em sell you out.

      Yours,
      Will Rogers.

2427   Mr. Rogers Would Revive
      The Old Police Methods

BEVERLY HILLS, Cal., May 14. — "The government is arranging a war chest of three million to hire and equip more men in the crime drive; 200 speedy armoured cars, submachine guns, bullet-proof vests and tear gas."

Two hundred armoured cars can't very secretly drive up to your place of hiding without being detected in advance.

In days when they caught these fellows, it was by one Pinkerton detective following them, or one Texas Ranger, or one Northwest Mounted Police.

I bet we got a lot of good man hunters in our various forces, if they were allowed to work without carrying an orchestra with 'em.

      Yours,
      Will Rogers.

2428   Will Rogers Offers A Tip
      On Catching 'Bad Men'

SAN FRANCISCO, Cal., May 15. — I don't want to brag, but we got mighty good policemen in Los Angeles. They have caught many a bad one.

It looks like every time you get one of these notorious ones now you get about two women to each man. Looks like about all the police would have to do is arrest every man that has more than one woman along.

Times do change. The old-time outlaw never mixed his women and business.

      Yours,
      Will Rogers.

2429   MR. ROGERS SEES PROGRESS
IN THE FIGHT ON CRIME

SAN FRANCISCO, Cal., May 16. — Looking over the beautiful San Francisco Bay here from a hotel window you can almost see San Quentin prison and three gentlemen kidnappers checking in for life on a crime committed not a week ago.

That leaves the State with a pretty good record. Out of two kidnappings, two down and three out. That must be heartbreaking to these "shyster" lawyers to not get a chance to defend this class of client.

But, I suppose, these fellows will be up before the parole board at its first meeting.

Yours,
Will Rogers.

2430   MR. ROGERS GOES NATIVE
AND FEELS MUCH BETTER

HOLLISTER, Cal., May 17. — Sure had a good time today. Been out to a calf branding at the "Quien Sabe" ranch. Forty thousand acres and one of the prettiest in California.

Didn't mind all the men beating me roping, but when a girl did it looks like golf will be coming on me pretty soon.

This is a real old cowtown, but prunes and Easterners are getting a hold in here and they are both hard to eradicate.

There is not a better day in the world to be spent than with a lot of wise old cowmen around—barbecued beef, black coffee and good free holy beans.

Cattlemen have lost more in the last few years than anybody and say less about it. When you ever have any doubt as to what might happen in these U. S., go to the country and talk with them and you will come back reassured.

Yours,
Will Rogers.

2431   ROGERS SAYS KIDNAPPERS
FIND "RACKET" UNPOPULAR

SAN FRANCISCO, Cal., May 18. — Well the kidnappers checked in at the hostelry across the bay and if you think kidnapping is popular, the other inmates all snubbed 'em and wouldn't even give 'em a tumble.

New flying boat makes a record, carrying 11,000 pounds flew at 22,000 feet altitude, built for South American trade. Now all we got to do is get some trade.

Congress been laying awful low lately, so we better look out, you can't house five or six hundred men in tight together, and the heat coming on, without having some catastrophe being caused by it. Roosevelt knows that, and would personally pay their way home, if he could get 'em out.

Yours,
Will Rogers.

2432   Mr. Rogers Solves Slump
In Church Attendance

SALINAS, Cal., May 20. — I read statistics every once in awhile and it shows maby how church attendance is sorter falling off on Sunday mornings.

But it's not lack of religious inclination. It's just that you can't beat Sunday morning to get the old car out and ramble.

A preacher can have the best sermon in the world, but he just has to deliver it to folks without any gas. I bet you we live to see the time when they will just hold services on rainy days and days when they are fixing the roads, and they will pack 'em in.

Folks are just as good as they ever were and they mean well, but no minister can move 'em like a second-hand car.

Yours,
Will Rogers.

2433   Mr. Rogers Offers Advice
On The NRA Squabble

BEVERLY HILLS, Cal., May 21. — The big argument now is between Mr. Darrow and Gen. Hugh Johnson. Now there is a couple of tough babies to run together.

Here is a thing that's in Johnson's favor. The report is 322 multigraphed pages. Now there can be an awful lot of things wrong with a thing, but 322 pages is kinder rubbing it in. It would almost have to be Dillinger to have that many things wrong with it.

Poor old NRA! If we all had spent as much time observing it as we have arguing over it, it would have worked, right or wrong. There is great good in it and evidently great ills in it.

Now if both sides are not broadminded enough to see and admit it, then let the argument continue, but charge admission for it.

Yours,
Will Rogers.

2434   Mr. Rogers Pays Tribute To A Senate Warrior

BEVERLY HILLS, Cal., May 22. — Senator Norris wanted to abolish the Electoral College.

This is a bad time to try and do away with anything connected with "college." He will have to wait till the low-brows get in.

Well, he is not a man to get discouraged. He was years trying to get them to abolish the lame-duck session. When you get down to common sense and level headedness and answerable to nobody but his own conscience, you just about got the definition of that quiet, fighting, old Senator.

Yours,
Will Rogers.

2435   Mr. Rogers Sees A Motive For Some NRA Criticism

BEVERLY HILLS, Cal., May 23. — Not long ago ex-Ambassador to Germany, Jimmie Gerard said there was fifty men running the country. Now they say they have let forty-nine of 'em go.

So, naturally, we have those forty-nine ex-country runners all on our hands, and dissatisfied. You can't let people out, no matter for what good reason and have them go away bragging on you.

I don't suppose there is any business with as many unemployed as the "advising" business. What gets these big fellows' goat is, Roosevelt listens to 'em all, but they can't tell whether he is paying any attention or not.

Yours,
Will Rogers.

2436   MR. ROGERS HAS HIS IDEAS
        ON HANDLING OF STRIKES

BEVERLY HILLS, Cal., May 24. — The government is trying to fix silver, gold, Wall Street, tariffs, how much to plant and a thousand other problems yet the greatest and most urgent need in our land now is the settlement of strikes.

It's so far above the needs of other legislation that there is no comparison. Can't the government make arbitration compulsory? Everybody knows that there is wrongs—everybody knows there are strikes with just cause and some that are not. But with the labor union, one man, the man that hires him, one man, and the government, one man.

It looks like the side that wouldn't agree to that there is something wrong with. Let everybody stay on the job during arbitration. If they get the raise of wages, it starts back from the day the complaint was made. If that was fixed all these other things wouldn't need fixing.

                              Yours,
                              Will Rogers.

2437   ROGERS URGES EVERYBODY
        TO BUY A VETERAN POPPY

BEVERLY HILLS, Cal., May 25. — If you haven't bought a poppy this morning as you read this, go right now and do so. The soldier boys in the hospitals make 'em and it's for a great charity.

The further we get in years away from the war, the less we think of it, but that's not these fellows' fault. They never thought so much of it even at the time.

A mother can come nearer saying the right, and most impressive thing, under any circumstance than all your great writers. The mother of the outlaw Parker girl, killed in Louisiana said, "She won't be buried with 'him,' he took her from me in life, but I will take her from him in death, she is mine from now on."

                              Yours,
                              Will Rogers.

2438   MR. ROGERS HAILS ZEPHYR
        AND PRAYS FOR FLIERS

SANTA MONICA, Cal., May 27. — Well, there is two Frenchmen trying to fly direct from France to California. Let's hope and pray they make it. New York is liable to find itself off the U. S. Franco Highway.

And, that train that went from Denver to Chicago at 78 miles an hour, that's the biggest news that we have had in transportation in years.

If railroads had woke up before, they wouldn't be so far behind today. Faster time than this was made thirty years ago by a train, but nothing was ever done about it.

They have done nothing since then but sell stock instead of speed.

Yours,
Will Rogers.

2439   MR. ROGERS'S HEART GOES
         OUT TO A CABINET MEMBER

BEVERLY HILLS, Cal., May 28. — Secretary of Agriculture Wallace is out our way here. He has got a tough job. It's by far the toughest job in the Cabinet.

Sec. of the Navy only has to deal with an admiral, Sec. of the Army with the generals, Postmaster General with the politicians, but when you deal with the farmer you are dealing with a man who is a dealer himself.

So if I was Wallace I would say, "Boys, you all are just too good farmers. You just raise too much. If you just wouldn't be so expert for a few years. It don't do any good to plow under every third row if you are going to raise more on the other two than you did on the three. Your efficiency is driving you to the poor house. So please don't be such good farmers."

Yours,
Will Rogers.

2440   MR. ROGERS IN HIS TRAVELS
         SEES SOME SAD SIGHTS

BEVERLY HILLS, Cal., May 29. — Walking Monday afternoon through one of the most famous of the historical California missions, San Juan Capistrano, half way to San Diego, and who should I find in meditation before a wonderful old picture depicting the joy of the harvest and the merrymaking at the sale of the crops?

It was Secretary of Agriculture Wallace.

Tears were in his eyes, and he kept murmuring lowly, as he turned to the altar, "Oh, what have I done, Father, that I couldn't have been Secretary of Agriculture in days like those?"
                              Yours,
                                Will Rogers.

2441   MR. ROGERS HAS PROGRAM
             OF HOME WORK FOR ARMY

SANTA MONICA, Cal., May 30. — President Roosevelt is giving Cuba a new treaty. The "godfather" clause is taken out. All their revolutions are to be strictly "home talent."

More news down that way. Porto Rica is to be "wet-nursed" by the Interior Department instead of the army. The Philippines are rehearsing for peace. It won't be long now till our army will all be visiting America at one time.

That's the dope. Get 'em all home, add to their number, add to their training, then just sit tight with a great feeling of security and just read about foreign wars.

That's the best thing in the world to do with them.
                              Yours,
                                Will Rogers.

2442   WILL ROGERS COMFORTS
             A BROKEN-HEARTED FRIEND

BEVERLY HILLS, Cal., May 31. — Our Governor "Jimmy" Rolph is very, very ill.

Writers who rose in such glee to denounce him for doing nothing but speaking from his heart and not from political tact, they broke his heart. Now let them, before commenting further, speak of some of the fine human qualities he possessed. Few men ever in public life will leave more real friends.

Our country's structure is built on "let the law take its course," but there has been more the matter with our laws, our courts and our justice than there has with Jimmy Rolph.

Editorial writers were against you, Jimmy, for they have to write for their public, but, gosh, it must do your old heart good to know how many mothers were for you.
                              Yours,
                                Will Rogers.

2443   ROGERS READY TO DISPLAY
'COWLICK' TO EVERYBODY

BEVERLY HILLS, Cal., June 1. — Among all the big news and headlines of today's news there was a little item that sure gave me great encouragement. It said that some great professor of the Smithsonian Institution had discovered that a person with a "cowlick" was human, and not like the person who had none, as they descended from the ape; as no ape ever had a cowlick.

So now instead of having M.D. and Ph.D. after your name (and all those things to publicly advertise your supposed knowledge) why we just take off our hat and show you the old "cowlick," and say, "There, you apes, take a look at a human."

                         Yours,
                         Will Rogers.

2444   MR. ROGERS FINDS SECRET
OF A DICTATOR'S SUCCESS

SANTA MONICA, Cal., June 3. — That Mussolini, who is the "sire" of the present dictator epidemic, knows just what to do to drive those other nations "nutty." He knows his sycology (that's not spelled right but it sounds right).

He asked his soldiers Saturday, "Are you ready to fight?" And, he did it so loud that the adjoining nations could hear.

Now, that is how he has kept out of a war all this time (when everybody predicted he would have one every week).

But, here is something that he did tell his people that will bear repeating all over the world, "We must accept hard times, we must get used to hard times."

                         Yours,
                         Will Rogers.

2445   WILL ROGERS PAYS TRIBUTE
TO A FRIEND AND EDUCATOR

HOLLYWOOD, Cal., June 4. — A sad wire this morning from Vice President O'Hara tells me of the death of a good friend, Father O'Donnell of the great Notre Dame University. What a fine, plain, human man.

What Rockne did with 'em when they got those football suits on, this man did with 'em while they was off the field, and turned out many "All Americans" in the game of life.

Some good news in the papers, however. It rained in the Middle West. Farmers are learning that the relief they get from the sky beats what they get from Washington.

Yours,
Will Rogers.

2446 WILL ROGERS IS PLEASED
THE DIPLOMATS NOW KNOW

HOLLYWOOD, Cal., June 5. — Well, America was finally notified "diplomatically" that England wouldn't pay the debt.

That's what practically all the people in both nations knew all the time, but even though a diplomat is the last person to find anything out, I knew the news would finally leak out to 'em.

The news hit us like the news that Babe Ruth bats left-handed.

But was we downhearted? No, sir. On that very day Congress voted seven billions. So our own credit is all right.

From now on we will do all our borrowing and loaning on the home grounds.

Yours,
Will Rogers.

2447 WILL ROGERS APPROVES
OF NEW G. O. P. LEADER

HOLLYWOOD, Cal., June 6. — Glad to see the Republican party honor Henry Fletcher, ex-Ambassador to Italy. He is a very able man.

They made him chairman of the Republican National Committee. Course, you got to use a little humor when you say it's an honor to hand a man the Republican party to run at this time. It's sorter like giving you an empty gun to protect yourself.

Henry will do 'em as good a job as anybody could, if he confines 'em to constructive criticism. Mr. Roosevelt has a unique position in the feelings of the people. They will let you throw a brick at him, but it's got to be loaded with something besides political mud.

Yours,
Will Rogers.

2448   WILL ROGERS PROTESTS
        THE BUCK-PASSING TREND

HOLLYWOOD, Cal., June 7. — Both sides in the steel business seem anxious to strike. Well, if they would only strike just each other it wouldn't be so bad.

Don't it look like there ought to be some civilized way of finding out what the employee and employer owed to each other?

The latest papers say that "It's up to the President now." Is there anything difficult under the sun that's not put up to that man? He will eventually be asked to decide if the five little babies born in Canada must go to the World's Fair in Chicago or not.

Yours,
Will Rogers.

2449   WILL ROGERS FINDS THIS
        INDEED AGE OF MIRACLES

HOLLYWOOD, Cal., June 8. — This is the age of "new deals" and miracles, at that. The Secretary of the Treasury informed all the Treasury Department people to keep out of politics. There wouldn't be any such luck as to have that spread to all departments.

Few good-health notes in today's press, the five girl babies are gaining weight, and Max Baer was reported out of danger.

If that Wheeler-Howard Indian bill don't pass there is no justice. I think we got a real Indian agent in this man Collier. The Indian has just lost 100 years in his civilization, and Collier is trying to get him back. However, I still think the old rich Indian's wife deserved her share. But I don't think that was Collier's department.

Yours,
Will-Rogers.

2450   WILL ROGERS IS PREPARED
        TO MAKE BEST OF THINGS

HOLLYWOOD, Cal., June 10. — Well, no good news along the steel strike front. Both unions are standing tight, the Amalgamated Iron, Steel and Tin Workers Union against the Iron and Steel Institute. Both unions were organized for the members' protection against the other.

It does look like there is some fair men in this country both sides would be willing to leave it to.

Well, if it comes to the worst, we can do like some old famous queen in Paris when she said, "Let 'em eat cake." We can build it out of wood instead of steel. Dillinger did.

       Yours,
        Will Rogers.

2451   Mr. Rogers Joins In Fuss
      Over NRA Labor Clause

HOLLYWOOD, Cal., June 11. — When the National Recovery Act (NRA) was drawn up there was one clause in there in regard to "collective bargaining" and it was known at the time that the thing could mean just about anything that anybody wanted it to.

Now, they never will get through with all these strikes till they send that clause to a Supreme Court that has a Webster dictionary and let them hold a final clinic and announce just what the thing means, in case it does mean anything.

It's always better to brand a calf plain the first time. You just can't brand him so he will belong to both outfits.

       Yours,
        Will Rogers.

2452   Will Rogers Rejoices
      As 'Dirt' Farmer Wins

HOLLYWOOD, Cal., June 12. — Well, the latest papers record the fact that Mr. Tugwell went through O. K. They tried him for being a "menace" and he come clear.

I am glad of that. It's a mighty hard thing to tell nowadays whether an idea is revolutionary, or downright conservative.

Tugwell proved that he had at one time been a "dirt" farmer. I think that's what got him clemency with the jury.

A soldier returning from a popular war don't carry as much sympathy as a "dirt" farmer, or for that matter even a prairie land farmer where there ain't no dirt.

       Yours,
        Will Rogers.

2453   WILL ROGERS WELCOMES
          ALL THE DEBT TALK AGAIN

HOLLYWOOD, Cal., June 13. — The debt thing bobbed up again today. The news never gets so dull that somebody can't bob up with a new proposal.

We can always revive talk of it and interest in it, but we just can't seem to revive payment of it. In fact, a great many of the ideas we have loaned 'em they haven't even paid back.

Well, it's good to get it all stirred up before the new Congressional elections. The following sounds awful good on the platform:

"Did the man you last sent to Washington make Europe pay? No, no. Well, elect me and I will make them pay."

So it will always be a good argument.

Yours,
Will Rogers.

2454   MR. ROGERS HAS HIS EAR
          TO THE GROUND JUST NOW

HOLLYWOOD, Cal., June 14. — Well, there ain't much news till we get the dictaphone records of what Mussolini and Hitler really talked about. They may have never said a word about France but you will never make France believe it.

They was supposed to travel and meet on neutral ground. They met on neutral ground, but it was Mussolini's.

To get even with 'em now, we will have President Roosevelt meet Mr. Plutarco Calles of Mexico and show those Europeans a couple of boys that really run their countries.

Yours,
Will Rogers.

2455   WILL ROGERS POINTS OUT
          THE OBVIOUS THING TO DO

HOLLYWOOD, Cal., June 15. — Now that the prizefight is out of the road, the American people can settle back down to the trivial things of life.

The steel strike looks better than it has in weeks, looks like a mighty fair proposal that Mr. William Green, president of the whole

American Federation of Labor, made, whereby the President is to appoint three disinterested men. Now if the steel men will agree to that, why it looks like they would finish it. Funny how long it takes people to see what to do, when there ain't but one thing to do.

If Mr. Roosevelt can just get that strike fixed, and get those Congressmen out from under those government-paid-for electric fans by July 1st, he will be sitting pretty.

Yours,
Will Rogers.

2456   MR. ROGERS FINDS WE TOO
       ARE PRONE TO 'SAVE FACE'

HOLLYWOOD, Cal., June 17. — See where one strike is ended. Nobody won anything, but you always word the agreement in such a way that it looks like both sides gained something.

China (by far the smartest nation in the world) has a word that I don't know how in the world we live without it. It's called "face," "saving face."

We have it just as much as China does, and call it by a hundred other things. But it all gets back to the same thing, "face."

"How can I do nothing and still make it look like I done something?"

Congress would have adjourned Saturday night and the country would have arose Monday morning in the happiest and most optimistic mood, but each Congressman tried to get his pet bill through, so he could go home and "save face."

Yours,
Will Rogers.

2457   MR. ROGERS IS ANNOYED
       BY THE PACE OF THE NEWS

HOLLYWOOD, Cal., June 18. — I just give up reading murders. You no more than get a few details of one murder than the afternoon paper brings you news of another.

The best read man in the country couldn't tell you who killed who last week.

The papers ought to list 'em by numbers.

"Murder Case No. 211" went to court this morning in order to make way for Case 212.

Case 211 is of the A Class (that is where the wife kills husband). Case 212 is of the B Class (husband kills wife). Killings of the C Class include all promiscuous other killings not embraced in A or B Class.

Yours for brevity,
Will Rogers.

2458   WILL ROGERS GETS THE AID OF COBB ON HIS DAILY JOKE

HOLLYWOOD, Cal., June 19. — We was all setting around on the moving picture "set" this afternoon. Irvin Cobb was entertaining us 100 per cent as usual.

I says, "Irvin, I got to write my daily mess; what's something komical in the day's news?"

"Well, Will, you couldn't get anything much funnier than England and France wanting us to use our influence with Germany to get them to pay France and England.

I wouldn't be surprised if they tried to show we was on the note, and they will be suing us."

When we read our papers today and found Congress had adjourned it reminded you of Armistice Day. They say ticker tape in New York was a foot thick.

Yours,
Will Rogers.

2459   MR. ROGERS FEARS A SLUMP IN BANK ROBBING INDUSTRY

BEVERLY HILLS, Cal., June 20. — You can't beat Oklahoma for originality.

Guess you read about the outlaws with a big truck (with a winch attachment on it) backed up to the bank to kidnap the safe. Everybody in town came down to see the show.

Due to the outlaws having done no physical work in so long they wasn't stout enough to load it. But they notified the bank that they will be back right away and that the bank is to have a smaller safe.

The future of bank robberies is to arrange some way to charge admission. So many people seeing robberies free is what's killing the business.

Yours,
Will Rogers.

2460   Mr. Rogers Rises To Ask
        'What Price A Degree?'

HOLLYWOOD, Cal., June 21. — Yale give President Roosevelt a degree. But they made him make a speech for it. Degrees are getting higher priced. That's the most anybody has given for one in years.

The President kinder held up for his brain trust. He said he would take brains any time in preference to politics. He just as good as admitted you couldn't get both in the same body.

He paid a very high compliment to Congress, and he should. They had just adjourned the day before.

Yours,
Will Rogers.

2461   Rogers Thinks Baruch
        Knows A Thing Or Two

HOLLYWOOD, Cal., June 22. — What's this I read in the papers today about Barney Baruch quitting Wall Street and starting writing?

That's what I call leaving a business when you are at the top. He knew more about it (and everything else) than anybody. But just think of the novelty of a man being in the writing game that knows what he is talking about.

Say, we are holding the American Olympic games here today. Every great runner and jumper are here. Nearly every State has sent one or more great athletes, yet in the big games that's held in Washington every year not a single State seems to be able to send a statesman.

Yours,
Will Rogers.

2462   Mr. Rogers Says It's Easy
To Get Money For A War

HOLLYWOOD, Cal., June 24. — Lots of news today about that South American war.

I was down there almost two years ago and they were going strong then. Now, how can they fight that long without getting all their war material from other nations?

That's why there will always be war. You got every nation that's not in it boosting for it, for everybody makes money out of a war but the nations fighting.

We used to think war couldn't last long because one or both sides had no money. Why, there is no industry under the sun you can get credit as quick for as you can war.

This war down there has been on credit since twenty-four hours after it started.

Yours,
Will Rogers.

2463   Mr. Rogers Sees Promise
Of Real News In Europe

BEVERLY HILLS, Cal., June 25. — The pictures of Hitler and Mussolini are pouring in on us from the press now and every one of 'em keep looking more like they are going to bite each other.

Sure glad to see where William Allen White had received the high award for Americanism. He is a mighty clear thinking man. That Kansas has more real newspaper men than all the rest of the States combined.

Mr. Roosevelt attended a meeting of Tammany Hall leaders. First time Tammany Hall's name has come up in months. I kinder thought they had given up their franchise.

Yours,
Will Rogers.

2464   Mr. Rogers Feels Sorry
For Weary Congressmen

BEVERLY HILLS, Cal., June 26. — Congressmen are coming dragging in from Washington. Some of 'em look like they had hitchhiked.

Now their real work starts. That is trying to get elected this fall. I tell you it's no easy life when you consider that battle to get back there.

I just don't know what they are going to promise the voters this fall. This is a tough time to think up something new. About a man's only chance is to just say, "Well, boys, I don't know what I will do. I will just have to wait till I get there and see what Mr. Roosevelt wants. He knows more about it than me."

Yours,
Will Rogers.

2465   MR. ROGERS IS ALL READY
        TO TUNE IN THE PRESIDENT

BEVERLY HILLS, Cal., June 27. — Well tomorrow night (or I mean tonight as you read this) Mr. Roosevelt is going to talk to the country.

I doubt if ever in the history of any country, at any time, was the talks of one man so earnestly listened to.

The best example we have that he actually feels that we are headed out of the brush is that he is going on this trip to Honolulu. Firemen don't stop for a nap in the middle of a fire.

If he feels like it's coming out all right, why the rest ought not to worry, for he has more invested in it than any man in it.

Yours,
Will Rogers.

2466   WILL ROGERS MOURNS
        A REALLY GREAT FLIER

BEVERLY HILLS, Cal., June 28. — And they lay to rest Jimmy Wedell, died as a soldier in the discharge of his duty, for he was teaching somebody else how to fly.

When you realize aviation is the greatest advancement in our times and America is spending the most money on it, yet our whole government, whole army, whole navy, had to wait to see how fast they could fly till Jimmy Wedell (through his own personality and personal honesty got financial backing from generous and public-spirited Mr. Williams) would make the plane.

Who knows but what aviation might not be permanently set back 100 miles an hour through the loss of this fellow, with the knowledge that was buried with him. Such men should be grabbed up at once and put into our government service.

He had one thing that was in keeping with all great aviators and that was his modesty.

Yours,
Will Rogers.

2467   ROGERS FINDS ROOSEVELT
       PLEASED MOST EVERYBODY

BEVERLY HILLS, Cal., June 29. — Headline says, "13 Bankers in Detroit Indicted." You would think Detroit was a bigger town than that.

The early afternoon edition that I got out here on the movie "set" says dear Marie Dressler is fighting yet. We are all just afraid to get the next paper. Those that don't offer a prayer for her, well, they just ain't human, that's all.

Mr. Roosevelt's speech seemed to satisfy all but those that had made up their minds in advance that they wouldn't like it, no matter what he said.

Yours,
Will Rogers.

2468   MR. ROGERS TAKES A LOOK
       AT THE WORLD'S EVENTS

SANTA MONICA, Cal., July 1. — Well, the President leaves on his cruise aboard what must be Jesse Jones's boat, for it's called the Houston.

I expect that guy Hitler would like to be on a boat headed somewhere about now. Germany has some sort of a custom where they allow you to commit suicide in case you have been found to be against the government. Over here we just let you go on making speeches, and it amounts to about the same thing in the end.

Well, they finally got that Astor wedding over with. There ain't nothing that will do more to add comedy relief to our reading of strikes, wars, revolutions and world uncertainty than to read about a society wedding.

Yours,
Will Rogers.

2469   Mr. Rogers Thinks Il Duce
                Gave Hitler Some Advice

HOLLYWOOD, Cal., July 2. — Hitler must have got his information about Germany from Mussolini. He didn't seem to know much about what was going on till he went down to see the old "daddy" of all the dictators.

Trouble with this killing a guy to get rid of him, there never was a fellow killed that didn't leave some friends.

Well, they will have to get their trouble in Germany over with pretty soon for it's just breaking France's heart? In fact, I expect they are feeling so bad they are offering ammunition and free burial to both sides.

                            Yours,
                            Will Rogers.

2470   Mr. Rogers Thinks G. O. P.
                Still Lacks Judgment

BEVERLY HILLS, Cal., July 3. — There is something about a Republican politician, they are smart but they just don't know much.

Now Henry Fletcher, their national chairman is smart and a durn nice fellow, but here he comes out with the Republican keynote speech for the coming election, and there is not a man, woman or child in the United States that has listened to, or read, one thing in the papers, in three days about Germany.

The eyes of the world are on Germany and Henry is trying to get somebody to take a backward glance at the Republican party.

                            Yours,
                            Will Rogers.

2471   Will Rogers Now Expects
                Excitement In The Fall

SANTA MONICA, Cal., July 4. — They say it takes a big man to admit he is wrong. Well, here is where I become a giant.

I said yesterday that the Republicans made their campaign speech when the whole U. S. was tuned in on Germany, or Amos and Andy, and that nobody heard it.

But, by golly, I was wrong. From some of the criticism I read of it from the Democrats they must have all been listening. I had no idea they were even paying any attention to the Republicans.

Get these Democrats on the defense and they are not so hot. A Democrat is a better fault finder than he is an explainer, so there is liable to be some excitement at this fall's election yet.

Yours,
Will Rogers.

2472   Mr. Rogers Is In Doubt
As To Borah's Objective

BEVERLY HILLS, Cal., July 5. — Senator Borah, I think, is a mighty able and self-thinking statesman (you notice I said statesman). A statesman is a man that can do what the politician would like to do but can't, because he is afraid of not being elected.

Well, Senator Borah, who has spent the past winter with the Democrats, is leaving their bed and board, and has given instructions that he won't be responsible for any bills they incur.

Now from the way his tracks led when he left their campfire it looked like he might be headed for the Republican chuck wagon again. Or he may just camp on a hill where he can roll rocks down on both of 'em.

Yours,
Will Rogers.

2473   Rogers Finds Roosevelt
Has Resorted To A 'Blab'

BEVERLY HILLS, Cal., July 6. — All I know is just what little I see in the papers. See today where Mr. Roosevelt is putting a "blab" (you know what a blab is? It's a thing you put over a calf's mouth to keep it from eating between meals) well, he is putting a "blab" on these socalled "officials" who are making speeches around the country trying to tell what the New Deal has in mind.

He has informed 'em, "you go ahead and deal and shut up about it. A dealer is not supposed to entertain along with his dealing."

So the next time you hear a fellow speaking for the White House, you just holler, "Yeah?"

Yours,
Will Rogers.

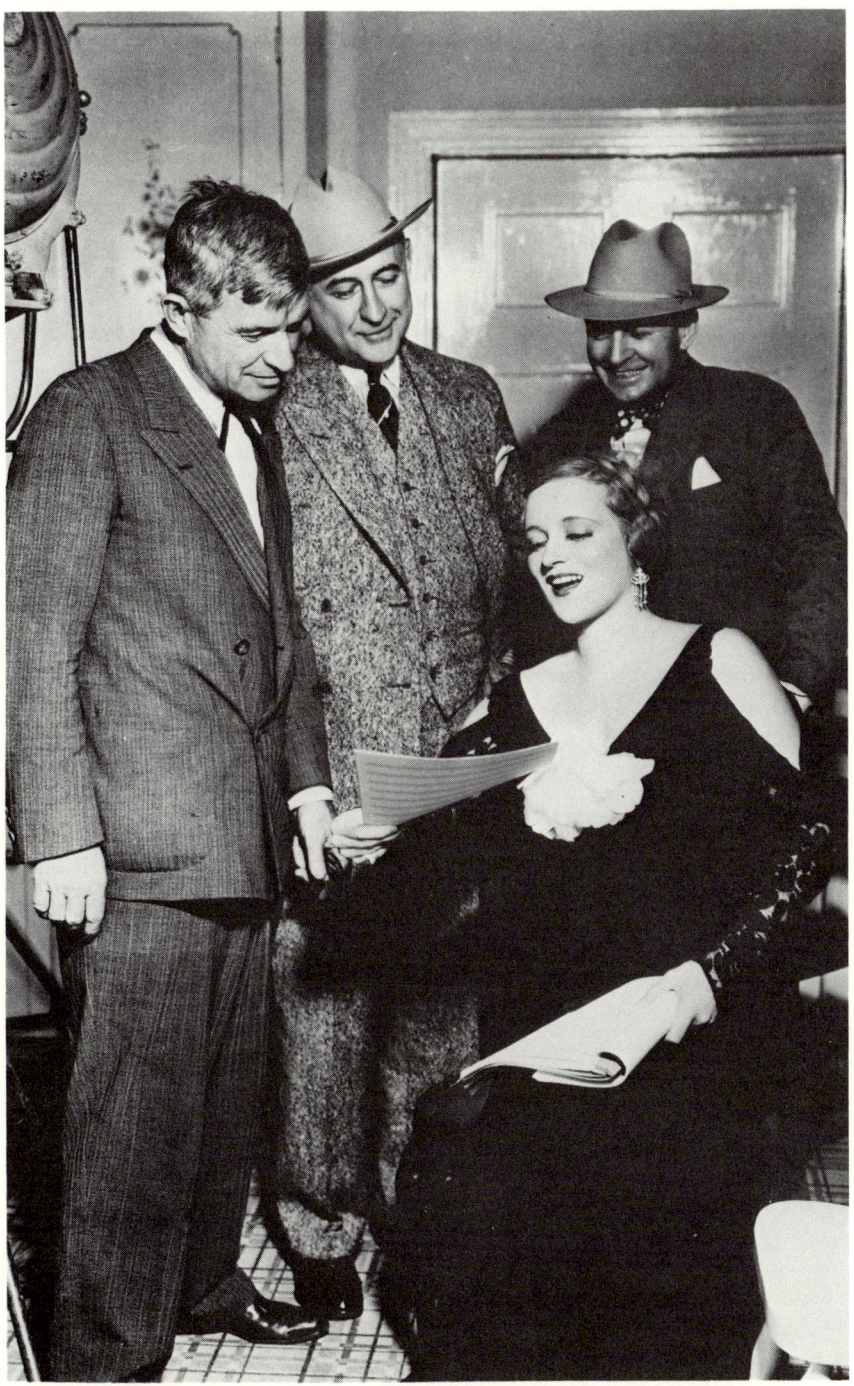

(l to r) *Will Rogers, Amon G. Carter and J. A. Wigmore, Cleveland builder and Pasadena polo player, with Peggy Wood on the Rogers set at Fox studio in Hollywood during filming of the motion picture* Merry Andrew.

2474   WILL ROGERS COMMENTS ON HERR HITLER'S VACATION

SANTA MONICA, Calif., July 8. — See by the papers that Hitler took a vacation. Most people doing the same thing would have took one too. The judge would have said, "Now you take a nice rest for about sixty days, and some morning at daylight the warden will call you, and from then on you can rest again."

Mr. Cordell Hull paid a mighty nice compliment to little Finland today, and incidentally did all he could to make the others feel ashamed, but Mr. Hull you are just wasting your breath. Those boys have been insulted by experts and it never fazed 'em.

Yours,
Will Rogers.

2475   WILL ROGERS THINKS HESS IS TOO GOOD TO BE TRUE

SANTA MONICA, Cal., July 9. — Every day we get new surprises from Europe. Sunday some fellow from Germany named Hess, who said he was speaking for Hitler, told France there wasn't any use of them fighting, and that they would like to make up, it all sounded so friendly that you started peeping under the bottom to see what was hid.

Mr. Roosevelt visited our Virgin Islands. He seems to have got away pretty good. Two or three years ago I flew into those islands just a couple of weeks after Mr. Hoover had been there, and those Virginis were sure sore. But Mr. Roosevelt promised 'em a distillery.

Yours,
Will Rogers.

2476   WILL ROGERS TO WITNESS BRANDING OF 5,000 CALVES

MULESHOE, Texas, July 10. — Flew all night just to get over here to the Mashed-O outfit to the calf branding at Ewing Halsell's, an old boyhood friend. They are branding 5,000 calves, but the whole cattle country is mighty dry. The government is doing what they can to help 'em out, but even a Democrat can't make it rain. But they are going to bring that up at the next Congress.

There is no finer and more satisfying business in the world than the cow business when you get half a chance, but when the elements are agin' you, you are just like a candidate that runs second.

This is a part of the famous XIT ranch that was the biggest in the world. An English syndicate got it for building "Ma" and "Jim" a State capitol in Austin.

Yours,
Will Rogers.

2477　　　　　WILL ROGERS REVIEWS
　　　　　　THE HOME TOWN SCENE

CLAREMORE, Okla., July 11. — I never get through the thrill of coming back home, seeing kin folks and old friends. Nature has been rough with the ranchmen and farmers here. The drought wilted the corn just as it was starting to "roastin' ear."

I asked about the wheat and oats, and some other Republican scourge had fallen on them. No grass for the cattle, but they did have an awful nice radish crop.

I never saw redder radishes. All I know is just what I read in The Claremore Progress. See where Speaker Rainey of the House of Representatives has been kinder beating the political bushes around here. Wish I had been home, he is a mighty lovely old gentleman. It's awful hot to be campaigning. I would let the Republicans do all the talking. You lose more votes this weather than you gain.

Yours,
Will Rogers.

2478　　　　　ROGERS SEES GREAT WORK
　　　　　　IN REPAIRING OF HOMES

WASHINGTON, D. C., July 12. — Just had a fine long visit (and incidentally a good lunch) with the kindliest, friendliest and most able of our diplomats in a long time, Secretary of State Cordell Hull. We talked much of South America, where he made many friends at that conference, and that's the country where we can use some friends, too. That's our alley, for our "drummers" down there.

They are finally starting something that should have been started a year ago, and that's this house building and repairing.

The local bank, or local organization loans the money, up to $2,000. The government don't spend anything. It only guarantees 20 per cent of it in case of loss. And these loans are made almost entirely on a man's name alone.

Well, just the idea of a man being trusted again is going to make the whole thing 100 per cent honest. It's the best of all the plans and Jimmy Moffett and a fine organization is working it.

Washington was never prettier, not a Senator or Congressman here.

Yours,
Will Rogers.

2479   WILL ROGERS FINDS MAINE
WAS BUILT TO BE ENJOYED

LAKEWOOD, SKOWHEGAN, Me., July 13. — Did you ever see a place that looks like it was built just to enjoy? Well, this whole State of Maine looks that way. If it's not a beautiful lake, it's a beautiful tree, or a pretty green hay meadow, and beautiful old-time houses with barns built right in with the kitchens.

Vacationers and everything have improved 30 per cent over last year. Roads have been fixed up with Federal money. Newspaper advertising has increased over 50 per cent. All these things have been done, yet the editorials say that the New Deal is a failure.

It's a funny world. You feed a dog and he bites you.

Yours,
Will Rogers.

2480   ROGERS THINKS ROOSEVELT
ONLY CAN SETTLE STRIKE

SANTA MONICA, Cal., July 15. — It would be pretty tough to ask Mr. Roosevelt to give up his well-earned vacation and come to San Francisco and stop this strike. But it looks like he is the only man can do it. The trouble is that both sides have negotiated so much that they are sick and tired looking at each other. It would be a great thing for him to do.

That's the tough part about our affairs, everybody seems to be willing to trust the President, but it just don't seem like there is anybody he can send that they will trust. I never saw a man that had to do as many things himself.

Yours,
Will Rogers.

2481   Mr. Rogers Philosophizes
On The Speed Of Travel

SANTA MONICA, Cal., July 16. — You know we are just finding out in lots of ways that we are not as "big" as we used to be. I had breakfast away up in Boston Saturday morning, and Beverly Hills for breakfast Sunday morning. All that would delay us would be waiting for the postoffices to bring the mail out. Farley is out here. I am going to speak to him about that. I missed the line that runs real sleepers. But then every one will have to come to it, or they will be like a railroad that runs nothing but day coaches.

And incidentally railroads since they made rates within reason are enjoying a big boom.

America is never in a better humor or feeling better than when moving. So all this traveling (even if it's walking) is a mighty good omen.

                      Yours,
                      Will Rogers.

2482   Will Rogers Finds Nothing
Happens In San Francisco

SAN FRANCISCO, Cal., July 17. — Well, for a little fresh air away from Hollywood, made a little two-hour flight up to Frisco last night. Lovely historic old place, but it seems nothing ever happens there. Never saw it as quiet. About the only news is that Max Baer, who lives near here, announces that he won't fight this fall. That set the old town kinder agog.

I see among the hotel arrivals is Gen. Hugh Johnson, who is passing through going to Los Angeles. He is lectioneering for the NRA. I want to see "Bobbie" before she gets out of town.

Some talk of President Roosevelt pulling in here for fuel, but I see where he has gone to Honolulu instead. Nothing ever happens in this town. Oh, yes, the National Guard is using the old town as a Summer camp, instead of Monterey. That brings in a little extra money. The Chamber of Commerce landed them to kinder stir up a little interest in the place. The Governor spoke on the radio last night on "civic pride." Certainly a quiet, restful old city, but nothing ever happens there.

                      Yours,
                      Will Rogers.

2483   WILL ROGERS REVEALS
                     HIS VIEWS ON STRIKES

BEVERLY HILLS, Cal., July 18. — Back from the strike. There is no doubt the "Reds" run away with the fair, conservative leaders in the union. The thing was not, as some try to make you believe, 100 per cent one-sided. They had some just kicks, and plenty of fair-minded people of San Francisco were in sympathy with 'em. They lost lots of that by calling the general strike. When you interfere with everybody's business, you can't get away with it.

Now, here is something that you don't read about, but there is a lot of 'em, and for lack of a name we might call 'em "Greens." That is, their whole system becomes green when the very idea of a union, or a strike, or anything pertaining to the betterment of labor is mentioned. He is the one that tells who should be took out and shot, if he makes any move to better his condition. So we got radicals on both sides, "Reds" on one and "Greens" on the other. Both of 'em ought to be run out, and leave it to men that know and feel that there is such a thing as a fair union and a fair employer.

The whole thing will prove beneficial, for it will prove that no general strike can win. People might be with you, but when it begins costing 'em their food and their convenience, they are going to quit you. Sometimes we think we don't know what kind of government we got, but it's always bigger than any group of people.

                                                Yours,
                                         Will Rogers.

2484   WILL ROGERS FINDS PLENTY
                     OF COMMON SENSE LEFT

SANTA MONICA, Cal., July 19. — In 1926 I was in England during their world-famous general strike. And brother it was general, not a paper printed, not a train, not a bus, not a wheel turned. Well, I never got through telling of the composure of these level headed people.

Well, I went to San Francisco, and I tell you we are not so "nutty" under stress as you might think. It was as quiet as the British. The only thing went haywire was the headlines in the out-of-Frisco papers. I hope we never live to see the day when a thing is as bad as some of our newspapers make it.

There is lots of sense in this country yet.

                                                Yours,
                                         Will Rogers.

2485   WILL ROGERS IS AMUSED
               BY STRIKING BARTENDERS

SANTA MONICA, Cal., July 20. — One of the funniest angles to the strike in San Francisco: bartenders had been out of work for fourteen years, just been back in for six months, then called out again.

I was working yesterday and missed all the lunches they gave my friend Jim Farley. Everybody in the State but Baby LeRoy is running for Governor, so Jim endorsed LeRoy. He arrived at 4 o'clock in the morning, an unearthly hour, but in spite of that there was over 200 men there, every one a postmaster.

It's a mighty poor town that Jim hasn't got one staunch friend in.

                    Yours,
                        Will Rogers.

2486   WILL ROGERS FINDS PLENTY
               OF ALIBIS IN SAN FRANCISCO

S. S. MALOLO, SAN FRANCISCO, Cal., July 22. — Just steaming out of beautiful San Francisco Bay. Putting a bridge across it. They will build a bridge to Honolulu if the government don't run out of credit.

Could wire later in the afternoon but better get this off while I am able. As a sailor, I am as big a success as a "red" trying to run a strike.

Drove to San Francisco and stayed all night. You have seen towns full of many things, but did you ever see one full of "alibis"? Everybody on both sides of the strike had nothing to do with starting it, and every one of 'em was responsible for stopping it. Everybody has a sore back from taking bows. Nobody seems to be responsible for starting this strike.

I just know it was that darn Dillinger again. That fellow should be deported. Ship ahoy.

                    Yours,
                        Will Rogers.

2487   ROGERS SAYS DILLINGER
                WOULD NOT TAKE ADVICE

ABOARD S. S. MALOLO, July 23. — Radio operator woke me, middle of night, telling me they got Dillinger. Like to be home. Guess it's like Armistice Day.

Well, the moral is, he just wouldn't take advice. The better element warned him to stay away from those movies, they would be a bad influence on him. Cable me at once (your expense) what picture it was got him. Hope it was mine.

Yours,
Will Rogers.

2488   MR. ROGERS LOOKS FORWARD
           TO THE RACE TO AUSTRALIA

ABOARD S. S. MALOLO, July 24. — The big thing you hear about on the Pacific side of the world is the great exposition at Melbourne, Australia, in October. It's the tourists' next great round-up. It's where that greatest of all air races is to end. Fifty-thousand dollar prize from London to Melbourne, 12,000 miles. We have over a dozen of our crack fliers and over half the ships in it will be American made. Wish the army and navy would put a boy apiece in there. Wiley Post hopes to make it in fifty hours, keeping the championship in Oklahoma. I would sho' love to be with Wiley. I could be his navigator. I have flown that very same route, 10,000 of the 12,000 from Singapore to London on the Dutch line. Hope to see lots of aviation on this trip.

Yours,
Will Rogers.

2489   MR. ROGERS FINALLY HEEDS
           THOSE WEATHER REPORTS

ABOARD S. S. MALOLO, July 25. — I used to dident pay much attention to reports of the heat all over the East and Middle West. Just naturally figured that it was the California papers using prevaricating license, but our ship radio newspaper every day says it's terrible, and naturally you got to believe them. They got no lots to sell.

Mr. Roosevelt is out here somewhere on Japan's ocean fishing. Awful long way to come to fish. I think he come away out here so he couldent hear the Republicans roar, and to get away from any new scheme that his own gang might cook up.

Yours,
Will Rogers.

2490   WILL ROGERS SAYS AUSTRIA
       NEEDS DIFFERENT NEIGHBORS

ABOARD S. S. MALOLO, July 26. — Poor old Austria! If ever a nation needed to move out and settle among different neighbors it's her. They divided her up so much after the last war till there was nothing left but this little game fighting cock Dolfuss; now they got him. There was a fellow that looked like he was doing a heroic job of trying to hold the few strands together of what had been a great nation. Now it's a fresh piece of meat to be thrown to the neighboring wolves.

Yours,
Will Rogers.

2491   WILL ROGERS IN HONOLULU,
       FINDS ROOSEVELT THERE

HONOLULU, Hawaii, July 27. — Well, we blew in here this morning on the first leg of our long hop, and imagine who we run into. You wouldn't guess in a year. You remember the President we lost just after Congress adjourned, the one that was so tickled that he disappeared? Well, he is out here at some Japanese islands in the middle of the Pacific.

Just looks fine. Same great smile that he used to use on those Congressmen and make 'em bring stocks out of the water for him.

These folks want their sugar quota raised. But he just smiles at 'em. He is the world's only man that can turn you down and you go out liking him. The whole of Honolulu is doing the hula, or riding a surf board, for him today.

If he don't raise their quota, I will go over his head and take it up with Gen. Hugh Johnson, and get it done for 'em. For we can't let the Garden of Eden be dissatisfied.

Yours,
Will Rogers.

2492   ROGERS FINDS GREAT RANCH
       ON ONE OF HAWAII ISLANDS

WAIMEA, Hawaii, July 29. — This is written out here on the world's famous Parker Ranch. There are marvelous cattle ranches on these islands, and these native cowboys are plenty salty with those rawhide riatas. Thirty thousand head of high grade Herefords on this

Parker Ranch. Over half a million acres. They have the best horses I ever saw on any ranch anywhere, nothing under seven-eighths thoroughbred, over 600 here just in the saddle-horse string.

You fly to these various islands in an amphibian plane on a well-managed and equipped line. They are all connected by wireless telephone. This is phoned to the Honolulu Islands.

Yours,
Will Rogers.

2493   ROGERS SAYS ROOSEVELT
DEEPLY IMPRESSED HAWAII

WAIMEA, Hawaii, July 30. — Well, they got rid of all the big Democrats now and the islands can settle down to steady gossip. They can't hardly figure Mr. Roosevelt's visit out. They can't tell if he come to see them or come to get some fish or come to impress somebody (I am not naming anybody, mind you) that he still would stand for no monkey business in the Pacific. Anyhow, whatever he come for it was a big success; that is, if it wasn't for fish. The fish didn't bite, but everybody else did.

Yours,
Will Rogers.

2494   ROGERS CALLS GOOD ROADS
THE TEST OF A POLITICIAN

KULAMAUI, Hawaii, July 31. — Did you ever hear of the Hawaiian Islands? Well, if you didn't, you have heard of Baldwins. Flew into an island here that is just chuck full of Baldwins. Frank Baldwin has the biggest sugar plantation and the most up-to-date and best run. A water pumping system that is big as San Francisco. Then they got a big cattle ranch. All riders and ropers and polo players.

These visitors that never get away from the Whykiki Beach when they come out here miss a lot. This island must have the best politicians. For they got the best roads. Over home a Congressman is never any better than his roads, and sometimes worse.

Yours,
Will Rogers.

2495   WILL ROGERS FINDS HAWAII
DOES THINGS IN A BIG WAY

HONOLULU, Hawaii, Aug. 1. — Back into the real city of Honolulu after a wonderful few days, "too few," on the big cattle ranches of the islands. These islands look little on the map, but they sure do things big.

Nowhere on the mainland (that's what they call the joint where we live), nowhere is there such signs of doing well as there is here. You don't have to be warlike to get a real kick out of our greatest army post, Schofield Barracks, and the navy at Pearl Harbor. If war was declared with some Pacific nation we would lose the Philippines before lunch, but if we lost these it would be our own fault.

Yours,
Will Rogers.

2496   WILL ROGERS SAYS IT TAKES
A RADICAL TO LIVE JUST NOW

HONOLULU, Hawaii, Aug. 2. — With Dollfuss the conservative gone and that fine level-headed old patriot von Hindenburg gone, it looks like it takes a radical to live.

England saying that her borders reached to the Rhine was good news to these islands, for that means that ours at least reach our own possessions.

The army and navy ought to be flying this hop all the time. It's like carrying the mail. We ask 'em to do something right now and then blame 'em because they have had no practice. If we ever had to fly here we would have to ask 'em to postpone the emergency till we learned it.

So don't blame the boys. They will have to wait now till commercial lines do it first.

Yours,
Will Rogers.

2497   WILL ROGERS HEADS AGAIN
INTO THE BROAD PACIFIC

HONOLULU, Hawaii, Aug. 3. — Well, we are heading today for the broad Pacific. It has been a wonderful week here, but it would take months to see it all. They do lots of playing here, but these old missionary families do lots of work too. One good thing about 'em they put all their money right back in the islands.

Attorney General Cummings got in yesterday. He is Roosevelt's lawyer, and I guess come out to straighten out some devilment his boss got in while here.

Huey Long is getting more publicity out here in the papers than Hitler. If I am seasick tomorrow you won't hear from me.

Yours,
Will Rogers.

2498   MR. ROGERS HEARS NOTHING OF WAR OUT IN THE PACIFIC

ABOARD S. S. EMPRESS OF CANADA, Aug. 5. — Fine boat. Fine trip. Interesting people from the four corners of the earth, going and coming.

Everybody feeling optimistic and telling of how their country is recovering. No war talk. That's all in the editorials at home.

Lots of Japanese and Chinese on board. Arrive in Yokohama next Saturday morning. Miss Floyd Gibbons on this trip. We had a great time coming out before.

Did the President ever get home? I think he had a great trip. He was feeling fine.

Yours,
Will Rogers.

2499   WILL ROGERS IS PUZZLED BY THAT MISSING DAY

ABOARD S. S. EMPRESS OF CANADA, Aug. 6. — Get this calendar mess:

Yesterday was Sunday. We had services on here and I sent a daily wire. Now last night they informed us, "Tomorrow morning when you get up it won't be Monday, it will be Tuesday."

Now what I want to know is, did I miss Tuesday's papers or is this one going in Tuesday or is it Wednesday? In fact I am not right sure about the month. Some man in a uniform could come up and announce, "We are skipping August," and I would believe him.

I bet the Republicans wish they could have skipped a year ago the 4th of last November.

Yours,
Will Rogers.

2500   Mr. Rogers Is Finding Life
On The High Seas Dull

ABOARD S. S. EMPRESS OF CANADA, Aug. 7. — We been on here just long enough for everybody to find out everybody else's business.

Brazil's new Ambassador to Japan just coming from Denmark says Ruth Bryan is doing fine.

Filipinos on here going home. Englishmen on here don't like it because we are giving Philippines freedom. It sets a bad example. It puts freedom into other folks' heads.

No news of Hitler's speech, not even any of Huey Long. Certainly a dull day.

I am going down and play fan tan with the Chinamen.

                       Yours,
                       Will Rogers.

2501   Mr. Rogers Is Becalmed
As Regards Spot News

ABOARD EMPRESS OF CANADA, Aug. 9. — I have lost all idea of days or time on here, but this ought to reach you for breakfast Saturday. That's the morning we reach Yokohama, and then to Tokyo, only twenty miles away.

The old Pacific has sure been behaving fine this trip. All our radio news on boat tells of the continued drought and hot weather at home.

I believe if they didn't scrub brass and paint on a ship they would run it with about one man.

Ought to have some news for you from Japan. There is never a dull moment in that country.

                       Yours,
                       Will Rogers.

2502   Mr. Rogers Takes Charge
Of Far East Situation

TOKYO, Aug. 12. — Had dinner and long chat with Roosevelt in Honolulu and he gave me practically same advice that Calvin Coolidge gave Dwight Morrow on Mexico.

The President told me, "Will, don't jump on Japan. Just keep them from jumping on us."

Arrived Saturday, everything peaceful and fine. They want a bigger navy and I think I will let 'em have it, for they are going to build it any way.

Yours,
Will Rogers.

2503   Mr. Rogers Has New Task
To Do For Us In Tokyo

TOKYO, Aug. 13. — Japanese Naval Committee announced today it was going ahead with ship building. If allowed at the next conference they will have them. If not allowed they will have them, too. You can't beat logic like that.

Japanese-American swimming meet here. Our backstroke boy won one swimming on stomach, but lost in tonight's races. I am coaching them all to turn over on back.

Sure hot here.

Yours,
Will Rogers.

2504   Mr. Rogers Reports Gains
In His Toyko Campaign

TOKYO, Aug. 14. — Got my American swimmers turned over on their backs last night and they broke a world's record and won three out of six final events.

We are coming back in swimming at the Olympic Games. In 1932 the Japanese could just throw a pair of trunks in the water and beat us.

Awful hot here. Plenty mosquitoes and American tourists.

Yours,
Will Rogers.

2505   Mr. Rogers Finds Toyko
Also Is Baseball Crazy

TOKYO, Aug. 15. — I thought during my long lifetime I had been awakened just at daylight by every known thing, but right under the Imperial Hotel window exactly at daylight five separate baseball games start. That goes on all day.

Will and Betty Rogers with son of Prince Fumimaro Konoe at the Imperial Hotel, Tokyo, 1934. Prince Konoe was premier of Japan, 1937-1941.

Harvard arrives tomorrow to play the Japanese colleges but about all they will win will be in English pronunciation.

Yours,
Will Rogers.

2506   Rogers Sees Beginning Of The End For Japan

TOKYO, Aug. 16. — Well, Japan won't have her world supremacy in business long.

I saw a lot of golf courses being put in. That's the beginning of a nation's commercial decline.

When we traded a spade for a putter that's the way we started in the red.

What you guys doing with silver over there? You got these folks about nuts, and I expect you got yourself the same way.

Yours,
Will Rogers.

2507   Mr. Rogers Finds A Lull In Affairs In Manchukuo

MUKDEN, Manchukuo, Aug. 17. — I'd heard how nobody seemed to be able to recognize Manchukuo, and there's been such a lot of trouble about it, but I recognized it the minute I got into the hotel here.

It's not near as exciting as you might think.

There's lots of news, but it don't seem to be originating around here.

Yours,
Will Rogers.

2508   Rogers Sees Week's Peace Assured In Manchukuo

HSINKING, Manchukuo, Aug. 19. — This country is so mad at Russia that they've broke off the diplomatic relations that never existed.

That makes the Soviets and Manchukuo such strangers that they can't even fight each other unless they can get Louisiana and Bolivia to act as seconds, so it looks like we're going to have peace over here all week long.

Yours,
Will Rogers.

2509   Mr. Rogers Has New Job
For Louisiana Kingfish

HARBIN, Manchuria, Aug. 20. — I see by the papers that Huey Long decided in favor of Paraguay and got a fort named after him down there.

I guess these folks heard about a big island near New York named for Long where there was a battle not long ago.

If Huey will intervene over here right quick I think I can get a country and two miles of railroad named after him.

Yours,
Will Rogers.

2510   Mr. Rogers Hails 'Benito'
As A First-Rate Teacher

HSINKING, Manchukuo, Aug. 21. — No more monkeyshines in Austria. The Austrian Chancellor has been visiting Mussolini and learning a lot.

This fellow Benito is running a free school for dictators. They all come to him to learn how to put it over.

You don't have to worry about dictators in America until Rex Tugwell passes his entrance exams at Mussolini's academy.

Yours,
Will Rogers.

2511   Mr. Rogers Finds Recruit
For Our Brain Trusters

IRKUTSK, Aug. 22. — Pine trees, low mountains, beautiful valleys today. Distances are far here and names have to be long to reach the next town—Petrovskyisavod and Verhneudinsk.

A mess of nationalities on this train, English, German, Russian, Swiss, Check, American Indians, Japanese, and, the smartest of all is a Chinese, a noted authority on Far Eastern affairs.

Nothing in the world's smarter than one Chinaman and nothing dumber than two.

Mr. Roosevelt told me to scout him some new brain material. I am signing this bird up.

Yours,
Will Rogers.

2512   WILL ROGERS, IN SIBERIA, FINDS AN AMERICAN WORD

CHITA, Siberia, Aug. 23. — Been waiting to reach a town that American readers could pronounce. Chita, that's an old American word.

Came up through Korea, then the length and breadth of Manchuria. Was two days on the Chinese Eastern Railway. That's the one Japan is trying to buy, but take this tip: Russia won't sell. She is just kidding them.

Tell you some time about all the military preparations on both sides. I said some time I would tell you.

This is the heart of Eastern Siberia. All a beautiful prairie, not a tree, not a fence, just grass up to your stirrups. Tomorrow we pass around beautiful Lake Baikal.

Yours,
Will Rogers.

2513   WILL ROGERS IMPRESSED BY SIBERIAN METHODS

NOVOSIBIRSK, Aug. 24. — These folks got an entirely different alphabet and it's only in a few towns where there is telegraph operators that can send messages in English. We are still in Siberia. If you think it's not big, we been for days and haven't made a dent in it. Wish I had Wiley Post here. This is his old round-the-world trail. Beautiful country.

They are just harvesting the wheat; women doing the harvesting and the men are at the depot. You know these folks got some good ideas at that.

Say, you know all these big beautiful rivers we cross run to the Arctic Ocean. Nine o'clock at night and the sun's shining.

Yours,
Will Rogers.

2514   WILL ROGERS IS PUZZLED
BY NEW MANCHUKUO LAW

IRKUTSK, Siberia, Aug. 26. — They just passed a law in Manchukuo that you mustn't mention the Emperor's name, but you got to call him His Majesty.

It's just like if they should pass a law in Kansas that you'd get your head cut off if you ever mentioned Bill White by name, but you'd have to call him "His Honor" instead.

I reckon that's one way to beat the depression, but you got to be born east of Claremore to understand it.

Yours,
Will Rogers.

2515   MR. ROGERS IS IMPRESSED
BY RESOURCES OF SOVIET

MOSCOW, Aug. 27. — From the Far East to Europe in seven and a half days, from Harbin, Manchuria. If you wanted to make no stop you can come from Tokyo in ten days.

It's a great trip, only way to go round the world; fine train, great diner, food enough for Primo Carnera and select enough for Dolly Gans.

Meals all start with a soupbowl full of caviar. Unfortunately I don't like the stuff, but it's still on the gold standard in society.

Never saw as many big rivers and all full of floating logs, and not an inch of land the whole way that couldn't be cultivated.

These birds have got nature with 'em anyhow.

Now for the city sights.

Yours,
Will Rogers.

2516   Mr. Rogers Finds A City
That Really Is Booming

MOSCOW, Aug. 28. — Talk about a town on a boom, this is it. I never saw as many buildings going up in my life.

You have heard of equality of sex in Russia. That's not so. The women are doing the work. They are digging a subway.

Have talked all day today with Maurice Hindus, Walter Duranty and Louis Fisher. Here are three men that know their Russia from A to Bolsheviki. I am so full of facts and statistics that I feel like a brain truster.

By the way, I got my little Chinese professor with me yet. They can fool me but they can't fool him.

Yours,
Will Rogers.

2517   Mr. Rogers Finds A Land
Where Authors Prosper

MOSCOW, Aug. 29. — Ambassador Bullitt just flew in a good old army plane from Odessa down on the Black Sea.

What a live bird this Bullitt is, and a tremendous favorite here. He did a smart thing. He picked George Hanson, our crack Consul General from Harbin, to come here and assist him.

The Soviet writers are holding a convention here. They are the richest people in the U. S. S. R. Maxim Gorky's royalties last year was 7,000,000 roubles.

I am trying to learn to write in Russian.

Yours,
Will Rogers.

2518   Mr. Rogers Goes To Races
In Moscow, Sees Plenty

MOSCOW, Aug. 30. — These Russians sure believe in mass production. Just come from the race meet and they had thirty-six races. They run the Soviet Derby today.

All the horses belong to the government but are raised and entered by different parts of the army and the collective farms.

Half of the races are running and half trotting. When the trotters come out old David Harum wanted to come down and take over the ribbons.

Tomorrow I am trying out Russia's commercial aviation, flying down through the Ukraine and Caucasus to the Black Sea.

Yours,
Will Rogers.

2519   WILL ROGERS RUNS ACROSS
AN OLD-TIMER IN RUSSIA

MOSCOW, Aug. 31. — I met a guy today that could remember back to the time when there was a Czar in Russia, Trotzky was pressing pants in New York, Upton Sinclair was away uptown, Texas steers had long horns and governments paid their debts.

Flying south through Soviet Russia, and the oil wells smell like regular capitalistic oil.

Yours,
Will Rogers.

2520   WILL ROGERS DISCOVERS
THE SOVIET HAS WINGS

ODESSA, Sept. 2. — Say, these old Russians can really fly.

We had about a 65 to 70 foot ceiling today and they stuck right under it.

That's what the Japanese are more afraid of than any other thing, is that these guys will outfly 'em.

Commercial aviation is not so hot but military is, and it looks like they got 'em by the thousands.

Who hasn't pictured Odessa on the Black Sea? Russia and Turkey have been fighting over this for a thousand years.

Do you remember it in the Russian picture Potemkin? That long row of steps from the ocean to the hill? Well, they are right into this hotel.

Yours,
Will Rogers.

2521   Will Rogers Quits Russia
                            Full Of Mixed Ideas

LENINGRAD, Sept. 3. — Well, we are finally on the track of Finland. Found a pilot who is going to leave here with us in the morning and take us by way of Estonia and land us in Helsingfjord. That's the place I been looking for for a month.

Just like these folks to move their capital from a beautiful city like this to Moscow. Saw the opening of the great opera in Moscow Saturday night. New drama last night there, and tonight the ballet in the real home of the Russian ballet.

Saw Leningrad's old Stock Exchange today. Would hate to tell you what it is now. Boys, you better behave!

                                  Yours,
                                  Will Rogers.

2522   Will Rogers, In Finland,
                            Gives It An A1 Rating

HELSINKI, Sept. 4. — This is Finland, integrity's last stand. They told our Minister, Mr. Albright, "You loaned us the money when we needed it and we are going to pay you back." Them's mighty scarce words.

I tell you, they got just about the most stable government right now of any of them.

It's a beautiful little city and clean. When these Finns aren't running a twenty-five-mile race they are scrubbing on something.

Haven't seen Nurmi yet. He is out a couple of hundred miles but is going to run down and see me tomorrow morning.

Yeh boy, don't miss Finland.

                                  Yours,
                                  Will Rogers.

2523   Will Rogers Continues
                            To Rave Over Finland

HELSINKI, Sept. 5. — I just saw the finest Capitol, or House of Parliament, in the world. Brand new. They vote by electric buttons. I got to get home to tell you about it.

Not just because they paid their debt, but these Finns are a knockout. Did you know they are the seventh biggest country in all Europe?

And eat? Brother, you haven't had a meal till you have one in Finland.

Viva Finland.

Yours,
Will Rogers.

2524   WILL ROGERS NOW SINGS
             THE PRAISES OF SWEDEN

STOCKHOLM, Sept. 6. — These Swedes are so hospitable they don't give you time to write or hardly even to read the papers.

They're the healthiest looking people you ever saw and they haven't been in a war for so long that they haven't got any word in their language for repudiation.

The King don't have much time to practice with a sword, but he swings a right smart tennis racket.

Yours,
Will Rogers.

2525   WILL ROGERS FLIES OVER
             THE FJORDS OF NORWAY

OSLO, Sept. 7. — You've heard of Norway's beautiful fjords, high-walled canyons of water that run back for miles into the land. I took a small seaplane and flew over them for hours. Landed on their lakes and chased herds of reindeer through the snow in the plane.

Minnesota can well be proud of its Fatherland. It's wonderful and substantial. Skol.

Yours,
Will Rogers.

2526   WILL ROGERS NOW GIVES
             THE DANES A BIG HAND

COPENHAGEN, Sept. 9. — Great flight down from Norway.

These Danes took nothing but a pig and cow and common sense enough to stay out of war for fifty years. Today they, along with Sweden, Norway and Finland, are an example to the world of how to live neighborly and tend to your own business.

There's lots to be learned from these Scandinavians.

Yours,
Will Rogers.

2527   Mr. Rogers Gets Ideas
             In London's Hyde Park

LONDON, Sept. 10. — These Englishmen are about the smartest white folks there is. It's one place where fascism, communism, Hitlerism or nudism will never get anywhere.

They have a park here. Hyde Park, that's just built for folks that are agin something.

Yesterday I saw it at its best. The biggest crowd in its history. The Black Shirts were holding one meeting and the Communists, 200 yards away, holding another, and all London in between laughin' at both sides.

Everybody went home satisfied for they had all had their say, for after all nobody wants his cause near as bad as he wants to talk about his cause, and England has solved the talking problem.

                        Yours,
                           Will Rogers.

2528   Mr. Rogers Reports Briefly
             On A European Hot Spot

VIENNA, Sept. 1. — This is Vienna, Europe's hot box.

If a war starts, this is supposed to be the place that it starts. It's a beautiful city.

Going to the opera tonight and I will last about one act and then start hunting a vaudeville show.

Flying on to Bucharest tomorrow. Got to see Queen Marie's country.

                        Yours,
                           Will Rogers.

2529   Mr. Rogers Gets A Shock
             On His Tour Of Europe

BUCHAREST, Sept. 12. — Say, this Rumania is a real place. This is a beautiful city of 800,000. The King is in the mountains and Queen Marie is at the seashore.

This is a corn country, the only civilized country in Europe that knows what a roasting ear is. They raise lots of hogs and everybody can talk English.

Here is some political scandal. Saw Senator Joe Robinson at the opera in Vienna last night. Democrats are going bushwa.

Yours,
Will Rogers.

2530   Mr. Rogers Finds A Job
            As King For The Kingfish

BUDAPEST, Sept. 13. — I am going to keep flying up and down this Danube River till I find a place where it's blue.

This is the star city of all Europe. Hungary is a kingdom, but got no king. They are looking for one.

I believe the old Kingfish will fit 'em. I can fix it for you, Huey.

Yours,
Will Rogers.

2531   Mr. Rogers Finds Plenty
            Of Excitement In Europe

LONDON, Sept. 14. — Budapest for breakfast and London for dinner. I have reached in my pocket for my passport in so many different countries today that I am all in. Crossed Hungary, Czechoslovakia, Austria, France, Belgium and England.

Poland upset Europe at the League of Nations more yesterday than anything that's happened over here. You never lack for excitement. There is twenty countries over here in a bunch all thinking of some trick to pull on the others. They do love each other.

Yours,
Will Rogers.

2532   Will Rogers Is Befogged
            By The Yacht Race News

LONDON, Sept. 16. — Will you please tell me what happened at the so-called yacht race Saturday?

I never saw as many conflicting statements as in the local papers today. Some say the race was in doubt to the last minute. Some say that cruisers, or Roosevelt, or somebody got in the way of the English boat.

They say our crew is professional and that theirs just work for the love of the sea air and that ours is not built right below decks.

Send all particulars to the League of Nations and let's get this thing straightened out.

Yours,
Will Rogers.

2533   MR. ROGERS FINDS LONDON
          YACHT RACING CONSCIOUS

LONDON, Sept. 17. — London is awaiting the news of the second day's yacht race.

They take yacht racing serious over here. It seems by today's papers that any bad sportsmanship was shown by the writers and not by the owners.

They are talking about holding an ammunition selling investigation over here. Ammunition is about the only export now. Wars ought to be awful equal for they all use the same guns and ammunition.

Best show in London is a colored show from Harlem.

Yours,
Will Rogers.

2534   WILL ROGERS, IN SCOTLAND,
          IS MOVED TO A 'HOOT MON!'

EDINBOROUGH, Sept. 18. — I been coming over since 1906 when I first worked on the stage in London, and do you know I had never been to Scotland before, and I want to apologize for being so dumb. It sho is pretty.

Saw all Glasgow, Lock Lomond and the big boat that Queen Mary launches next week. Yes they are up here in this country with us, too.

Edinborough, which we are doing now, kinder high-hats Glasgow. There is quite a mess of class to Edinborough.

Hoot mon,
Will Rogers.

2535   WILL ROGERS FINDS SCOTS
          LIBERAL AND HOSPITABLE

EDINBURGH, Sept. 19. — You get these Scotchmen wrong. Why they are the most liberal and hospitable people you ever saw.

Course I have to carry an interpreter to tell me what they say, but they are awful friendly.

Grouse is Scotland's principal export. You got to rent a castle. Then rent some drivers to drive the grouse by the castle.

The grouse have been shot at so much they know just about who can hit 'em and who can't.

It's a racket, and the grouse and the Scotchmen work together and the Americans and the Englishmen pay the bill.

Yours,
Will Rogers.

2536   Mr. Rogers Is Heading
For The Home Corral

LONDON, Sept. 20. — On the track of a bed on a boat so headed home.

Besides these English are making life miserable for us poor Americans since we can't even win a race where wind is involved, a thing we were preeminent in. Can't make 'em believe we been wanting to lose that cup for forty years.

What's this about my Western boys losing a polo game? I got to get home and start brain trusting 'em. Hold 'em, cowboys.

Yours,
Will Rogers.

2537   Rogers Finds Europe Quiet;
Sure Sign Of War, He Says

ABOARD S. S. ILE DE FRANCE, Sept. 21. — I tell you you can't beat England for her justice. Brought some English papers on board and it tells of a man who killed his nagging wife and the judge give him a year, but apologized for it. Said he was compelled to do it under the law.

Europe's awful quiet now. Don't hear much war talk so I guess that means one will break out. That's when they have 'em when there ain't any reason.

Sure hate to miss that polo game tomorrow, Saturday. In Russia, if they send you out on a mission and you don't perform it, you better not come back. So if you birds lose this game don't come home letting a lot of dudes beat you.

Yours,
Will Rogers.

2538   MR. ROGERS IS A BIT PAINED
         BY JITTERY BUSINESS MEN

S. S. ILE DE FRANCE, via Chatham, Sept. 23. — You know the American business man or traveler from home is a queer duck. All over Europe and a couple of days ago on the boat, they was saying:

"I tell you I am afraid of things at home. It don't look good to me."

Well, for the last couple of days the market has picked up and today's news said the strikers went back to work.

Now they are running around the boat grinning like a possum.

Imagine people who's whole idea of our country is gained from what it does every day in a stock market.

Yours,
Will Rogers.

2539   MR. ROGERS PUTS IN A BID
         FOR SOME RFC MONEY

ABOARD S. S. ILE DE FRANCE, Sept. 24. — Now out here somewhere is where they ought to have one of those floating aeroplane stations so they could drop you off and pick up a day.

If Jesse Jones is still loaning out money on self-liquidating projects, here is one that would be worthy and plenty liquid.

Say, where is your referee in this yacht racing? Can't he see the fouls, if there is any?

I got to go up there and see what kind of racket that is anyhow.

Wish that foghorn would shut up. I can't hear the typewriter.

Yours,
Will Rogers.

2540   MR. ROGERS DOCKS IN TIME
         TO SEE HIS POLOISTS LOSE

NEW YORK, N. Y., Sept. 25. — Well the old boat docked in time to rush to see the East-West polo game, and it was a real game.

And hats off to the Eastern kids, for they are a fine bunch of young fellows. They played a great game and deserved to win.

Fourteen to thirteen, you can't get it much closer than that. Our team did mighty nobly, and this fine thing about it there was no protests and no hard feeling.

Our boys have just got to go home and dig up a couple of more goals by next year.

Yours,
Will Rogers.

2541   MR. ROGERS FINDS THINGS
        AT HOME MIGHTY LIVELY

HEMPSTEAD, N. Y., Sept. 26. — Boy, it's great to get back into a country where something happens. Talk about Japan, Russia and Europe, why even a society reporter could cover their news. With us something is cracking every minute.

Hugh Johnson's retirement? Why that's like Hitler stepping out.

Hugh has never put any men to death, but he has certainly scared some of our biggest industrialists half to death. He has cussed 'em all, collectively and individually.

You told many big guys the truth that had never been told it before. Good luck to you Hugh.

Yours,
Will Rogers.

P. S. — And best to Bobby.

2542   MR. ROGERS IN WASHINGTON
        FINDS GREAT GOINGS-ON

WASHINGTON, D. C., Sept. 27. — Flew in here this afternoon and what greets my eye? Washington's Monument has a scaffold built up around it. I said to Jesse Jones, "Jesse, don't tell me the New Deal is rebuilding George's monument."

Lobby of the hotel full of badges and found out it's the police chiefs from everywhere, getting their code. They was afraid to come and get it under Johnson.

The President is picking five men to replace Johnson and run the NRA. I think that's what these police chiefs are all doing here. They are going to help him arrest the men that he appoints, for nobody would like a job like that voluntarily.

Yours,
Will Rogers.

2543   ROGERS THINKS JOHNSON
        WILL GO TO PHILIPPINES

WASHINGTON, D. C., Sept. 28. — Just been helping work on a new NRA board. Mr. Richberg is the head of it, replacing "Bobby." Three executives and two college professors take Hugh Johnson's place, in addition to an "exec" committee composed of the Cabinet and the President himself.

It looked for a while like they was going to have to call in the marines to replace Johnson.

Everybody wonders what Johnson will do next? I think he will be sent to the Philippines to replace the Governor General, the army and the navy, and on days off supervise the Hawaiian Islands.

Yours for accurate tips,
Will Rogers.

2544   MR. ROGERS IS QUITE UPSET
        OVER THIS 'LIBERTY' STUFF

NEW YORK, N. Y., Sept. 30. — The greatest aid that I know of that any man could give the world today would be a correct definition of "liberty."

Everybody is running around in a circle announcing that somebody's pinched their "liberty."

Now what one class's "liberty" might be another class's "poison." Course I guess absolute "liberty" couldn't mean anything but that anybody can do anything they want to, any time they want to.

Well any half wit can tell that that wouldn't work. So, the question arises "how much liberty can I get and get away with it?"

Well you can get no more than you give. That's my definition, but you got perfect "liberty" to work out your own, so get in.

And let's get this "liberty" business settled.

Yours,
Will Rogers.

2545   MR. ROGERS DROPS SEARCH
        FOR WISDOM TO SEE DIZZY

NEW YORK, N. Y., Oct. 1. — This morning The New York Times kidded me about my wanting to know the definition of "liberty."

Well, read the very last paragraph of Mr. Roosevelt's radio speech last night. It says:

"I am not for a return to that definition of liberty under which for many years a free people were regimented into the service of the privileged. I prefer that broader definition of liberty under which we are moving forward to greater freedom."

So Mr. Times Man, I am not the only one that thinks the definition of liberty is kinder flexible. So if you don't know, ask your Congressman.

I am leaving here right now to see Mr. Henry Ford and a gentleman named Dean who is to be in Detroit, too.

Yours,
Will Rogers.

2546   MR. ROGERS FINDS DETROIT PLUM DIZZY AND DAFFY

DETROIT, Mich., Oct. 2. — A German town on Hitler day couldn't be any nuttier than Detroit. There is only two sane, quiet, well-mannered people in the whole city today and they are visitors from Oklahoma, Jerome and Paul Dean. Why they are the most likeable boys you ever saw. Jealousy and not facts nicknamed them "Dizzy" and "Daffy."

Been out with Mr. Henry Ford today. He give $100,000 for the broadcasting privilege, so he is dizzier than the Deans spending money like that when other rich men are buying Canadian and English bonds.

He must be just plum dizzy, for he believes the country is improving and that if he had to vote tomorrow he would vote for Roosevelt. That he had never heard of a person that offered a single constructive plan of what they would do.

His endorsement is not only verbal, for he is spending millions and millions on new plants. Queer duck, this fellow.

I attribute his success to selling motor cars exclusively and not selling stock. He don't dread inflation and he don't fear it if it comes. In fact he don't seem to fear anything.

What a relief to meet the richest man in the world and him not worried. Well I will take that back. I think these two Dean boys have got him worried.

Yours,
Will Rogers.

2547   MR. ROGERS FILES A REPORT
          ON AN OKLAHOMA WONDER

DETROIT, Mich., Oct. 3. — Mr. Jerome Dean of Holdenville, Okla., who Alfalfa Bill Murray sent here to quell this riot, did so today. And he had to do it with his head instead of his arm, for he was tired from his season's work. When you can beat Mickey Cochrane's great team with your head alone, you ain't dizzy.

Tomorrow is test of higher education. We get High School Boy Rowe against Grammar School Boy Paul Dean. And it will be a test of whether you should go to high school or go to work. It's going to be a real game, with the score 3 to 2 or 2 to 1, in anybody's favor.

I sit by Mr. Henry Ford and he paid $100,000 and he said it was two great teams and that he had had his money's worth. So certainly nobody else has a squawk.

But tomorrow you will see a baseball game.

Yours,
Will Rogers.

2548   MR. ROGERS RAVES A BIT
          OVER THAT SECOND GAME

DETROIT, Mich., Oct. 4. — I told you what the score would be today, 3 to 2, and that it would be a great game. Anybody's game.

Frankie Frisch crossed me up by pitching Bill Hallahan instead of Grammar School Paul Dean. "Student" Rowe of Smackover, Arkansaw, pitched. And brother, did he smack 'em over. He certainly earned his diploma. He ain't Schoolboy any longer. He goes right into the brain trust.

The St. Louis batters didn't know any more about what he was doing than do some of them in Washington. Yes, sir, he goes into brain trust. He comes from my wife's home State.

Everybody played ball today and that kid pitched a great game. And don't forget Bill Hallahan. He was very, very hot too. A muffed ball in the center field, a questionable hit over third base, and toughest of all a little pop-fly dropped on the first-base line. The breaks were just against Bill.

But it would have been a national calamity for the kid from Smackover to have lost. I bet I am the only one's been to that town.

Well, I hear that plane whistling for the crossing.

Yours,
Will Rogers.

2549   Mr. Rogers Confesses All
        And Doesn't Try To Alibi

FT. WORTH, Texas, Oct. 7. — Last Saturday I was absent from these parts in this paper. Teacher, I can't tell a lie. I wasent sick, or away from a telegraph station.

Friday afternoon after watching Paul Dean almost shut out Detroit, rush to the hotel, write my piece, and predict that Detroit was still plenty tough.

Then start rushing off to my old home in Okla, and forget to file my telegram. It never happened before. So I can only plead old age.

But here is what really hurt. The world moved along Saturday (even better) than any other day lately. I tell you it's surprising how many of us it can get along without. I dont want to appear rude, but I actually believe it could get along great without all of us.

Yours,
Will Rogers.

P. S. — That world series is getting really hot. I got to go get the finish of it.

2550   Will Rogers Now Looks
        For A Nine-Game Series

DETROIT, Mich., Oct. 8. — It was a great game, good to win and tough to lose.

Detroit has been watching "Dizzy" when it should have been "Daffy." "Daffy" has walked in unobserved and packed off two arms full of bacon. "Highschoolboy" Rowe was mighty good, but old McGuffey's Third Reader Paul Dean was a little better. It just shows you got to leave school earlier and take up your profession.

Mickey Cochrane was a real hero. He got crippled, but went right on and blocked 'em off that plate when they come with spikes blazing in his face.

Mr. Ford wanted to bet me $40, but there ought to be a law against folks betting that can't afford it.

Now about tomorrow. That's going to be a real game. Ball players say that Bill Hallahan pitched one of the finest games in this whole mess.

Then there is a chance of Dizzy coming back. He wants to get the Dean name back to "Dizzy" and "Daffy" instead of going through the Winter with it "Daffy" and "Dizzy." Then for Detroit it looks like "Gen." Crowder, who looked good in his game.

I look for the series to go nine games, with a couple of ties in there.

Yours,
Will Rogers.

2551   MR. ROGERS MAKES HIS OFFICIAL REPORT
ON THE WORLD SERIES FINALE AND THE RIOT

CHICAGO, Ill., Oct. 9. — We had a ball game, we had a riot, we had Judge Landis hold court right on the field. And we had "Dizzy" Dean. Anywhere "Dizzy" is there is something happening, either for or against.

The courtroom scene didnt last long because neither ball player had time to call their lawyers, quick. I believe I am the only fellow who talked with both boys in their dressing rooms directly after the game.

Medwick, whom I already knew, is a fine boy. And he felt very sorry, said it was just in the excitement of the game and he did it before he realized what he was doing, and that he had no hard feelings at all toward Owen.

Owen was mighty nice about it and said there was no attempt at a fight or argument, and that he thought that Medwick had done what he did in the excitement, it was the crowd that wanted to fight not the ballplayers.

The Tigers put up a fine fight and darn it I did feel sorry for 'em in their dressing room. Nobody slapping 'em on the back, in fact nobody in there but them.

Game Mickey Cochrane sitting there just removing bandage after bandage from almost all over himself. Real he men, in a he mans game, with almost tears in their eyes but not squawking. They just said "Old 'Diz' had everything." I can applaud a winner as loud as anybody, but somehow a loser appeals to me.

Over in the St. Louis dressing room it was a madhouse. "Dizzy" had on one of those Indian helmets, and a stuffed rubber tiger by the tail. He says, "Will, the championship remains in Oklahoma." "Pepper" Martin and all the others just plain "nutty."

It's been a great series. I used to know all the old-time players and it was like a reunion for me. "Dizzy" aint dizzy, and "Daffy" aint daffy. They're plenty smart and fine boys.

Will Rogers in scenes from Judge Priest, *the motion picture based on Irvin S. Cobb's character "Judge Priest"* (Fox Film Corporation, 1934).

My old friend, Joe E. Brown, didnt wound anybody by a handshake. If he did he must have hit 'em.

         Yours,
         Will Rogers.

2552   Mr. Rogers, Home At Last, Reviews A Dizzy Series

BEVERLY HILLS, Cal., Oct. 10. — See a ball game in Detroit, and home for early breakfast. Felt plum lost this afternoon without the Deans to watch.

Every sport is looking for outstanding players with "color." Well, old "Diz" is a "rainbow." "Rainbow" Deans, for Brother Paul while quiet and timid is a great team-mate for "Dizzy." And ball players say there is darn little difference in their pitching. They both got the old, long, free-arm Walter Johnson swing.

By the way I saw Walter up there, looks great, and Tris Speaker, the one man that has never been approached in his playing of center field. And "Rabbit," saw Rabbit, he looks great and says he will be in there next year.

With the Deans success and these little soda fountain colleges beating the big ones in football it looks like a country boys year.

         Yours,
         Will Rogers.

2553   Mr. Rogers Glad To Hear Of New Political Blood

BEVERLY HILLS, Cal., Oct. 11. — Say the Republicans have turned the coming election into a real "youth's movement."

Just signed up for the coming sorority hop is those ex-White House co-eds, Mrs. Benjamin Harrison, Mrs. Theodore Roosevelt, Mrs. William Howard Taft, Mrs. Calvin Coolidge and Mrs. Herbert Hoover. And nothing is any more gratifying to America than to welcome back into the fold all those gracious and sturdy American women.

Funny thing about that White House. It wears down the most hardy of our men folks, but the women seem to thrive on it.

By the way, this is Mrs. Franklin Roosevelt's birthday. I wish I knew where she was today, I would send her a message of good wishes as I am very fond of her.

So here is a kind of blanket good wish to all of 'em, and Mrs. Woodrow Wilson. Sure you should all keep up your political affiliations and public interests. Don't retire. We want you to keep on living.

      Yours,
      Will Rogers.

2554   WILL ROGERS FOUND CROATS
     LIKE OUR LIBERTY LEAGUERS

SANTA MONICA, Cal., Oct. 12. — In my late world pilgrimage in search of a definite platform for the Republican party, I hit about a half dozen of those Balkan nations, and Yugoslavia, where this murdered king come from, was one of 'em. I learned quite a little bit about him and his country.

He was the only king over there that really did his own "dictating." Generally those kings just do a little "kinging" and let somebody else do the "rough stuff." He was a Serbian, but there's another band of people in this country called the Croats. Well the Croats are sorter like the "liberty leaguers" are here. They say they are downtrodden. But the one thing their whole country is united in, is that they hate Italy.

Well a Croat killed the King, and it was in France. But the whole country is united in saying that Mussolini furnished the ammunition. Well why not blame poor old Mussolini? Didn't Roosevelt bring on the drought?

Yours for European news that's fit to print,
      Will Rogers.

2555   MR. ROGERS GIVES HIS IDEA
     OF AFFAIRS IN EUROPE

SANTA MONICA, Cal., Oct. 14. — There is not going to be any war in Europe now, for nobody knows just who they would fight. Nations are not signed up.

In the big war before, they already had their sides picked, and the war was booked long before it come off, but since that war, nations have kinder wanted to do like a lot of our moving picture stars do. They won't sign exclusively with one company. They take a chance on what we call "free lancing," that is, waiting for the best offer.

So that's what most European nations are doing. They are going to wait till war starts, then "free lance." Sit and wait for the best.

That's what France had this King come over there for, they were trying to get an option on his services. France had Poland signed up, but there was a cancellation clause, so now Poland is "free lancing."

Yours for all the European news that's fit to print,
Will Rogers.

2556   MR. ROGERS FINDS RELIGION AND POLITICS MIXED A BIT

BEVERLY HILLS, Cal., Oct. 15. — This is Monday and I have been sitting here reading sermons delivered yesterday. On Sundays politics is transferred from the platform to the rostrum.

In October on election years it's awful hard for a sinner in search of spiritual advice to drop into a church and receive any of it, but instead he can hear an awful pretty theological talk on "The NRA," "Fundamental Principles" and "Elect Brother Jones, he will lead us out of this mire of misery."

Yours,
Will Rogers.

2557   WILL ROGERS SEES MORAL FOR US IN HUNGARY STRIKE

BEVERLY HILLS, Cal., Oct. 16. — Saw a mighty pleasing Associated Press dispatch from Washington in the papers this morning, saying Fred Stone was a sensation in a straight dramatic play.

Those self-entombed miners in Hungary had to starve practically to death to get a raise from $2 a week to $3.50 a week. An impartial board in San Francisco gave the longshoremen 95 cents an hour with $1.40 per hour overtime.

So you see these old boys that get up and tell you what the rest of the world is doing, well, that's just about what they are doing.

Yours,
Will Rogers.

2558   MR. ROGERS IS ENJOYING
                     POLITICS IN CALIFORNIA

SANTA MONICA, Cal., Oct. 17. — In most places it's awful hard to get folks to go and register to vote, but out here in Los Angeles where we do everything "big" why each qualified voter is allowed to register himself and ten dead friends. If he hasn't got ten dead friends, why he is allowed to pick out ten live ones, just so they don't live in this State.

The Republicans are kicking on this arrangement, as they claim that system of registration gives the Democrats the best of it, as very few Republicans have ten friends.

You ought to come out here some time. We do have the most fun.

                                            Yours,
                                           Will Rogers.

2559   WILL ROGERS POINTS OUT
                     'BLESSINGS' OF PAROLES

BEVERLY HILLS, Cal., Oct. 18. — There must not be such a thing in this country as what you would call an "amateur crook." Every person that is caught in some terrible crime you find where he has been "paroled, pardoned and pampered" by every jail or insane asylum in the country. Some of these criminals' records and the places they have been freed from, it sounds like the tour of a "one-night stand theatrical troupe."

It must be awfully monotonous belonging to one of these State pardon boards. There is days and days when they just have to sit around waiting for new criminals to be caught so they can pardon 'em.

                                            Yours,
                                           Will Rogers.

2560   WILL ROGERS INSPECTS JOB
                     GOING ON AT HOOVER DAM

LAS VEGAS, Nev., Oct. 19. — The madame and I just been visiting "Hoover Dam." That's not a typographical error, it's Hoover Dam, there must be some justice left among us.

Well you should see it under construction, it will be finished in less than a year, two and one-half years ahead of time. They have done a great job. If they decide to plow under every third dam they are going to have a tough time with this one.

Found the best way I ever went to Arizona, by a cable and bucket. The dam grows a foot high a day, that sounds like Oklahoma weeds.

One old boy got fired from down in there the other day, and as he walked out he got on a high peek and declared, "I hope she leaks."

That sounds like a rich Republican's wish to the New Deal. They "hope it leaks."

Yours,
Will Rogers.

2561   Mr. Rogers Is All Astir Over The Big Air Race

SAN FRANCISCO, Cal., Oct. 21. — This race to Australia, I can just picture it. If I wasn't making a movie I would be stowed away in there.

Rome, Athens, Bagdad, Jask, Karachi, Allahabad, Calcutta, Allostar, Singapore! I stayed all night in every one of those in 1932, including Cairo, flying with these same Holland Dutch that are in this race. Took us eleven days from Singapore to London. Some improvement, eh?

Am pulling for Roscoe Turner, but those Dutch in an American Douglas, knowing the route, it's their regular line, they know it like Sinclair knows his voters.

I wish we had old "One-Eye, No-Sleep" Wiley Post in there flying solo, or Frank Hawkes, or Jimmy Doolittle, or "Ex-Navy" Williams.

Yes, and an old-time flyer by the name of, I think it's Lindbergh or something like that. I would like to see that old timer pin his whiskers back out of the propeller and be in this heat.

Yours,
Will Rogers.

P. S.: Speaking of aviators, there is one coming breezing in here from Australia any day now that's a little more than a green hand at the controls.

2562   MR. ROGERS IS OUT STRONG
                 FOR REAL PREPAREDNESS

SONORA, Cal., Oct. 22. — Walked into a barber shop in this beautiful and historical little mountain town. I heard the radio going and somebody raising Old Ned with somebody. I says:

"Who's that talking? Merriam against Sinclair or Sinclair against Merriam, or Haight against the field?"

They says:

"Why no. That's the President giving some folks fits for being against military preparedness."

I says:

"Amen."

Sic 'em Franklin. Pour it on 'em. If they want to show what "not having a gun" will do for you, they can point out China and India.

                         Yours,
                            Will Rogers.

2563   WILL ROGERS HANDS PALM
                 TO THE FLYING BRITONS

SONORA, Cal., Oct. 23. — By golly you got to hand it to those flying Englishmen, they run express, and cut out all the local stops.

They must have been in great physical shape for it. That's where Wiley Post would have shined; he never sleeps till he gets back to Oklahoma.

And they must have had a real plane. Flying a two-motored plane on one motor is what they all advertise but few do.

I picked the Dutch in our Douglas, but they seem to be laying back waiting for something to happen to the Englishmen. It did; they won.

Turner and Pangborn did a great job. Third in that race was some accomplishment.

Watch my good friend Brisbane. He will have Japan flying into California for lunch.

                         Yours,
                            Will Rogers.

2564   WILL ROGERS GIVES A HAND
                 TO 'STRATHASCOPE' FLIERS

SONORA, Cal., Oct. 24. — "Strathascope fliers land safely in tree top."

Mighty glad, for they are awful pleasant, nice folks. During the late "Dizzy" Dean carnival in Detroit, Mr. Henry Ford introduced me to these Picards, and I crawled in that thing (but, brother, she was anchored to old Mother Earth). They are just about as game as anybody that went to Australia.

Tonight Mr. Roosevelt is to speak to the bankers. That shows a mighty broad-minded spirit on his part, for there has been times that we all thought he never would speak to 'em again. I hope he treats 'em with mercy, and don't shoot for the poor devils are licked.

                         Yours,
                         Will Rogers.

2565   MR. ROGERS REPORTS TODAY
                 FROM A HISTORIC SPOT

ANGELS CAMP, Cal., Oct. 25. — This is in Angels Camp, that original home of Mark Twain's high leaping frog.

Every old gold town that you have read about in Twain's or Bret Harte's stories is right around in this country. The adventure and romance of half a continent is in these very hills. Good roads, good hotels and great people and history to burn.

So come in and see 'em mining gold on these original grounds and with descendants of the original casts.

P. S. — Read President's speech the bankers are still in the doghouse.

                         Yours,
                         Will Rogers.

2566   MR. ROGERS SAYS IT'S TIME
                 RAILROADS SHOWED SPEED

SONORA, Cal., Oct. 26. — That was a great record run that Averill Harriman's train made, and it will be a great boost for all railroading. You know, it's astonishing, but the record that he broke held for 30 years. With all our speed for the last 20 you wonder where the folks that manage railroads were. It wasn't the RR workers' fault, there was never a more efficient worker than they have been, but this will just wake 'em up and it will mean a lot to the whole country to see the RR doing well.

The bankers finally made up with Mr. Roosevelt when they give up hope of him making up with them. Thay thanked him for coming over and doing an act for 'em at their banquet.

Yours,
Will Rogers.

2567   MR. ROGERS HAS A PROPOSAL
             FOR THE ROSE BOWL GAME

SANTA MONICA, Cal., Oct. 28. — Football was the headliner over the late news.

Huey Long joined Louisiana and annexed Tennessee.

Yale and Harvard can get the rich socialites, but they just can't seem to get a good line.

It looks like the Army and Navy both got good teams, and I hereby make this as a motion—a Congressional motion—that if they both breeze through, and even after playing each other (and if it's a good close game), that both teams be brought out to the Rose Bowl.

It would be a new and great thing to see two football teams meet twice in a season and see what happened, (baseball teams play each other twenty-two games each season).

It would be a shame to bring one team out and not the other. Do I hear a seconder?

Yours,
Will Rogers.

2568   MR. ROGERS'S GREAT HEART
             IS MOVED TO PITY AGAIN

BEVERLY HILLS, Cal., Oct. 29. — Well sir there was an awful heart rendering little item of news in the papers this morning. It's just as well you mayby didn't see it.

The New York Stock Exchange lost $287,986 last year, according to their own press sheet. They state that it's the first time in history that they have ever published their winnings or losings.

Well, in fact, they haven't printed any of their winnings yet.

But, it's encouraging to the bread line to have such a prominent new member join 'em.

Yours,
Will Rogers.

2569   Mr. Rogers Gives A Hand
            To The Australian Fliers

BEVERLY HILLS, Cal., Oct. 30. — In case you might have overlooked it, there is a fellow flying this Pacific Ocean with Kingsford-Smith and his name is Taylor, Captain Taylor. All he does is pick out these little specks in the Pacific Ocean that they are to land at, so he is not exactly what you would call excess baggage.

This is a great flight. This Smith is a real aviator, and there is glory enough for both of 'em. They would have looked pretty good in that Australian race.

This is a single-motored American plane. Gosh, I hope they make it.

                            Yours,
                            Will Rogers.

2570   Will Rogers Takes Note
            Of Election Psychology

BEVERLY HILLS, Cal., Oct. 31. — Well with election coming on all over the country about next Tuesday, folks only got five more days to tell other folks what to do.

Ain't it funny, we can see our friends or neighbors go out, make bad investments, do fool things, but we never say a word. We let him risk his life and his money without any advice. But his vote? We got to tell him about that, for he is kinder ignorant and narrow-minded and don't see things our way. So we advise him.

Well, hurry up and tell him, for he ain't going to pay any attention to you anyhow. But it's a great satisfaction to think you are advising him anyhow.

                            Yours,
                            Will Rogers.

2571   Mr. Rogers Notes Revival
            Of The Old Chicago Spirit

BEVERLY HILLS, Cal., Nov. 1. — Say, did you read about 300,000 grown folks in Chicago going Halloween? They tore down a fair that it took 'em two years and Sally Rand to erect. Women grabbed $200 potted plants under their coats and ducked with 'em. Be a good joke on 'em if they forget to water 'em.

Didn't say how Mr. Henry Ford's wonderful exhibit fared. Hope they didn't put a lot of those in their pockets and duck with 'em.

It's just the old kittenish Chicago spirit. They just love pranks, shooting each other or something, then too modern plumbing has about done away with Halloween fun anyhow.

Yours,
Will Rogers.

2572   WILL ROGERS REMARKS

BEVERLY HILLS, Cal., Nov. 2. — Just had a long chat with Mr. O'Connor, Comptroller of the Currency, who is a mighty big man in the Roosevelt administration, he is out here to vote? "Yeah" and try and do a couple of other little odd chores for the boys back at the big county seat.

Funniest gag in the paper today was that woman Mrs. Frooks, or maybe it's Miss. Well the she Democrats were having a dinner, and there is nothing, (not even bad food) can ruin a Democratic dinner like some Republican sneaking in. Well they finally told her that if she would be still that later on she could ask some questions, and the meeting busted right in her face and there was nobody to ask 'em of, but the waiters cleaning up. That will break Miss Frooks from horning into these sorority dinners.

Yours,
Will Rogers.

2573   MR. ROGERS SAYS THE FLIERS
          DID CALIFORNIA A FAVOR

SANTA MONICA, Cal., Nov. 4. — The radio (God bless it) just tells us that Sir Charles Kingsford-Smith finished his wonderful flight, and it is one of the outstanding ones of history.

Great piloting, perfect navigation, and America gets in on it, too, for he had a real plane.

And he got here at the right time. It takes people's minds in California off this election. They were getting entirely too serious. They think this election is making history, when as a matter of fact it's only marking time.

Yours,
Will Rogers.

P. S. — I am pretty sore today. Am looking for the ones that reminded me that 55 years ago today at Oolagah, Indian Territory, on Nov. 4, 1879, a boy baby was born. Well anyhow played a game of polo and roped calves all day, so there is life in the old nag yet.

2574   Mr. Rogers Reports A Case
Of Pre-Election Jitters

BEVERLY HILLS, Cal., Nov. 5. — This last night before election California puts you in mind of the young husband waiting at the maternity ward for news of the first born. They are walking up and down, lighting one cigarette after another, and looking anxiously toward the voting booth.

Brisbane has bought some land and is moving all us movie folks to Florida. I am trying to get our company to drop off in Oklahoma. I got some cheap stuff there that would look awful pretty with a studio and Janette Gaynor and Warner Baxter on it.

Claremore, Okla., would read awful pretty on all these marriage and divorce notices.

Yours,
Will Rogers.

2575   Mr. Rogers's Early View
Of The Election Results

BEVERLY HILLS, Nov. 6. — It's kinder early in the evening out here, and not much news yet. I would rather have a man counting for me at the polls than I would voting for me.

History has proven that there is nothing in the world as alike as two candidates. They look different till they get in, and then they all act the same.

I am anxious to see how they classify these newly elected. Some are Republicans, but New Dealers; some are Democrats, but not New Dealers; some are Democrats, just to use the label; some are Republicans, just to try and keep an old custom alive.

This next Congress is sure going to be a pack of mongrels.

Yours,
Will Rogers.

2576   WILL ROGERS IS CONVINCED
                   'HONEYMOON' ISN'T OVER

BEVERLY HILLS, Cal., Nov. 7. — The Republicans have had a saying for some time, "The Roosevelt honeymoon is over."

They were might poor judges of a love-sick couple. Why he and the people have got a real love match, and it looks like it would run for at least six years.

If there is one thing the Republican party has got to learn it is that you can't get votes by just denouncing. You got to offer some plan of your own. They only had one platform, "Elect us, and maybe we can think of something to do after we get in, but up to now we haven't thought of it, but give us a chance, we may."

                         Yours,
                         Will Rogers.

2577   MR. ROGERS SETS EXAMPLE
                   TO EXULTANT DEMOCRATS

BEVERLY HILLS, Cal., Nov. 8. — You know as all these late precincts keep coming in (where they can't count very fast) the Democratic lead keeps piling up.

It's just kinder kicking a fellow when he is down. In the heat of the moment they have kicked out some awful good Republicans. And then, too, too big a victory ain't so good. We need quite a few in there just as detectives or watchdogs.

Then too you want to remember that an awful lot of these Democratic votes this time were really at heart Republicans, and they can revert back to type mighty quick.

So don't rub it in boys, for there ain't any finer folks living than a Republican that votes the Democratic ticket.

                     Yours for tolerance,
                     Will Rogers.

2578   YOU CAN'T BEAT SOMETHING
               WITH NOTHING, ROGERS SAYS

BEVERLY HILLS, Cal., Nov. 9. — The day after election I said the Republicans lost because they had nothing to offer but criticism. No plan. Denounce, but don't suggest.

Now comes along Mr. Brisbane and says the same, Mr. Borah, young Bob La Follette and Hiram Johnston.

Now I don't want any better approval than that. It's nothing but the old saying, "You can't beat something with nothing."

We had a man in California that polled eight hundred thousand votes not because that many thought he was right, but simply because he at least had a plan.

I imagine Roosevelt is wrong, but there ain't nobody just smart enough to tell where he is wrong.

Yours,
Will Rogers.

2579   MR. ROGERS AND THE COAST
GREET RETURNING FLEET

SANTA MONICA, Cal., Nov. 11. — We got our navy back this week. It's been off on some kind of a world tour, making a kind of a good-will tour of various places. I think they got as far away from home as New York and Philadelphia.

They were mighty glad to get back, I tell you. You can travel all you want to in all these curious old places, but there is nothing like steaming into the old home port.

We are mighty proud of our navy. Some nearsighted folks kick on the cost, but by golly, it's worth the price to see 30,000 men spotlessly clean, and a "cocky" walk that you don't find on any other animal but a peacock.

There is only one whisker, and that on popular Admiral Reeves. He looks more like Robert E. Lee every day. God bless him.

Yours,
Will Rogers.

2580   MR. ROGERS BASKS PROUDLY
IN A BRAND-NEW SPOTLIGHT

BEVERLY HILLS, Cal., Nov. 12. — Well you actors and politicians can have all the race horses and cigars and perfume named after you, but I got some clippings from down in South Carolina that was mighty gratifying to me.

Will Rogers, an old pot hound, was voted the best hunting dog in the State, and he took another prize for the finest looking dog. So my regards to the champion of South Carolina.

There ain't nothing better than to ride up on a little hill at night and stop and hear 'em running. You don't need to see 'em, you know who is ahead, who's running second and third, and just how close they are to old man fox.

        Yours,
        Will Rogers.

2581   MR. ROGERS OFFERS A BIT
        OF ADVICE TO HUEY LONG

BEVERLY HILLS, Cal., Nov. 13. — Well, let's see what we got in today's papers that will hold up till tomorrow.

Huey Long (Huey will stand up) is trying to make Senators out of football players. He better be trying to make something out of Senators. I don't blame that boy for not wanting to be demoted.

Awful lot of predictions in the papers every day as to what is the outlook for political success in 1936. The ins, and the outs, too, better concentrate on what's going to happen next month or next week. No country in the world was ever further away from 1936 than we are.

        Yours,
        Will Rogers.

2582   WILL ROGERS ACCLAIMS
        PAUL REVERES DE LUXE

BEVERLY HILLS, Cal., Nov. 14. — Well we was just feeling fine and we thought we had listened to our last campaign speech out here for two more years, when who come in here on a barnstorming tour but John J. Raskob, Irénée du Pont and Edward F. Hutton. Three hundred million dollars worth of talent.

They got a plan called (no not Epic) theirs is called Liberty League. They feel that under the New Deal that the United States Constitution is the forgotten man.

So they are doing a modern Paul Revere and are going down the valleys in three private railway cars arousing the people.

"Block that kick! Block that kick! The Democrats are kicking our Constitution around."

They are all three mighty fine, estimable men and if they happen to play your town get all the big wigs out. They are darn nice fellows and got the best show on the road this season.

        Yours,
        Will Rogers.

2583   MR. ROGERS, IT APPEARS,
         IS LOOKING FOR AN OUT

BEVERLY HILLS, Cal., Nov. 15. — This is rather a personal affair but I feel that there is enough besides me interested in it that we would like to have an answer publicly.

Does this Huey Long debt cancellation apply to a man that moves in from another State? If it does the Sinclair movement into California will be made to look like a lone hitch-hiker compared to the pilgrimage going into the old State of Louisiana.

Don't let the Bank of America of Beverly Hills know anything about this, but I am thoroughly interested. Wire collect, Huey (and that means that I am desperate).

Yours,
Will Rogers.

2584   MR. ROGERS HAS PROPOSAL
         FOR THE ROSE BOWL SHOW

BEVERLY HILLS, Cal., Nov. 16. — Huey Long hung one on me. He stopped me. He asked me for a thousand dollars for his legal opinion. He could have stopped me for fifty just as easy. But I am sending him my note for a thousand for, according to his own law of Longiana, he can't collect it anyhow.

Minnesota, from what we can all hear, is the best team east of any mountains, and if professional jealousy among their own conference don't stop 'em, they should be in the Rose Bowl New Year's. But if they don't, I am pulling for Huey's kindergarten. Stanford will play 'em, and we will have Sinclair debate Huey between halves and Sister Aimee and myself will referee the debate.

Yours,
Will Rogers.

2585   WILL ROGERS GETS A KICK
         OUT OF A LIVESTOCK SHOW

SANTA MONICA, Cal., Nov. 18. — With all the "haywire" ideas we have, ever once in awhile we hit on a good one like old age pensions (which is sure to come at the next Congress).

Well I was down to the Los Angeles livestock show and I saw these hundreds of farmer boys that had fattened and cared for a calf, or pig, or sheep themselves. It's a thing called the 4-H Club. Somebody was inspired when they founded that. It's all over the country.

By golly they are a great bunch of kids, and don't they have some fine stock. Look how young and he is starting in his business.

We got the most thorough training in every line of business in this country but statesmanship and that you just decide overnight yourself, "I am a statesman."

Yours,
Will Rogers.

2586   Mr. Rogers Is Impressed
          By The President's Talk

BEVERLY HILLS, Cal., Nov. 19. — The President made one of his best speeches in Tupelo, Miss., Sunday. He told that the people could make their own electric energy cheaper than they were getting it. And say, by Monday morning he had the companies talking "new rates."

They all say the government can't do anything toward running any business, but they break their necks to see that it don't try.

They never will find out who that Vanderbilt child belongs to till both sides go plum broke.

Yours,
Will Rogers.

2587   Mr. Rogers Gets Behind
          A New Pageant Idea

BEVERLY HILLS, Cal., Nov. 20. — Well sir, here is something I would like to see all your cities and towns do.

The L. A. Bar Association put on a pageant called "The Making of the Constitution." (They say it was originated in Kansas City). Well it's a great thing. It shows Benjamin Franklin, Washington, Madison, Hamilton, and all those old "rope wigs" fighting during the making of our Constitution. Young as well as the old will profit by it, and really enjoy it.

Write and get your information from the L. A. Bar Association. You can put it on for some good charity, or free admission.

I am not press agent for any bar association. I just saw it and thought it was great, and it's a great thing to do at this time. It's not expensive to put on, just the renting of the costumes is all.

Do this, and you will thank me some day.

Yours,
Will Rogers.

2588 Mr. Rogers Is All Ready
    To Bat For Gen. Butler

  BEVERLY HILLS, Cal., Nov. 21. — If Smedley Butler don't take that job of marching down Pennsylvania at the head of Wall Street's fighting brigade, I would like to get my application in. I got the gray horse. It won't be such a novelty as people think. It's not the first time that Wall Street has had the country.

  Well, sir, you can find dead folks in automobiles and in brush piles here at home and the news don't last but a day, but find 'em off on an island somewhere and they get about a week's run in the papers.

         Yours,
         Will Rogers.

2589 Mr. Rogers Pays Tribute
    To A Noted Horseman

  BEVERLY HILLS, Cal., Nov. 22. — "Mexico, Mo. — Tom Bass, well-known Negro horseman, aged 75, died here today."

  Don't mean much to you, does it? You have all seen society folks perform on a beautiful three or five gaited saddle horse, and said, "My, what skill and patience they must have had to train that animal."

  Well, all they did was ride him in. All this Negro, Tom Bass, did was to train him. For over fifty years America's premier trainer. He trained thousands that others were applauded on. A remarkable man, a remarkable character.

  Many Negroes have been great horsemen. Every big ranch has its traditional stories of what its famous Negro rider used to do. Negro Add of the L. F. D. ranch was perhaps the most famous.

  If old St. Peter is as wise as we give him credit for being, Tom, he will let you go in horseback and give those folks up there a great show, and you get the blue ribbon yourself.

         Yours,
         Will Rogers.

2590 Will Rogers Finds Reason
    At Last For Another War

  BEVERLY HILLS, Cal., Nov. 23. — It's been hard for nations to start another war because they didn't have any particular reason or alignment. But now it looks like the next war will be between the nations that were invited to the big English wedding and those that were not.

The funny part about it is, the whole mess of 'em are all kin folks, and nobody can fall out and get as sore at each other as kin folks. That Queen Marie strain seems to have run a more direct line and stayed in the ermine than any strain in Europe.

Well, the whole thing makes good reading and that's about all society things are for.

Yours,
Will Rogers.

2591 MR. ROGERS TIRES OF NEWS
OF APPEALS TO PRESIDENT

BEVERLY HILLS, Cal., Nov. 25. — Just sitting here reading in all parts of the papers where "so-and-so appealed to the President."

Is there nothing that anybody in our country can do themselves any more? If a strike is on, if strike is even threatened, away goes the "appeal to the President." The American Chamber of Commerce sends about three appeals a week, "Can you guarantee our members so and so?"

We have a hard time finding good stories in the movies. I suppose we ought to "appeal to the President." And the movie companies ought to appeal to him for a guarantee as to what conditions will be by the time the picture is out.

If you must appeal to somebody, appeal to the Supreme Court. That's all they are paid for.

Yours,
Will Rogers.

2592 MR. ROGERS FEELS SORRY
STILL FOR HIS G. O. P. PALS

BEVERLY HILLS, Cal., Nov. 26. — Well sir guess who showed up out here yesterday. It wasn't a soul but my good old friend Pat Hurley, Secretary of War. He seemed awful pleased that I remembered him.

You know there is one thing about these Republicans, if you are just the least bit nice to 'em, or show 'em the least little courtesy, why they are awful appreciative. They know they didn't do right, but they are repentive now, and I just haven't got the heart to speak to 'em.

Pat told me what their big mistake was in the last campaigns.

"Will, we went on the theory, that Barnum was wrong, and that one wasn't born every minute. But now we see our mistake."

Yours,
Will Rogers.

2593   Mr. Rogers Recalls 'Gag' That Wasn't Far Wrong

SANTA MONICA, Cal., Nov. 27. — I wrote a little "gag" the other day about "appealing to the President for a guarantee," and I bet a lot of you thought it was just to be writing.

Well, get this headlines in the papers today. C. L. Bardo, president of the National Association of Manufacturers, asks the President the following:

"Business must have more definite ideas as to the direction in which the government is headed."

I can just see Mr. Roosevelt rushing in with a guarantee reading about as follows: "Nobody guaranteed me anything when I took over this job, no man gambles more than a President of the U. S., so you will pardon me if I am not able to guarantee business that it won't lose."

Yours,
Will Rogers.

2594   Mr. Rogers Thinks People Are Less Thankful Now

BEVERLY HILLS, Cal., Nov. 28. — Thanksgiving Day.

In the days of its founders they were willing to give thanks for mighty little (for mighty little was all they expected). But now neither government or nature can give enough but what we think it's too little.

Those old boys in the Fall of the year, if they could gather in a few pumpkins, potatoes and some corn for the winter, they was in a thanking mood.

But if we can't gather in a new Buick, a new radio, a tuxedo and some government relief, why we feel like the world is agin us.

Yours,
Will Rogers.

2595   MR. ROGERS SCANS THE LIST
          OF THOSE AT THE WEDDING

SANTA MONICA, Cal., Nov. 29. — Reading the list of guests at big wedding in London, Grand Duke Dimitri of Russia, Grand Duchess Xenia of Russia, Grand Duke Vladimir of Russia. Moscow will get a kick out of that.

There was a big bunch of German ex-nobility. It was really a pre-war gathering.

It was a very gracious thing of King George of England to dig up all these old "has beens" and let 'em live over again past glories, even if it was just for a day.

Not a Stalin, a Hitler, or a Mussolini to mar the proceedings.
             Yours,
                  Will Rogers.

2596   ROGERS SEES INFLATION
          AS STILL A LIVELY TOPIC

BEVERLY HILLS, Cal., Nov. 30. — When you don't know what to write, or talk about, you can always resort to two subjects, weddings and inflation. I once heard Lady Astor say "only two things get the House of Lords excited, a tax on liquor and a tax on landed estates, then the old Lords really come to life."

Well, about the only time you can get our "big houses of finance" interested is to start talking about cutting that dollar up into little ones. The big fellows say, "Mr. Roosevelt, we think you mean well, but your ideas are wrong and we are not going to play with you."

He can say, "I am sorry, gentlemen. Love to have you with me. In fact, I think you are still playing with me. It's a game called heavy, heavy, hangs over your head, and it's not an axe. It's just a printing press which stops all government interest, don't slam the door as you go out."
             Yours,
                  Will Rogers.

2597   MR. ROGERS SEES A BIG JOB
          FOR 'COACH' ROOSEVELT

SANTA MONICA, Cal., Dec. 2. — With football about ending, we have no major sport going now till January 3 when Congress holds its opening game.

There'll be a lot of interest in Congress this season, for they are giving away more free tickets than ever before. Coach Roosevelt has been South for three weeks training with some of his star players. His problem is to make his team realize they haven't got it too easy, then to keep from getting dissention on the team. They all feel they are "all American" and each one will want to pack the ball every time.

Coaching prima donnas is no cinch.
Yours,
Will Rogers.

2598   MR. ROGERS TAKES UP NEWS
        OF IRELAND AND OKLAHOMA

BEVERLY HILLS, Cal., Dec. 3. — Ireland rioted in the movie theatres when they showed pictures of the wedding of the Duke and Marina. When that Ireland don't like anything, they don't even like the picture of it. Well, they missed seeing a mighty pretty couple.

Our own Wiley Post went up to break the altitude record. He drifted from Bartlesville, Okla., to Muskogee. Went square dab over Claremore. He was up ten miles, just high enough to clear the buildings.

In case any of you happen to be keeping statistics on it, Japan issued another ultimatum to the world today.
Yours,
Will Rogers.

2599   MR. ROGERS IN HIS RESUME
        GOES QUITE COLLEGIATE

BEVERLY HILLS, Cal., Dec. 4. — In a legal game, two California college students versus U. S. Supreme Court, U. S. Supreme Court wins. Score, court, 9; students, 0. College boys get awful smart nowadays, but that old Supreme Court has still got quite a bit on the ball.

Speaking of colleges, I feel real sorry for Huey Long. I believe his team was as good as Tulane (if not better), but they **didn't** kick goal after touchdown.

The first bill to be passed by the next sovereign State of Louisiana's Legislature will read as follows: "In accordance with, and in defense of State rights, any football kicked through goal after touchdown is null and void, unless done so by University of Louisiana."

It's the one bill that he overlooked last fall, so he has nobody to blame but himself for not being in the Sugar Bowl New Year's Day.
Yours,
Will Rogers.

2600   WILL ROGERS DISCUSSES
        THE TRANSPACIFIC FLIGHTS

BEVERLY HILLS, Cal., Dec. 5. — Having lunch in the studio cafe Tuesday with Sir Kingsford-Smith, the great Australian aviator. He was called to the phone. He come back and said, "They have missed the Hawaiian Islands and are down. That's too bad."

Then he told how important navigation was, especially over the ocean. He paid great tribute to the American that took him to Australia and the Australian that brought him over this time.

Gatty is a great navigator; Lindbergh and Post are a couple of the best pilot-navigators.

Thousands can fly, but few can find a speck in the ocean. You got to be on intimate terms with astronomy. Never mind the carburetors or the feed line or the R. P. M. It's old man sun, moon and stars that you want to be on speaking terms with.
Yours,
Will Rogers.

2601   MR. ROGERS IS PESSIMISTIC
        ON THE MUNITIONS INQUIRY

BEVERLY HILLS, Cal., Dec. 6. — The investigation season opened earlier than usual this season.

The Ammunition Investigating Committee had an awful exciting session yesterday. That committee has got a job for life. The ammunition concerns sell it faster than the committee can investigate it.

No nation will buy anything to eat or anything to wear from you, but if you got a gun they will buy it and more than likely shoot it back at you.

Looks to me like if every nation made their own ammunition it would relieve their unemployment.

Well, there ain't no use arguing about it. Nothing is going to be stopped anywhere that there is any money in.

Yours,
Will Rogers.

2602   WILL ROGERS SEES DANGER
IN THE NEWS FROM EUROPE

BEVERLY HILLS, Cal., Dec. 7. — Certainly news in the papers today.

"Russian firing squad executes 200."

"Thousands of Hungarians driven from Yugoslavia."

"Norman H. Davis gives warning to Japan that ship ratio will not be changed."

Now there is three separate events, each enough to start its own war, but time will tell which one of the three proved the most costly. Two of these are dealing with their own internal affairs, and I just sorter hate to see us dictate beyond our own borders.

Yours,
Will Rogers.

2603   MR. ROGERS TAKES NOTICE
OF NOTRE DAME'S UPSWING

SANTA MONICA, Cal., Dec. 9. — Notre Dame popped in here and started heaving 55-yard passes and 60-yard kicks. Wait till the Irish Free State hear they have a guy named Shakespeare playing with those Irish.

Notre Dame lost their great coach and their great president, but Father O'Hara and Elmer Layden are worthy successors. One more year and they will be right at the top again. A great school and a great spirit.

The war news today mostly concerns Italy and France. That's one thing about European arguments. The trouble is never between the two nations most concerned. It's always among those who want to make it their business.

                              Yours,
                              Will Rogers.

2604   Mr. Rogers Tries To Advise
           One Of Our Big Bankers

HOLLYWOOD, Cal., Dec. 10. — One of New York's very very leading bankers was visiting our studio (and incidentally his studio) and he accused me of being an inflationist.

I told him I wasn't an inflationist, that to be honest with him I didn't know anything about it, but that the thing that I felt was that if industrialists and business men didn't start investing and helping the President, and not keep hollering for a guarantee of the value of their money, they would force the President to do the very thing that they kept hollering and asking him not to do.

This fellow had an economist with him. Pretty near everybody's got one, either that or a police dog, and the more wealthy have got both.

                              Yours,
                              Will Rogers.

2605   Will Rogers Remarks

BEVERLY HILLS, Cal., Dec. 11. — The biggest news in the papers today was furnished by the Japanese Ambassador. It was pretty strong medicine. He just said that if England and America made Japan mad enough they would go and take all of North China; in other words, if Max Baer the world's champion does anything to me, I am going to jump onto little Shirley Temple and give her a good spanking.

Well, if America is just even half smart diplomatically, they will laugh the whole thing off and stall things along till Russia is ready, and just say "Sic em Tige, he is your meat."

                              Yours,
                              Will Rogers.

2606   Mr. Rogers Pays Tribute To A Great Old Cowman

HOLLYWOOD, Cal., Dec. 12. — A fine old friend and one of the last of the great cowmen died in Fort Forth, Texas, W. T. Waggoner.

One of two biggest ranches in the United States. It had oil all over it, and it made him sore every time they found a new well, for he said it was always on the best grass land and just spoiled it for that many cattle. He would rather lose a dollar on a cow than make a thousand on an oil well. He loved good horses and had the best in Texas.

There will never be any class of people in our country that can replace the old western cowman for common sense, shrewdness, humor and fine citizenship.

The Three D lost a real boss.

Yours,
Will Rogers.

2607   Mr. Rogers Is Convinced Conferences Are Futile

HOLLYWOOD, Cal., Dec. 13. — Another disarmament conference wending its way home labeled "no fish."

In London in 1930 we had 100 writers and fifty on the delegation from here. We are getting a little wiser. Roosevelt hired a fellow named Davis (Norman Davis) and he just pays him so much a conference and gives him the contract to attend all there is.

They all go home sore at each other now, that's one thing that conferences always succeed at, each nation finding out just how "ornery" the others are.

I bet you that history don't record any two nations ever having war with each other unless they had had a conference first.

Yours,
Will Rogers.

2608   Mr. Rogers Sees Aviation Changing Map Of World

HOLLYWOOD, Cal., Dec. 14. — Monday is aviation day. Thirty-one years ago Monday the Wrights made their famous flight at Kitty Hawk. It was a box kite put together with barrel staves and putty. He sat on a stool out in front of the thing, hoping that it wouldn't get excited and run over him. He didn't get very high, but he started something that will change many a map in this world.

Aviation is sorter like the old .45 pistols, which made little men as dangerous as big men. It's a sort of equalizer. You could give little Switzerland enough airplanes and she would worry the old Ned out of the big ones. There is no end to how many we ought to have. Buy about fifty thousand.

And take the profits out of war, and you won't have any war.

Yours,
Will Rogers.

2609   WILL ROGERS RUNS ACROSS
          AN HONEST DIVORCE PLEA

SANTA MONICA, Cal., Dec. 16. — One of the most honest divorce reasons I ever heard was given the other day by some fellow, "She suits me fine, but I just can't afford her."

I guess Florida is destroyed by the cold beyond any hope of ever coming back, from what I read in the papers out here.

I see where somebody has started a movement to "unrecognize" Russia. We didn't sell 'em as much as we thought we would. I imagine their recognizing us hasn't turned out so hot for them either.

Yours,
Will Rogers.

2610   WILL ROGERS DISCUSSES
          THE 'PLAN TO END PLANS'

BEVERLY HILLS, Cal., Dec. 7. — The other night over the radio for the Salvation Army, I was blathering away about a short piece I had read in the paper that very night telling of a plan to give everybody work.

Well, friends been kidding me since then, "Will, where is your plan you was telling about?"

Well today it broke out. It was gotten up by the National Resources board. It plans to spend 105,000,000,000 (now all those naughts belong on there, that 105 is billions) and it's called a "plan to end all planning."

That will knock these old rich boys in the creek that have been hollering about a debt of a mere 28 billion.

That is a plan to do away with all small figures.

Yours,
Will Rogers.

2611   MR. ROGERS FINDS SAVIORS
         OF THE NATION SLOWING UP

BEVERLY HILLS, Cal., Dec. 18. — Read all the papers through today and I can't find a new plan to save the country. Kind of slack season before Xmas, I guess. The boys ain't thinking as pert as they usually are.

That Yogoslavia, they just seem to want to fight anyhow. Be a good joke on them if nobody prevented 'em.

We had heard of all kinds of likely wars between nations, but this one that Mussolini dug up is a new one. Italy versus Ethiopia. That's going a long way for an enemy.

Yours,
Will Rogers.

2612   MR. ROGERS IS OUT ALREADY
         WITH FIRST '35 FORECAST

BEVERLY HILLS, Cal., Dec. 19. — It seems by today's papers that Dillinger's escape gun wasn't exactly all wood. It was loaded with $11,000.

The city of Los Angeles was doing away with some mules to use motors. They auctioned 'em off. They brought big prices. Now let 'em drive one of the motor cars around the corner and back and see what they can sell it for.

The old span of mules won't get you to town as often as the car, but they will get you there as often as you ought to go and you can drive them back empty.

Everybody is predicting something for '35. I predict it will be a great mule year.

Yours,
Will Rogers.

2613   MR. ROGERS LOOKS FORWARD
         TO THE BATTLE OF JAN. 3

BEVERLY HILLS, Cal., Dec. 20. — See where the doctors say "President Roosevelt is in great physical shape and ready to face Congress on Jan. 3."

Well, that being the case from one training camp, I would like to report from the other training camp, I have examined Congress and they are in great shape physically. (I said physically.) Mentally the boys are befuddled, but they are in the "pink." (That's what the fellows with the dough are afraid of there is too many of 'em in the "pink.")

Remember the date and tune in on the biggest show on earth, bar none.

Yours,
Will Rogers.

2614   ROGERS SEES MANY PLANS
        BUT HOPE FOR ONLY ONE

BEVERLY HILLS, Cal., Dec. 21. — You know I told you Wednesday that it seemed kinder like an off day, nobody had turned in a plan. Well they made up for it Thursday; 90 leading industrialists met at Sulphur Springs and drafted a new plan of recovery. One thing about these recovery plans, the same man can draw one up every week and no two of 'em will be alike.

Trouble with these plans is, the plan is generally to assist the planner's own business. Anyhow there is no use to get excited about any of 'em, for the one that Mr. Roosevelt uses will be the one that he dropped in the hat himself.

Yours,
Will Rogers.

2615   MR. ROGERS FINDS THE WARS
        AT HOME AND AFAR ALIKE

BEVERLY HILLS, Cal., Dec. 23. — For international wars this lovely Sunday morning we have Russia and Japan. For civil war we have Donald Richberg versus Hugh Johnson.

Both wars are rather similar in that there is really a third party mixed up in 'em. Russia's and Japan's argument is over Manchuria and Richberg's and Johnson's is over what The Saturday Evening Post can say.

Richberg says if Johnson tells the truth about him he has to prove it and Johnson says that he can lie about him and still prove it.

There ain't nothing that breaks up homes, country and nations like somebody publishing their memoirs.

Yours,
Will Rogers.

2616   WILL ROGERS REMARKS

BEVERLY HILLS, Cal., Dec. 24. — If rumor is any good at all it looks like England will have their best Christmas present in years. Between Ireland annoying the life out of 'em (I think more for pure devilment than anything else,) and the Prince not marrying, and Lloyd George's memoirs, they have had a pretty uneasy life. I imagine he has met a lot of girls that looked good enough to 'em, but in the language of royal ritual, they were "mongrels." When you have to take one that is sired in the purple, it kinder cuts your field of operation down, but this Swedish Princess looks mighty lovely, and they are a great people, all those Scandinavians. So we will all cheer with England.

                                       Yours,
                                         Will Rogers.

2617   MR. ROGERS REPORTS SIGNS
          OF PROSPERITY OUT WEST

PASADENA, Cal., Dec. 25. — Beautiful afternoon, marvelous race track, magnificent, stanch and sleepy old mountains in the background (sounds like Graham speaking). It is all of that, and some of the coyotes that I was persuaded to make a small wager on are as stanch and sleepy as the mountains.

Actors and actresses are thick here today, but they'd just as well be bankers as far as being noticed. Female screen stars are just some more women. Madam and Señor Horse is king. Hollywood just as well be Skiatook, Oklahoma. The currycomb has replaced the lip rouge. Even Garbo would have to ride Twenty Grand to get a look in.

It's the old oat-eaters' day. And the suckers. And it's proof positive that there is plenty of money to feed and clothe everybody.

It's only a rumor that everybody has been taxed to death.

                                         Yours,
                                         Will Rogers.

2618   MR. ROGERS OFFERS A FORM
          FOR A NEW YEAR FORECAST

SANTA MONICA, Cal., Dec. 26. — Well, Christmas is all over and they say there was more buying and more money spent than any time in four years.

Now comes New Year's and along with it comes New Year's predictions of our leading men. This year they will read as follows, all of 'em:

"I am an optimist, and always have been, but we must be assured of no inflation and a fair return on our investment. If the government will just lay off us everything will be fine."

Now watch New Year's and see how far this misses it.

Yours,
Will Rogers.

2619   Mr. Rogers Cites His Idea
Of A Nice, Steady Job

HOLLYWOOD, Cal., Dec. 27. — Talk about a steady job during these hard times, get this one.

President Roosevelt sent a letter yesterday to the Federal Trade Commission asking them for a report. They been investigating six years. He told 'em:

"I don't want to hurry you boys, but I thought maybe you had a few preliminary notes made that you could hand me. Of course I expect nothing thorough at this early date, just any little casual information that you might have picked up accidentally during your mere six years of holding the office."

They have just about been introduced to each other by now.

Yours,
Will Rogers.

2620   Will Rogers Would Plead
Guilty For Investigations

HOLLYWOOD, Cal., Dec. 28. — The only trouble about this suggesting that somebody or something ought to be investigated is that they are liable to suggest that you ought to be investigated. And from the record of all our previous investigations it just looks like nobody can emerge with their nose entirely clean.

I don't care who you are, you just can't reach middle life without having done and said a whole lot of foolish things.

If I saw an investigating committee headed my way, I would just plead guilty and throw myself on the mercy of the court.

Yours,
Will Rogers.

2621   MR. ROGERS SEES PROGRESS
IN THE WAR ON CRIME

HOLLYWOOD, Cal., Dec. 30. — Here is about the best crime prevention news I have seen:

"The California Bar Association is to rid its ranks of any attorney found to have connection with the underworld."

The first thing they do now if they are taking up crime as a profession (even before they buy the gun) is to engage their lawyer. He works on a percentage. He acts as their advance agent, too, he picks out the banks they are to rob. Bar associations invented the word "ethics," then forgot about it.

                                       Yours,
                                       Will Rogers.

2622   WILL ROGERS WAITS TO SEE
WHAT NEW YEAR WILL BRING

SANTA MONICA, Cal., Dec. 31. — Well, the old year will be passing out in a few hours, and I don't know personally of a thing that I can do about it. I guess there will be a lot of people will take it up with the government, as they look to them to do everything else.

I have received in pamphlet and small book forms several plans to prolong the old year. They all say if they can just get their plans adopted that it will do the work. Of course the question arises as to whether it has been a year that the brain trusters want to prolong. I have no doubt they have schemes to do it, so we will have to just wait till tomorrow to see if they have done it.

                                       Yours,
                                       Will Rogers.

DAILY TELEGRAMS — 1935

2623   Mr. Rogers Was Too Busy
                 Yesterday To Work Much

BEVERLY HILLS, Cal., Jan. 1. — Well, it looks like none of the schemes worked, and we are going right on ahead just letting the new year come.

I am on my way out to the football game. I imagine it will be in the papers anyhow about who won. I will be too busy blathering with the players after the game to do much reporting.

It's real Chamber of Commerce weather, and I look for those old Arkansaw boys (that are playing under the name of Alabama) and those Pennsylvania ones playing under the nom de plume of Stanford to put up a great game.

Anxious to hear about the team that Huey Long imported to beat Tulane.

Yours from the shady side of the bleachers,
Will Rogers.

2624   Mr. Rogers Has Some Tips
                 For Coaches Of Football

HOLLYWOOD, Cal., Jan. 2. — Just last Sunday I wrote an article about the pro football becoming so popular because they did something besides just run up into the line and butt their heads together all afternoon.

Audiences like clever passing and lots of scoring, not 0 to 0, or 6 to 7. Open up your rules and let a man pass from anywhere behind the line.

Well, Alabama must a been able to read for they just said it's easier to throw this thing over there than it is to carry it over and, as a consequence, 85,000 people went nutty.

So the quicker you coaches start imitating the pros the quicker you will start filling your stadiums again.

I don't blame Stanford for not getting in the way of those passes. Why, those things would kill you if they hit you.

Yours,
Will Rogers.

2625   Mr. Rogers Defines Again
The Roosevelt New Deal

HOLLYWOOD, Cal., Jan. 3. — You hear people say, "what is this new deal, anyhow?"
Well, there was a headline today that explains it.
"Wall Street Anxiously Awaits the President's Message."
Well, in the "old deal" it was the President that was anxiously waiting till Wall Street sent him the message to read.
If Arizona, Texas or Arkansas hear something whizzing over your heads, it won't be a plane. It's Dixie Howell passing some autographed footballs back to friends in Tuscaloosa.

Yours,
Will Rogers.

2626   Rogers Heard Republicans
Applauding The President

HOLLYWOOD, Cal., Jan. 4. — When I wasn't making faces at a movie camera this morning I was hustling out to hear the President's message in the car on the radio. I don't blame him for bringing his message up in person, it would have been a shame to have to turn that over to some reading clerk. They read good, but they're not like that baby.
It wouldn't ever do any good to try to impeach Roosevelt. All he would have to do would be to go on the radio and the whole thing would die out.
When he hit those "holding companies" he must have hit a popular note for I could hear even a few scattering Republican hands. He dug up three new initials for a new unemployment work program.
"Big business" had its ear to the ground, but all they got in it was dust.

Yours,
Will Rogers.

2627   Mr. Rogers Notes A Lull
On The News Fronts

BEVERLY HILLS, Cal., Jan. 6. — Well, there is not much news today. It's what might be called a watchful waiting Sunday.
Congress met last week, but they really didn't have time to do any damage. But tomorrow the taxpayers will start suffering.

The Hauptmann case is at the waiting stage.

Japan ought to come through with another ultimatum by Monday or Tuesday.

The President is to send another message to Congress Monday. It's really not a message. It's a working schedule.

So that leaves us today to meditation and worship.

Yours,
Will Rogers.

2628   MR. ROGERS IS SURPRISED
         ANY ONE WANTS A KING

HOLLYWOOD, Cal., Jan. 7. — See where Mussolini and Foreign Minister Laval have decided to let Austria have a king.

You know I didn't know this till I was in Vienna last Fall, but Austria really wants a king. Can you imagine that?

The nearest we can come to understanding that is an American girl wanting a man for a title.

It's a musical city, cafes and a lot of bright-colored uniforms and a king and some waltzes is about all they want.

So France and Italy are going to give 'em Archduke Otto. You would wonder what they have to do with it. Well, that's Europe for you. Austria and Hungary's business is everybody's business. These Hapsburgs have gummed up about all of Europe.

Yours,
Will Rogers.

2629   MR. ROGERS HAS HIS THIRST
         FOR BIG NEWS ASSUAGED

SANTA MONICA, Cal., Jan. 8. — I told you there would be some news popping Monday. Well, it exceeded all expectations.

President Roosevelt made the biggest touch in history. "Brothers, can you spare eight and one-half billion?"

Betty Gow wins the decision over Hauptmann's lawyer. She broke him of getting sarcastic.

Hugh Johnson after deviling the life out of big business finally joined 'em.

Then, to top off the day, the Supreme Court went Republican and said: "There is nothing you can do about the oil business by law."

So it was a great day.

Yours,
Will Rogers.

2630   Mr. Rogers Is Cheerful
             In Face Of Rising Debt

BEVERLY HILLS, Cal., Jan. 9. — Last week it was "How did you like the President's message?" This week it's "How did you like his figures?"

I never thought we would live to see a Democrat that would put down that many figures and get 'em right. Well, it goes for relief, and there is nobody can legitimately kick on that.

By the end of next year, '36, our per capita debt will be $270 each. (Course, if you think that's too high, you gota perfect right to die and beat it.)

Well, England, the country we point out as being the most prosperous at this time, theirs is exactly double that. Why, we are just amateurs at being taxed.

                              Yours,
                              Will Rogers.

2631   Mr. Rogers Makes A Bow
             To The Auto Industry

SANTA MONICA, Cal., Jan. 10. — Dispatch in paper today, "Ford employs ten thousand more men, highest since the peak of '29." And the auto show here and in New York was booming.

Now, how does it come that the auto industry don't just sit still and holler, "We could recover if the government would just lay off us a while."

No industry is restricted and taxed more than autos, so the government certainly ain't "laying off them."

Say, I see where the Supreme Court is about to put the gold back in the dollar. I didn't know it had been out of there till I went to Europe. (Where I didn't have any business anyhow.)

Anyhow, we are living during an exciting week.

                              Yours,
                              Will Rogers.

2632   Rogers Sees Revolution
             In Prize-Fighting Game

BEVERLY HILLS, Cal., Jan. 11. — You talk about the Supreme Court not signing the "New Deal's" mortgages. That ain't nothing. If you want to see an industry that's been absolutely ruined,

Will Rogers as "Jim Hackler" in the motion picture adapted from George Ade's play The County Chairman *(Fox Film Corporation, 1935).*

it's the prize fight racket. Why, this champion Max Baer has thrown a skunk right in their living room. Why, just think of a champion that wants to do nothing but fight and don't want to wait a couple of years for one big purse? Such a thing is, unheard of. Why, he even wanted to fight two men in one night. Why, the promoters like to dropped dead.

So it looks like Maxie has just revolutionized the prize fight game by introducing fighting.

Yours,
Will Rogers.

2633   MR. ROGERS EXPECTS NEWS
FROM CONGRESS PRESENTLY

BEVERLY HILLS, Cal., Jan. 13. — Congress ought to really get into the main show next week. This past week was just the overture. They will get settled down this coming week to "steady taxing."

All the "lobbies" are gathered in there to see that the tax is put on somebody else's business, but not on theirs.

Congress got all their committees made up last week and they are composed of two Democrats to each one Republican, so what a pleasant year that poor fellow will be in for.

Course, there is an awful lot of different breeds of Democrats. I bet you before the session is over President Roosevelt will trade you two or three Democrats for one Republican.

Yours,
Will Rogers.

2634   MR. ROGERS CALLS FOR VOTE
ON WHAT TO DO WITH U. S.

SANTA MONICA, Cal., Jan. 14. — It would be interesting if they would allow every country to do like they did yesterday with this Saar — vote on whether they wanted to go back with who they come from or go with somebody else, or go with the League of Nations, or go it alone? Australia, India, Canada, Philippines, Manchuria and Louisiana.

In fact, I make this in the nature of a motion. I think you would see a lot of changes. In fact, I think you would see our own country given back to the Indians.

Yours,
Will Rogers.

2635   MR. ROGERS FINDS SECRET
         OF NOTRE DAME SUCCESS

NOTRE DAME, Ind., Jan. 15. — Well, here we are in the famous Notre Dame. You know why these kids can play football? No cars, no roadsters here. When you're driving to town in all these other colleges, here you are either studying or catching forward passes. There is a great spirit that makes this such an institution.

Say, I am so tickled about Jimmy Doolittle cracking the passenger plane record. You know, there is more flyers (real flyers) that will tell you that Jimmy is the greatest all-around flyer there is. Wiley Post told me so last week.

Wiley is getting ready to come across pretty soon, at 35,000 feet, using an oxygen suit. He will make it in about seven hours.

                          Yours,
                              Will Rogers.

2636   MR. ROGERS GETS A SHOCK
         ON REACHING WASHINGTON

WASHINGTON, D. C., Jan. 16. — Say, I flew in here away in the middle of last night with a female co-pilot. She is the only one in existence on a regular organized line, from Cleveland to Washington, and she was O. K.

Well, I get in here and what do you think I find this Senate arguing over? The World Court!

Now, I don't want to split the party, but the World Court is the deadest thing in this country outside of prohibition.

It's all right to fix the world, but you better get your own smokehouse full of meat first.

                          Yours,
                              Will Rogers.

2637   MR. ROGERS FINDS SENATE
         GROPING IN DARK AGAIN

PHILADELPHIA, Pa., Jan. 17. — Well, I just this minute come out of Washington.

The Senate opened at twelve o'clock. Huey grabbed 'em by the ears at 12:05 and shook 'em till four o'clock. Well, when he turned 'em loose they was ready to go home and behave themselves. They was talking on the World Court.

I don't know what the World Court has got to do with pulling us through the rest of this Winter. It's the Supreme Court we are interested in right now, not the World Court.

But, that is just about like the Senate to make that mistake in the names and be arguing over the wrong court.

Philadelphia is booming.

Yours,
Will Rogers.

2638 WILL ROGERS FINDS INDIANA
IS COMING THROUGH 'GREAT'

INDIANAPOLIS, Ind., Jan. 18. — It had been bad flying weather and I had to be in Indianapolis for a hospital benefit tonight. It seemed like good old times to be back on a train, fine train, fine service! The railroads are recovering. Then an accident at one of those grade crossings which really seemed to be the fault of no one.

In giving people work, that eliminating of grade crossings looks like it would be a great thing, for the worker and for the lives saved.

Old Indiana, the home of politics, is coming through great. They are getting by without any new taxation. Any news from the Supreme Court?

Yours,
Will Rogers.

2639 MR. ROGERS ARRIVES HERE
WITH NEWS OF CAPITAL

NEW YORK, N. Y., Jan. 20. — Left Washington this afternoon.

There is two Texans down there that have certainly made good. One is Jack Garner, who is Vice President and don't care whether you know it or not. After over thirty years of sound common sense he knows more about the running of this government than any man outside of President Roosevelt. Ask any old time Congressman or Senator what they think of Garner.

And this fellow Jesse Jones, head of the Reconstruction Finance. I like to hear the big bankers cuss him, for he can loan more money and collect more of it back than they can.

You don't leave all your assets behind when you go to Jones. You leave all your assets with Jones. Outside the income tax (brother, they are efficient), the R. F. C. is the most business-like run thing in Washington.

Yours,
Will Rogers.

2640   MR. ROGERS QUITS THE CITY;
IT'S TOO FAST FOR HIM

LANCASTER, Pa., Jan. 21. — Headed west. New York is too fast for me.

The evening press relates that the Supreme Court give in a decision on Mooney, not on the gold clause. Well, they forget Mooney has been in for about twenty years and the gold has only been out for one year.

So don't get impatient. You can't go rushing those fine old gentlemen. They are liable to turn you in a decision any year.

Whatever the decision is, it will break these Democrats from sucking eggs without first finding out the condition of the egg.

Yours,
Will Rogers.

2641   MR. ROGERS IS IN A LAND
THAT IS RICH IN ROMANCE

AUSTIN, Texas, Jan. 22. — It looked early this morning in Cincinnati in all that snow like I wasn't going to be able to make a worthy benefit here tonight, but the American Airways was all ready to make it, weather or no weather, and we took off. But it cleared up by St. Louis and we had a fine trip in here.

This is historic old Austin, the capital. When you want to read of excitement read the history of Texas. It's just mangy with romance. Here is Jack Garner's first stepping-stone, and, by the way, did you notice that President Roosevelt endorsed him Monday morning, the same morning I had a little oration on him.

When you are thinking with Roosevelt you are thinking in pretty fast company.

Yours,
Will Rogers.

2642   Mr. Rogers Raves A Bit
         Over Wonders Of Texas

CLARENDON, Texas, Jan. 23. — Texas is having a big centennial next year and while you are sorter planning your vacation ahead, you want to come to our biggest State.

You ought to read a list of what this State produces, and her modern and up-to-date cities, and size and distances.

Plenty of ranches here as big as Germany or France. Horse pastures as big as England. Your Belgiums and Switzerlands would get lost in some farmer's cotton patch in Texas. And oil? They are the only State that can serve you oil hot or cold.

Sam Houston, the most colorful man in all American history, made this his arena.

Yes, sir, brother, this is a State.

Yours,
Will Rogers.

2643   Mr. Rogers Finds The West
         Uninterested In Europe

ALBUQUERQUE, N. M., Jan. 24. — Well, all I know is just what I read in the Amarillo, Texas, Daily News.

Cattlemen are feeling better than in years. No rain, but the Senate will get to that as soon as they get us all set in the World Court. That will just about be the breaking of this depression. Yes, sir.

Wish they could get out and talk to the people. Think they would learn something rather surprising about how little interested they are in Europe. If it was put to a vote of the people, you would think that it was some Republican running for something.

Yours,
Will Rogers.

2644   Will Rogers Glad Congress
         Won't Spend That Money

PASADENA, Cal., Jan. 25. — Glad Congress give Mr. Roosevelt permission to spend that four billion, eight hundred million himself. Just imagine if they had decided they would spend it themselves.

That would be an awful lot of money if you was paying it, but when you are just borrowing it, it ain't so much.

Everybody in Washington seems to be apologizing to each other. In Washington they just generally figure that one hatred offsets the other and they are both even.

Yours,
Will Rogers.

2645   MR. ROGERS HAILS FETES
ON PRESIDENT'S BIRTHDAY

SANTA MONICA, Cal., Jan. 27. — Only a couple of days now till the President's birthday.

This year some one has conceived a fine idea to keep the fine cause going and also allow every community to be able to do something for its very own in the home town. Seventy per cent of all funds raised stays right among the ones that raised it.

There is so much gayety, so much dancing and fun going on that it's a fine tribute to try and raise all they can to help this marvelous case. Any illness is terrible, but there is something about this particular affliction that makes you just a little more sympathetic.

To do all in his power to help the victims of infantile paralysis is one Roosevelt policy where there can't possibly be a dissenting vote.

Yours,
Will Rogers.

2646   MR. ROGERS A-WING AGAIN
AND VISITS BATTLEFIELD

BATON ROUGE, La., Jan. 28. — Say, have you slept in one of these aeroplane sleepers? Left Los Angeles last night at 7:30 for Fort Worth (Texas), Phoenix, El Paso, Tucson. Why, they just land and get gas and you sleep right through it.

Passing over here this afternoon headed for New York and Washington, and I just couldn't pass up this beautiful and historic old capitol city. Mussolini has his Rome, Stalin his Moscow, but Huey has his Baton Rouge, and it's the prettiest of all. I landed on the very air field where the famous tear-gas war was fought last week.

Huey has a beautiful new capitol building here that is just six inches lower than Al Smith's Empire Building.

The National Guard have the town "well in hand."

Yours,
Will Rogers.

2647   MR. ROGERS IS IN THE THICK
        OF THE LOUISIANA HUBBUB

NEW ORLEANS, La., Jan. 29. — Well, sir, I had a unique experience today. I was literally run out of a town through too much kindness. I just had to leave Baton Rouge. These Louisiana people are the most friendly and hospitable you ever saw.

Of course, there is two sides down here (but that has nothing to do with their hospitality). There is what I would call the "Longs" and the "Shorts" (There is no mediums). Now they are trying to make "Shorts" out of the "Longs" and Huey is trying to make "Longs" out of not only the State "Shorts" but all the United States "Shorts."

I visited their Capitol today, the finest in the world outside Finland. They have buttons on the desks and they vote by electricity. It's a marvelous way to vote, but Huey runs the switchboard, so it don't matter much which button the boys press, all the answers come out yes.

But they are great folks.

Yours,
Will Rogers.

2648   MR. ROGERS IS HERE AGAIN
        WITH NEWS OF THE SENATE

NEW YORK, N. Y., Jan. 30. — New Orleans got the finest airport I ever saw. Built on made land from the lake. Just what Chicago or any water town could do.

Flew in a little two-cylinder plane from Baton Rouge to New Orleans. Top speed of seventy. Flew up to Washington last night.

I had no idea in the world but what the World Court would pass. Lots of Senators feel better about it. They was voting through promise and not by conviction for it. Senator Joe Robinson made an outstanding fight for it and he didn't have much whole-hearted help, either.

Well, today they were all settled down to see if they couldn't do something for America.

Yours,
Will Rogers.

2649   Mr. Rogers Takes A Look
         At The City's Streets

NEW YORK, N. Y., Jan. 31. — Now, listen, this Mayor La Guardia is a good friend of mine but he has just moved his snow from one side of the street to the other. He didn't seem to want to take it far from its old home.

Headline in the financial page says, "This week's clearings rise to five billion, one hundred million."

So the Roosevelt Administration people are not the only ones that are talking in billions.

We had been led to believe that there was no "billions" only in a government "deficit," but there is just as much money as there ever was. Nobody eat any during the depression. It's just planted deeper in the rat hole, that's all.

Yours,
Will Rogers.

2650   Rogers Learns Why Work
         Is Better Than The 'Dole'

NEW YORK, N. Y., Feb. 1. — Say, my friend the Mayor wasn't to blame about the snow. He couldn't get the labor. They were all on relief.

Now moving snow in New York City used to be the one big job that they laid for. But no more. Now that's what's going to turn some of the sympathy of relief away. When the impression gets around that people are being fed who won't work, you will have an about face on this relief situation.

Nobody can kick on honest deserving relief, and nobody can be blamed for kicking on relieving somebody when they won't work. The governments and towns have got to find some way of telling them apart. Maybe fingerprinting would do it, or one of those "lie detectors."

Anyhow all this shows where public works beats the straight "dole."

Yours,
Will Rogers.

271

2651   MR. ROGERS SEES NO REASON
        TO FEAR RED MENACE NOW

NEW YORK, N. Y., Feb. 3. — Good deal of Russian news. They say our debt negotiations fell. One of the principal reasons these debt deals fall down is we won't loan 'em enough money to pay us with.

Then I see where Russia is taking to dress suits. They are broadcasting to their people where they can and must buy a ready-made tuxedo.

That's their finish. The world don't have to worry about them being a menace any longer. Nothing makes people more alike than putting a dress suit on 'em.

When I was there last Summer they was going to the opera with no top shirt, just an undershirt.

Yours,
Will Rogers.

2652   MR. ROGERS'S MEDITATIONS
        AS HE FLIES WESTWARD

MEMPHIS, Tenn., Feb. 4. — Heading west at 200 miles an hour on a great aeroplane and Mr. Douglas right across the isle from me. Two little children on here come clear from Boston, playing up and down the isle all afternoon. Then we get the plane sleeper at 9.

Washington is still agog over the gold decision. It would be a great thing if they would decide unanimously, 9 to 0. The country have so much confidence in that learned body. Folks look on this as a point of law with no politics, or no emergency cutting any figure.

It shouldn't be so complicated that they can't all see it alike, but law is complications and complications are law. If everything was just plain there wouldn't be any lawyers.

Yours,
Will Rogers.

2653   WILL ROGERS GETS A SLANT
        AT THINGS FROM OUT WEST

SELIGMAN, Ariz., Feb. 5. — Yesterday afternoon I was flying out of New York and Washington with every principal newspaper to read, all the high-grade editorials and all the news from Washington.

This evening as I have to send my message I am at a little railroad division point and real cowtown out in Arizona, no paper, no editorials.

Will Rogers and Donald Douglas, President of Douglas Aircraft Corporation.

But just to talk to these old boys beats all your New York dailies, all your learned editorials. They want no part of Europe, they think our markets are at home, they want to see our country pay its way. That is, they want to see Congress every time it votes an appropriation to vote what is to be taxed to raise the money, and interest rates are so high that the banks can't lend, for nobody can make more than that.

Gosh, I wish some of you folks would talk to somebody besides who is just in your own little claque.

Yours,
Will Rogers.

2654   WILL ROGERS REMARKS

BEVERLY HILLS, Cal., Feb. 6. — Guess who I found when I got to the Coast this morning, Max Baer and Roger Babson. A couple of my favorites. Max likes to fight (a rare combination in a modern prize fighter,) and Babson is a predictor (and a good one) and he likes to predict. He is the only man that can meet a chamber of commerce face to face and out predict 'em. While in the East I had a two-hour talk with Frank Kent. He said I wouldent listen to him, but I did, and I learned a lot that Frank knows and Lippmann knows, too. I missed Mr. Brisbane, a fact of which I was sorry. Met Mr. Martin the editor of "Time" magazine. Saw the very first showing of March of Time on the screen. It interferes with nothing, but supplies much that we should know.

Yours,
Will Rogers.

2655   WILL ROGERS TELLS HOW
RUSSIA ERRED ON DEBTS

BEVERLY HILLS, Cal., Feb. 7. — I see where the government is all excited because the debt negotiations with Russia fell through. They are bringing home a lot of our representatives from there.

Where the Russians made their mistake was in even talking about paying the debt. If they had never said anything about it, and never had any idea of paying it, why they would have the same standing as all the others.

There is a lot to be said for, and against the recognition of Russia, but I never talked to a well informed man in the Far East who didn't tell me that it absolutely prevented a Russian-Japanese war.

Yours,
Will Rogers.

2656   WILL ROGERS PAYS TRIBUTE
         TO AMERICA'S BOY SCOUTS

SANTA MONICA, Cal., Feb. 8. — Well sir, I pick up my papers and find that today is the twenty-fifth anniversary of the founding of the Boy Scouts. Course I will be a day late with my congratulations, but it is such a wonderful thing that you can compliment it every day and then not be giving it half credit.

Baden Powell, an Englishman, conceived and carried out the idea. What a monument to a man that is.

This year I think their international convention is held in Washington, D. C., and you will see the pick of the kids of the world assembled there. It's the only purely democratic thing I know of, no accident of birth, no pull, no nothing but just merit and manhood.

Yours,
Will Rogers.

2657   WILL ROGERS IS SKEPTICAL
         OF THE 'DEAD MEN' TALES

SANTA MONICA, Cal., Feb. 10. — These old boys that's claimed they been dead and then come back to life, they seem to be getting all the play in the papers.

The fellow in England claimed he got to heaven and that it was great, and he is sorry they revived him. Well, it's not much trouble to get dead again. A little street crossing without being alert will do the job.

Then we got an old boy out here in Hollywood that claimed he was dead for twenty-two minutes, and he says he was glad to get back alive again. Sounds like a Chamber of Commerce ad for Hollywood to me. Course coming from where he does he might have got in the wrong place. That's very probable.

Anyhow they're both maybe lying, but it helps kill the time till the Supreme Court acts.

Yours,
Will Rogers.

2658   Mr. Rogers Makes Guesses
On 2 Impending Verdicts

BEVERLY HILLS, Cal., Feb. 11. — Still arguing in the Senate committee over whether in trying to relieve the unemployed, the Roosevelt way, which is to pay 'em so much (I think it's fifty dollars a month) until they can get other employment, or the Senate way is to have Mr. Roosevelt match anybody else's offer that will hire you.

For instance, if you was unemployed, and they give you a job making speeches for some cause or another, they would have to pay you a Senator's salary. Some of 'em kinder look for the gold decision to be handed in tomorrow (Tuesday). Whenever they do, I predict a six-to-three decision in favor of upholding what has been done. A Hauptmann hung jury, but why it should be the good Lord only knows.

Yours,
Will Rogers.

2659   Mr. Rogers Gives Views
On The Hauptmann Case

BEVERLY HILLS, Cal., Feb. 17. — Just reading Prosecutor Wilentz's speech and it was greater than Reilly's.

By the way Wilentz wired me that no prosecution attorney had talked over the radio about the case.

It's in the jurors' hands now and not ours, so all our getting messed up in anger and arguments won't do us any good. I wonder if the jurors' minds were made up early like all the rest of ours were.

I have had a hunch somehow that it would be a hung jury. If it is, I wonder if they couldn't just sneak off in a back room somewhere with a judge, a jury and a few witnesses, and then do it like the Supreme Court handles theirs, don't let us know anything till the decision.

Yours,
Will Rogers.

2660   Mr. Rogers Is Set Right
On The Relief-Job Issue

BEVERLY HILLS, Cal., Feb. 13. — I wrote a little gag from New York the other day about them not being able to get any snow shovelers on account of everybody on relief. Well I got a lot of letters explaining it. They say that if you are on relief and accept any work (even a day or so) that it knocks you off the relief rolls and you can't get back on. So all I know is just what I read in the letters.

We been unlucky with our dirigibles, but what makes it look so bad is we only have one at a time and when we lose that, it makes us look 100 per cent inefficient. Maybe if we didn't have but one aeroplane at a time we might lose that, too. They did a good job of landing it, and the navy of rescuing the men.

Yours,
Will Rogers.

2661   MR. ROGERS IS AN ADMIRER
        OF THE NEBRASKA PLAN

BEVERLY HILLS, Cal., Feb. 14. — Comptroller of the Currency O'Connor is visiting his home out here. He is very enthusiastic about the Nebraska plan and says other States are watching it.

They did away with the State Senate and House, too, and formed a smaller single body, and also cut down the amount of counties in the State. The whole thing cuts down expenses tremendously.

It's a marvelous idea but tough to get through, for look at those jobs lost. Some States, Georgia and Texas (if I remember right), their Constitution gives every ten signers to an application a county of their own.

Yours for the Nebraska plan,
Will Rogers.

2662   MR. ROGERS ASKS A PRAYER
        FOR A GREAT AIR VENTURE

BEVERLY HILLS, Cal., Feb. 15. — Wiley Post is leaving here any morning now on the most hazardous flight yet, the most beneficial to aviation of any since Lindbergh's. He is pioneering a new world, flying a long course at 35,000 feet. Never attempted before. Eight hours on oxygen is new. He drops his landing gear on leaving. He has to come in on (pardon the expression, but it's all he has to land on) his "belly." His propeller spins lower down than the bottom of his plane. He has to stop it and get it exactly crossways before landing or it will hit first and turn him a somersault.

It's a real scientific flight. If it works everybody will fly up there. It's an old-style ship, five years old. He has flown it around the world twice.

So a prayer, or at least a good wish, for Wiley.

Yours,
Will Rogers.

2663   MR. ROGERS GROWS SERIOUS
OVER TOWNSEND'S PLAN

SANTA MONICA, Cal., Feb. 17. — See by today's papers Mr. Townsend appeared before the Senate committee and they had a lot of fun and laughter at his plan. Well they can have some fun with the amount, but they can't have much fun with the idea of paying a pension.

You see it's not just some idealistic crank or Bolsheviki idea. All the rest of the world are doing it but us. We thought we had a better idea, we called it a "poor farm" and everybody that could afford it, or had any political influence, put their old relatives there.

Now Townsend may have to take only 25 or 15 per cent of his original idea, but the Senators are not going to laugh themselves out of paying an old age pension.

Yours,
Will Rogers.

2664   MR. ROGERS SENDS S O S
FOR A COUNTRY MOTOR

SELIGMAN, Ariz., Feb. 18. — This is an open letter to Henry Ford. It goes to him first and if he don't pay any attention to it, why, then it goes to General Motors or any worth-while automobile manufacturer.

What this country needs is a high-centered automobile. You would be surprised at the amount of the U. S. that has not got a boulevard by their door. They making cars so low that you can't run over a fellow without hurting him and if you want to drive out of towns anywhere you got to use a span of mules.

Come on, Mr. Ford, do something for the country folks.

Yours,
Will Rogers.

2665   Mr. Rogers Saw Warning
In The Decision On Gold

CHICAGO, Ill., Feb. 19. — Papers full of gold decision. Folks couldn't be more excited if they had any gold.

Quite a few of the editorials have shown what the court ought to have done. We are always saying let the law take its course, but what we mean is, "Let the law take our course."

I have told a lot of alleged little jokes about the court splitting 5 to 4 on everything including the weather, so I have been vindicated in this decision. But, regardless of that, I think they are a mighty trusty pillar for our country to lean on.

But I do think there was just a slight warning in that decision to the Democrats to not try any more monkey business.

Yours,
Will Rogers.

2666   Rogers Finds An Industry
That Is Not Asking Relief

CHICAGO, Ill., Feb. 20. — What would you say was the biggest and most prosperous convention held in Chicago?

It's not autos, steel or bankers. The only industry that has never asked for governments relief.

Frank Behring, manager of the big Sherman Hotel, says it's the only convention that paid their room rent since '29.

It's the slot machine convention, manufacturers and operators. Those games where you put in a nickel, pull a lever and play marbles with yourself. It's replaced golf, bridge, kelly pool and the N. Y. Stock Exchange for exercise and gambling.

Your next Ambassadors and Senators are coming right from this business, for they got the political campaign dough.

They are showing 'em here that have lunch wagon attachments, where you can play twenty-four hours a day.

We will win the next war in a walk if they let us shoot marbles at 'em.

Yours,
Will Rogers.

2667   Mr. Rogers Gives Details,
Intimate, Of An Air Trip

BEVERLY HILLS, Cal., Feb. 21. — Well I was trying to snooze on the ship coming into Albuquerque this morning early and what keeps me awake but some big guy snoring.

I look and if it's not Wally Beery. He had climbed on somewhere during the night. He is a good pilot himself and generally flies his own plane. He wasn't so good to look at laying there snoring, but he is by far the most popular person, man or woman, on the screen. Behind us was Jockey Meade flying from Florida to ride in the big race.

We just now flew over the track and we can look down and see 'em racing. Writing this just as we landed.

                       Yours,
                       Will Rogers.

2668   Mr. Rogers Gives Reason
For Clash On Relief Bill

BEVERLY HILLS, Cal., Feb. 22. — Was out at daylight to see Wiley Post take off. Was in the camera plane and we flew along with him for about thirty miles. We left him at 8,000 feet right over the mountains. He soon after had to land. He brought her down on her stomach. That guy don't need wheels.

Lots of Washington news. The Senate overruled the President and say that the government must pay you as much for unemployed work as the regular wages of that business. How they come to disagree on it was, the President was thinking where the money was coming from and that little detail never entered the Senate's head.

                       Yours,
                       Will Rogers.

2669   Mr. Rogers Sees Evidence
Of Recovery Out West

SANTA MONICA, Cal., Feb. 24. — Well they had the big horse race out here Saturday. For the most money any race ever paid, and an Irish horse won it. He was seven years old. He had been a steeplechase horse and he was Saturday. He jumped over 20 American horses.

There was eight hundred thousand dollars bet at that track on the eight races. The stores of Los Angeles put on a dollar sale and they played to more money than the races did, and Iowa had a picnic the same day out here and they had more people than the races and the dollar sale combined.

With all these going on in one town, I wouldn't worry too much about the country going Bolsheviki.

Yours,
Will Rogers.

2670   WILL ROGERS HAS A PLAN
THAT SOUNDS REASONABLE

BEVERLY HILLS, Cal., Feb. 25. — Papers say 60,000 Filipinos want to go home. Well you can't blame a person for being homesick, and fare is cheaper than relief.

Why wouldn't that be a good move for the government to make, send anybody home that wants to go, or any American citizen that craves a change. (They say citizenship here now is not so hot.)

So while everybody is introducing a bill, or a plan, the Rogers plan read as follows:

"Party of the first part (the U. S. A.) will ship anybody, anywhere, if they won't come back."

So come on folks rally around the Rogers plan.

Yours,
Will Rogers.

2671   MR. ROGERS INTRODUCES
THE GREATEST ECONOMIST

HOLLYWOOD, Cal., Feb. 26. — Was down last night with Charlie Chaplin listening to our friend Will Durant, the philosopher, debate on world economics.

Charlie has made a study of that. He is the greatest economist in the world. Every nation has lost its export trade. Yet stop and think of it, Chaplin manufactures the only article in the world that hasn't depreciated. The world is his market the same as before the depression, but he has never let the supply equal the demand. While all the world's big industrialists were greedy, Charlie never went in for mass production.

Seems odd that a comedian can do what governments are not smart enough to do.

Yours,
Will Rogers.

2672   MR. ROGERS IS NOT FOOLED
BY MUSSOLINI'S REMARKS

BEVERLY HILLS, Cal., Feb. 27. — I get a kick out of Mussolini. Now today he says that he has so many million and is ready for the world.

Now he ain't talking to the world at all. He is talking to that little king down there in Abyssinia, the stepchild to Cleopatra, and he is talking to keep his own folks steamed up. He don't want war. His record shows that he don't. And it's because he is ready for it, he hasn't had any.

I think he is too smart to go in there and even conquer this Aba-dab-ba country. He would lose a lot of friends if he pounces on that country, and besides Mussolini likes to do these things just to devil the life out of France. He has kidded France seriously more than any man alive.

Yours,
Will Rogers.

2673   MR. ROGERS HAS ANSWER
TO A PUZZLING QUESTION

BEVERLY HILLS, Cal., Feb. 28. — Quite a few of our writers are wondering why J. P. Morgan is selling his paintings. He is getting more for them than he give. That might be a small possible clew.

Headline in paper says he is "letting his miniatures go." Then I guess he is letting that midget go. Did you ever see pictures in the paper where a fellow had left his wife for another woman that the wife he left wasn't better looking than the new one.

All you read about Washington is how are they going to spend that four billions. There hasn't been even one suggestion as to where it was to come from.

It must be marvelous to just belong to some legislative body and just pick money out of the air.

Yours,
Will Rogers.

2674   Mr. Rogers Philosophizes
On The News Of The Day

BEVERLY HILLS, Cal., March 1. — Good deal of news today. King of Siam abdicates. He always seemed like a pretty nice little fellow, but a king is sorter like a politician, it's hard to tell when he is making good or bad.

The Saar Valley was officially turned back to Germany today. Too bad they don't allow the islands they took away from Germany to vote on whether they wanted to go back too. You know that's always been a sort of a touchy point with these big allied nations. They don't like to have anybody bring up the subject of the gobbling up Germany's possessions. That's the skeleton in their closet that they are not so proud of.

You can get you a baby bond, or a pound of baby beef, they both cost the same.

Yours,
Will Rogers.

2675   Mr. Rogers Recalls A Chat
With A Grand Old Greek

SANTA MONICA, Cal., March 3. — Greece has got some kind of a little cotton-tail revolution on over there. I flew through Athens in January, 32, coming from India, and went up with one of our officials there and had a couple of hours chat with this old statesman Venizelos. He speaks good English (better than me), got a lot of humor and is a mighty interesting old gentleman. They call him the grand old man of Greece. You see he is about the last one outside of Lloyd George that was with President Wilson during those historic old Versailles days.

Greece has got a lot of old ruins, but he is not one of 'em.

Yours,
Will Rogers.

2676   Mr. Rogers's Meditations
Take A Military Turn

BEVERLY HILLS, Cal., March 4. — Say, these Greeks have a word for it, and it's bullets.

There is one thing in common with all revolutions (in fact they are pretty near like wars in that respect) nobody ever knows what they are fighting about.

Too bad we (so foolishly) split up the old Negro Tenth Cavalry. We could have loaned them to this King Aba-Dab-Ba down there and Mussolini would have "shinnied over on his own side."

When we get through paying the Senate for arguing over the relief bill there won't be any money left.

Yours,
Will Rogers.

2677   MR. ROGERS SEES A MENACE
        TO AN AMERICAN TRADITION

BEVERLY HILLS, Cal., March 5. — A real old standpat Republican Governor of the great State of California reached the Townsend plan age yesterday, and I am a telling you that I am on the waiting list not many years away.

I don't know where the money would come from. In fact I don't know where any of all this money is coming from we are spending now, any more than a Congressman does, but if Americans are going to stop and start worrying about whether they can afford a thing or not, you are going to ruin the whole characteristic of our people.

There wouldn't have been a dozen automobiles sold if that was the case.

Yours,
Will Rogers.

2678   MR. ROGERS TAKES NOTICE
        OF THE SENATORIAL STORM

BEVERLY HILLS, Cal., March 6. — The United States Senate may not be the most refined and deliberative body in existence but they got the most unique rules.

Any member can call anybody in the world anything he can think of and they can't answer him, sue him, or fight him.

Our Constitution protects aliens, drunks and United States Senators.

There ought to be one day a year (just one) when there is an open season on Senators.

Yours,
Will Rogers.

P. S. — Huey, you better lay off Joe Robinson. That's like me getting in an argument with Dempsey.

2679 WILL ROGERS IS PUZZLED
BY AT LEAST THREE THINGS

BEVERLY HILLS, Cal., March 7. — It's the usual custom for a writer or speaker to tell how much better England or France or Zululand have handled their money than the U. S.

Well in today's paper France is prohibiting the shipment of gold out of their country, and still they say they are not going off the gold. No, but they are not letting the gold go off them either. Then last week England had to put up millions of pounds to stabilize their money.

So I guess over there they are pointing to the excellent way our system is working. Your own country always looks like they are the only one doing the wrong thing.

This thing called money has got the whole mess of 'em buffaloed.

Money, horse racing and women are three things the boys just can't figure out.

Yours,
Will Rogers.

2680 WILL ROGERS IS IMPRESSED
BY CAMPBELL'S NEW RECORD

BEVERLY HILLS, Cal., March 8. — That Englishman, Malcolm Campbell, sure deserves a lot of credit, 276 miles an hour in an automobile; very few airplanes have beat that. About all the credit we get out of it is, we furnish the beach. It seems strange that we don't hold the automobile speed record, for we have millions trying to break it every day.

Huey is setting fine now. The Republican papers have all adopted him. They took him in as their white hope.

Whatever become of the four billion relief bill?

Yours,
Will Rogers.

2681 ROGERS USES HOLMES'S WILL
TO POINT A MORAL FOR ALL

SANTA MONICA, Cal., March 10. — Wasn't that a remarkable will that Oliver Wendell Holmes left? Imagine a man giving his money to the government at a time when 120 million people are trying to get it away from the government, or trying to keep from paying 'em what we owe 'em.

At least eighty years of service to his country and he accumulates some money, and is so appreciative of what his country has done for him that he wants to return it.

All we hear is "What's the matter with the country?" "What's the matter with the world?" There ain't but one thing wrong with every one of us in the world, and that's selfishness.

>Yours,
>Will Rogers.

2682   WILL ROGERS REDISCOVERS
        GIRL OF 'SEPTEMBER MORN'

BEVERLY HILLS, Cal., March 11. — Well Washington is not doing anything, so we have to turn to other things in the day's news. Remember "September Morn"? Sure you do. Well she is fat and she has got three children. And I bet none of 'em can swim.

The paper says the Prince of Wales danced with a Baltimore woman in a "multi-colored dress of spun glass, and just a single diamond in her hair." If that made international news, what would it have been if he had dropped her in that glass dress. Some day there is going to be a society gal that didn't dance with him. Then you going to hear of real fame.

>Yours,
>Will Rogers.

2683   ROGERS FINDS WAR TALK
        MORE ABUNDANT THAN WARS

SANTA MONICA, Cal., March 12. — All you read is war, war, war, but over 99 per cent are predictions and not wars. Everything considered, the world has been pretty peaceful toward each other since the Big War. Outside of Japan and China, Bolivia and Paraguay, there hasn't been much between nations.

If you just stop and figure it out, all the wars are home talent. Greece is frying in her own fat, Cuba is operating on herself, the Russians have shaved each other, Germany's trouble has been internal and infernal, England has succeeded in India in keeping the Mohammedans fighting the Hindus and not her.

All our wars since 1918 have been with the NRA. Our neighbors, Mexico and Canada, have both behaved like gentlemen.

So most wars are in the newspapers.

Yours,
Will Rogers.

2684   MR. ROGERS MAKES A PASS
          AT THE HOLDING COMPANIES

BEVERLY HILLS, Cal., March 13. — Say did you read about what Mr. Roosevelt said about those "holding companies?" I wouldn't want my worst enemy to call me names like that.

Now Huey Long and Father Coughlin and General Hugh Johnson can call each other names, but theirs is all in good clean fun. They don't really mean it, any of 'em. But Mr. Roosevelt ain't kidding.

And what makes it worse is that it's true. A holding company is a thing where you hand an accomplice the goods while the policeman searches you.

Yours,
Will Rogers.

2685   ROGERS SEES SOME STATES
          DOING NOTHING ON RELIEF

SANTA MONICA, Cal., March 14. — I was reading a rather surprising thing. Of course you knew that a lot of the States are bonding themselves very heavily to pay their proportionate share of their own relief. But did you know that some of 'em don't do anything? They just let the Federal Government pay the whole thing.

Now that thing can't go on. You are going to hear a howl like a pet 'coon, if they find the government is handing out a whole biscuit to one State and just a half to another State.

They going to testify at the ballot box in 1936.

Yours,
Will Rogers.

2686   WILL ROGERS REMARKS

BEVERLY HILLS, Cal., March 15. — I have often said that with all our kidding or cussing our public elected officials, that they are as good or better than we who elect 'em. Well we got a fine example of it in the papers this morning. John Steven McGroarty, who wrote California's famous Mision Play. A great writer, a real humanitarian, and fine and beloved type of real gentleman, (I expect Los Angeles' most universally popular citizen) one of his voters wrote him an insulting letter wanting to know why he hadn't put trees on the Sierra Madre Mountains. McGroarty's reply: "One of the drawbacks of being a Congressman is that I have to receive impertinent letters from a jackass like you. Will you please take two running jumps and go to h___." Score one for Congress.

Yours,
Will Rogers.

2687   ROGERS BURSTS INTO GAELIC
             AFTER THIMBLEFUL OF IRISH

SANTA MONICA, Cal., March 17. — Well, we just wake up in the morning to see who will get the headlines. "Mussolini is moving into Abasynia," "Stalin builds up the Red army to one million," but today Hitler took the play away from not only the dictators but away from St. Patrick, and say that old gentleman St. Patrick was no slouch as a fighting man himself.

Today I am dipping me shamrock into a thimbleful of old Irishowen. And may you be seven months in heaven before the devil knows you're dead. Fag a bealach.

Yours,
Will Rogers.

2688   ROGERS TELLS ONE LESSON
             PRESIDENT HAS LEARNED

SANTA MONICA, Cal., March 18. — Democrats in Congress want to get the President to abandon all his humanitarian schemes, and center on just the old-age pensions. In other words the kittens have arrived at such an age that it's time to pick out the one that will be the biggest and strongest by November, '36, and drown the others.

They would drown some fine helpful brotherly love schemes, but the one thing that I would stake my life on that Mr. Roosevelt has learned since he has been in there, is that the people are willing to cooperate, but they are not going to willingly pay to do it. You can bet that his faith in human nature has had quite a jar.

Yours truly,
Will Rogers.

2689   MR. ROGERS IS NOT EXCITED
                OVER EUROPE'S TROUBLES

BEVERLY HILLS, Cal., March 19. — It ought to feel awful good to us (even as bad off as we think we are) to be away off over here and not have to send a protest because Germany has decided to put on some extra help.

Those nations over there just get up every morning and start writing protests. If Mussolini ain't deviling the life out of 'em why Hitler is. Whether you got a man in the army before the war starts or after it starts don't make much difference, he is going to be in there if it does start anyhow.

The trouble with the Versailles peace treaty is that the men that made it are dead, and the ones living say, "we didn't sign that mortgage."

So it looks like our worries are mostly all tax worries.

Yours,
Will Rogers.

2690   MR. ROGERS KEEPS AN EYE
                ON THE EUROPEAN MUDDLE

BEVERLY HILLS, Cal., March 20. — I was gabbing to you yesterday about the big nations over in Europe protesting to Germany. Well, this morning they are so busy protesting, that they are protesting to each other.

France and Italy said, "You didn't scold Germany enough," and they also told 'em, "Before you go to talk with Germany, come and talk with us."

Of all the scheming and of all the conniving. We are putting on more soldier help, and neither of our neighbors have paid any attention to us. They just figure, "They are your men. We don't care whether you dress 'em in a uniform or dress 'em in tights. Either way they could shoot a gun if they had to."

Yours,
Will Rogers.

2691 MR. ROGERS FINDS ISSUES
OF MOMENT BEING SOLVED

BEVERLY HILLS, Cal., March 21. — I don't know what all your different State Legislatures are doing. Guess they are figuring out schemes to slip up on the taxpayer with a blackjack. Ours worked a week on finding out how long a freight train ought to be. They finally compromised on seventy-four cars.

Now that we got that settled I don't see anything can hold us back from recovery. I know the railroads will feel proud of the compliment and will start immediately to get seventy-four empties ready.

Why don't they pass a bill as to how long a bus can be? It takes two minutes for one to pass a given point.

Yours,
Will Rogers.

2692 MR. ROGERS URGES CAUTION
ON TWO LIVELY SUBJECTS

BEVERLY HILLS, Cal., March 22. — I was shooting off the other day about holding companies. Mr. Roosevelt and lots of folks may think they are uncalled for, but the folks working for 'em think mighty well of 'em. It's the old fault of not calling your shots by naming the bad ones and not shooting into the whole covey.

I tell you another argument a fellow wants to keep out of, and that's this printing money thing. It's a subject where nobody knows just exactly what it would do, and every person thinks he knows exactly what it would do. All I know it's easier to print than to make by work. But please don't write or wire explaining it.

If you know all about money, you are awful lucky, and it's a secret you should cherish and not let even your grandchildren know about.

Yours,
Will Rogers.

2693   Mr. Rogers Hails Return
Of Two-Party System

SANTA MONICA, Cal., March 24. — Just been reading Mr. Hoover's message to the underprivileged Republicans and I gathered from reading between the lines that he wasn't just exactly 100 per cent sold on all that's going on.

Now mind you I may be wrong. That may have been just a wrong interpretation that I put on the message. But it did look like he was bringing out some stuff that the Democrats would like to keep buried in the ash can.

Mr. Hoover is a mighty honorable and respectable citizen, and his parables should be given mighty serious consideration, for he is about half right. There is some schemes that haven't exactly percolated for the Democrats.

And how it's good to hear that we have again after a relapse returned to a two-party system.

                               Yours,
                               Will Rogers.

2694   Will Rogers Is Saddened
By Week-End Auto Toll

BEVERLY HILLS, Cal., March 25. — When you pick up a Monday paper it's just like in the old days when we only got a telegram when there was bad news. We are afraid to open our paper. We know that a loved one, a friend, or at least an acquaintance has met death in a car over the week-end.

Before we had this high type of civilization which we are so thoroughly enjoying, why we used to have wars to get rid of the surplus number of people.

California is all excited about a baby who could work a dial telephone at the age of 2 years. Well, I bet I could come as near doing it at two as I can now. There is only one difference with a dial phone, you have to cuss yourself instead of some innocent girl.

                               Yours,
                               Will Rogers.

2695   Mr. Rogers Gives Credit
To Hitler As Humorist

BEVERLY HILLS, Cal., March 26. — Today's best bit of humor in the papers come from Mr. Hitler who said the reason he was engaging more men with guns was solely on account of Russia.

I guess France didn't enter into it at all. Russia is in enough devilment, we all readily admit. But I wonder what the world did for somebody to lay everything onto before Russia come along. (Well as a matter of fact they used to lay most of it onto us.)

I guess no individual ever invented can pass the buck as quick as a nation can.

> Yours,
> *Will Rogers.*

2696   Mr. Rogers Takes A Stand
In A Monumental Clash

BEVERLY HILLS, Cal., March 27. — Have you been reading this college women argument?

Secretary Perkins spoke to Cal University, but a Miss Ijams objected about two columns worth. She held out for May West instead. She can't see a Democrat even if it was Jane Addams.

Then through some curious turn of events, Mrs. Roosevelt got into it.

Well I was going to remain neutral, but today, according to her mother, Miss Ijams sleeps till afternoon.

Well I can readily see how women like Mrs. Perkins and Roosevelt (who get up with the birds) would get in Ijams' hair.

So Ijams has either got to get her a husband or an alarm clock to catch those two.

> Yours for the early birds,
> *Will Rogers.*

2697   Mr. Rogers Reaches Town,
Wafted East In The Dust

NEW YORK, N. Y., March 28. — Flew through these dust storms last night with the pilot flying entirely by instruments.

Where in the world is it going to? It's a terrible thing, and it's going to bring up some queer cases in law.

If Colorado blows over and lights on top of Kansas, it looks kinder like Kansas ought to pay for the extra top soil, but Kansas can sue 'em for covering up their crops.

Now, this week's wind has picked up Colorado which was in Kansas, taking Kansas with it, and that's what's in the air looking for a new place to light.

In the Middle West now you got to put a brand on your soil, then in the Spring go on a round-up looking for it.

Yours,
Will Rogers.

2698 LORD MAYOR'S HORSE SENSE
IMPRESSES WILL ROGERS

WASHINGTON, D. C., March 29. — Last night, Thursday night, Mrs. Rogers, Mary and I saw a fine comedy show in New York called "Three Men on a Horse." The idea is that a man that is not betting can dope out the winners.

Well now get this for a coincidence. I fly down here this morning, and I meet the Lord Mayor of Dublin, Ireland, a lovely fine little Irish gentleman. Well you would naturally ask an Irishman about the Grand National race at Aintree, for all the good horses in it are Irish. Well, this little Lord Mayor gave them this morning the following winners, Reynoldstown, Blue Prince, Thomond II.

By golly, if he didn't pick 'em one, two, three. So if the Lord Mayor of Dublin should be coming your way, no matter if he tells you "The Republicans have a chance," listen to him.

Yours,
Will Rogers.

2699 MR. ROGERS GENTLY CHIDES
THE NEW YORK GRUMBLER

NEW YORK, N. Y., March 31. — Here is New York City where all the money in the world is, and where every guy with a dollar is doing better than he was a year ago.

"Say, what's this country coming to? I tell you this income tax is terrible."

"My business is picking up every day, but I am scared."

"I am doing better than I have since '29, but when are we going to get back to the good old days?"

Well, the good old days with most of us was when we didn't earn enough to pay an income tax.

Yours,
Will Rogers.

2700   MR. ROGERS GIVES A BOOST
TO THE OLD HOME STATE

CLAREMORE, Okla., April 1. — I tell you Oklahoma has got 'em all beat. Looking mighty good. Good Governor, good crops. Cattle a good price.

Just flew in over Kansas. Say, Kansas has got 'em a fine Republican Governor that you are awful liable to hear a lot about for President.

You know the Republicans here lately have decided to put out a ticket. You know an awful lot of folks are predicting Roosevelt's downfall, not only predicting but praying.

We are a funny people. We elect our Presidents, be they Republican or Democrat, then go home and start daring 'em to make good.

Yours,
Will Rogers.

2701   MR. ROGERS STILL RATES
OKLAHOMA A GARDEN SPOT

TULSA, Okla., April 2. — All I know is what I read in the Claremore Progress. Towns booming, fine aeroplane field all lighted, Oklahoma Military Academy best polo team in the country.

Claremore is the flowered city and the exilirating odor of roses are entrancing. The sweetest smelling town in the U.S.

Government loaning farmers enough to get teams, seed oats or corn and a milk cow. That don't seem such a terribly nutty scheme.

Everybody that is making money has it in for Roosevelt. You will have to explain that one yourself.

Yours,
Will Rogers.

2702   WILL ROGERS FINDS SIGNS
OF BETTER TIMES IN WEST

SANTA MONICA, Cal., April 3. — Flying through Phoenix, Ariz., this morning and an old boy standing there that I got to talking to, as I always do, as to how things were going. He said they shipped 190 cars of lettuce out of that one valley yesterday. Now a carload of lettuce is considerable lettuce, but 190 cars. And at a good price.

Talking to a cattleman in Claremore yesterday. He had just shipped a bunch of steers to Kansas City and netted $128 a head. Three months ago he tried to sell 'em for $30.

These just show you how quick your business can change.

Now a sheep man wires me that mutton hasn't gone up. Now I don't want to be caught helping out a sheep man, but it sounded like he may be right.

Yours,
Will Rogers.

2703   MR. ROGERS TALKS OF ARMS
        AND GOES A BIT O'NEILLISH

BEVERLY HILLS, Cal., April 4. — Well, today Austria says they want a gun. Yesterday it was Germany.

England's got a gun, France has got a gun, Italy's got a gun, Germany wants a gun, Austria wants a gun. All God's children wants guns, going to put on the guns, going to buckle on the guns and smear up all of God's heaven.

All these come from treatys which say, "I will have two guns, and you have one."

It just don't make sense to say that one nation shall have more than another in anything.

Yours,
Will Rogers.

2704   ROGERS RECORDS THE FATE
        OF ONE ANTI-LOBBYING BILL

BEVERLY HILLS, Cal., April 5. — Got a wire from my sheepherder friend today and he says that our Saviour was a sheepherder once, and that not only is the sheep business a mighty ancient business, but makes mighty good food. So give the old wooly boys a break. And hogs, say, hog meat is so high that even the gentiles have gone "kosher."

California had a bill in to investigate lobbying, and the lobbyists bought off all the votes and they can't even find the bill now. Putting a lobbyist out of business is like a hired man trying to fire his boss.

Yours,
Will Rogers.

2705   MR. ROGERS HAS AN IDEA
                       REGARDING RELIEF WORK

BEVERLY HILLS, Cal., April 7. — Well the Relief Bill is all passed. Now, all we got to do is just sit back and see who it relieves. I hope the real needy get at least their 10 per cent out of it anyhow.

We have ways and means of gathering any sort of information, how much money you earned to a nickel, how many rabbits were born in the Dakotas, how much rainfall fell between here and Honolulu, but we just can't seem to get even a fairly reliable count of who really needs helping and who don't.

What would be the matter with taking all our guys who do nothing but gather useless statistics and put 'em on this relief work.

                              Yours,
                                   Will Rogers.

2706   SUPERIORITY OF MAN
                           SUFFERS A SETBACK

BEVERLY HILLS, Cal., April 8. — Girl aviator teaching stronger sex to fly, he froze controls and was about to crash. She picks up fire extinguisher and used it in a way that would do the most good, just casually bent it over his head, causing temporary unconsciousness. As my good old native son of Florida Arthur Brisbane would say, "There is a lesson in that." Man is not as mighty as he thinks he is, the gorilla is mightier, and a woman with a fire extinguisher is not only mightier than the man, but we all know a lot of 'em without an extinguisher that can worry a gorilla till he says, "Maybe I am wrong."

                              Yours,
                                  Will Rogers.

2707   WILL ROGERS MOURNS LOSS
                      OF TWO VERY GOOD FRIENDS

BEVERLY HILLS, Cal., April 9. — My boss is dead. My friend is dead.

Adolph Ochs, owner of the great New York Times, is the first man that I ever wrote for, and it was him personally that got me to try it.

Think of being lucky enough to break in at the top, for that paper is the tops. He was a fine friend and a fine citizen.

Then another good friend, Warren Robbins, our Minister to Canada, is gone too. He is the man who took me in to see Mussolini, when I got the famous castor oil interview. He next took me in to see the President of little San Salvador, when he was Minister there. A fine fellow, Warren, and our diplomatic service will miss him.

Yours,
Will Rogers.

2708   WILL ROGERS EXPLAINS
        THE DULLNESS OF STOCKS

BEVERLY HILLS, Cal., April 10. — That was certainly nice of Hitler to appear at that wedding today and not be the groom.

No wonder the New York stock market can't ever go up to amount to anything. The minute it starts everybody starts selling to take a little profit. Suppose every cowman sold his cattle the minute they started up.

Just been chatting out here at the studio just now with an awful fine man, Fielding Yost of Michigan. I think some of our great coaches like him and Stagg and Warner have been a great influence on thousands of their boys through life.

Yours,
Will Rogers.

2709   MR. ROGERS HAS NO SILVER,
        BUT STRESA INTERESTS HIM

BEVERLY HILLS, Cal., April 11. — Silver went up to 71 cents, so the papers say today, which don't mean much to all of us, for I doubt if we knew what it was before it went up. I guess the 70 cents was what it's worth, and 1 cent tax.

Down in Stresa, Italy, the nations only met yesterday, and by noon were 100 per cent in discord. Somebody suggested inviting Russia, Germany and Poland. It seems in mailing out the original invitations they had overlooked them.

It's awful hard for three nations to entirely agree on how the other three will be run by them.

And this is the kind of a mess that some folks wanted us into.

Yours,
Will Rogers.

2710 ROGERS IS READY TO ADVISE
DEMOCRATIC POSTMASTERS

BEVERLY HILLS, Cal., April 12. — Among my mail this morning was a telegram marked urgent, it says: "The Democratic postmasters of Los Angeles County are getting together." It says very specifically that it's the "Democratic" postmasters. I would love to see a dinner given by the Republican postmasters. I think these boys are kinder getting together to draw up ways and means of prolonging their stay. You see their employment calls for four years (with an option). Well I think it's this option that they want a little rough and tumble advice from me on. I am suggesting that they deliver no mail to anyone of Republican faith. Why should hard working deserving Democrats take up their valuable time handing out what is no doubt anti-Democratic propaganda. And I am so advising 'em.
Yours,
Will Rogers.

2711 MR. ROGERS IS A BIT TIRED
OF DECIDING EUROPE'S FATE

SANTA MONICA, Cal., April 14. — Well the papers are all saying today "The fate of Europe will be decided this week at Stresa, Italy."

I have never remembered in my whole long life of ever picking up a paper where in there wasn't somewhere in it, "The fate of Europe is in the balance."

It looks to me like Europe hasn't got any fate. They go from one mess to another. It's been cut up, subdivided, resold and resubdivided, let and sublet.

Europe is just like a bunch of checkers on a checkerboard. One minute the reds are in the king row. The next minute somebody is jumping over 'em.
Yours,
Will Rogers.

2712 MR. ROGERS EXPLAINS WHYS
AND WHEREFORES OF TREATY

BEVERLY HILLS, Cal., April 15. — Now here is where this Hitler kinder has these other nations in the hole when they start yelling about this arming when he was supposed not to. In the treaty

Germany wasn't to arm for so many years, but — and here is the but — they were to disarm down to a certain point by then. Now it's a question of "who has broke who's treaty?"

Trouble with all these treaties is that the guys that make 'em are generally kicked out by the time they get home, and the new bunch says, "That's not our signature." But nobody is fighting, so what's all the worry about?

Yours,
Will Rogers.

2713   MR. ROGERS FEELS FORCED
TO DECLINE A HIGH HONOR

BEVERLY HILLS, Cal., April 16. — Got a wire today from an old boy in Parsons, Kansas, and he wanted me to enter in a hog-calling contest.

You know I used to be an awful good hog-caller when hogs were cheap. But the way hogs have gone up in price it's changed the whole system of calling 'em. It would take Henry Ford hollering with his check book to get one to come to you nowadays. I hollered all morning just for three slices of bacon and it didn't come.

So there ain't much use of me hollering my head off to try and get a whole hog to come.

Yours,
Will Rogers.

2714   MR. ROGERS SEES REAL NEWS
WITH RUTH AND DIZZY BUSY

BEVERLY HILLS, Cal., April 17. — Well you can have all your European entanglement conference news, all your war talk, all your aviation exploits, all your Congressional aba-cadaba; Ickes and Huey can fight a duel two columns long. All these bits of news you can throw in the ash can when Babe Ruth steps to plate and knocks a home run.

That interests everybody. We expected Dizzy to do something out of the ordinary and he did.

The country is all right now. We get real news every morning from now on.

Yours,
Will Rogers.

2715   ROGERS IS LOUD IN PRAISE
                         OF THE FLIGHT TO HAWAII

BEVERLY HILLS, Cal., April 18. — That was a great flight the Pan-America made. They will do some great work out there. I have often wondered why the army and navy don't make that flight almost regularly.

A night or so ago I went to listen to Amelia Earhart tell of making it. Don't miss it. Her personality equals her flying skill.

Huey has the greatest chance he has had now. The government is spending too much. A State, if it had the will and the leadership, could work itself out. So if he refused any money, pitched in and did it, then he would prove something. It could be done.

                                      Yours,
                                      Will Rogers.

2716   MR. ROGERS TAKES WARNING
                         FROM THE FATE OF GEORGIA

BEVERLY HILLS, Cal., April 19. — I see where a Governor down in Georgia has also ceceeded from the Union. That gets his State off the relief rolls. Well that means more to divvy up among the rest. I tell you I am going to try and get Oklahoma and California to do nothing in any way that will cause Secretary Ickes to shut off our water.

And speaking about people calling people things, did you see what Hitler called England and what Mussolini called everybody. But Hugh Johnson was the hero yesterday, he took the rap himself.

                                      Yours,
                                      Will Rogers.

2717   WILL ROGERS SEES EUROPE
                         FINDING HER GOAT AS USUAL

SANTA MONICA, Cal., April 21. — That Europe is funny. The leader of one country, maby Hitler, maby Mussolini, will say something, then all the others will run together and hold a conference.

"What did he say, do you think he meant it, do you think he will fight or is he bluffing?"

Then they all go home again and then in a couple of days somebody else will make a statement, then the huddle starts all over again. Of course before each gathering adjourns it's understood and goes on the minutes of the meeting automatically that we (the U. S.) are indirectly to blame, that if we would just meet with 'em they would blame it on somebody else.

Yours,
Will Rogers.

2718   WILL ROGERS SEES A WAY
TO MAKE CHURCH POPULAR

BEVERLY HILLS, Cal., April 22. — I bet any Sunday could be made as popular at church as Easter is if you made 'em fashion shows too. The audience is so busy looking at each other that the preacher just as well recite Gunga Din. We will do anything, if you just in some way turn it into a show.

They say children in kindergarten must play in order to get 'em to learn. What do you mean children? Crossword puzzles learned grown folks more words than school teachers. And what arithmetic the women folks know they got at a bridge table. Our splendid English comes from attending the movies. My geography comes from an airplane window. Yes sir there is 120 million in the American kindergarten.

Yours,
Will Rogers.

2719   WILL ROGERS SIZES UP
THE BRITISH AND BRITAIN

BEVERLY HILLS, Cal., April 23. — Here is the latest racket if you are so rich you don't know what to do with your money.

They are putting it in annuities in England. They feel it's safer there. Then they wonder how it is that England recovers.

It recovers because you couldn't in a hundred years get an Englishman to do what these folks are doing. England will bet you on England to their last penny. In England they invest most of their money in income tax. Read what their rate is.

With this money invested over there it's not hard to see where all the influence comes from to get us to keep joining something over there.

Yours,
Will Rogers.

2720   Mr. Rogers Tries To Answer
          The Question Of The Day

BEVERLY HILLS, Cal., April 24. — Up to a day or so ago this country really had some problems. "Where is all this money coming from?" was on the lips of every man who had any. "Should business be allowed to recover first and then reform, or visa versa?" "Who will the Republicans nominate?" "Is Kent right or is Lippman right?"

But all those momentous things are washed up now. They are as dead as a balanced budget. The problem that hits every man, woman and child in the face today is, "Was Mae Married?" It's splitting this country like a Supreme Court decision.

Personally, I don't believe she was, for I can't see why the fellow would have ever left her.

Yours,
Will Rogers.

2721   Mr. Rogers Makes A Bow
            To A 'Cap And Gown Boy'

BEVERLY HILLS, Cal., April 25. — Well there has been great suspense and much guessing as to who would really handle the "big Roosevelt bankroll."

Mr. Tugwell has got the last laugh on all his critics. In fact, Tugwell is the only one of all "cap and gown boys" that the boss has ever really trusted with any dough. The other professors could recite their piece but couldn't get their fist in the till.

A professor's theories have often been considered workable, but not when they applied to actual cash. So, this will be any professor's first chance of betting on a face with real money. They have always just done it in their heads.

Yours,
Will Rogers.

2722   Mr. Rogers Has Solution
            For The Bonus Squabble

BEVERLY HILLS, Cal., April 26. — Having a time with the bonus. Congress wants to pay it, the soldiers want to receive it, but every person wants it paid or received according to his own particular plan.

Looks like soldiers can't agree any more than congressmen can. Better put General Pershing in charge again. He was the only man we ever had that could tell a soldier and a Senator too where to head in.

Don't hold those dimes, quarters and halves you may have too lightly, for by tonight Mr. Roosevelt may have thought of a new price for 'em.

Yours,
Will Rogers.

2723   MR. ROGERS CONSIDERED US
            A NATION OF BUCKPASSERS

SANTA MONICA, Cal., April 28. — This is dispatched just before the President goes on the air tonight.

I am anxious to hear the comments in the press. Even if it's good there is plenty of 'em won't like it, he can speak on the Lord's supper and get editorials against it.

Never in our history was we as willing to blame somebody else for our troubles.

America is just like an insane asylum. There is not a soul in it will admit they are crazy. Roosevelt being the warden at the present time, us inmates know he is the one that's cuckoo.

Yours,
Will Rogers.

2724   WILL ROGERS COMPARES
            TALKS OF TWO LEADERS

BEVERLY HILLS, Cal., April 29. — The President made a very encouraging and hopeful speech. On the same day Mussolini spoke to his people.

It's interesting to compare the two speeches, not so much on account of the two men, but on account of difference in temperament of the two races.

Mussolini said, "You have many lean years ahead. You must sacrifice and bear it."

Now nobody could make that speech to us. We don't want to be told we must "sacrifice," and that we might have "lean years coming."

But Mussolini's plan is the best. If he brings his people any little benefits they are tickled to death. If we don't receive every benefit we are hollering.

Yours,
Will Rogers.

2725   MR. ROGERS GETS AROUND
         TO THE SUBMARINE SCARE

BEVERLY HILLS, Cal., April 30. — You know the other day I had a little "gag" in the papers about every time some nation sneezed a little louder than usual the others run into a huddle.

Well, that might sound like a joke, but look at 'em today. Germany announced some submarines and now these diplomats' heads are closer together than a barber shop quartet.

The one thing these old boys with a big navy are scared of, and that's submarines. They are always claiming they are inhuman and not a civilized mode of warfare.

It would be rather interesting to see published the names of the weapons that are considered a pleasure to be shot by.

Yours,
Will Rogers.

2726   MR. ROGERS FEELS BETTER
         OVER HIS ISOLATION STAND

SANTA MONICA, Cal., May 1. — The great argument with all Americans who want to join in with Europe and help set the world right was that any one that was not in favor of it was pretty narrow-minded and selfish. In plain words, it's the dumb folks that are "agin'" it.

Well, read today's papers. The Premiers of Canada, Australia, South Africa and New Zealand have never been considered anything but intelligent, yet they notified England to quit messing around on the opposite bank of the English Channel.

So the American dumb ones are in pretty good company.

Yours,
Will Rogers.

Will Rogers as "Kenesaw H. Clark" in the motion picture Life Begins At 40, suggested by the book by Walter B. Pitkin (Fox Film Corporation, 1935).

2727   Mr. Rogers Isn't Surprised
By F. D. R. C. Of C. Divorce

BEVERLY HILLS, Cal., May 2. — The papers said today, "The President breaks with U. S. Chamber of Commerce."

That's the oldest news I have seen in a long time.

Through habit of the last few administrations the U. S. Chamber of Commerce is supposed to be wedded (in an advisory capacity) to each President. But this particular union was never consummated.

It was an unhappy alliance on both sides from the start. And the break didn't come in the last day or so. Incompatibility developed as early as March 4, 1933.

Both are headstrong and used to running things their own way, and it will be a divorce well worth reading about.

Up to now Roosevelt is ahead, for he is collecting five billion temporary alimony.

                      Yours,
                      Will Rogers.

2728   Rogers Sees Honors Equal
In A Notable Argument

BEVERLY HILLS, Cal., May 3. — I don't know which one was the littleist in this U. S. Chamber of Commerce versus Roosevelt argument. The President he got sore and the "leading industrialists" they got sore and it ended in a tie that brought no glory on either one. Mr. Roosevelt should have kidded 'em, for they left a great opening.

Governor Lafoon of Kentucky, I wish I could be there tomorrow watching the great Kentucky Derby, but this dime letter mail that Jim Farley invented to boost his business has just got me swamped. I have received everything in the world but a dime. Kentucky, stay with Bradley.

                      Yours,
                      Will Rogers.

2729   Mr. Rogers Would Book
Our Wars On Home Lots

SANTA MONICA, Cal., May 5. — Well, the Kentucky Derby is all over now, and maby Congress can settle down to work again.

Our big fleet has pulled out to practice. I don't know where a lot of these writers get the idea that we haven't got any army, or navy, or aviation. Course we could use a lot more of 'em, but to read some writers you would think that our whole defense force was sorter "Mickey Mouse."

I believe these boys can keep everybody off, if we just know enough to book all wars on the home grounds.

The place we need our re-enforcements is in the diplomatic end.

Yours,
Will Rogers.

2730   MR. ROGERS CANNOT WIN
          A BET ON A MOVIE RACE

MONROVIA, Cal., May 6. — This is the home of the famous Santa Anita race track. We are over here shooting some race scenes. I can't even pick the winner in a movie race where it's fixed.

Just reading of a fund the government has called the "Conscience Fund." If you feel that you have cheated the government you send the money. It now has $618,000. Now, offhand that sounds like a lot of conscience, but it figures out to just one-half cent apiece. So I imagine we still got quite a little bit on our mind that we haven't settled for.

Say how about the government having a "Conscience Fund"? They have skinned us many a time.

Yours,
Will Rogers.

2731   MR. ROGERS THINKS PLANES
          WILL CONQUER FOG YET

BEVERLY HILLS, Cal., May 7. — My old flying pardner Frank Hawks just breezed in here from Buenos Aires, Argentina, in 48 flying hours. Think of Buenos Aires being only two days away.

Air lines just coming in or out of Los Angeles alone have flown 243,000,000 miles, carrying 1,900,000 passengers. Accidents to passengers have been less than one to 25,000 that travel.

That "old devil" fog is tough, not only on aeroplanes, but ships, autos, horseback or afoot. But planes will be the first thing to lick it.

Yours,
Will Rogers.

2732   MR. ROGERS PINS A BOUQUET
                  ON A GREAT WOMAN FLIER

BEVERLY HILLS, Cal., May 8. — Amelia is streaking it from Mexico. When you take off from Mexico City you have already gained 7,500 feet altitude, even before you get your feet off the ground.

When you take a fast ship loaded with 400 gallons of gas off that field, you are an aviator, be you man or woman.

I bet you Amelia is the only woman that Mrs. Roosevelt could possibly in any way envy. If she could fly like her, Monday she would speak to the French in Paris, Tuesday the Female Comrades Club in Moscow, Wednesday to the Tokio Women's Club, next morning the whalers in the Bering Sea, New Orleans that night to address the Anti-Long Society.

                              Yours,
                                 Will Rogers.

2733   MR. ROGERS SUPPLIES DATA
                  ON THAT PACIFIC FLIGHT

BEVERLY HILLS, Cal., May 9. — As this editorial goes to press we have forty-six naval planes headed from Honolulu to the Midway Islands.

This flight is not only going to be great training for the navy fliers, but it's going to drive millions of Americans to a geography.

The reason they didn't send fifty planes was there is only room on the island for forty-six.

The way you tell a navy plane from an army plane is the naval planes are made to land on the land and the army has the ones that are made to land on the water.

These boys are getting over there pretty close to Japan. I look for the next Japanese manoeuvres to be held off Catalina Island.

                              Yours,
                                Will Rogers.

2734   ROGERS NOTES A MYSTERY
                  IN PACIFIC AIR MANOEUVRE

BEVERLY HILLS, Cal., May 10. — Yesterday as I went to press we couldn't find the Midway Islands; today as I go to print we can't find the islands or the forty-six airplanes either. Maybe the Japanese hid the islands on 'em.

Correction note: Frank Hawkes says I beat him out of nine hours, his flight from Buenos Aires to Los Angeles was thirty-nine hours, and not forty-eight. He says Brazil has the best air force in South America, says England and France have peddled a lot of old planes to a lot of those countries, that the U. S. is the only one sells 'em the latest model ones. Their own army and navy takes all their factories can make.

Yours,
Will Rogers.

2735 MR. ROGERS TAKES A STAND
ON A QUESTION OF THE DAY

LOS ANGELES, Cal., May 12. — Well, big headline today says Barbara is marrying a count, or a duke or something, and we get all excited and start criticizing as though she was a ward of the people.

It's her money. It's her life. She must pay a tremendous lot of taxes to our government. She deserves some right. Her fortune was made from ten cent purchases, so nobody got stuck very much.

So if she wants to pick up where the United States Government left off and finance all Europe it's her own business.

Yours,
Will Rogers.

2736 MR. ROGERS GIVES WARNING
OF ANOTHER DARK HORSE

ARCADIA, Cal., May 13. — Say Huey, you and all these other third-party guys better look out. This fellow Talmadge, Governor of Georgia, although a late starter among all these Presidential self-starters, is coming strong. Some of his talks make pretty good sense.

This coming election is going to be lots of fun when all these third-party candidates meet head on. All Roosevelt will have to do is just sit back and watch 'em cut each other's throats.

All of 'em will claim they are running on the real Democratic ticket and I expect Thomas Jefferson was about the very last real Democrat.

Yours,
Will Rogers.

2737   Mr. Rogers Finds A Reason
                For Uncle Sam Horning In

ARCADIA, Cal., May 14. — In these days of everybody hollering about the government butting into their business or the labor unions trying to run it there is just plenty of cases in America like this one that happened yesterday.

An old gentleman, Mr. Van Brunt that for sixty-five years has run his factory in Horicon, Wis., never had one speck of labor trouble, he just gave ninety old-time workers and five widows $3,000 apiece.

If everybody was Van Brunts there would be no need for anything, but there is men in business that don't belong in business any more than the government does and that's why the government has got to go in.

                          Yours,
                              Will Rogers.

2738   Mr. Rogers Joins The Cry
                For Bonus Greenbacks

BEVERLY HILLS, Cal., May 15. — Soldiers going to get their bonus, and I think they should have the first money we print.

There are so many different (and honest) opinions as to what more money would do to us that the only way we can find out is to print some.

Anyhow, that $2,000,000,000 is going to change hands so fast and so many times in the first few weeks, and with taxes getting higher and higher, it's going to wind up right back where it started, in Mr. Morgenthau's locker.

                          Yours,
                              Will Rogers.

2739   Mr. Rogers Is Exploring
                New California Wonders

SANTA MARIA, Cal., May 16. — Eddie Vail, one of California's real cowmen, and I are prowling through here.

This is a mighty pretty little town. They raise more different things, in this part of the country. At Lompoc near here is great fields of flowers (thousands of acres) for commercial use. Think of seeing a thousand acres of just flowers. Then out of the same ground they take a kind of sandstone for insulation. Then a big sugar beet factory and the biggest mustard fields in America. Cattle by the thousands.

Piece in the local paper about Mr. Hoover coming out against the NRA; also one about Jack Garner issuing a statement. I don't believe that. Garner thinks but don't talk.

Well, got to get up on the road.

Yours,
Will Rogers.

2740 ROGERS FINDS WHERE GARLIC
IS PRODUCED AND CONSUMED

SACRAMENTO, Cal., May 17. — Well, just been prowling along up the road. I found out how to cut out fast driving and worry and hurry. Just get up and start about two hours earlier than you had intended. That ought to be made a law.

Yesterday as I told you I run into a little town where all the mustard comes from that eventually goes on your fingers off the hot dog. Well, last night I stayed all night at Gilroy, and over 90 per cent of all the garlic is raised there. But here is the big astonishment. Boston is one of the greatest consumers of garlic in America.

So what you detect when you are speaking to a Harvard Bostonian is not all culture.

Yours,
Will Rogers.

2741 WILL ROGERS KEEPS FAITH
IN THE SOVIET'S AVIATORS

SACRAMENTO, Cal., May 19. — That was a terrible thing about that big Russian plane.

I saw it when I was there. They said themselves over there that it had never been much success as far as flying. But Russia is just at that stage like we used to be where they want the "biggest" of everything. So it made good "reading" when they would write how big it was.

It was a warehouse with six engines on it. They could jack it up and get it above the field in Moscow, but I don't think it had ever been out of town.

311

The great sport in Russia is parachute jumping. They used to take half the town up in this and let 'em jump.

But don't get the impression that all the planes there can't get out of town. It's the most air-ambitious nation in the world, and those old "Rushions" can fly.

Yours,
Will Rogers.

2742 MR. ROGERS MARKS TIME
NOW ON THE BONUS VOTE

SACRAMENTO, Cal., May 20. — On Wednesday is the big day of the bonus.

I am not following the usual custom and saying, "Wire your Senator." Any Senator that hasn't got his mind already made up by now, he would have to be one that couldn't read anyhow.

Besides, I doubt if this new method of "government by telegraph" which we are developing is quite as effective as it's advertised to be.

There is a good deal of difference between a vote and a telegram. In our system of voting they generally stop you after about once, or maybe twice, but any one person can send as many telegrams as they have money and can think up names to sign to 'em.

Yours,
Will Rogers.

2743 MR. ROGERS THINKS DANIEL
HAD A BREAK, AFTER ALL

SACRAMENTO, Cal., May 21. — In two adjoining columns today was:

"Mrs. Roosevelt goes down in coal mine to see operations 'in the raw.'" "Mr. Roosevelt goes to see Senate." The last item should have "in the raw" after it, too.

Mrs. Roosevelt has got the best of these two family visits. With her sympathy for the less fortunate she is bound to come away with admiration and pity. The President is liable to come away with just pity.

This is a cage he is going into. When he thinks he can go in there with 96 assorted animals and tell 'em where and when to lay down, he is confusing himself with Daniel.

Yours,
Will Rogers.

2744 MR. ROGERS IS IMPRESSED
BY THE PRESIDENT'S LOGIC

PASO ROBLES, Cal., May 22. — Mrs. Rogers and I poking down the road and we were listening to the President's speech.

I don't care if you are for or against the bonus, you have to admit he made what the lawyers call a mighty good brief, and he made Mr. Long swallow his boast that the President "was nothing but a politician and wouldn't dare to veto the bill."

The best line he had was, "We have enough for everybody, but we haven't got all that they want."

And, say, you got to give that Hitler credit. He come through with some facts that these other nations are going to have to do some studying to think up answers to.

His best line was, "A tank is a tank, a bomb is a bomb, no matter what nation has it."

Yours,
Will Rogers.

2745 WILL ROGERS'S TRIBUTE
TO 'MOST USEFUL WOMAN'

HOLLYWOOD, Cal., May 23. — Two or three weeks ago the very popular novelist Mrs. Kathleen Norris wrote me an awful nice letter asking me to say something about—I think it was the birthday of Jane Addams.

I wrote her I would and I fully intended too, but rattle-brain like, I just forgot it till I saw pictures of it in the paper. Then I felt terribly sorry. Now she is dead and I feel sorrier still.

Irvin Cobb just tells me she was the woman that remembered the people who everybody else forgot. I imagine that she was the most useful woman of this generation.

Yours,
Will Rogers.

2746   MR. ROGERS MAKES A NOTE
         OF WOMEN'S TOLERANCE

HOLLYWOOD, Cal., May 24. — Was reading today where the Federation of Women's Clubs was going to have a hot election. The woman in line for the presidency (she is now first vice president) they all admit has every qualification. Worked up for thirty years in the club. High class, talented, cultured lady, but she is an Indian.

You would expect intolerance from some organizations, but not from the most civilized one we have. Even one of the two great uncivilized tribes (the Republicans) elected dear old Charley Curtis.

So I don't believe these ladies are going to get bias. Course there is some of 'em that would love to meet around the convention campfire and shout: "Well, sisters, we scalped another Indian. We have to keep this club 100 per cent American." They can't afford to do that.

Yours,
Will Rogers.

2747   MR. ROGERS SPENT SUNDAY
         WITH THE SPORTING PAGES

LOS ANGELES, Cal., May 26. — The sporting pages were where the news was this Sunday morning.

Dear old Babe Ruth, God bless him, stepped into three fast balls and put 'em all out of bounds. Lawson Little, a Stanford boy, for the second year in succession collected a small portion of the British debt with a golf club.

A Mr. Owens, a colored lad of 21 years from Ohio State University broke practically all the world records there is, with the possible exception of horseshoe pitching and flagpole sitting.

Congress laid dormant, Hitler was refueling and Mussolini was changing records. But a man in California sued his wife for non-support.

Yours,
Will Rogers.

2748   MR. ROGERS TAKES NOTE
         OF THE NRA SLAUGHTER

HOLLYWOOD, Cal., May 27. — Poor old "New Deal." She went to bat three times today with the Supreme Court pitching and she struck out each time.

There was a bill called the Frazier-Lemke bill, where a farmer didn't have to pay his mortgage for five years. The court said Frazier and Lemke were both wrong.

Then come the NRA and they washed that up. And to make it a Republican holiday, they decided that a Mr. Humphrey that used to work for the Federal Trade Commission should be working there yet, even if he was a Republican.

So the Supreme Court just stole the spotlight from Jesse Owens.

Yours,
Will Rogers.

2749   MR. ROGERS WOULD AMEND
THE GOOD OL' CONSTITUTION

HOLLYWOOD, Cal., May 28. — Hurray for the old Constitution. Nobody wants to see that old lady led astray. But wouldn't this amendment to her be helpful?

"When Congress passes a law or a President exceeds his authority, have some person notify the Supreme Court what has happened and get them to examine the medicine and see if it's poison before it's given to the patients and not at the funeral."

This amendment would make the Supreme Court a preventive and not an autopsy jury.

Yours,
Will Rogers.

2750   MR. ROGERS ALSO LAUGHS
AT THE NRA AFTERMATH

HOLLYWOOD, Cal., May 29. — We are a funny people.

Business men have howled from every luncheon table the evils of the whole NRA. Then all at once the Supreme Court says, "The bridle is off, boys: from this day on every man for himself."

Now the same men are rushing back to the banquet tables and unoccupied microphones and shouting, "Wages must be maintained," "Cut-throat competition must be curbed," "Child labor is wrong," "The sweat shop must not return."

You just can't please some people.

Yours,
Will Rogers.

P. S. — Then the stock market went down six points.

2751   WILL ROGERS OFFERS EPIC
                FOR SUPREME COURT RULING

SANTA MONICA, Cal., May 30. — Our State Assembly is having a terrible fight. There is twenty-seven EPICs (Eliminate Poverty in California), the Sinclair ticket, that is out of a membership of eighty in the lower house. Well, the fight is just among these twenty-seven. It's a bill to stop all these unemployed that's flocking into the State (it passed the lower house). Some EPICs say they can eliminate the poverty in the State, but they can't eliminate all the poverty that come in. Others say that one State can't bar people of other States.

All of which gets back to my plan, that is of being able to wire the Supreme Court and ask them. They reply with a night letter and the whole thing is settled once and for all.

                          Yours,
                          Will Rogers.

2752   MR. ROGERS CROWS A BIT
                OVER HIS OWN JUDGMENT

HOLLYWOOD, Cal., May 31. — We all like to crow when a prediction turns out good. I been saying for fifteen years that Jack Garner was as common sense man as we have. Nick Longworth told me Garner was the smartest man in the House. Now our very popular (and usually up to date) Time magazine just this week, finds Garner quite a fellow.

Say, just talk to some small merchants or druggists and get them to tell you what's going on now in the price cutting, chiseling and conniving line.

It's terrible to have a law telling you you got to do something. But you ain't going to do it unless there is.

                          Yours,
                          Will Rogers.

2753   MR. ROGERS JOINS IN TASK
                OF TRYING TO SALVAGE NRA

LOS ANGELES, Cal., June 2. — Well sir a forlorn looking gentleman come to my house this Sunday afternoon. Said he was one of Roosevelt's cabinet, and he looked it. It was Mr. Roper, Secretary of Commerce.

I try to make it a point to never turn anybody away. First one of the New Deal I had seen since the Supreme Court took their matches away from 'em. But he was a game Southern gentleman. No kicks, no squawks.

He and I searched around through the burned embers to see if any little New Deal object might be salvaged. We decided that with big business operating under the old "dog-eat-dog" plan, so many dogs would eventually get bit that parts of the NRA would look like a halo by 1936.

Yours,
Will Rogers.

2754   MR. ROGERS CASTS AN EYE
             OVER THE CURRENT NEWS

HOLLYWOOD, Cal., June 3. — France won't have to go off the gold now. Their new boat broke the record, so that means all Americans with nothing to do when they get over there will want to go on the fastest boat.

The United States Treasury says that expenditures are running a billion and a half under estimates. That means more money than schemes.

These baccalaureate addresses given to graduates don't offer 'em much encouragement outside of advising 'em to vote the straight Republican ticket.

Yours,
Will Rogers.

2755   MR. ROGERS SEES NO HOPE
             OF MENDING CONSTITUTION

HOLLYWOOD, Cal., June 4. — Looks to me like Washington always asks the wrong man when they want to know something. Now today they called in all the big Democratic leaders to see what THEY "think" can be done. Well, why didn't they just quietly ask the Supreme Court what "could" be done?

Now, if nothing can't be done under the present Constitution, why they better just forget it, for I bet you a span of old gray mules that you ain't going to get folks to change that Constitution. That's like asking an old man to change the brand of his chewing tobacco.

Yours,
Will Rogers.

2756   Mr. Rogers Notes A Turn
In The Tide Of Our Luck

HOLLYWOOD, Cal., June 5. — The U. S. finally got an even break with all Europe today. Americans won $2,745,000 and all the rest of the world combined only $2,966,000 on the big Irish sweepstake, a lottery on the great English Derby.

They are going to try to retain the best features of the NRA by persuasion. Hours and wages.

You got to admit Roosevelt is trying to get a semblance of fairness. But they wouldn't even do it by law, so this scheme looks doubtful.

                    Yours,
                    Will Rogers.

2757   Mr. Rogers A Bit Amazed
By Two Remarks Of A Day

BEVERLY HILLS, Cal., June 6. — Two kinder amazing statements in the papers today.

The President was supposed to be quoted as saying, "Unless the Wagner bill and the Guffey-Snyder bill passes, it might be necessary to call out the militia."

The other was before the great Federation of Women's Clubs convention at Detroit. Mrs. Thomas G. Winter, who has represented the Federation in Hollywood, reported:

"Pictures have been cleaned up, and it was by the help of the solid middle classes, and not by the intelligensia. Society classes are the dirtiest-minded people in America."

The social order received a couple of pretty tough blows from two different sources.

                    Yours,
                    Will Rogers.

2758   Rogers Finds We Are Not
So Badly Off After All

HOLLYWOOD, Cal., June 7. — To read what all these critics of our country write, you would naturally think that everybody else was just sitting pretty.

But France has offered their Premiership to everybody over there but Chevalier, and they know he is too smart to take it.

England just today traded horses right in the middle of Thames River. Half of Italy has gone to Africa with a gun on their shoulder.

Japan is just looking over Chinese maps to see where to send their army.

Russia must be in some devilment, we never hear of 'em any more.

So you see there's none of 'em that we can point with pride to. It's just a bad time to be in the government running business anywhere.

Yours,
Will Rogers.

2759   MR. ROGERS CITES EXPERT
ON CONSTITUTION LAW

LOS ANGELES, Cal., June 9. — See where my old friend Alfalfa Bill Murray says he is with the Constitution if he has to be a Republican to do it.

With Bill joining the Supreme Court, that makes ten men on it. The very thing that must be avoided is to raise the number.

But now that my little joke is over, let me tell you something about Bill Murray. My daddy was a member of the Constitutional Convention that made Oklahoma's scenario, and he told me: "Willie, this Murray guy that's running this convention is smart on constitutional law."

Say, Bill has majored in that, with a 40-year course.

Yours,
Will Rogers.

2760   MR. ROGERS HAS HIS FEARS
IN THIS KIDNAPPING CASE

HOLLYWOOD, Cal., June 10. — Hope nobody don't appeal this kidnapping case to the Supreme Court, for it certainly interferes with State rights, and as they have just decided that the Federal Government has no more standing than Santa Claus, why, they might make 'em turn 'em loose.

It kinder shows that the government can do something. They ought to turn all crime over to 'em and take it out of local politics.

But all they have to do to find out who the criminal is nowadays is just find the one that's been pardoned the most times.

These two guys seemed to just have made one-night stands out of all the jails in the Northwest.

Yours,
Will Rogers.

2761   MR. ROGERS STILL PONDERS
THE WAYS OF POLITICIANS

BEVERLY HILLS, Cal., June 11. — Well, I got a kick out of that bunch of unemployed old-timers who call themselves the "Grass Root boys." They just met and "denounced" and "redenounced." Give a prize to the fellow that called the President the most names.

But they all do it. When Mr. Hoover was in why the other side did the same thing. In fact I think it's the same names they called him, for neither side has ever been original enough to think of new ones.

That's what makes politics such a high-class gentlemanly game. Prize fighters meet and fight and then are considered lowbrows for saying, "Well, the best man won."

Yours,
Will Rogers.

2762   MR. ROGERS IS HOBNOBBING
WITH SOME FAST PEOPLE

BEVERLY HILLS, Cal., June 12. — Setting here on the running board of my car, about a hundred people sitting around, we are all trying to make a movie to try to make the world laugh.

Step and Fetchit just come up with Jesse Owens, the Cleveland colored boy of Ohio State, who breaks world's records as easy as the rest of us break commandments. He is a very, very modest fellow. Says he will be tickled to death if he can just win these events here Saturday as he thinks these are the best boys he has met. He is entered in four events. He holds the world's record in three of 'em and is tied for the other.

Funny thing, on the picture with us is Jim Thorpe, our greatest all-around athlete of all time.

Yours,
Will Rogers.

2763   Mr. Rogers Must Admit
          That A 'Hero' Is Slipping

BEVERLY HILLS, Cal., June 13. — I hate to report any shortcomings in one of my heroes, but Huey is going back. Imagine only being able to talk sixteen hours. Why before he was fattened by the luxury of senatorial life, he would have talked right on into July.

But at that he pulled the biggest and most educational novelty ever introduced in the Senate. He read 'em the Constitution of the U. S. A lot of 'em thought he was reviewing a new book.

Headline says, "Japanese by Thousands March Further Into China." Yes and in forty years they will all be Chinamen.

Yours,
Will Rogers.

2764   Rogers Finds Kate Smith
          Right, The Experts Wrong

BEVERLY HILLS, Cal., June 14. — If you have seen a fellow entirely hidden behind a thin lamp post today, it's your favorite sporting writer, who predicted Max Baer in the early part of the first round. From what I can hear Kate Smith was the only one guessed it right. So Katie, from now on I am for you no matter which side the mountain the moon is on.

I am glad the judges told us who won, for you couldn't tell from the broadcasting. Broadcasting for all big sporting events should be sold to Henry Ford, for he only tells you who is paying for it, and don't try to sell you a car, or name Dizzy Dean's dog.

Yours,
Will Rogers.

2765   Mr. Rogers Takes A Look
          At The World Picture

SANTA MONICA, Cal., June 16. — They have such a thing among nations, like they do among people, called "chickens come home to roost."

England and all the big nations are awful sore at Italy about Abyssinia, and Italy is just as wrong as she can be, but all these others have gobbled up something at some time, and Mussolini reminds 'em of it, and that makes 'em sorer than ever.

321

Reading history has put all these ideas in Japan's head. Us giving back the Philippines may ease our conscience a little. It almost pays a nation to remain small and point with pride that they haven't gobbled up anything.

                              Yours,
                                Will Rogers.

2766   MR. ROGERS REPORTS FATE
            HAS SMILED ON CALIFORNIA

HOLLYWOOD, Cal., June 17. — I don't know how you all are fixed with your State Legislatures, but we finally had some luck with ours at last. It adjourned last night, and there is a spontaneous celebration going on today that is bordering on Armistice Day.

Now if they can just get the main one to adjourn in Washington things will just go a sailing and then all the politicians will have to do is just sit back and argue over who the credit belongs to for recovery.

I was asked to deliver a commencement day address, but I couldn't do it. The pupils knew more about politics than I did.

                              Yours,
                                Will Rogers.

2767   MR. ROGERS IS MADE HAPPY
            BY AN ITEM IN THE NEWS

HOLLYWOOD, Cal., June 18. — That's great news about those two South American nations that have been fighting for three years, Bolivia and Paraguay. According to the terms of peace, neither side has to take any of the land that they were fighting over. Bolivia thought for awhile that she was going to have to take it. It goes back to the Indians.

Hurrah for Judge Landis. The old judge made a mighty wise decision. Especially in not allowing them to exploit this boy just for publicity alone. You young blades might not know it, but in us fellows' younger days this same Judge Landis hung a 21 million traffic fine on the Standard Oil Company.

                              Yours,
                                Will Rogers.

2768   Mr. Rogers Puts Us Down
               As A Nation Of Fleas

SANTA MONICA, Cal., June 19. — At the great San Diego World's Fair yesterday Mr. Hoover received a tremendous ovation.

There is no country in the world where a person changes from a hero to a goat, and a goat to a hero, or vice versa, as they do with us. And all through no change in them. The change is always with us.

It's not our public men that you can't put your finger on. It's our public. We are the only fleas weighing over 100 pounds. We don't know what we want, but are ready to bite somebody to get it.

                       Yours,
                       Will Rogers.

2769   Mr. Rogers Hails A Tax
               He Considers Painless

HOLLYWOOD, Cal., June 20. — All the big influential papers this morning are full of the "soak the rich." And you can tell from the tone of their voices they have been "soaked."

But as the scheme is mostly on inheritance, he don't really hit 'em good till they die, so I would call that the nearest to a painless tax that could be invented. You don't pay it till you die and then you don't know it.

I would sure liked to have seen Huey's face when he was woke up in the middle of the night by the President, who said, "Lay over Huey, I want to get in with you."

                       Yours,
                       Will Rogers.

2770   Mr. Rogers Finds Just One
               Requirement For Senate

BEVERLY HILLS, Cal., June 21. — Mr. Roosevelt went to see Yale race Harvard in boats today. Funny he don't go to see the big league row at Poughkeepsie. These Western colleges can drag an anchor and beat Yale or Harvard.

They are seating a new Senator today. The whole argument is whether he is 30 years old or not. West Virginia keeps no records and they can't remember back that far.

Funny thing about being a U. S. Senator, the only thing the law says you have to be is 30 years old. Not another single requirement necessary. They just figure that a man that old got nobody to blame but himself if he gets caught in there.

         Yours,
         Will Rogers.

2771   Mr. Rogers Wants To Hear
      All The Bad News Now

BEVERLY HILLS, Cal., June 23. — Well this "soak-the-rich" program is about all you hear about now and you can tell just to a dollar how much a man has got by how sore he is.

They are supposed to put the thing over till next Congress, but Senator Joe Robinson in this morning's paper had the best suggestion, as he generally always does, for he is mighty level-headed and plenty smart. Joe says to thrash it out at this session, "Why go home leaving everybody in fear of the next session?"

Hold the clinic now and operate if they are going to operate. You won't help business by postponement. Why not go ahead and let everybody know just what it's going to cost 'em to die, for the way it is now, a fellow don't know whether to die or not.

         Yours,
         Will Rogers.

2772   Mr. Rogers Is In Favor
      Of One Soak-Rich Move

BEVERLY HILLS, Cal., June 24. — See there is a bill in Congress to do away with tax exempt bonds.

That's the best bill of all of 'em. The way it is a man could have a million-dollar income from tax-free bonds, own no property or nothing else, and not pay one cent of tax. And it's all lawful.

If you can make all these bonds pay tax they will be doing one of the most fair share-the-wealth plans there is.

It was put in so that a town, or a State, or the government could sell more bonds than it ought to.

         Yours,
         Will Rogers.

2773   MR. ROGERS DOESN'T THINK
        THAT WE ARE SO SMART

BEVERLY HILLS, Cal., June 25. — In schools they have what they call intelligence tests.

Well if nations held 'em I don't believe we would be what you would call a favorite to win it.

The chain letter thing lasted just two days in England. Over here it took us a whole month to figure it out. And Mexico laughed the thing out of their country before lunch.

Then there was "technocracy," which we took serious for over three months.

There is still a lot of monkey in us. Throw anything you want to into our cage and we will give it serious consideration.

                                Yours,
                                    Will Rogers.

2774   MR. ROGERS, HISTORIAN,
        RECORDS A NOTED BATTLE

BEVERLY HILLS, Cal., June 26. — The first battle of the next war was fought in N. Y. City Tuesday night. Big Italy met Little Abysinia and Mussolini's first Spring drive was halted in its tracks.

General Joe Louis, head of the Ethiopian forces, met El Duce Carnera (the biggest Roman of them all) and treated him like a Christian of gladiatorial days.

Now there is a movement on to send "Lion" Louis to Abysinia to meet Mussolini's whole army. His trip is being gladly paid for by several American philanthropists, new friends of Abysinian liberty.

A Mr. Braddock, a Mr. Baer (not Bugs) and even a German, a Mr. Schmelling have contributed to make Mr. Louis's trip to Africa more permanent.

                                Yours,
                                    Will Rogers.

2775   MR. ROGERS HEARS OF PLAN
        WHICH HE THINKS IS GOOD

BEVERLY HILLS, Cal., June 27. — One thing you got to say for an administration that tries out a lot of plans, some of 'em are apt to be pretty good.

325

Now this one that broke out yesterday where they help out these young folks, that sounds awful good. Course I look for bountiful editorial condemnation, for it's going to cost money. But if you help out the young folks up to 20, and the old ones over 60, that only gives a fellow a little stretch in between of about forty years where he has to do any worrying for himself (or herself as the sex may be).

If we can keep the young happy and the old satisfied, why all the middle-aged have to look out for is its women automobile drivers.

Yours,
Will Rogers.

2776   MR. ROGERS SEES ROOSEVELT
             KEEPING THE CONGRESS BUSY

BEVERLY HILLS, Cal., June 28. — Every day now Congress gets a message from the White House. Congress opens the letter with about the same enthusiasm as we do one with a "please remit." He sure keeps those old boys going. Every time they start looking toward home he slips 'em another odd chore to do.

Today's message he told 'em: "There is some folks that's suing us about the gold. Now there is a ruling that you can't sue us unless the government says you can. Now today's chore for you boys is to say that they can't. That's all for today. Your section boss, Franklin."

Yours,
Will Rogers.

2777   WILL ROGERS IS TOUCHED
             BY PLIGHT OF CONGRESS

BEVERLY HILLS, Cal., June 30. — It's geting the time of year in Washington, D. C., when the old Senator or Congressman begins to wonder if his opponent wasn't really the winner after all.

If those babies oozed knowledge like they will perspiration for the next month, we would be a great nation.

Mr. Roosevelt's got the laugh on 'em. He has a swimming pool in the White House, and he just sends 'em a message and then dives off in a nice cool pool while they sweat and cuss and fight off the professors.

You know this administration has shown that there is no insect that can bother a statesman like a professor.

Yours,
Will Rogers.

2778   Mr. Rogers Is Worrying
About Italy's Troubles

BEVERLY HILLS, Cal., July 1. — You got to hand it to Mussolini. He is at least honest. He says that the war in Abyssinia will last about five years, and that it will take an additional fifteen years to mop up loose odds and ends.

But suppose they don't strike oil? And the whole thing will have been for nothing. The Lord help his geologists who have misled him.

War talk in Europe has pretty near died out on account of no international conferences being held. They haven't got much chance of getting sore at each other.

Yours,
Will Rogers.

2779   Mr. Rogers Has A Theory
On The 'Sucker' Business

BEVERLY HILLS, Cal., July 2. — If you are holding in a holding company why you are still a holding this morning. Congress voted yesterday that as bad as a lot of 'em are, they are better than nothing.

I imagine the President knows that there has been swindling and crookedness and he wanted to protect people from it, but there they go trying to do something against human nature. Anytime a slick salesman meets a ten dollar bill there is a deal made. All it has to be is on the instalment plan.

There is something about American folks that they think it must be on the level or the company wouldn't trust us to pay the other payments. It's never entered our head that the first payment more than pays for it.

Yours,
Will Rogers.

2780   Mr. Rogers Is Heartened
By A Trip To The 'Sticks'

STAMFORD, Texas, July 3. — Cowboy sports and contests are about the most popular thing there is, especially where they know what it's all about.

I had often heard of the great time this little city holds every year. It's called a cowboy reunion and it is. It's put on by real ranch hands. This is the heart of the old Texas ranch country. The outfits send in their chuck wagons and they have a great time. Lots of good horses and lots of good ropers. Grass is high and cattle are a good price and everybody feeling fine.

If Mr. Brisbane don't want to use his old slogan any more I will take "Don't Sell America Short."

Yours,
Will Rogers.

2781   Mr. Rogers Finds We Live
In An Interesting Period

BEVERLY HILLS, Cal., July 4. — Well, breakfast in Fort Worth this morning. Did kinder want to go on and see what the boys in Congress was doing as there was a plane standing there that would have put me there this afternoon.

Another leaving for Brownsville, Texas, and old Mexico. I looked longingly at it. Another leaving for Tulsa and Claremore. I did want to go on it, but finally settled on one for California, as that's what I should do, come on home.

In here at 4 o'clock this afternoon, fifteen hundred miles. It don't take you long to go a long distance and get back nowadays.

Lot of hollering among the rich and near-rich. We are living in a great time, something to get excited about every minute.

Yours,
Will Rogers.

2782   Rogers Suggests Reform
For July 4 Celebrations

SANTA MONICA, Cal., July 5. — That liberty that we got 159 years ago Thursday was a great thing, but they ought to pass a law that we could only celebrate it every 100 years, for at the rate of accidents yesterday we won't have enough people to celebrate it every year.

And the speeches? Did you read them? Never was as much politics indulged in under the guise "freedom and liberty." They was 5 per cent what George Washington did, and 95 per cent what the speaker intended to do.

What this country needs on July the fourth is not more "liberty or more freedom," it's a Roman candle that only shoots out of one end.

Yours,
Will Rogers.

2783   WILL ROGERS IS PROUD
             OF BOTH THE HELENS

SANTA MONICA, Cal., July 7. — How are some of these sporting writers going to ever get through apologising for the things they said about Helen Wills's gameness?

They didn't think she could have been hurt that day in '33, for she never died on the court. Two long years of hearing jibes at her sportsmanship and nursing herself back to health, just to show 'em, is a long time.

And don't forget that other Helen. She put up a great fight and it was tough for her to lose. We can sure swell up and be mighty proud of both of 'em. And they are even—they both met the Queen and King.

And say I bet if the truth was known those two girls don't hate each other any worse than any other two star rival athletes in any line.

Yours,
Will Rogers.

2784   MR. ROGERS PAYS TRIBUTE
             TO A GRAND OLD GENTLEMAN

BEVERLY HILLS, Cal., July 8. — Hurrah for Mr. Rockefeller, 96 years old today, one of the very few men that knew how to give money away so that every dollar does good. That's more than our government can do. It's more than anybody can do.

All over the world there is a Rockefeller doctor swatting at a mosquito or trapping a poisonous fly. I flew the whole east coast of Brazil and they have eliminated mosquitos. However, I do wish he would spread some of that Standard oil (or even Gulf) on some of these home-talent mosquitos.

There is no end to that old gentleman's talents. He beat insurance without dying. They just got discouraged and paid him. He will make the 100 and some to spare.

Yours,
Will Rogers.

2785   Mr. Rogers Raises To Greet
           A Long-Neglected Party

SANTA MONICA, Cal., July 9. — Well sir, funny thing showed up in the papers yesterday. Something we hadn't heard of in so long that it seemed like reviving an article from King Tut's tomb. It was "the budget."

Remember old budget? Well they dug him up, and they are even talking about balancing him. Course they won't be able to do that. You take a rope walker that's laid off for years and they never come back.

But it's good just to hear the old boy's name mentioned again. Young folks won't know who he is, but he was quite a useful fellow in his day.

Budget is the name, spelled B-U-D-G-E-T, pronounced bud-jet.
                    Yours,
                         Will Rogers.

2786   Mr. Rogers Has Discovered
           Il Duce Is Not A 'Mudder'

BEVERLY HILLS, Cal., July 10. — Well, we often heard of folks waiting for a dry day to hold a picnic, but Mussolini waiting for a dry day to hold a war is sorter new.

That makes a great ad for good roads. Our Chambers of Commerce can put out a slogan, "Build good roads in our part of the country, then in case of war we won't have to lay off at all, we can fight every day. Remember be patriotic, have good roads and fight rain or shine."

I wonder if this Abysinian King could sue and get his dues back that he has paid into the League of Nations for protection.
                    Yours,
                         Will Rogers.

2787   Mr. Rogers, The Reporter,
           Covers A Typical Inquiry

BEVERLY HILLS, Cal., July 11. — It looks like you don't make a good witness or committee member in a Washington investigation unless you call each other a liar or insult the President of the United States.

Will Rogers as "Doctor John Pearly" in Steamboat Round the Bend, *one of Rogers' last motion pictures, adapted from the novel by Ben Lucien Burman* (Fox Film Corporation, 1935).

Chairman of the committee: "Mr. Jones, we are led to believe you know something about the matter we are investigating."

Mr. Jones: "You are a liar and the President of the United States is a horse thief."

Call the next witness.

"Mr. Smith, what do you know of lobbying about holding companies?"

Mr. Smith: "You are all liars and the President is fooling you. His mother was a Stalin and his father was a Mussolini and he is taking the money away from us to send to Hitler."

And this goes on day after day.

Yours,
Will Rogers.

2788   WILL ROGERS DIAGNOSES
         THE CRISIS IN ABYSSINIA

SANTA MONICA, Cal., July 12. — Now they find that Italy is after the trade of Abyssinia. The Japanese are in there. They are underselling everybody all over the world. Well a few years ago when we thought we had a patent on "mass production" we was underselling everybody.

England wants Italy to lay off Abyssinian territory. Yet look at the map. They control three sides of Abyssinia themselves. They have already got theirs.

So you see there is two sides to every argument, and it's all a matter of "whose dog is bit."

Yours,
Will Rogers.

2789   WILL ROGERS REMARKS

SANTA MONICA, Cal., July 14. — California has been lucky, we escaped the winds, the floods, the drouths, and the heat, but pestilence finally caught us, the boweevil descended on us in trainloads, 3500 laywers of the American Bar Association are here eating us out of house and home. They are here, they say, "to save the Constitution, to preserve State rights." What they ought to be here for, that would make this convention immortal, is to kick the crooks out of their profession. They should recommend a law that every case that went on trial, the lawyer defending should be tried first, then if he come clear, he was eligible to defend. As it is now they are trying the wrong man.

Yours,
Will Rogers.

2790   MR. ROGERS FINDS A CHANGE
         IN THE REPUBLICAN MOOD

BEVERLY HILLS, Cal., July 15. — Pat Hurley called me up last night. Remember Pat, Secretary of War during the time when we had no trouble with the Constitution but had it with everything else.

Well sir, there was a cheerful, and in fact an arrogant ring in Pat's voice. You know Republicans' voices are changing. They are not whispering any more. You meet one now and he hollers across the street:

"Hello, Hello, did you know that our free American institutions are in greater danger today than ever before? Did you know that our Constitution is in jeopardy? Did you know they are going to take our Rolls Royces away from us and make us ride in a mere Cadillac? Did you know that six months ago there wasn't a Republican Presidential candidate in a car load, and now there is over a million.

"Happy days are here again."

Yours,
Will Rogers.

2791   MR. ROGERS IS HOBNOBBING
         WITH LEADERS OF THE BAR

BEVERLY HILLS, Cal., July 16. — Say, wait a minute. This heat out here is just about as tough as it is anywhere.

Went down and spoke at some lawyers' meeting last night. They didn't think much of my little squib yesterday about driving the shysters out of their profession. They seemed to kinder doubt just who would have to leave. Pretty serious, some of 'em. But the big percentage are regular guys.

Had three ex-Cabinet members there from three different Presidents, Hurley, Secretary of War under Mr. Hoover, Wilbur, Secretary of Navy under Mr. Coolidge, and Will Hays, who elected, who served under Mr. Harding.

New Governor of Maryland, Governor Nice, seemed a fine fellow and he accomplished something. I told him, "You beat Man of War, ex-Governor Ritchie."

Yours,
Will Rogers.

2792   WILL ROGERS DISCUSSES
COURTS AND COURTSHIPS

SANTA MONICA, Cal., July 17. — Every morning some State court declares "so and so tax declared illegal." If this keeps on everybody will get back everything they paid in.

In other words the way the courts are going now they may declare this whole depression and everything connected with it illegal, and that it all has to be done over again.

Say, that judge sure give European fortune hunters fits. It's generally men that do it, but this time it was a girl who led our rich young hopeful astray, which proved that the young American male can be as sappy as the female.

Yours,
Will Rogers.

2793   MR. ROGERS TAKES A LOOK
AT THE DAY'S DISPATCHES

SANTA MONICA, Cal., July 18. — News today, papers say that the market stood still. Yes, and so did Congress. Rain and no war in Abyssinia. Heat not so bad as it was. Now that the AAA raised prices on all products they are about to say it's not constitutional.

England let our chorus girls out. Well, that's all right. Every country should be allowed to protect its own labor. Be nobody more broke up over it, however, than the English "Johnnies." American Bar Association yesterday come out very strong against unethical and shyster lawyers. Looks like I been vindicated.

Yours,
Will Rogers.

Will Rogers and Wiley Post at Fairbanks, Alaska, August 15, 1935, prior to take off for Point Barrow.

2794   Mr. Rogers Sees Lawyers
          Ready To Run The Country

SANTA MONICA, Cal., July 19. — Well the lawyers of the American Bar Association convention are leaving us. Think they had a good time. Like all conventions, they didn't do a thing. No convention ever did anything.

If this country ever becomes civilized the first thing eliminated would be people gadding around to get to a convention. And the humorous thing about 'em is they always wait and hold 'em in the hottest weather. Convention slogans should be, "Let's meet and perspire together."

It seemed to be the unanimous opinion of the convention that the management of the United States should be entirely in the hands of lawyer judges, and that elected representatives of the people didn't know what they was doing.

                                       Yours,
                                       Will Rogers.

2795   Mr. Rogers Sees Sure Sign
          That Congress Nears End

SANTA MONICA, Cal., July 21. — Mexico's President stopped gambling in Tiajuana and the whole town is left unemployed. It's just like if they stopped lobbying in Washington thousands would be thrown out of employment.

Mrs. Vice President Garner has gone home to Uvalde. That's the best tip that Congress won't run much longer. She has gone home to clean the gun and feed the bird dog. Congress will blow up about the 10th of August.

You can all have your Einsteins, your Edisons and your Robert Fultons, but yesterday somebody invented a safety pin that flies shut instead of open, and you can feed 'em to your babies with oatmeal. If that's not a contribution to the world there never was one.

                                       Yours,
                                       Will Rogers.

2796   Mr. Rogers Is Excited
          Over That Soviet Flight

SANTA MONICA, Cal., July 22. — Say there is some "Rushians" that's taking-off soon to fly to San Francisco from Moscow. They are cutting across and coming right over the North Pole. It's about a sixty to seventy-hour non-stop flight. (One across the Atlantic is about half that long.)

If they make it they going to just about go to the head of the class in flights. Wouldn't it be wonderful if they did finally turn that North Pole into a filling station.

If they make it we want to give 'em a great welcome, not hold anything back just because they might be Bolsheviki Rushians. Great achievement is non-political. I believe in giving credit even to a brain trust professor if he should happen to do something worth while.

Yours,
Will Rogers.

2797   Mr. Rogers Arises To Deny
A Bit Of Exaggeration

BEVERLY HILLS, Cal., July 23. — Wiley Post and I been blathering about flying over to a ranch in New Mexico and some guy with poor slant on geography got it mixed up with Siberia in Russia. Looks like New Mexico has got a suit.

England says the old armament treaties of Washington in 1922 are dead, that it wounded the pride of nations to be told that they were inferior. That's right. A nation can be small, but it don't want it put in treaties that it's small. Besides, it's the little nations that should be allowed the most armament.

Lack of armament has got nothing to do with wars. Abyssinia has just got so many six-foot bows and arrows and so many nine-foot ones.

Yours,
Will Rogers.

2798   Mr. Rogers Has A Digest
Of The Political News

BEVERLY HILLS, Cal., July 24. — Good deal of news in the papers last day or so.

Republicans feel very confident of taking over the government in a year and a half from now, but some of 'em like Bert Snell and Ham Fish, think that's a little long to wait, and they are suggesting letting Roosevelt out now and taking the thing over themselves at once.

They holler about the Constitution. Well it says you are elected for four years. But what's a Constitution when your boys need the work now?

Ham and Bert are giving Mutt and Jeff a run.

Yours,
Will Rogers.

2799   MR. ROGERS IS NOW HOPEFUL
         OF OUR STAYING NEUTRAL

SANTA MONICA, Cal., July 25. — Here is how getting into wars starts. Italy warned England that they were not to sell arms to Abyssinia That's verging on fighting talk.

Guess we will be able to keep out of it, for we don't seem to have anything anybody wants (of course, only on credit).

Went down last night to a world's championship wrestling match. Us movie actors are advised to go there by our producers so we can learn how to act. It was a fine show, everybody enjoyed it, but wrestling managements are overlooking an extra big revenue, for folks would pay even more to see them rehearse with each other before the match.

Yours,
Will Rogers.

2800   ROGERS ON A FLYING TRIP
         SEES A BEAUTIFUL COUNTRY

VERMEJO PARK, N. M., July 26. — This sure is a beautiful country up in here, lakes, streams, mountains, fish, deer, elk, everything. Every time we would see a good looking ranch and a little meadow down in the canyon Wiley Post would set his Lockheed down on it.

Visited our old friend Waite Phillips first. He has a marvelous place, and 325,000 acres of pretty country.

Now we are at the famous Vermejo ranch, the greatest fishing and game place in the whole Southwest. Wiley is fishing, and I am out looking at cattle.

Yours,
Will Rogers.

2801 MR. ROGERS IS SEEING LOTS
       ON TRIP WITH WILEY POST

DURANGO, Col., July 28. — Towns are like people. They are proud of what they have. Trinidad, Col., with enough coal to melt the North Pole down till it runs.

Then Wiley hit a beeline over the tops of the mountains to Durango, a beautiful little city, out of the way and glad of it. Gold, silver and Mesa Verde cliff dwelling ruins, where civilization flourished before it started to go backward.

Today Wiley is flying over Brice Canyon, Zion Canyon, over, down, and through the Grand Canyon, Hoover Dams, New Lake.

No wonder American people are filling roads, trains and air. There is so much to see. What we lack in reading we make up in looking.

Yours,
Will Rogers.

2802 MR. ROGERS WANTS ANYONE
       HE FIGHTS TO BE CIVILIZED

BEVERLY HILLS, Cal., July 29. — Say did you read about Mussolini's army being camped on a stream and the Abyssinians went above 'em and diverted the creek and left 'em with no water (that's a dry country down there).

I can't imagine anything any more disconcerting to an army than to wake up in the morning and find the river hid from you.

Modern armies have everything, but there is just something about a native in any country in the world, where he seems to have more sense than any general army corps. Our old Apache Geronimo drove nineteen sets of United States Army officers "nuts." The Boers hid the Englishmen's tea for two years. Cortez's great, great grandchildren in Mexico are still trying to whip the Yaquis.

If I was going to fight somebody I would pick out the most civilized one I could find, cause they are the dumbest.

Yours,
Will Rogers.

2803 MR. ROGERS IS A BIT IN AWE
       OF THE ARKANSAS NATIVE

SANTA MONICA, Cal., July 30. — Aimee Semple McPherson's daughter is in the Ozarks and the Arkansawyers notified her that she was welcome but that they didn't want to be "redeemed, saved or liquidated."

That's right, too. There is pretty strong characters down there. You can't redeem 'em, you just join 'em. That's what I had to do about 27 years ago with one of 'em.

Joe Robinson is another one, leader of 96 picked men of the whole United States who are in the Senate.

Anytime you tangle with an Arkansaw hillbilly or hillbillyess, you are going to run second.

Yours,
Will Rogers.

2804   Mr. Rogers Thinks A Lot
        Of Talk Is Being Wasted

SANTA MONICA, Cal., July 31. — Here is your headlines in the papers every day.

"Jim Doakes delivers blistering attack on Roosevelt," "Woodruff, Republican of Michigan, denounces heartily New Deal in its entirely," "Colonel William A. Bohunk says unless country returned to good old Republican rule Moscow will annex us," "Dr. Jasbo, the well-known infantile paralysis specialist, a man of great means and a life-long Republican, says there is something about the affliction and it's after effects that delusions the patient to want to bring equality, it's purely a mental disease and should be kept out of office."

Now, it's sixteen months till election. You think they going to feed people on that for sixteen long months? No. The boys started their race too early. The time to make your plea to the jury is just before they go out. You can't lecture a jury for a year and four months.

Yours,
Will Rogers.

2805   Rogers Struggling Along,
        Rallies To 'Soak Rich' Cry

BEVERLY HILLS, Cal., Aug. 1. — Here is rather an amazing statement. It didn't get much publicity in the press, but it was in there. It was made by the President, who has access to the records and must know:

"Fifty-eight of the richest people in the U. S. paid no Federal tax on 37 per cent of their incomes."

This soaking the rich has got two sides to it. Roosevelt gets him a pack of humorously called "brain trusters" to help him devise ways and means of trying to get at this extra 37 per cent and the rich get them some lawyers that are just as smart as Roosevelt's tribe, and their job is to cook up an antidote.

So up to now most of the soaking has been done in the papers and not at the cash register.

Yours,
Will Rogers.

2806   ROGERS REPORTS ONE SPORT
                BOOMING THESE DAYS

SANTA MONICA, Cal., Aug 2. — Well, haven't got much time to do any editorializing today. Tomorrow (Saturday) the big world's championship cowboy contest starts, and I am busy setting on the fence blathering with 'em (which is about all I can do along cowboy sports line).

Some of 'em are right from my home range in Oklahoma, and I think learned to rope on some of my stock.

It's like baseball, it's a sport you can attend and now know that it's not "in the bag." You can't put a calf or a bucking horse in a bag.

It's not like prize fighting or wrestling, where the loser gets a big slice too. Nobody is paid a nickel but the winners.

The depression hit everything but horseback riding. There was never as many people riding and interested in ranch life, but I must get back to me blathering, "now Crosby can you?"

Yours,
Will Rogers.

2807   MR. ROGERS EXPLAINS WHY
                JIM FARLEY SEEMS HAPPY

SANTA MONICA, Cal., Aug. 4. — Jim Farley went through here yesterday by mail. He seemed mighty cheerful for a dog that every rich kid is trying to tie a can to his tail. I think the main thing that makes Jim feel so good is that he is so tickled that all this is coming up this summer instead of the next summer, in other words it looks like the general in command of the opposition forces didn't have a calendar, and he started his sprint in '35 instead of '36.

I am just waiting to see Farley's picture on a surf board playing a ukulele.

> Yours,
> *Will Rogers.*

2808   WILL ROGERS DISCOVERS
                ORGY OF BRIDGE BUILDING

SAN FRANCISCO, Cal., Aug. 5. — Folks live down around Los Angeles way got to come to town every once in awhile. We got the numbers down there, but San Francisco has got the class.

This town is going through a "wild orgy" of bridge building. You know how a town is when it decides to pave. Well San Francisco is that way with bridges. You daren't leave a few buckets of water out overnight or somebody will build a bridge over it by morning.

San Diego has done so well with her fine fair this summer that this town is going to hold one. When folks' minds turn to fairs and expositions, why it's a sign of better times.

> Yours,
> *Will Rogers.*

2809   WILL ROGERS DISCOVERS
                SEATTLE IS A REAL CITY

SEATTLE, Wash., Aug. 6. — Seattle is a real city, the end of the main line, New York in miniature, boats for China, Japan, Los Angeles seven hours by plane, Spokane, Minneapolis, and Chicago by plane. Sixty lakes are in sixty-minutes drive by car from City Hall.

Saw the world's greatest bombing plane being finished. If we don't want it Abyssinia does.

Also has here the only streamlined ferryboat.

You know the money Mr. Roosevelt is going to make, with holes in it, worth a fifth of a cent, well this State has already got it. It's called "tokens."

The Lieut. Governor of the State is a fiddle player, the only politician in America with a legitimate profession.

> Yours,
> *Will Rogers.*

Scenes of the plane accident.

2810   ROGERS FINDS A PLACE
                      ROOSEVELT MIGHT LIKE

JUNEAU, Alaska, Aug. 7. — Well that was some trip. Thousand-mile hop from Seattle to Juneau. Was going to stop at Ketchikan for lunch, but mist and rain and he just breezed through, never over 100 feet off the water.

And talk about navigating. There is millions of channels and islands and bays and all look alike (to me) but this old boy turns up the right alley all the time.

Nothing that I have ever seen is more beautiful than this inland passage, by either boat or plane, to Alaska. You know, I just been thinking about things at home. You know who I bet would like to be on this trip. Mr. Roosevelt.

                             Yours,
                             Will Rogers.

2811   WILL ROGERS SEES ALASKA
                      AS A DEMOCRATIC HEAVEN

JUNEAU, Alaska, Aug. 8. — This is Juneau, the capital of the whole territory of Alaska. The Governor is a nice fellow, a Democrat but a gentleman. In their government there is sixteen Congressmen and eight Senators. Fifteen of the Congressmen are Democrats and all the Senators. It's about the nearest to an ideal existence you can get.

The Chamber of Commerce will shoot me for this, but I have been buying raincoats since early morning.

We are going to Skagway now and see the famous Chilkoot Pass. We will do it in ten minutes and it took the pioneers two and three months.

                             Yours,
                             Will Rogers.

2812   MINING ACTIVITY IN ALASKA
                      IMPRESSES WILL ROGERS

JUNEAU, Alaska, Aug. 9. — Bad weather. Not a plane mushed out of Juneau yesterday.

I had a great visit last night. Rex Beach, a mighty dear old friend, arrived from Vancouver. Alaska welcomed him like an old brother. He did more to popularize it than any one. The first movie

Point Barrow Eskimos and Captain Henry F. Thomas at monument marking site of plane crash on Arctic coast line.

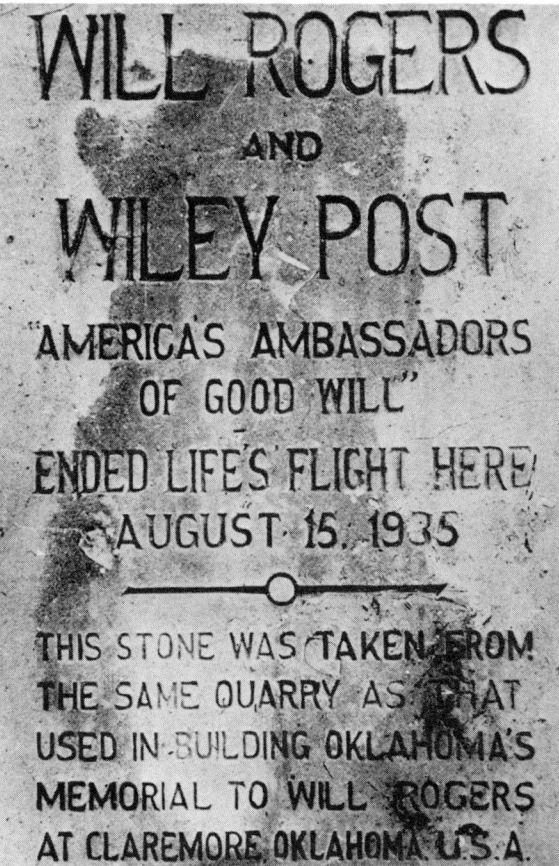

Inscription on the Rogers-Post monument near Point Barrow.

I ever made was in '18, an Alaskan story by Rex called "Laughing Bill Hyde."

Tourists are still arriving by the boatload. Mining activity everywhere. Not much news of Congress and what we do get is mostly bad. Guess it's about the same down there.

Yours,
Will Rogers.

2813 ROGERS AND WILEY POST
FLY INTO THE FAR NORTH

AKLAVIK, N. W. T., Aug. 10. — Get your map out and look this up. The mouth of the Mackenzie River, right on the Arctic Ocean. Eskimos are thicker than rich men at a "Save the Constitution convention."

This is sent from one of the most northerly posts of the Northwest Mounted Police, a great body of men, like the "G" men.

We are headed for famous Herschel Island in the Arctic. Old Wiley had to duck his head to keep from bumping it as we flew under the Arctic Circle. What, no night? It's all day up here.

Yours,
Will Rogers.

2814 WILL ROGERS DESCRIBES
ADVENTURES IN FAR NORTH

AKLAVIK, N. W. T., Aug. 12. — Was you ever driving around in a car and not knowing or caring where you went? Well, that's what Wiley and I are doing. We are sure having a great time. If we hear of whales or polar bears in the Artic, or a big herd of caribou or reindeer we fly over and see it.

Friday and Saturday we visited the old Klondyke district, Dawson City, Bonanza, Eldorado. Say there is a horse here; the furthest north of any horse, and he eats fish and travels on snowshoes. Maybe Point Barrow today.

Yours,
Will Rogers.

2815   ROGERS DECIDES ALASKA
WAS A PRETTY GOOD BUY

FAIRBANKS, Alaska, Aug. 13. — This Alaska is a great country. If they can just keep from being taken over by the U. S. they got a great future.

This is the greatest aviation-minded city of its size in the world. There is only 30,000 white people in Alaska and there is seventy commercial planes operating every day, in winter on skis.

Edmonton, Canada, is similar for their country run clear to the Arctic. Both countries have developed marvelous pilots. What they need now is a mail line from Seattle up here.

There may be some doubt about the Louisiana purchase being a mistake, but when Seward in '68 bought Alaska for $7,000,000 he even made up for what we had overpaid the Indians for Manhattan Island.

Yours,
Will Rogers.

2816   ROGERS TAKES A DAY OFF
TO FLY UP MT. MCKINLEY

ANCHORAGE, Alaska, Aug. 14. — Well, we had a day off today and nothing to do, so we went flying with friend Joe Crosson, Alaska's crack pilot, who is a great friend of Wiley's and helped him on his difficulties up here on his record trips, and Joe Barrows, another fine pilot. In a Lockheed Electra we scaled Mount McKinley, the highest one on the American Continent. Bright sunny day and the most beautiful sight I ever saw.

Crosson has landed on a glacier over half way up it in a plane and took off. Flew right by hundreds of mountain sheep, flew low over moose and bear down in the valley. Now out to visit Matanuska Valley, where they sent those 1935 model pioneers.

Yours,
Will Rogers.

2817   ROGERS ON FLIGHT VISITS
OUR NEW SPINACH PIONEERS

FAIRBANKS, Alaska, Aug. 15. — Visited our new emigrants. Now this is no time to discuss whether it will succeed or whether it won't, whether it's farming country or whether it is not, and to enumerate the hundreds of mistakes and confusions and rows and arguments and management in the whole thing at home and here.

As I see it, there is now but one problem now that they are here, and that's to get 'em housed within six or eight weeks. Things have been a terrible mess. They are getting 'em straightened out, but even now not fast enough. There is about 700 or 800 of 'em. About 200 went back; also about that many workmen sent from the transient camps down home (not CCC) and just lately they are using about 150 Alaskan workmen paid regular wages. But it's just a few weeks to snow now and they have to be out of the tents, both workmen and settlers.

Plenty food and always has been and will be. They can always get that in, but it's houses they need right now and Colonel Hunt in charge realizes it.

You know after all there is a lot of difference in pioneering for gold and pioneering for spinach.

Yours,
Will Rogers.

NOTES

2054   *New York Times (NYT)*, Monday, March 6, 1933, 15:7. The editors throughout used *NYT* as the main source; however, variations appeared when other newspapers were examined. In that event, we relied upon the *Los Angeles Times (LAT)* primarily and the *Tulsa Daily World* and the *Kansas City Times* secondarily. Variants indicated generally come from *LAT*, although conflicting variants from *NYT* are given in the footnotes when appropriate. Unless otherwise indicated, the heading of each Daily Telegram (DT) is from *NYT*.

Franklin Delano Roosevelt was inaugurated as president of the United States on March 4, 1933. He served until his death on April 12, 1945.

Bank failures occurred regularly in the United States in early 1933, and general banking conditions suggested the probability of a widespread breakdown. The situation was eased somewhat in California when the governor declared a three-day "bank holiday" in early March to allow banks in the state to reorganize their finances.

2055   *NYT*, Tuesday, March 7, 1933, 17:7.

The Treasury Department planned to issue "clearing-house scrip," paper certificates intended as a substitute for statutory currency, to enable banks to make change and to honor small withdrawals for personal necessity. The plan was never implemented, however.

Roosevelt issued a proclamation on March 5, invoking emergency powers under a war-time act of 1917 and declaring a national bank holiday until March 9.

2056   *NYT*, Wednesday, March 8, 1933, 15:7.

Anton Joseph Cermak, Democratic mayor of Chicago since 1931. Cermak was wounded critically in Miami, Florida, on February 15, by an assassin's bullet intended for President-elect Roosevelt. He died nineteen days later.

Thomas James Walsh, Democratic United States senator from Montana from 1913 to 1933 and attorney general-designate in Roosevelt's cabinet. Walsh, who was known primarily for his fair and thorough investigation during Senate hearings in the 1920s of the scandal involving the Teapot Dome and Elk Hills oil reserve leases, died of a heart attack on March 2.

2057   *NYT*, Thursday, March 9, 1933, 15:7.

2058   *NYT*, Friday, March 10, 1933, 17:7.

Fred Bennett Balzar, Republican governor of Nevada from 1927 until his death in 1934. The first banking holiday in the nation was proclaimed in Nevada on November 1, 1932.

2059   *LAT*, Saturday, March 11, 1933, I:1:3. *NYT* did not print the DT.

John Davidson Rockefeller, Sr., founder of Standard Oil Company who used his great wealth in the establishment of numerous industrial, commercial, and philanthropic corporations.

John Davison Rockefeller, Jr., eldest son and namesake of the billionaire oilman. Together, the two men controlled the largest block of stock in Chase National Bank of New York City.

Winthrop Williams Aldrich, president of Chase National Bank from 1930 to 1934.

J. P. Morgan & Co., one of the most powerful banking houses in the world, was founded in 1895 by American financier John Pierpont Morgan. After Morgan's death in 1913, his son and namesake, John Pierpont Morgan, Jr., succeeded to his father's position as head of J. P. Morgan & Co., remaining in control until his death in 1943.

2060   *NYT*, Monday, March 13, 1933, 15:7.

Arthur Brisbane, American newspaper columnist and editor. He began his nationally syndicated editorial column, "Today," in 1917 and continued it until his death in 1936.

A severe earthquake shook Southern California on March 10, causing 130 deaths and $41 million worth of property damage.

For J. P. Morgan, Jr., see Note 2059.

2061   *NYT*, Tuesday, March 14, 1933, 17:7.

Roosevelt, in the first of his famous "fireside chats," addressed the nation on March 12, outlining plans to reopen financially secure banks. His proposals, coupled with his warm and reassuring radio voice, did much to restore his countrymen's confidence in the American banking system.

2062   *NYT*, Wednesday, March 15, 1933, 19:7.

Roosevelt sent a terse message to Congress on March 13 in which he recommended immediate modification of the Volstead Act to legalize the manufacture and sale of beer and light wines; he asked also for substantial taxes on these beverages. Congressional Democrats rallied around this popular move, enabling the Senate to pass the beer bill on March 16.

2063   *NYT*, Thursday, March 16, 1933, 19:7.

Several international disarmament conferences, most of which proved unsuccessful, were held throughout the 1920s and 1930s. In 1933 delegates from fifty-nine nations attended the Geneva World Disarmament Conference, which had first convened in 1932 and which was held irregularly until 1937. The conference ultimately failed because of disagreements over definitions of categories of war materials, the reluctance of France to agree to any form of military limitation, and the desire of Germany to achieve military equality.

Much of northeastern China in early 1933 was under the military domination of the Japanese, who had invaded the region two years earlier. Open fighting between Chinese and Japanese forces expanded southward in March of 1933 as Japanese troops moved closer to Peiking and Tientsin.

Germany had experienced severe economic and political instability since World War I. The National Socialist (Nazi) party solidified its control of the government in early 1933 and initiated a virtual war upon its political opponents. The country remained in turmoil throughout the year.

2064   *NYT*, Friday, March 17, 1933, 19:7.

The Senate passed a $500 million economy bill on March 15 that allowed the president to reduce federal salaries and veterans' benefits. The measure, which was signed into law on March 21, provided for a 15 percent cut in congressmen's pay.

Huey Pierce "Kingfish" Long, Democratic United States senator from Louisiana from 1931 until his death in 1935.

Bennett Champ Clark, Democratic United States senator from Missouri from 1933 to 1945.

The California state assembly passed a bill on March 15 to legalize pari-mutuel betting in the state. The measure later passed the state senate, but was vetoed by the governor. Voters in California, however, approved pari-mutuel betting in an initiative election in June of 1933. Texas also legalized pari-mutuel betting in 1933.

The House voted on March 15 to legalize the manufacture and sale of beer. On the same day the Senate Finance Committee, considering a similar bill, voted to include wine on a list of legal alcoholic beverages.

Greta Garbo, Swedish motion picture actress. Garbo, noted for her beauty and sultry sexuality, arrived in Hollywood in 1926 where she soon became one of the highest paid performers in films. She left the United States for Sweden in July of 1932 but returned to Hollywood in 1933 to begin work on a new motion picture.

Aimee Semple McPherson, controversial American evangelist, self-proclaimed faith healer, and founder of the International Church of the Foursquare Gospel in Los Angeles.

Film stars and other motion picture employees accepted salary and wage reductions of 25 to 50 percent in 1933 to help revive the financially plagued industry. To aid the equally troubled theatrical business, vaudeville and other stage performers accepted salary cuts of up to 25 percent.

2065 *NYT*, Saturday, March 18, 1933, 15:7.

Roosevelt summoned Congress into special session on March 9, and from then until its adjournment on June 16, Congress acted virtually without opposition to enact Roosevelt's entire legislative program. Before the session—the so-called "Hundred Days"—ended, Congress had enacted more than a dozen pieces of significant legislation.

2066 *NYT*, Monday, March 20, 1933, 17:7.

A bill to legalize mild beer was passed by the Senate on March 20, a few days after its passage by the House. The return of beer in April of 1933 after a thirteen-year absence and while the country was still in the grips of a severe depression seemed to many Americans to be a happy omen for the future.

The Treasury Department was authorized by the new law to collect a manufacturers' tax on beer. The new levy yielded about $150 million in 1933.

2067 *NYT*, Tuesday, March 21, 1933, 19:7.

2068 *NYT*, Wednesday, March 22, 1933, 19:7.

Federal income tax receipts for the calendar year 1932 totaled slightly more than $481.5 million, compared to $233.9 million in 1931. A decline in taxable income in 1932 was more than offset by the increased taxes under the revenue act of that year.

2069 *NYT*, Thursday, March 23, 1933, 19:7.

2070 *NYT*, Friday, March 24, 1933, 19:7.

A farm relief bill providing for compulsory restrictions on crop production was passed by the House on March 21. Signed into law on May 12, the new act established the Agricultural Adjustment Administration (AAA) which paid farmers for withdrawing part of their land from cultivation.

Several unemployment measures were introduced into Congress in early 1933. The most significant included an act passed in March which established the Civilian Conservation Corps (CCC) to provide jobs for young men in reforestation and other conservation projects and the National Industrial Recovery Act (NIRA) which created a $3.3 billion public works program and provided for industrial codes of fair business and labor practices.

The technocracy movement was a short-lived (1931-1932) effort to arouse popular support for a political-industrial organization of American society based on advanced technology.

2071 *NYT*, Saturday, March 25, 1933, 19:7.

George Bernard Shaw, Irish playwright, novelist, and literary critic noted for his satirical wit; winner of the Nobel Prize for literature in 1925. Shaw arrived in the United States on March 23 on his first visit to this country.

James Matthew Barrie, Scottish novelist and dramatist famous for his play *Little Minister* (1891) and for his adventure story *Peter Pan* (1904).

2072 *NYT*, Monday, March 27, 1933, 17:7. Variant: *NYT* omits "Arizona's Mother Superior," in sixth sentence.

John Joseph "Black Jack" Pershing, Army general who commanded the American Expeditionary Force in Europe during World War I.

Isabella Selmes Greenway, Democratic United States representative from Arizona from 1933 to 1937. The first woman member of Congress from Arizona, Greenway was the widow of an Arizona copper-mining magnate.

Benjamin Baker Moeur, Democratic governor of Arizona from 1933 to 1936. Moeur practiced medicine in Tempe, Arizona, for thirty-six years before his unexpected election to the governorship in 1932.

2073 *NYT*, Tuesday, March 28, 1933, 21:7.

Adolf Hitler, chancellor and *Fuehrer* (leader) of Germany from 1933 until his death in 1945. The supreme dictator of Germany, Hitler based much of his political philosophy on racial bigotry, especially anti-Semitism.

Benito Mussolini, founder and leader of the Fascist movement and dictator of Italy from 1922 to 1943.

2074 *NYT*, Wednesday, March 29, 1933, 17:7.

The World Court, the popular name of the Permanent Court of International Justice, was established in 1921 as part of the League of Nations. The United States never joined the judicial body.

2075 *NYT*, Thursday, March 30, 1933, 19:7. Variant: *LAT* gives "hardly wait" in third sentence.

2076 *NYT*, Friday, March 31, 1933, 21:7. Variant: *NYT* gives "than the income tax men." to end ninth sentence.

For the reforestation bill establishing the CCC see Note 2070.

2077 *NYT*, Saturday, April 1, 1933, 17:7. Variants: *NYT* omits "little country" in ninth sentence/*NYT* gives "hero." to end tenth sentence, omitting next eight words.

Roosevelt appeared to have persuaded the French on March 30 to pay their overdue war debt installment of $19,261,432. France did not pay the overdue obligation and defaulted on the two installments which came due later in 1933.

Morgan (see Note 2059) appeared before the Senate Banking and Currency Committee which was conducting an investigation of security dealings on the New York Stock Exchange. Revelations of questionable activities on stock exchanges led in part to the enactment of the Securities Act of 1933, which provided basic regulations of the issue and sale of stocks and bonds.

2078   *NYT,* Monday, April 3, 1933, 17:7.

Walter Lippmann, influential American editor, columnist, and author who served on the editorial staff of the *New York World* from 1921 to 1931 and later contributed columns to the *New York Herald-Tribune* and the *Washington Post.*

2079   *NYT,* Tuesday, April 4, 1933, 19:7.

Ruth Bryan Owen, Democratic United States representative from Florida from 1929 to 1933. The daughter of William Jennings Bryan, Owen was appointed by Roosevelt as ambassador to Denmark. The first woman ever to achieve ministerial rank, she served as ambassador from 1933 to 1936.

For Greta Garbo see Note 2064.

William Jennings Bryan, American statesman and orator known as "the Great Commoner." A three-time Democratic presidential nominee, Bryan served as United States secretary of state from 1913 to 1915.

2080   *NYT,* Wednesday, April 5, 1933, 21:7.

The bill to legalize beer (see Notes 2064 and 2066) was signed by Roosevelt on March 22. A mandatory fifteen-day waiting period expired on Friday, April 7.

2081   *NYT,* Thursday, April 6, 1933, 19:7.

William Adger Moffett, American naval officer who had headed the Bureau of Aeronautics of the Navy Department since 1921. Considered by many to be the "Father of American Naval Aviation," Rear Admiral Moffett died in the crash of the United States naval dirigible *Akron* on April 4, 1933.

2082   *NYT,* Friday, April 7, 1933, 21:7.

2083   *NYT,* Saturday, April 8, 1933, 15:7.

2084   *NYT,* Monday, April 10, 1933, 15:7. Variant: *LAT* gives "in a hurry." in fourth sentence.

2085   *NYT,* Tuesday, April 11, 1933, 21:7.

2086   *NYT,* Wednesday, April 12, 1933, 21:7.

2087   *NYT,* Thursday, April 13, 1933, 19:7. Variant: *NYT* gives "left with a police" in eighth sentence.

The Century of Progress Exposition, a world's fair to mark the centennial of Chicago, opened in that city on May 27 and continued into November of 1933. By popular demand, it reopened in May of 1934, finally closing permanently in October of that year.

Alphonse "Scarface Al" Capone, Italian-born American gangster whose crime syndicate terrorized Chicago from 1920 until his conviction for federal income tax evasion in 1931. Imprisoned in October of 1931, he was released in 1939, an invalid.

For George Bernard Shaw see Note 2071.

2088 *NYT,* Friday, April 14, 1933, 21:7.

George Higgins Moses, Republican United States senator from New Hampshire from 1918 to 1933.

James Eli Watson, Republican United States senator from Indiana from 1916 to 1933. Both Moses and Watson opposed repeal of prohibition.

2089 *NYT,* Saturday, April 15, 1933, 15:7.

Anna Eleanor Roosevelt, wife of Franklin Roosevelt. Charming and outgoing, Eleanor Roosevelt greatly expanded the duties of a first lady by undertaking innovative and precedent-setting responsibilities.

2090 *NYT,* Monday, April 17, 1933, 15:7.

Long faced charges in Louisiana of political and moral unfitness for office.

For the Japanese-Chinese conflict see Note 2063.

France announced on April 15 that it would meet its past and future war debt obligations.

Mystic Knights of the Sea, the name of a fictional fraternal organization to which the male characters on the popular radio serial "Amos 'n Andy" belonged. The program, first broadcast in 1928, featured two white comedians, Freeman Fisher Gosden and Charles J. Correll, in every male role, including that of the conniving Kingfish. The escapades of two Harlem taxi drivers and their friends attracted an enormous and faithful listening audience.

2091 *NYT,* Tuesday, April 18, 1933, 17:7.

Six British engineers working in the Soviet Union were arrested by the Soviet government in mid-March of 1933 on charges of espionage, bribery, and sabotage. On April 19 a Soviet court convicted five of the men. Three of them were deported and two were sentenced to prison. The latter two were released in July of 1933 after Great Britain agreed to lift an embargo against Soviet goods.

2092 *NYT,* Wednesday, April 19, 1933, 19:7. Variants: *LAT* gives "coast at night" in second sentence/*LAT* gives "this bustling" in third sentence.

2093 *NYT,* Thursday, April 20, 1933, 19:7.

Clarence Marshall Young, United States assistant secretary of aeronautics in charge of civil aviation from 1929 until his resignation in 1933.

The Wright brothers, Orville and Wilbur, made the first successful flights in a power-propelled, heavier-than-air machine at Kitty Hawk, North Carolina, on December 17, 1903.

2094 *NYT,* Friday, April 21, 1933, 19:7.

Gold as a medium of exchange was outlawed by an executive order by Roosevelt on April 20.

2095 *NYT,* Saturday, April 22, 1933, 15:7.

2096 *NYT,* Monday, April 24, 1933, 17:7. Variant: *NYT* gives "paper dollars" in ninth sentence.

For Arthur Brisbane see Note 2060.

2097 *NYT,* Tuesday, April 25, 1933, 19:7. Variant: *LAT* gives "beads (are wampum)" in eighth sentence.

2098 *LAT,* Wednesday, April 26, 1933, I:1:5. *NYT* did not print the DT.

James Ramsay MacDonald, Scottish-born British Labour party leader and statesman who served as prime minister of Great Britain in January of 1924 and from 1929 to 1935.

Edouard Marie Herriot, premier of France from 1924 to 1925 and from June to December of 1932. He was one of the few French statesmen to advocate payment by France of war debts to the United States.

2099 *NYT,* Thursday, April 27, 1933, 19:7.

Frances Perkins, United States secretary of labor from 1933 to 1945; the first woman member of a presidential cabinet.

2100 *NYT,* Friday, April 28, 1933, 19:7.

2101 *NYT,* Saturday, April 29, 1933, 15:7.

2102 *NYT,* Monday, May 1, 1933, 17:7.

Ogden Livingston Mills, United States secretary of the treasury from 1932 to 1933.

2103 *NYT,* Tuesday, May 2, 1933, 19:7.

2104 *NYT,* Wednesday, May 3, 1933, 19:7. Variant: *LAT* omits "tomorrow" in second sentence.

2105 *NYT,* Thursday, May 4, 1933, 19:7. Variant: *NYT* gives "the House pass" in fifth sentence.

John Nance "Jack" Garner, vice president of the United States from 1933 to 1941. A Texas Democrat, Garner served as Speaker of the House of Representatives from 1931 to 1933.

Henry Thomas Rainey, Democratic United States representative from Illinois from 1903 to 1921 and from 1923 until his death in 1934. Rainey took office as Speaker in March of 1933.

Congress passed a $6 billion inflation bill on May 3 as an amendment to a farm relief measure. The legislation gave Roosevelt unprecedented authority to expand the currency.

William Hartman Woodin, United States secretary of the treasury from March of 1933 until his resignation because of ill health in December of 1933.

Lewis William Douglas, director of the federal budget from 1933 to 1934. Member of a pioneer Arizona mining family, Douglas served in the House of Representatives from 1927 to 1933.

Joseph Taylor "Joe" Robinson, Democratic United States senator from Arkansas from 1913 until his death in 1937.

Thomas Terry "Tom" Connally, Democratic United States senator from Texas from 1928 to 1953.

2106 *NYT,* Friday, May 5, 1933, 17:7.

Guido Jung, Italian minister of finance who attended discussions in Washington, D. C., in May concerning the worldwide depression.

William Henry "Alfalfa Bill" Murray, Democratic governor of Oklahoma from 1931 to 1935. Murray sent a delegation of Oklahomans to Washington, D. C., in the spring of 1933 to lobby for continued restrictions on foreign imports of petroleum and petroleum products.

2107 *NYT,* Saturday, May 6, 1933, 15:7.

Jesse Holman Jones, Houston political and civic leader who chaired the Reconstruction Finance Corporation (RFC) from 1933 to 1939. The RFC was established in 1932 as a governmental lending agency to provide financing for banking institutions, life insurance firms, railroads, and farm mortgage associations.

Roosevelt told the Chamber of Commerce delegates on May 4 that "we have a new national word, 'got.'" In conversations with Prime Minister MacDonald (see Note 2098), the president had emphasized the need for international economic recovery, telling MacDonald that "we have got to do it." Translated into several languages, "got" quickly became an international code word for recovery.

"Forgot" referred to the delay by France in paying its war debt obligations.

2108 *NYT,* Monday, May 8, 1933, 17:7.

2109 *NYT,* Tuesday, May 9, 1933, 19:7.

Roosevelt delivered his second national radio address on May 8, outlining his programs for economic recovery, inflation, and international cooperation.

2110 *NYT,* Wednesday, May 10, 1933, 19:7.

2111 *NYT,* Thursday, May 11, 1933, 19:7.

For the Chicago World's Fair, or Century of Progress Exposition, see Note 2087; for the Chicago teachers' pay dispute see Note 2087.

2112 *NYT,* Friday, May 12, 1933, 19:7.

Excessive oil production glutted the American market in the early 1930s, forcing prices downward. Secretary of the Interior Harold LeClare Ickes was appointed federal oil administrator in the spring of 1933.

For John D. Rockefeller, Sr., see Note 2059; for Arthur Brisbane see Note 2060.

2113 *NYT,* Saturday, May 13, 1933, 15:7. Variant: *NYT* gives "is fifty cents" in fourth sentence.

Oklahoma had scheduled a statewide election for June 11 to consider the legalization of mild beer in the state. Both the governor and the state legislature, however, insisted that advocates of legalized beer pay for the cost of the election.

2114 *NYT,* Monday, May 15, 1933, 15:7.

The Rockefeller family commisioned Diego Rivera, a world-renowned Mexican artist, to paint a mural at the Rockefeller Center in New York City. Desiring to depict the emancipation of mankind through technology, Rivera portrayed Vladimir Ilich Ulyanov, "Lenin," leader of the Communist Revolution in Russia, as the key figure of the tableau, representing him as the leader of mankind. Offended by the portrait, John D. Rockefeller, Jr., paid Rivera in full, dismissed him from the project, and covered the incomplete fresco with an empty canvas.

2115   *NYT,* Tuesday, May 16, 1933, 19:7.

Alfred Emanuel "Al" Smith, governor of New York from 1919 to 1921 and from 1923 to 1929; Democratic presidential nominee in 1928.

2116   *NYT,* Wednesday, May 17, 1933, 19:7.

2117   *NYT,* Thursday, May 18, 1933, 21:7.

Roosevelt sent a personal appeal to the heads of fifty-four nations in May of 1933 asking that they enter into a nonaggression pact, eliminate offensive weapons, and sharply curb arms and armies. Hitler (see Note 2073) responded unexpectedly in a conciliatory manner, welcoming the president's message as supportive of German viewpoints.

2118   *NYT,* Friday, May 19, 1933, 19:7.

2119   *NYT,* Saturday, May 20, 1933, 15:7.

The Bonus Army, several thousand unemployed veterans who assembled in Washington, D. C., in the summer of 1932 to demand cash payment of their military compensation certificates. Many refused to evacuate when ordered to do so and were driven from the city by federal troops in July of 1932. Thereafter, a number of veterans reappeared in Washington each year to seek payment of the certificates.

Carter Glass, Democratic United States senator from Virginia from 1920 until his death in 1946. Glass, an expert on banking legislation, sponsored the Glass-Steagall Act of 1933 which provided for the Federal Deposit Insurance Corporation.

2120   *NYT,* Monday, May 22, 1933, 17:7.

Stephen Samuel Wise, American rabbi and Zionist. Founder in 1907 of the Free Synagogue of New York City, Wise addressed an emergency session of the American Jewish Congress in Washington, D. C., on May 21, asking that international pressure be brought upon Germany to restore the civil liberties of German Jews.

2121   *NYT,* Tuesday, May 23, 1933, 21:7.

2122   *NYT,* Wednesday, May 24, 1933, 23:7.

For Lewis W. Douglas see Note 2105.

2123   *NYT,* Tuesday, May 25, 1933, 21:7.

J. P. Morgan, Jr. (see Note 2059), appeared before the Senate Committee on Banking and Currency in the spring of 1933 to explain why he and twenty financial partners had failed to pay income taxes in 1931 and 1932.

The names of bank officials to whom the Morgan firm had made loans and the names of those who were sold securities issued by the company at prices below the listed market rate appeared on a so-called preferred list released publicly during the Senate investigation of the stock exchanges.

2124   *NYT,* Friday, May 26, 1933, 21:7.

For J. P. Morgan, Jr., see Notes 2059 and 2123.

2125   *NYT,* Saturday, May 27, 1933, 15:7.

For the "preferred list" see Note 2123.

For the Century of Progress Exposition see Note 2087.

2126 *NYT,* Monday, May 29, 1933, 15:7.

For the Century of Progress Exposition see Note 2087; for Arthur Brisbane see Note 2060.

Walter Winchell, syndicated columnist for the *New York Mirror* from 1929 to 1963. Winchell, one of the best-known journalists and radio commentators in the country, specialized in show business gossip and political commentary.

Amon Giles Carter, publisher of the *Fort Worth Star-Telegram* from 1909 until his death in 1955; powerful and energetic booster of Fort Worth and West Texas.

2127 *NYT,* Tuesday, May 30, 1933, 17:7.

Mary McElroy, the twenty-five-year-old daughter of the city manager of Kansas City, Missouri, was kidnapped on May 27 and held for twenty-nine hours until the payment of a $30,000 ransom. Public outcry against such crimes prompted Congress to pass an act in 1933 which made kidnapping a federal offense, punishable by long terms of imprisonment.

2128 *NYT,* Wednesday, May 31, 1933, 19:7.

For J. P. Morgan, Jr., see Notes 2059 and 2123.

2129 *NYT,* Thursday, June 1, 1933, 21:7.

The World Monetary and Economic Conference, held in London in 1933, had as its main object the checking of the world depression by means of currency stabilization and economic readjustments. Persistent disagreements among the participants made the meeting a failure; instead, adverse tariff and currency policies became increasingly commonplace.

James Couzens, Republican United States senator from Michigan from 1922 until his death in 1936. Couzens was one of several American delegates to the World Monetary and Economic Conference held in London in 1933.

George V, king of Great Britain from 1910 until his death in 1936.

2130 *NYT,* Friday, June 2, 1933, 21:7. Variant: *NYT* gives "when the flattery starts." in fourth sentence.

Robert Worth Bingham, United States ambassador to Great Britain from 1933 until his death in 1937. Bingham shocked many American isolationists when he suggested that the United States should abandon its traditional policy of noninvolvement in European affairs.

Edward Albert, the Prince of Wales, eldest son and heir apparent to the throne of King George V of Great Britain.

Ferdinand Pecora, Italian-born American lawyer and jurist. Pecora served as chief counsel from 1933 to 1934 of the Senate Banking and Currency Committee investigating banking and stock market practices.

2131 *NYT,* Saturday, June 3, 1933, 15:7.

A circus press agent placed a female midget in the lap of J. P. Morgan, Jr. (see Note 2059), during the proceedings of the Senate stock market investigation. Although flabbergasted, the multimillionaire financier dismissed the publicity stunt good-naturedly.

For the "prefered list" see Note 2123.

2132 *NYT,* Monday, June 5, 1933, 17:7.

2133 *NYT,* Tuesday, June 6, 1933, 23:7.

2134 *NYT,* Wednesday, June 7, 1933, 23:7.

Pecora (see Note 2130) was denied authority by the Senate on June 5 to expose fully the income tax transactions of partners in the Morgan banking firm. The Senate finally relented a week later, and Pecora resumed the probe.

James J. "Jimmy" Mattern, American long-distance flyer who took off from a Long Island airstrip on June 3, 1934, in an attempt at the first successful around-the-world solo flight. The adventure ended twelve days later when his plane crashed in Siberia; Mattern finally was rescued by Soviet flyers in early July.

2135 *NYT,* Thursday, June 8, 1933, 21:7.

Charles Augustus Lindbergh, internationally acclaimed American aviator who in May of 1927 made the first solo, nonstop transatlantic flight.

For Jimmy Mattern see Note 2134.

Amelia Mary Earhart Putnam, American aviator who in May of 1932 became the first woman to fly the Atlantic Ocean alone. Known as Amelia Earhart, she was the wife of a prominent American publisher.

2136 *NYT,* Friday, June 9, 1933, 19:7. Variant: *NYT* omits seventh sentence.

2137 *NYT,* Saturday, June 10, 1933, 15:7. Variants: *NYT* gives "night (Saturday)." in fifth sentence/*LAT* gives "Connolly" in ninth sentence.

Arthur "Bugs" Baer, American newspaper columnist and popular humorist.

Maximilian Adelbert "Max" Baer, American boxer who held the world heavyweight title from 1934 to 1935. Baer knocked out Max Siegfried Schmeling of Germany in ten rounds on June 8 in New York City.

Max Siegfried Schmeling, German pugilist who held the world heavyweight championship from 1930 to 1932. The most successful professional boxer in Germany history, Schmeling was the undisputed sports hero of Nazi Germany.

One-eyed Connolly, boxer of the early 1900s who was noted for his ingenious and highly commercial schemes at self-promotion.

2138 *NYT,* Monday, June 12, 1933, 17:7.

For the "preferred list" see Note 2123.

2139 *NYT,* Tuesday, June 13, 1933, 21:7. Variant: *LAT* gives "King George" to begin first sentence.

For George V see Note 2129.

2140 *NYT,* Wednesday, June 14, 1933, 21:7.

MacDonald (see Note 2098), in his opening remarks at the World Monetary and Economic Conference on June 12, declared that although war debts were not on the conference agenda the problem had to be considered by the conferees before obstacles to general world recovery could be removed. The semi-annual installment of war debts came due on June 15. With the token payment or outright defaults occurring on that date, the issue was eliminated temporarily from the conference arena.

²¹⁴¹ *LAT*, Thursday, June 15, 1933, I:1:5: heading from *NYT*, 19:7. Variant: *NYT* omits second paragraph.

Alexis Zachary Mdivani, member of a Russia-Georgian family of princes who moved conspicuously in international society circles during the 1920s and 1930s. Prince Alexis married American dime-store heiress Barbara Hutton on June 20 in Paris.

²¹⁴² *NYT*, Friday, June 16, 1933, 19:7.

The semi-annual installment of war debts came due on June 15. Only one country, Finland, paid its obligation in full; six others made partial payments, and another six nations, including France, defaulted completely. The amount paid represented less than 8 percent of the total due.

John Calvin Coolidge, president of the United States from 1924 to 1929. Coolidge, whose New England Yankee qualities of conservatism, frugality, and common sense endeared him to many Americans, died in Northampton, Massachusetts, on January 5, 1933.

²¹⁴³ *LAT*, Saturday, June 17, 1933, I:1:5; heading from *NYT*, 15:7. Variant: *NYT* omits first through fourth sentences.

²¹⁴⁴ *NYT*, Monday, June 19, 1933, 17:7.

²¹⁴⁵ *NYT*, Tuesday, June 20, 1933, 21:7. Variant: *NYT* omits "and peeping in the keyhole." in seventh sentence.

²¹⁴⁶ *NYT*, Wednesday, June 21, 1933, 19:7.

²¹⁴⁷ *NYT*, Thursday, June 22, 1933, 21:7.

²¹⁴⁸ *NYT*, Friday, June 23, 1933, 19:7.

²¹⁴⁹ *NYT*, Saturday, June 24, 1933, 15:7.

Smith (see Note 2115) received an honorary doctor of laws degree from Harvard University on June 22.

Ernst Udet, German aviator and army officer who was credited with destroying sixty-two enemy planes in World War I. Udet achieved a wide reputation as a fearless pilot who performed the most hazardous flying stunts.

²¹⁵⁰ *LAT*, Monday, June 26, 1933, I:1:6.

Aimee Semple McPherson (see Note 2064) underwent an intestinal operation in Paris in late June. In order to discover the source of news leaks in her evangelistic organization, she sent a hoax telegram to her husband in Los Angeles, announcing the "birth" of a nine-pound son. News of the miraculous conception swept the nation on June 24, only to be denied and corrected by McPherson one day later.

²¹⁵¹ *NYT*, Tuesday, June 27, 1933, 19:7.

Hugh Samuel Johnson, administrator of the National Recovery Administration (NRA) from 1933 to 1934. A brigadier general and World War I veteran, Johnson was appointed on June 16 as administrator of the NRA, a major New

Deal agency that was empowered to make voluntary agreements with employers dealing with hours of work, rates of pay, and the fixing of prices. The NRA was ruled unconstitutional in 1935.

Bernard Mannes Baruch, American financier and an adviser to the federal government on economic matters.

2152   *NYT,* Wednesday, June 28, 1933, 23:7.

For Ernst Udet see Note 2149.

Tito Falconi, lieutenant in the Royal Italian Air Corps who represented Italy in the National Air Races in Los Angeles in 1933. Falconi held the world record of one hour for flying upside down.

2153   *NYT,* Thursday, June 29, 1933, 21:7.

Californians overwhelmingly voted on June 27 to repeal prohibition. One day earlier, West Virginia became the first in the southern tier of states to vote anti-prohibition. By July 1, 1933, sixteen of the necessary thirty-six states had voted to ratify the Twenty-first Amendment for repeal of prohibition.

2154   *LAT,* Friday, June 30, 1933, I:1:2; heading from *NYT,* 19:7. Variant: *NYT* omits third paragraph.

American wheat farmers suffered greatly in 1933 from a widespread blight of wheat rust.

Roscoe Conkling "Fatty" Arbuckle, youthful-looking American film comedian of the silent era whose career was ruined after his involvement in a scandal in 1921 in which a woman died. Though he never again appeared before the camera, he directed a few motion pictures before his death from a heart attack on June 29, 1933.

2155   *NYT,* Saturday, July 1, 1933, 15:7.

2156   *NYT,* Monday, July 3, 1933, 13:7.

The National Air Races opened in Los Angeles on July 1. The highlight of the first day's program was the completion of the annual transcontinental Bendix Trophy Race from New York City to Los Angeles.

For Tito Falconi see Note 2152; for Ernst Udet see Note 2149.

Betty Blake Rogers, wife of Will Rogers. The couple was married on November 25, 1908, at the Blake home in Rogers, Arkansas.

2157   *NYT,* Tuesday, July 4, 1933, 15:7.

For the World Monetary and Economic Conference see Note 2129.

2158   *NYT,* Wednesday, July 5, 1933, 21:7.

Roosevelt's rejection on July 3 of a proposal that all countries participating in the World Monetary and Economic Conference return to the gold standard as soon as possible nearly precipitated the complete collapse of the London conference. The bluntness as well as the content of the president's message angered the conferees and brought a closer unity among the gold countries, which took active measures to defend the gold standard.

2159   *NYT,* Thursday, July 6, 1933, 23:7. Variant: *LAT* gives "anything, that's" in fifth and sixth sentences.

2160   *NYT*, Friday, July 7, 1933, 19:7.

For the World Monetary and Economic Conference see Note 2129; for George V see Notes 2129 and 2139.

2161   *NYT*, Saturday, July 8, 1933, 13:7.

Mattern (see Note 2134) was found safe at Anadyr, Siberia, on July 7 after having crashed several days earlier during his attempt to set an around-the-world solo flight record.

John Herbert "Jack" Crawford, Australian tennis champion and Davis Cup competitor (1928 to 1939).

Henry Ellsworth Vines, Jr., American amateur tennis star of the 1930s who won the Wimbledon singles championship in 1932 and held the United States singles title in 1931 and 1932. In a classic match on July 7, Crawford defeated defending champion Vines in five sets to win his first Wimbledon singles crown. Crawford had defeated Vines in the finals at Melbourne in 1932.

American golfer Densmore "Denny" Shute won the British Open championship on July 8 after a thirty-six-hole playoff against fellow American Craig R. Wood.

For John Rockefeller, Sr., see Note 2059.

Harvard, Yale, Cornell, and the University of Washington competed in the National Intercollegiate Sprint Championship Regatta at Long Beach, California, on July 8. Washington won in a nearly bow-to-bow finish with Yale.

2162   *NYT*, Monday, July 10, 1933, 15:7.

A wheat processing tax of thirty cents went into effect on July 9. The revenue collected from this and similar levies went toward funding the newly established Agricultural Adjustment Administration (AAA).

Cordell Hull, United States secretary of state from 1933 to 1944; recipient of the Nobel Peace Prize in 1945. Only the tactful diplomacy of Hull, who headed the American delegation at the World Monetary and Economic Conference, prevented a premature collapse of the conference.

2163   *NYT*, Tuesday, July 11, 1933, 19:7.

2164   *LAT*, Wednesday, July 12, 1933, I:1:6. *NYT* did not print the DT.

Frank Phillips, Oklahoma banker and oil producer who was appointed in late 1933 as chairman of General District Commission No. 2 of the petroleum industry. Phillips and other prominent oilmen helped to draw up a code of fair practices for their industry, similar to 500 other industrial codes formulated by the NRA in 1933 and 1934.

Mary McCormic, American concert and opera star. McCormic sued in July for separate maintenance from her husband, Prince Serge Mdivani, brother of Alexis Mdivani (see Note 2141) and David Mdivani, husband of American actress Mae Murray. McCormic was granted a divorce in November of 1933.

2165   *NYT*, Thursday, July 13, 1933, 21:7. Variant: *NYT* gives "Guard when the folks voted on beer." in first sentence.

Oklahomans voted nearly two to one on July 11 for the legalization of beer in the state. To insure that there would be no premature celebrating, Governor Murray (see Note 2106) ordered the National Guard into the streets of Oklahoma City on election night.

For the Prince of Wales see Note 2129.

2166 *NYT,* Friday, July 14, 1933, 19:7.

Roosevelt signed an executive order on July 12 that placed all postmasters in the United States under the civil service system, thus removing thousands of government positions from patronage politics.

2167 *NYT,* Saturday, July 15, 1933, 13:7.

Delegates to the World Monetary and Economic Conference voted to adjourn temporarily on July 27. Once adjourned, the conference never reconvened.

For Edouard Herriot see Note 2098; for Cordell Hull See Note 2162.

2168 *NYT,* Monday, July 17, 1933, 15:7.

An air armada of twenty-five twin-engined seaplanes, under the command of General Italo Balbo, left Italy on June 20 bound for Chicago and the Century of Progress Exposition. One plane crashed en route, but the remainder of the epic armada landed in Chicago on July 15.

Theodore Roosevelt, president of the United States from 1901 to 1909. Roosevelt sent the American fleet on a world cruise (1907-1908) to give the squadron experience, to demonstrate its might to the Japanese, and to publicize the need for increased naval expenditures.

Wiley Hardeman Post, American long-distance and high altitude flier. Post, who with Harold Gatty, had circled the globe in less than nine days in 1931, set off from New York City on July 15 for a solo trip over the same route. During the flight, Post, a native of Oklahoma who had lost an eye several years before in an oilfield accident, utilized a newly-developed automatic pilot for holding the plane on course while he rested. He returned to New York City on July 22, having set a new around-the-world record of seven days, eighteen hours, and forty-nine seconds.

2169 *NYT,* Tuesday, July 18, 1933, 19:7.

Will Harrison Hays, chairman of Motion Pictures Producers and Distributors of America from 1922 to 1945. Called the "czar" of the film industry, Hays was engaged in writing a code for the industry under the provisions of the National Industrial Recovery Act.

William Harrison "Jack" Dempsey, American prizefighter who held the world heavyweight title from 1919 to 1926. Dempsey married American singer Hannah Williams, popularly known as the "cheerful little earful," in an impromptu ceremony at Elko, Nevada, on July 18.

For Wiley Post see Note 2168.

2170 *NYT,* Wednesday, July 19, 1933, 19:7.

Prices on the New York Stock Exchange reached their highest levels of the year in mid-July in the heaviest trading in three years. The surge lasted only a few days; by July 20 shares of stocks had declined significantly.

2171 *NYT,* Thursday, July 20, 1933, 21:7. Variants: *NYT* omits first sentence/*NYT* gives "papers out here" in seventh sentence/*NYT* gives "paper here when" in eighth sentence.

For Jack Dempsey see Note 2169.

Balbo (see Note 2168) and the Italian air armada left Chicago on July 19 for the return flight to Italy. They landed at Rome on August 14, after a round-trip flight of 12,000 miles in forty-five days.

Alabama and Arkansas voters elected by wide majorities on July 18 to repeal prohibition. The victory for repeal in those states represented the first test of the issue in the so-called Solid South.

For Wiley Post see Note 2168.

Aimee Semple McPherson (see Note 2064) returned to the United States from Paris on July 19.

2172 *NYT*, Friday, July 21, 1933, 19:7. Variant: *NYT* gives "tax high" in fourth sentence.

2173 *NYT*, Saturday, July 22, 1933, 13:7.

Tennessee on July 20 became the nineteenth state to vote for repeal of prohibition. The vote of wets in urban areas barely offset that of prohibitionists in their mountain stronghold of East Tennessee.

For Wiley Post see Note 2168.

2174 *NYT*, Monday, July 24, 1933, 17:7. Variant: *NYT* gives "office, its the first they been in office, its the first reforestation" in fourth and fifth sentences.

Roosevelt served as governor of New York from 1929 to 1933.

The National Governor's Conference, was held at various sites in California in late July. Rogers was a member of the state welcoming party and attended and hosted many of the official functions.

Guy Brasfield Park, Democratic governor of Missouri from 1933 to 1937.

2175 *NYT*, Tuesday, July 25, 1933, 21:7. Variant: *NYT* gives "headed for Frisco," in third sentence.

Roscoe Turner, American flier who during a long and colorful career broke seven transcontinental speed records and collected most of the top aviation awards. A lieutenant colonel in the Nevada National Guard, Turner served on the staff of the governor of Nevada.

For Fred Balzar see Note 2058.

Theodore Francis Green, Democratic governor of Rhode Island from 1933 to 1937. A Phi Beta Kappa, Green held degrees from Brown and Harvard universities.

George White, Democratic governor of Ohio from 1931 to 1935.

Leslie Andrew Miller, Democratic governor of Wyoming from 1929 to 1931 and from 1932 to 1939.

Wilbur Lucius Cross, Democratic governor of Connecticut from 1931 to 1939. A former professor of English at Yale University, Cross served as dean of the Yale Graduate School from 1916 to 1930.

For Alfalfa Bill Murray see Note 2106.

Miriam Amanda Wallace Ferguson, Democratic governor of Texas from 1925 to 1927 and from 1933 to 1935.

2176 *NYT*, Wednesday, July 26, 1933, 19:7.

For Roscoe Turner see Note 2175.

A strike by motion picture sound men, which began on July 22 and stemmed from a jurisdictional dispute between rival unions, ended peaceably on July 26 after strike leaders sought the mediation of film producers.

2177 *LAT,* Thursday, July 27, 1933, I:1:2; heading from *NYT,* 19:7. Variant: *NYT* omits sixth and seventh sentences.

For Wiley Post see Note 2168.

The move to reduce the operation hours of the stock exchange was taken to relieve overburdened and overworked brokers as activity on the stock market continued at a high pace.

2178 *NYT,* Friday, July 28, 1933, 17:7.

For the World Monetary and Economic Conference see Note 2129.

2179 *NYT,* Saturday, July 29, 1933, 13:7.

A Missouri jury delivered a death verdict against Walter McGee, leader of a gang that kidnapped twenty-five-year-old Mary McElroy of Kansas City. McGee's sentence, the first death decree in the United States for kidnapping, was commuted in 1935 after McElroy had issued a plea that her kidnapper be saved from death on the gallows.

For Aimee Semple McPherson see Note 2064.

2180 *NYT,* Monday, July 31, 1933, 15:7.

Roger Ward Babson, American businessman, statistician, and business prognosticator.

2181 *NYT,* Tuesday, August 1, 1933, 19:7.

Murray (see Note 2106), who frequently summoned the Oklahoma National Guard to enforce his decisions, threatened in late July to call out the Guard to prohibit the construction of a federal dam in Texas which threatened to destroy valuable farm land in Oklahoma.

For Miriam Ferguson see Note 2175.

2182 *NYT,* Wednesday, August 2, 1933, 17:7.

2183 *NYT,* Thursday, August 3, 1933, 19:7.

Santa Barbara, California, annually hosted thousands of visitors at its presentation of Old Spanish Days, a three-day fiesta complete with a colorful pageant parade that emphasized events in the history of the city.

2184 *NYT,* Friday, August 4, 1933, 17:7.

The California legislature passed a 1 percent income tax in late July that aroused considerable protest from state residents saddled at the same time with a new $2\frac{1}{2}$ percent sales tax. The income tax, the least popular of the revenue measures, was vetoed by the governor.

2185 *NYT,* Saturday, August 5, 1933, 13:7.

A young attorney from Boston, hoping to attract publicity for a newly-formed, radical political party, placed tear gas bombs in the cooling system of the New York Stock Exchange on August 3, driving members and employees into the streets and forcing the suspension of trading for the remainder of the day.

2186 *NYT,* Monday, August 7, 1933, 15:7. Variant: *NYT* gives "and all disputes to be" in second sentence.

2187   *NYT,* Tuesday, August 8, 1933, 19:7.

For Cordell Hull see Note 2162.

Raymond Charles Moley, American political economist and magazine editor. A central figure in Roosevelt's circle of advisers, Moley was appointed in early August to head a special anti-crime force, organized to combat the rising tide of kidnappings in the country.

For the Missouri kidnapping case see Notes 2127 and 2179.

Hugh Johnson (see Note 2151)) was born in Fort Scott, Kansas, and was a graduate in 1901 of Northwestern Oklahoma Teachers College.

2188   *NYT,* Wednesday, August 9, 1933, 19:7.

The Spanish-American War of 1898 was caused in part by Americans' desire to help liberate Cuba from "Spanish tyranny." Cuba became an independent republic in 1902, although the Platt amendment, reluctantly accepted by Cuba, kept the island under United States protection until the abrogation of the amendment in 1934.

A revolution in Cuba raged with increasing intensity from January of 1933 until August 11, 1933, when the army withdrew its support of President Gerardo Machado y Morales. The Machado regime thereupon collapsed, and the deposed leader fled the country.

2189   *NYT,* Thursday, August 10, 1933, 19:7.

The American ambassador to Cuba, Sumner Welles, asked President Machado on August 8 to appoint a responsible official to run the Cuban government and then to depart the island on a "leave of absence." Roosevelt issued a similar plea the next day. See also Note 2188.

2190   *NYT,* Friday, August 11, 1933, 17:7.

For Cuba and the United States see Notes 2188 and 2189.

2191   *NYT,* Saturday, August 12, 1933, 13:7. Variant: *LAT* omits "whose father . . . in Cuba," in second sentence.

Hamilton Fish, Jr., Republican United States representative from New York from 1920 to 1945. Fish's father, Hamilton Fish, practiced law in New York City and served in Congress from 1909 to 1911. A cousin, also named Hamilton Fish, served in Theodore Roosevelt's Rough Rider Regiment during the Spanish-American War and was the first American soldier killed in the campaign against Santiago, Cuba. Representative Fish informed President Roosevelt on August 10 that the president could rely on the entire Republican minority of the House Foreign Affairs Committee to support any action the president decided to take in Cuba, including that of armed intervention.

2192   *NYT,* Monday, August 14, 1933, 15:7.

For Italo Balbo and the Italian air armada see Notes 2168 and 2171.

Machado resigned as president of Cuba on August 11 (see Note 2188) and fled the island by plane on August 12. He first flew to Nassau in the Bahamas and then to Montreal, Canada.

2193   *NYT,* Tuesday, August 15, 1933, 19:7.

Roosevelt ordered three American warships to Cuban waters on August 13 to protect American citizens on the war-torn island.

Albert Lebrun, president of France from 1932 to 1940.

2194 *NYT,* Wednesday, August 16, 1933, 19:7.

The newest event in American polo, the East-West matches, began at Lake Forest, Illinois, on August 13. The western all-stars won the first match of the best two-of-three match series, 15 to 11.

For the flight of Gerardo Machado see Note 2192.

2195 *NYT,* Thursday, August 17, 1933, 19:7.

The East all-star polo team took the middle game of the three-match series on August 16 by a score of 12 to 8. See also Note 2194.

Hubert W. "Rube" Williams, American polo player and race horse trainer who starred on several championship polo teams during the late 1920s and early 1930s. Williams, who played on the West team in the East-West series, suffered a fractured right leg when he collided with two other players and fell from his galloping pony during the second match of the series.

Eric Pedley, champion California polo player and one of the top American poloists in the history of the sport. Pedley, who often competed with Rogers at clubs in the Los Angeles area, flew to Illinois to replace the crippled Williams.

2196 *NYT,* Friday, August 18, 1933, 17:7.

For J. P. Morgan, Jr., see Notes 2059 and 2123; for Hugh Johnson see Note 2151.

2197 *NYT,* Saturday, August 18, 1933, 13:7. Variant: *NYT* gives "this guy" in fifth sentence.

For Hugh Johnson see Note 2151.

2198 *NYT,* Monday, August 21, 1933, 15:7.

For Hugh Johnson see Note 2151.

The final game of the East-West polo series was played on August 20.

For Huey Long see Note 2064.

2199 *NYT,* Tuesday, August 22, 1933, 19:7.

The West team defeated the East in the final game of the East-West series, 12 to 6. The victory gave the West the series, 2 games to 1. An all-star team from the East won a rematch series in 1934.

2200 *NYT,* Wednesday, August 23, 1933, 19:7.

The Agriculture Adjustment Act, which went into effect in May of 1933, provided for production-control programs for major crops and some stock animals in order to raise prices for farmers and established the AAA. As part of the plan, the Department of Agriculture proposed the controlled slaughter of some 5 million hogs, with the meat to go for relief.

Henry Agard Wallace, United States secretary of agriculture from 1933 to 1940. Son of a prominent Iowa farm editor, Wallace served as vice president of the United States from 1941 to 1945.

Blue Boy, the mammoth prize-winning Iowa boar which "starred" with Rogers in the motion picture *State Fair.* The film was released nationally in late August of 1933.

2201 *NYT,* Thursday, August 24, 1933, 17:7.

For Hugh Johnson see Note 2151; for Frances Perkins see Note 2099.

2202 *NYT*, Friday, August 25, 1933, 17:7.

Smith (see Note 2115) believed that the National Industrial Recovery Act and the NRA were unconstitutional, although he saw some virtue in the legislation. He spoke on national radio on August 22, for example, to laud the NRA for its role in increasing wages and employment in the country.

Robert Rutherford McCormick, editor and publisher of the *Chicago Tribune* from 1920 until his death in 1955. Fiercely anti-Nazi, McCormick visited Germany to study how Hitler had attained power and why the Nazis had begun a program of persecution of the Jews. He returned in mid-August of 1933 and wrote a series of articles for the *Tribune,* describing the life of the German people under Nazi rule.

2203 *LAT*, Saturday, August 26, 1933, I:1:6; heading from *NYT*, 13:7. Variant: *NYT* omits "(some . . . wife,) . . . dirt," in first sentence.

The murder trial of David A. Lamson, a Stanford University publications executive who was accused of the brutal slaying of his wife Allene, opened on August 22 in San Jose, California. The month-long trial, complete with gruesome photographs and glaring headlines, ended in Lamson's conviction. In April of 1936, after two appeals and retrials had resulted in hung juries, Lamson was freed and all charges were dismissed.

For Hugh Johnson see Note 2151; for Henry A. Wallace see Note 2200; for Cordell Hull see Note 2162; for Frances Perkins see Note 2099.

2204 *NYT*, Monday, August 28, 1933, 15:7.

Helen Newington Wills Moody, popular United States women's singles tennis champion from 1923 to 1929—with exception of 1926—and eight-time winner of the British Open title. During the finals at the United States Open on August 26, Moody retired suddenly in the third set because of a painful leg injury, defaulting the title to defending champion Helen Hull Jacobs.

Texas voters on August 26 elected twenty-three repealist delegates-at-large. They later met in state convention and declared adoption of the repeal of prohibition.

2205 *NYT*, Tuesday, August 29, 1933, 19:7.

Moley (see Note 2187) resigned as assistant secretary of state on August 27 to become editor of *Today* magazine. Before entering government service, he had been professor of public law at Columbia University.

2206 *NYT*, Wednesday, August 30, 1933, 21:7.

Ernestine Roessler Schumann-Heink, Austrian-born American operatic contralto who first appeared with the Metropolitan Opera Company in New York City in 1898 and reappeared with the Metropolitan in 1926 at the age of sixty-four. Because of the anti-Semitic policies of the German Nazi government, Schumann-Heink proclaimed herself an "exile" from Germany on August 29.

Long received a black eye from a punch thrown by an unidentified fellow guest at a party on Long Island, New York, on August 28. Long's detractors immediately launched a Reward-the-Socker-of-Huey-Long movement.

2207 *NYT*, Thursday, August 31, 1933, 19:7.

For Henry A. Wallace see Note 2200; for the Long Island party see Note 2206.

2208 *NYT,* Friday, September 1, 1933, 19:7.

Washington became on August 30 the twenty-fourth state to vote for repeal of prohibition.

2209 *NYT,* Saturday, September 2, 1933, 13:7.

John Jakob Raskob, wealthy Du Pont and General Motors executive who served as chairman of the Democratic National Committee during the campaign of 1928.

2210 *NYT,* Monday, September 4, 1933, 13:7.

2211 *NYT,* Tuesday, September 5, 1933, 19:7.

William Vincent Astor, American financier, magazine publisher, and yachtsman who supported the early New Deal policies of Franklin Roosevelt. Roosevelt sailed along the East Coast aboard Astor's yacht, the *Nourmahal,* in early September.

2212 *NYT,* Wednesday, September 6, 1933, 23:7.

Henry Ford, pioneer American automobile manufacturer and founder in 1903 of Ford Motor Company. Ford never joined the automobile code of the NRA, although he already had instituted or later would adopt many of its provisions and principles.

A "buy now" campaign was launched by Hugh Johnson, the colorful director of the NRA, on September 4. Johnson hoped that increased consumer purchasing, especially of the products of NRA-member firms, would serve to stimulate the sluggish economy.

A hurricane struck southern Texas on September 4; 22 persons were killed and 1,500 injured. The damage to property was estimated at $5 million. On the same day a less severe storm swept across south central Florida, causing several deaths and more than $1 million in property damage.

2213 *NYT,* Thursday, September 7, 1933, 23:7.

The August revolution in Cuba (see Note 2188) was followed by another revolt in September in which enlisted men of the Cuban army and navy overthrew the twenty-three-day-old government of Carlos Manuel de Cespedes and installed in power a military and student backed junta.

2214 *LAT,* Friday, September 8, 1933, I:1:6. *NYT* did not print the DT.

Edward Grey, British statesman who served as minister of foreign affairs from 1905 to 1916. Viscount Grey consolidated the Triple Entente before World War I, uniting Great Britain, France, and Russia, and took an important role in the negotiation of Balkan problems at the London Peace Conference of 1912 to 1913.

Edward Mandell House, American politician who as friend and close confidant of President Woodrow Wilson served as personal representative of the president at wartime conferences in Europe in 1914, 1915, and 1916. House's private papers were incorporated in a four-volume set titled *The Intimate Papers of Colonel House* (1926-1928).

David Lloyd George, prime minister of Great Britain from 1916 to 1922. The first volume of Lloyd George's memoirs of World War I appeared on September 6.

2215 *NYT,* Saturday, September 9, 1933, 15:7.

The Roosevelt administration, fearing that the Cuban revolution of September 5 (see Note 2213) presaged widespread disorders, sent twenty-nine vessels to Cuban waters and concentrated 1,000 marines at Quantico Naval Base in Virginia.

Claude Augustus Swanson, United States secretary of the navy from 1933 until his death in 1939. At the outbreak of disorders in Cuba, Swanson sailed for the island to direct American naval operations in the area. The American naval action, however, aroused resentment in some Cuban circles and much criticism in the United States and Latin America. Roosevelt met the protests by ordering Swanson not to land at Havana and by making public assurances that the United States would avoid intervention.

For Gerardo Machado see Notes 2188 and 2192.

2216 *NYT*, Monday, September 11, 1933, 19:7.

For the Cuban revolution see Notes 2213 and 2215; for George V see Note 2129.

2217 *NYT*, Tuesday, September 12, 1933, 25:7. Variant: *NYT* gives "little move preferred" in fourth sentence.

Oscar Lawler, California lawyer and corporations director who was an attorney for and close friend of Rogers.

2218 *NYT*, Wednesday, September 13, 1933, 21:7. Variant: *NYT* omits "Superior" from fifth sentence.

For the Cuban revolution see Note 2213.

2219 *NYT*, Thursday, September 14, 1933, 25:7.

2220 *NYT*, Friday, September 15, 1933, 21:7.

The State of California went to court in early September to halt the tapping of a state oil pool at Huntington Beach by private operators using the "whip-stock" method of drilling.

For Miriam Ferguson see Note 2175; for Alfalfa Bill Murray see Note 2106.

The New York Giants and the Washington Senators were battling in mid-September to win the pennants of their respective baseball leagues. The Giants clinched the National League title on September 19, and the Senators won the American League pennant two days later.

2221 *NYT*, Saturday, September 16, 1933, 15:7.

For the Cuban revolution see Note 2213.

2222 *NYT*, Monday, September 18, 1933, 21:7. Variant: *NYT* gives "drink it straight." in sixth sentence.

For the Lamson murder trial see Note 2203.

2223 *NYT*, Tuesday, September 19, 1933, 23:7.

2224 *NYT*, Wednesday, September 20, 1933, 23:7.

Herbert Clark Hoover, president of the United States from 1929 to 1933. Hoover and his wife, Lou Henry Hoover, arrived in Chicago on September 19 to visit the Century of Progress Exposition. Upon arrival the former president was met by numerous reporters, but he refused to discuss political affairs.

2225   *NYT,* Thursday, September 21, 1933, 21:7.

2226   *LAT,* Friday, September 22, 1933, I:1:4. *NYT* did not print the DT.

Several prominent members of the New York Stock Exchange threatened to form a new exchange in New Jersey to escape emergency taxes proposed by New York City on stock transfers and gross profits of brokers. The move was averted on September 26 when the Tammany-backed mayor of New York City vetoed the stock tax measure.

2227   *NYT,* Saturday, September 23, 1933, 17:7.

The Federal Emergency Relief Administration (FERA), an agency authorized by an act of May 12, 1933, and which eventually granted $3 billion to state governments to be used as public assistance to the unemployed, either as direct benefits or as wages on public works projects.

The Public Works Administration (PWA), an agency which was authorized under the National Industrial Recovery Act of 1933 and which administered a $3.3 billion program of extensive public works projects on federal state, and municipal levels. The huge works program provided a stimulus to the economy and reduced unemployment.

2228   *NYT,* Monday, September 25, 1933, 17:7.

The Iowa Farmers' Holiday Association declared a strike on October 23 as a protest against Roosevelt's refusal to adopt proposals for an inflationary issue of greenbacks and for a guarantee of a fixed price for agricultural products. Strikers broke into freight cars, and several railroad bridges were burned and dynamited.

The Frazier-Lemke Farm Bankruptcy Act, designed to prevent mortgage foreclosures, provided additional relief to farmers by enabling them to secure credit extensions. Passed in June of 1934, the act was declared unconstitutional in May of 1935. A modified version was enacted in August of 1935 and subsequently upheld in court.

2229   *NYT,* Tuesday, September 26, 1933, 23:7.

Ramón Grau y San Martin, head of the provisional junta (see Note 2213) and provisional president of Cuba from September 10, 1933, to January 15, 1934, and president from 1944 to 1948.

Joseph Vincent McKee, New York City attorney and public official. As aldermanic president, McKee became acting mayor of New York City in 1934 when Major James John "Jimmy" Walker resigned during a state investigation of graft and corruption in his administration. McKee chose not to run in a special election for the mayoralty but was a candidate in 1933 on the Recovery party ticket; he was defeated in a four-way race.

2230   *NYT,* Wednesday, September 27, 1933, 23:7.

Turner (see Note 2175) flew from Los Angeles to New York City on September 25 in a world record time of ten hours, five minutes, and thirty seconds. He also held the westbound transcontinental record.

The Union Pacific and the Chicago, Burlington, and Quincy railways put into operation in 1933 new lightweight, streamlined, electric-powered trains capable of traveling 100 miles-per-hour.

Ringgold Wilmer "Ring" Lardner, American satirist, journalist, author, and playwright. He contributed many sketches for the *Ziegfeld Follies,* including a memorable one in 1922 in which Rogers portrayed a veteran baseball pitcher. Lardner died on September 25, 1933, at age forty-eight.

Florenz "Flo" Ziegfeld, Jr., American theatrical producer best known for the elaborately-staged *Ziegfeld Follies*. First produced in 1907, these musical revues featured a troupe of beautiful chorus girls and many of the leading stage performers of the day. Rogers appeared with the *Follies* from 1916 to 1924.

2231 *NYT*, Thursday, September 28, 1933, 23:4.

For the New York Stock Exchange see Note 2226.

2232 *NYT*, Friday, September 29, 1933, 21:3. Variant: *NYT* gives "$69,000" in fourth sentence.

A white rat was placed in a rattlesnake cage in a zoology laboratory at a Pennsylvania college. The rodent was intended to be the cage occupants' evening meal. The rat, instead, killed the seven youngest reptiles and backed the remaining two into a corner; lab assistants finally came to the rattlers' rescue and removed the rat.

Federal agents recovered $74,250 in ransom money on September 27 from a Texas cotton field. The cache was part of a $200,000 ransom paid out earlier in the year for the return of a kidnapped Oklahoma oilman.

A special Senate committee revealed on September 27 that from 1929 to 1932 an American steamship company had received an average of $66,000 in government subsidies for each pound of United States mail it had carried on its ships. The payments generally were considered a legal pretext for subsidies to the merchant marine.

2233 *NYT*, Saturday, September 30, 1933, 17:3.

Irvin Shrewsbury Cobb, American journalist, humorist, and playwright. Cobb, who was born in Paducah, Kentucky, in 1876, was a close personal friend of Rogers. In 1934 the Oklahoman starred in the motion picture *Judge Priest* for which Cobb wrote the screenplay as well as the book (1915) upon which the box-office hit was based.

2234 *NYT*, Monday, October 2, 1933, 21:3.

For Roscoe Turner see Notes 2175 and 2230.

Francis Monroe "Frank" Hawks, American aviator who established numerous transcontinental and point-to-point speed records in the 1920s and 1930s.

James Harold "Jimmy" Doolittle, American flier noted for his speed marks set in the 1920s and 1930s, his interest in commercial aviation, and his heroism during World War II.

For Wiley Post see Note 2168; for Jimmy Mattern see Note 2134; for Charles Lindbergh see Note 2135.

2235 *NYT*, Tuesday, October 3, 1933, 25:3.

Roosevelt, in an address at the annual convention of the American Legion on October 2, defended his policy of paying benefits only to veterans who had been disabled in actual service or to those who had incurred disabilities after their service had ended.

2236 *NYT*, Wednesday, October 4, 1933, 25:3.

2237 *NYT*, Thursday, October 5, 1933, 23:3.

Fire swept through the Griffith Park section of Los Angeles on October 3, trapping more than 200 county workers struggling to fight the blaze. Twenty-eight of the men, most of whom came from the ranks of the unemployed, were killed.

William Lawrence "Young" Stribling, American prizefighter who fought his first professional bout in 1921 at the age of sixteen and who went on to record 126 knockouts in 286 fights. Stribling, son of circus performers, died on October 3 of injuries received in a motorcycle accident.

Engelbert Dollfuss, chancellor of Austria from 1932 until his death in 1934. Dollfuss, who came into conflict with Nazi interests because of his plans to maintain Austrian independence, was shot by a young Austrian Nazi on October 3. Dollfuss survived the attack, only to be assassinated by Austrian Nazi rebels in a raid on the Chancellery in July of 1934.

2238   *NYT*, Friday, October 6, 1933, 19:7. Variant: *NYT* gives "versus N. Y. N. Y. at" in second sentence.

In the World Series of 1933, the New York Giants defeated the Washington Senators, 4 games to 1.

2239   *NYT*, Saturday, October 7, 1933, 17:3.

2240   *NYT*, Monday, October 9, 1933, 19:7.

Augustín Pedro Justo, president of Argentina from 1932 to 1938.

2241   *NYT*, Tuesday, October 10, 1933, 23:7.

2242   *NYT*, Wednesday, October 11, 1933, 25:7. Variants: *NYT* omits eighth sentence/*NYT* omits "crazy" from tenth sentence.

The University of Kansas football team held a highly-touted Notre Dame squad to a scoreless tie on October 7. It was the first time since 1901 that a Notre Dame team had been tied in the opening game of the season.

William Harold "Bill" Terry, steady hitting infielder for the New York Giants from 1923 to 1936 and manager of the Giants from 1932 to 1941. Terry, who guided the Giants to a world championship in 1933, signed a new five-year contract on October 9.

Joseph Edward "Joe" Cronin, player-manager of the Washington Senators from 1932 to 1934, batted .309 and drove in 118 runs in 1933 to lead the Senators to the American League pennant. Cronin, who later managed the Boston Red Sox for eleven years and served several years as American League president, signed a three-year contract with the Senators on October 10.

James Rolph, Jr., Republican governor of California from 1931 until his death in 1934.

2243   *NYT*, Thursday, October 12, 1933, 27:7. Variant: *NYT* omits "anxious" from seventh sentence.

For James Watson see Note 2088.

Walter Evans Edge, United States ambassador to France from 1929 to 1933; former Republican governor of New Jersey and United States senator.

2244   *NYT*, Friday, October 13, 1933, 21:7.

Christopher Columbus, Genoese sailor, explorer, and discoverer of the New World (October 12, 1492).

Eric the Red, Norse mariner and explorer who discovered Greenland about A.D. 986. His son, Leif Ericson, is believed to have been the first European to visit (A.D. 1000) the American continent.

For Greta Garbo see Note 2064.

Charles Spencer "Charlie" Chaplin, English comedian and motion picture star who won international acclaim for his film portrayal of the human condition as "The Tramp."

Emil Ludwig, German biographer and playwright. Among his notable biographies, are *Goethe* (1920), *Napoleon* (1924), *Wilhelm II* (1925), and *Christ* (1928).

For Walter Winchell see Note 2126.

Napoleon I, emperor of France from 1804 to 1814 and in 1815. Napoleon was born on the Mediterranean island of Corsica in 1769.

Marie Joseph Paul Ives Roch Gilbert du Motier, marquis de Lafayette, French general and political leader who became enamored with the American Revolution and offered his services to the American patriots. Commissioned as major general, Lafayette distinguished himself in battle and won the admiration of the American people.

For John J. "Black Jack" Pershing see Note 2072.

2245   *NYT,* Saturday, October 14, 1933, 17:7.

2246   *NYT,* Monday, October 16, 1933, 19:7.

The German government unexpectedly announced its withdrawal from the League of Nations and the Geneva World Disarmament Conference on October 14, citing the refusal of the Allied powers and the United States to concede arms equality or to reduce materially their own armaments as reasons for its actions.

2247   *NYT,* Tuesday, October 17, 1933, 23:7.

The Versailles Peace Conference, an international peace conference at Versailles, France, at which the treaty to end World War I was negotiated and signed (1919).

The Washington Conference of 1921-1922 produced several treaties limiting tonnage of major war vessels, outlawing the use of poison gas, and establishing rules for naval warfare.

For the Geneva World Disarmament Conference see Note 2063.

2248   *NYT,* Wednesday, October 18, 1933, 23:7.

For Bernard M. Baruch see Note 2151.

2249   *NYT,* Thursday, October 19, 1933, 21:7.

Le Roy "Baby Le Roy" Winnebrenner, American infant who appeared in several light-hearted motion pictures in the early 1930s.

Jackie Cooper, American child actor of the 1930s famous for his performance in the "Our Gang" series; later became a noted television actor, director, and producer.

2250   *NYT,* Friday, October 20, 1933, 21:7

For Jack Garner see Note 2105.

James Aloysius Farley, American businessman and politician who served as chairman of the Democratic National Committee from 1932 to 1940 and as United States postmaster general from 1933 to 1940. Farley was Roosevelt's campaign manager in 1932 and 1936.

For Miriam Ferguson see Note 2175.

Horse racing with legalized betting returned to Texas on October 19 after an absence of twenty-five years.

For Amon G. Carter see Note 2126.

2251   *NYT*, Saturday, October 21, 1933, 17:7.

For Jack Garner see Note 2105; for James A. Farley see Note 2250.

Randolph Field, the chief training center for the United States Army air forces, was dedicated in June of 1930 and soon thereafter became known as the "West Point of the Air."

Kelly Field, the largest flight training center in the world during World War I, was the site of the Army Air Corps Flying School for Advanced Instruction from 1922 through World War II.

2252   *NYT*, Monday, October 23, 1933, 17:7.

2253   *NYT*, Tuesday, October 24, 1933, 23:7.

2254   *NYT*, Wednesday, October 25, 1933, 21:7.

For Bernard M. Baruch see Note 2151.

2255   *NYT*, Thursday, October 26, 1933, 21:7.

For Jesse Jones see Note 2107.

The RFC, in an effort to increase the value of the American dollar, began buying newly-mined United States gold on October 25 at prices above the world market price.

2256   *NYT*, Friday, October 27, 1933, 21:7.

2257   *NYT*, Saturday, October 28, 1933, 17:7.

2258   *NYT*, Monday, October 30, 1933, 19:7.

2259   *NYT*, Tuesday, October 31, 1933, 23:7.

2260   *NYT*, Wednesday, November 1, 1933, 23:7. Variants: *LAT* gives "Boris" in fourth, fifth, and sixth sentences/*NYT* gives "better marry" in ninth sentence.

Boris III, king of Bulgaria from 1918 to 1943.

Carol II, king of Rumania from 1930 to 1940. Carol and Boris met on October 30 to discuss ways to improve relations between their two countries. While the leaders conferred, newspapers reported that Carol, well-known for his escapades with women, and Boris's sister, Princess Eudoxia, planned to marry. The news story, however, proved erroneous.

2261   *NYT*, Thursday, November 2, 1933, 23:2.

Jay Norwood "J. N. Ding" Darling, political cartoonist and illustrator for the *Des Moines Register* and the *New York Tribune;* winner of Pulitzer prizes in 1924 and 1943.

²²⁶² *NYT,* Friday, November 3, 1933, 21:7.

For Jesse Jones see Note 2107.

²²⁶³ *NYT,* Saturday, November 4, 1933, 17:7.

After Ford refused to participate in the NRA program, General Johnson (see Note 2151) threatened to reject bids from Ford dealers for government contracts. The National Labor Board, however, announced on November 3 that Ford had adopted collective bargaining for his employees and had met all other federal standards necessary to qualify for government contracts.

For George V see Note 2129.

²²⁶⁴ *NYT,* Monday, November 6, 1933, 21:7.

Roosevelt rejected on November 4 a proposal offered by five Midwestern governors that he guarantee a fixed price for agricultural products. The president considered the price-fixing plan impractical and unacceptable to most farmers.

Gerald Swope, president of General Electric Corporation from 1922 to 1939 and from 1942 to 1944. In 1931 he proposed the so-called Swope plan for the stabilization of industry through the formation of national trade organizations representing each industry and functioning under federal supervision. Despite pressure to replace the ailing NRA, Roosevelt announced on November 4 that the administration would continue to support it in hopes that it eventually would succeed.

²²⁶⁵ *NYT,* Tuesday, November 7, 1933, 25:7.

The states of Kentucky, South Carolina, Pennsylvania, Ohio, Utah, and North Carolina voted on the prohibition repeal amendment on November 7. Wets carried Kentucky, Pennsylvania, Ohio, and Utah by margins as wide as four to one. Voters in North and South Carolina chose to remain dry.

In the mayoralty election in New York City on November 7, Congressman Fiorello Henry La Guardia, Republican-Fusion candidate, defeated former acting mayor Joseph Vincent McKee and incumbent John Patrick O'Brien by an impressive margin. La Guardia, who served as mayor from 1934 to 1945, candidly admitted before the election that he would defeat anyone but Al Smith (see Note 2115). Smith, however, had resisted all efforts by the leaders of Tammany to run him on the Democratic ticket.

²²⁶⁶ *NYT,* Wednesday, November 8, 1933, 28:7.

General Italo Balbo, commander of the Italian air armada which made a mass transatlantic flight to the United States in the summer of 1933 (see Notes 2166 and 2171), was removed suddenly on November 6 as Italian aviation minister, a post he had held since 1929, and was appointed instead to be governor of the Italian colony of Libya. With Balbo's departure, Mussolini assumed the aviation portfolio; he now held six of the thirteen cabinet ministries, including the premiership.

²²⁶⁷ *NYT,* Thursday, November 9, 1933, 23:7.

For Fiorello La Guardia see Note 2265; for prohibition repeal in North Carolina see Note 2265.

²²⁶⁸ *NYT,* Friday, November 10, 1933, 23:7.

On election day, November 7, Utah became the thirty-sixth state to vote for repeal of prohibition, completing the necessary number of states required to ratify the Twenty-first Amendment.

2269 *NYT*, Saturday, November 11, 1933, 17:7.

A five-member special Senate committee met in Los Angeles in November to investigate stock swindles involving a bankrupt Southern California real estate empire.

Sally Rand, American vaudeville dancer and motion picture actress who created a sensation with her electrifying fan dance routines at the Century of Progress Exposition in Chicago in 1933. Rand made her Southern California debut in February of 1934.

2270 *NYT*, Monday, November 13, 1933, 19:7.

2271 *NYT*, Tuesday, November 14, 1933, 21:7.

The first plebiscite in Germany under Nazi auspices was conducted on November 12. Managed by the Nazis, it resulted in an 88 percent vote of support for Hitler's decision to quit the Geneva World Disarmament Conference and the League of Nations.

2272 *NYT*, Wednesday, November 15, 1933, 23:7. Variant: *LAT* gives "statesmen (sic)." in fourth sentence.

Stephen John Maher, American physician and pioneer in tuberculosis research, reported on November 13 that he had bred the so-called "A. Y. Bacteria," which had been used successfully in the treatment of tuberculosis cases complicated with symptoms of bronchial pneumonia.

2273 *NYT*, Thursday, November 16, 1933, 23:7. Variant: *NYT* gives "lives let's just" in eighth sentence.

2274 *NYT*, Friday, Novmber 17, 1933, 19:7.

For Al Smith see Note 2115.

Royal Samuel Copeland, Democratic United States senator from New York from 1923 until his death in 1938. A physician, Copeland formerly had served as president of the New York City Board of Health.

Jesse Isidor Straus, United States ambassador to France from 1933 to 1936 and son of a former owner of R. H. Macy & Co., a major New York City-based mercantile firm.

For James A. Farley see Note 2250.

Herbert Henry Lehman, Democratic governor of New York from 1932 to 1942. An investment banker and noted philanthropist, Lehman later served in the United States Senate.

For John J. Raskob see Note 2209; for William H. Woodin see Note 2105.

2275 *NYT*, Saturday, November 18, 1933, 17:7. Variant: *NYT* gives "out that people will" in fourth sentence.

A special Senate committee, conducting an investigation in New Orleans into the election of Senator John Holmes Overton of Louisiana, often found itself besieged by political factionists. On November 16, a crowd of several thousand surrounded the building where the committee was conducting its hearings, forcing some members of the committee to enter and leave the building by a fire escape and through a women's restroom.

For Tom Connally see Note 2105; for the Senate Banking and Currency Committee investigation see Note 2077; for Ferdinand Pecora see Note 2130; for the Senate investigation of California real estate transactions see Note 2269.

2276 *NYT,* Monday, November 20, 1933, 17:7.

For J. P. Morgan, Jr., see Note 2059.

2277 *NYT,* Tuesday, November 21, 1933, 21:7. Variants: *NYT* gives Troyanovsky" in second sentence/*LAT* gives "Bullett" in fourth sentence.

The United States and the Soviet Union officially established diplomatic relations on November 16 as the result of an exchange of notes between Roosevelt and Soviet representatives in Washington, D. C. Alexander Antonovich Troyanovsky, Soviet ambassador to Japan since 1927, immediately was designated as the new ambassador to the United States, a post which he held until 1939. William Christian Bullitt, appointed United States ambassador to Moscow, had been sent by Woodrow Wilson on a special mission to Russia as early as 1919 and later had served as a special assistant to the secretary of state. He remained as ambassador to the Soviet Union until 1936.

2278 *NYT,* Wednesday, November 22, 1933, 21:7.

Baruch (see Note 2151), in an article in the November 25 issue of *Saturday Evening Post,* upheld the monetary policies of the Roosevelt administration and chastised those who had called for employment of inflationary practices as a remedy for the nation's economic woes.

George Horace Lorimer, editor-in-chief of the *Saturday Evening Post* from 1899 to 1936. The *Post* traced its origin to Benjamin Franklin's *Pennsylvania Gazette,* which was first published in Philadelphia in 1729.

2279 *NYT,* Thursday, November 23, 1933, 21:7.

Two American balloonists, Lieutenant Commander Thomas Greenhow Williams Settle of the Navy and Major Chester L. Fordney of the Marine Corps, established a world altitude record of 11.17 miles on November 21.

2280 *NYT,* Friday, November 24, 1933, 21:7.

Cuba and other Western Hemisphere nations participated in a Pan-American Conference at Montevideo, Uruguay, in the fall of 1933. The Montevideo meeting was significant for denying the right of any nation to interfere in the affairs of another.

Oliver Mitchell Wentworth Sprague, American economist who, while on leave of absence from his teaching position at Harvard University, served as financial assistant to the secretary of the treasury from June to November of 1933. Sprague resigned in protest against the inflationary policies of the Roosevelt administration.

2281 *NYT,* Saturday, November 25, 1933, 17:7. Variant: *LAT* gives "interest," in fourth sentence.

2282 *NYT,* Monday, November 27, 1933, 19:7.

Al Smith (see Note 2115), who had become increasingly anti-administration, attacked Roosevelt's monetary policies in a public statement on November 24. Brushing party regularity aside, Smith charged that Roosevelt had forfeited government responsibility by his program of dollar depreciation.

William Edgar Borah, Republican United States senator from Idaho from 1907 until his death in 1940. Former chairman of the Senate Foreign Relations

Committee, Borah came to the defense of the gold policies of the Roosevelt administration in a formal statement issued on November 25. "The ones you hear howling about sound money," the maverick Republican stated, "are those who own securities."

²²⁸³ *NYT,* Tuesday, November 28, 1933, 23:7. Variant: *NYT* omits first sentence.

Many Californians were shocked when a mob at San Jose battered its way into a local jail on the night of November 26 and seized the two men who had confessed to the kidnapping and brutal murder of Brooke L. Hart, son of a prominent local merchant. The next day, Governor James Rolph, Jr., who had been appraised of the movement of the mob and who had refused to send state aid to the local authorities, aroused worldwide criticism with a statement praising the mob's act.

The Army football team of 1933 was one of the most successful in the history of the Academy. Until the final game of the season, Army sported an unbeaten and untied record that included seven shutouts. On December 2, however, a Notre Dame team, with a record of five losses, defeated Army by scoring thirteen points in the final ten minutes. The Rose Bowl of 1934 featured Stanford and Columbia; the latter was the first New York City team ever chosen to play in the prestigious post-season football classic.

²²⁸⁴ *NYT,* Wednesday, November 29, 1933, 21:7. Variant: *NYT* omits first sentence.

²²⁸⁵ *NYT,* Thursday, November 30, 1933, 31:7.

²²⁸⁶ *NYT,* Friday, December 1, 1933, 21:7.

William Surrey Hart, American actor who made his first motion picture in 1914 and soon thereafter became the foremost western hero of the silent screen. A close friend of Rogers, Hart retired from acting in 1926.

Homer Croy, American novelist and screen writer, best known for his humorously warm portrayals of small-town America. His book, *They Had to See Paris* (1926), was produced in New York City as a musical comedy and then in 1929 as a motion picture, Rogers' first talking film. Croy wrote the scripts for most of the pictures that Rogers made after that time, including *Down to Earth* (1932) and *David Harum* (1934).

Mary William Ethelbert Appleton "Billie" Burke, American stage and motion picture actress who appeared in more than eighty films before her retirement in 1960. She married theatrical producer Florenz "Flo" Ziegfeld (see Note 2230) in 1914.

Louis Ferdinand, second son of the former German crown prince, Freidrich Wilhelm Viktor August Ernst, and grandson of the exiled kaiser of Germany, Wilhelm II. Prince Louis Ferdinand worked in the sales department of Ford Motor Company in Detroit, later becoming an executive with the German branch of Ford.

²⁷⁸⁷ *NYT,* Saturday, December 2, 1933, 15:7.

²²⁸⁸ *NYT,* Monday, December 4, 1933, 19:7.

Rolph (see Note 2242) aroused criticism from many sections of the nation by an emotional statement issued on November 27 praising the action of a San Jose lynching mob (see Note 2283).

Ethel Barrymore, American stage and screen actress and a member of a family prominent in American theater and motion pictures. Barrymore, in an appearance before a Philadelphia lecture group, outraged members of her audience by characterizing them as ignorant, ungrateful, and "moronic." Long noted for her outspokenness, Barrymore issued the rebuke because of criticism previously leveled at her and an associate by members of the study group.

Oscar Odd McIntryre, American syndicated writer whose daily column "New York Day by Day" appeared in more than 550 newspapers from 1921 until his death in 1938. A well-known lover of dogs, McIntyre wrote of the death of his pet Sealyham in his column of December 2.

2289   *NYT*, Tuesday, December 5, 1933, 23:7.

Manuel Luis Quezon y Molina, Philippine statesman and independence leader. President of the Philippine Senate from 1916 to 1935 and later president of the Commonwealth of the Philippines, Quezon chaired a delegation of Filipinos which lobbied actively in the United States in late 1933 and early 1934 for Philippine independence.

The Philippine independence measure, the Tydings-McDuffie Act of 1934, provided for the independence after ten years of self-government under United States tutelage. Complete independence was granted on July 4, 1946.

2290   *NYT*, Wednesday, December 6, 1933, 23:7.

"The noble experiment," the term Herbert Hoover originated to describe prohibition. The Eighteenth Amendment to the Constitution was terminated officially on December 5 when the Twenty-first Amendment repealing prohibition was ratified by the convention of Utah, the thirty-sixth state required for the purpose.

2291   *NYT*, Thursday, December 7, 1933, 23:7.

2292   *NYT*, Friday, December 8, 1933, 23:7. Variant: *NYT* gives "These so-called big" in second sentence.

A Mexican delegate to the Pan-American Conference caused a furor on December 6 by charging that the United States had kept its diplomatic policies secret. Supported by other Latin American representatives, the Mexican diplomat, Manuel Puig Casauranc, denounced the American practice of holding closed meetings.

2293   *NYT*, Saturday, December 9, 1933, 17:7.

Heartley W. "Hunk" Anderson, head football coach at Notre Dame University from 1931 to 1933. Anderson succeeded the legandary Knute Rockne as coach in April of 1931 and went on to compile a three-season record of 16-9-2. His record was not successful enough, however; he was forced to resign on December 8.

Elmer Francis Layden, football star at Notre Dame University in the early 1920s who won fame as one of the celebrated "Four Horsemen" in the Fighting Irish backfield. Successful as football coach at Duquesne University since 1927, Layden was named on December 8 to replace Hunk Anderson as head coach at Notre Dame. Layden remained in that post through 1940 and led the Irish to a 47-13-3 record.

Knute Kenneth Rockne, head football coach at Notre Dame University from 1918 to 1931. Personable and popular, Rockne compiled a remarkable 105-12-5 record at Notre Dame. He and seven other persons died in a plane crash in southeastern Kansas on March 31, 1931.

Columbia University surprised most football experts by compiling a record of 7-1-0 in 1933 and by being selected to play in the Rose Bowl against a powerful Stanford University team. Columbia, the first school from New York City ever to appear in the post-season classic, won the game 7 to 0.

Nicholas Murray Butler, president of Columbia University from 1902 to 1945, corecipient of the Nobel Peace Prize in 1931, and veteran of Republican politics.

2294   *NYT,* Monday, December 11, 1933, 21:7.

2295   *NYT,* Tuesday, December 12, 1933, 23:7.

2296   *NYT,* Wednesday, December 13, 1933, 23:7.

Harry Carr, reporter and columnist for the *Los Angeles Times* from 1897 until his death in 1936.

2297   *NYT,* Thursday, December 14, 1933, 23:7.

For the Pan-American Conference at Montevideo, Uruguay, see Notes 2279 and 2292.

The Chaco War, a conflict between Bolivia and Paraguay (1932-1935) over possession of the Gran Chaco north of the Pilcomayo River. A truce finally was signed in 1935 after more than 100,000 lives had been taken and both sides were exhausted. A peace treaty signed in 1938 gave the greater share of the disputed territory to Paraguay.

2298   *NYT,* Friday, December 15, 1933, 23:7. Variant: *LAT* gives "$34" in sixth sentence.

For Roscoe Turner see Note 2175.

Jones (see Note 2107) announced on December 14 that the RFC had bought 446,000 ounces of domestic, newly-mined gold at $34.01 per ounce.

2299   *NYT,* Saturday, December 16, 1933, 17:7. Variant: *NYT* gives "the boys say things" in first sentence.

The "boss" to whom Rogers refers is probably James Hamilton "J. Ham" Lewis, picturesque senator from Illinois, who arrived in Los Angeles on December 14, whereupon he enthusiastically affirmed his faith in Roosevelt's policies and predicted imminent prosperity.

2300   *NYT,* Monday, December 18, 1933, 21:7. Variant: *NYT* gives "money, but got good" in fifth sentence.

2301   *LAT,* Tuesday, December 19, 1933, I:1:6. *NYT* did not print the DT.

Jones (see Note 2107) indicated on December 18 that the board of directors of the RFC was studying a plan to extend direct loans to industry to meet payrolls and to increase employment. Although such action was never taken by the RFC, the rumors regarding it prompted many bankers to loosen their credit policies.

2302   *NYT,* Wednesday, December 20, 1933, 23:7.

2303   *NYT,* Thursday, December 21, 1933, 23:7.

"Darb," an American slang term infrequently used in the 1920s and 1930s to mean any remarkable or excellent person or thing.

2304   *NYT,* Friday, December 22, 1933, 23:7.

French authorities arrested two Americans, Robert Gordon Switz and his wife, the former Marjorie Tilley, in Paris on December 20, 1933, on charges of spying for the Soviet Union. During the next few months, the American couple steadfastly maintained their innocence, but in March of 1934, faced with incriminating evidence, they finally admitted their guilt and named their accomplices. The Switzes were found guilty but, because of their willingness to cooperate, were released unpunished.

2305 *NYT,* Saturday, December 23, 1933, 17:7.

Bryan (see Note 2079) first attracted national attention in 1896, when, in discussing the Democratic platform, he made his notable "Cross of Gold" speech, in which he narrated the history of the silver movement and called for the free and unlimited coinage of silver. This speech so swayed the silverites that he won the presidential nomination, even though he was only thirty-six years old.

Sectional demands for the monetization of silver was organized in the fall of 1933, with a view to swaying Congress in 1934. Roosevelt made a welcome concession on December 21, 1933, by ordering the purchase annually of 24,241,410 ounces of newly-mined domestic silver at a price far higher than the existing market rate.

2306 *NYT,* Monday, December 25, 1933, 25:7.

2307 *NYT,* Tuesday, December 26, 1933, 17:7. Variant: *NYT* omits third sentence of P.S.

A French express train crashed on December 23 into the rear of a local train crowded with holiday passengers and halted by fog; 180 persons were reported killed in the greatest railway tragedy of the year.

Edward Townsend Stotesbury, American financier and philanthropist who was a member of several major banking and investment firms and chairman of the executive committee of Reading Railroad.

2308 *NYT,* Wednesday, December 27, 1933, 21:7.

For Edward T. Stotesbury see Note 2307.

William Wallace Atterbury, American railway executive who served as president of Pennsylvania Railroad from 1925 to 1935.

Hirosi Saito, Japanese career diplomat who was appointed as ambassador to the United States in December of 1933; he remained in that post until 1938.

2309 *NYT,* Thursday, December 28, 1933, 21:7.

2310 *NYT,* Friday, December 29, 1933, 23:7.

For the Pan-American Conference see Notes 2280 and 2292.

Hull (see Note 2162)), head of the United States delegation, left the Pan-American Conference on December 27 for a tour of Argentina and Chile. By the time he returned to Washington, D. C., in early January of 1934, he had completed the most extensive Latin American tour ever made by a United States secretary of state.

2311 *NYT,* Saturday, December 30, 1933, 15:7.

Roosevelt declared in an address on December 28 that the United States would no longer pursue a policy of armed intervention in the affairs of the Latin American republics. The president's statement, a reiteration of the Good Neighbor Policy set forth in his inaugural address, reflected the agreements made at the recently adjourned Pan-American Conference in Montevideo.

For the United States and Cuba see Notes 2189, 2193, and 2215.

²³¹² *NYT,* Monday, January 1, 1934, 25:7.

²³¹³ *NYT,* Tuesday, January 2, 1934, 17:4.

In the Rose Bowl game of 1934, the Columbia University football team defeated Stanford, 7 to 0, in a surprising upset accomplished with only fifteen players.

For Nicholas Murray Butler see Note 2293.

²³¹⁴ *NYT,* Wednesday, January 3, 1934, 21:7.

For the Columbia-Stanford game see Note 2313.

Hoover graduated from Stanford University in 1895.

²³¹⁵ *NYT,* Thursday, January 4, 1934, 21:7. Variant: *NYT* omits "(the little . . . white ones)" in third sentence.

Roosevelt, in his "State of the Union" message delivered before a joint session of Congress on January 3, assured his listeners of the permanence of the New Deal and of the continuing progress of the country toward complete recovery. The message was received for the most part enthusiastically; however, some congressmen complained that Roosevelt had not given them an inkling of his current policy.

²³¹⁶ *NYT,* Friday, January 5, 1934, 23:7.

²³¹⁷ *NYT,* Saturday, January 6, 1934, 17:7.

"Brother, Can You Spare a Dime?" memorable, moody depression song; melody by Jay Gorney and lyrics by E. Y. "Yip" Harburg.

Roosevelt sent to Congress on January 4 an unprecedented $10 billion budget that showed a contemplated excess of expenditures over receipts of about $7 billion.

²³¹⁸ *NYT,* Monday, January 8, 1934, 19:7.

The on-going Franco-German arms controversy (see Note 2063) continued to hamper the resumption of discussions at Geneva. Germany sought arms equality with an army of 300,000, but France would allow the Reich an army of only 200,000, with limited, supervised rearming. Gradually, Hitler abrogated the Versailles Treaty, building a powerful war machine and remilitarizing the Rhineland and other formerly restricted areas.

For Roosevelt on expansion and intervention see Note 2311.

²³¹⁹ *LAT,* Tuesday, January 9, 1934, I:1:6. *NYT* did not print the DT.

Cary Travers Grayson, former medical director and retired rear admiral of the United States Navy. A native of Culpepper, Virginia, and the personal physician to President Woodrow Wilson, Grayson underwent successful surgery at the Mayo Clinic on January 8 for the removal of a kidney tumor.

Charles Horace Mayo, American surgeon who with his brother, William James Mayo, cofounded in 1889 the famed Mayo Clinic in Rochester, Minnesota.

Thomas Woodrow Wilson, president of the United States from 1913 to 1921. Wilson and an entourage that included Grayson and Jesse Jones (see Note 2107) went to Europe in 1918 to participate in the peace treaty deliberations following World War I.

For Carter Glass see Note 2119.

²³²⁰ *NYT,* Wednesday, January 10, 1934, 23:7. Variant: *LAT* gives "The same day the deficit" in second sentence.

The California state supreme court ruled on January 8 that all male students at the University of California would have to take compulsory courses in military training regardless of their anti-military convictions.

²³²¹ *NYT,* Thursday, January 11, 1934, 23:7. Variant: *NYT* omits "and high stepper." in fifth sentence.

David Harum, motion picture released in late February of 1934 in which Rogers played the title role of a country banker and horse trader. One of the best scenes in the film is a trotting race in which Rogers drives his horse to victory by singing "Ta-ra-ra-boom-de-ay."

The Grand Circuit of harness racing in the 1930s included the Hambletonian at Goshen, New York, and the Kentucky Futurity at Lexington, Kentucky.

Edward Franklin "Pop" Geers, famed and picturesque American harness driver known as the "Grand Ole Man of the Trotting Turf." Geers died in a racing mishap in 1924 at age seventy-three.

²³²² *NYT,* Friday, January 12, 1934, 25:7. Variant: *LAT* gives "Finland's new" in third sentence.

The Senate passed an amendment to a liquor tax bill on January 10 which provided for a special penalty on liquor imported into the United States from countries that had defaulted on their debt payments. Aimed especially at wines from France, the debt-default penalty was stricken from the tax bill before the final passage of the measure on January 11.

Finland was the only country that paid its war debt obligation in full.

Paavo Nurmi, Finnish long-distance runner and gold medal winner at the Olympics of 1920, 1924, and 1928.

²³²³ *NYT,* Saturday, January 13, 1934, 15:7.

For the Liquor Tax Act see Notes 2322 and 2324.

²³²⁴ *NYT,* Monday, January 15, 1934, 17:7.

The Liquor Tax Act of 1934 (see Note 2322) raised the tax on distilled liquors by more than 80 percent and on wines by as much as 150 percent, depending on alcoholic content.

Nobumasa Suetsugu, vice admiral of the Japanese Navy and commander-in-chief of its combined fleet, created an international stir in January of 1934 when he charged in a Japanese magazine article that the United States and the Soviet Union were scheming to encircle Japan and that Charles Lindbergh and his wife, Anne, had spied for the United States during a trip to Japan in 1931.

²³²⁵ *NYT,* Tuesday, January 16, 1934, 23:7.

The Chicago Bears professional football team defeated a Southern California collegiate all-star team at Los Angeles on January 14 by a score of 26 to 7. This was the first game ever between the defending National Football League championship team and a college all-star squad in a post-season contest for charity.

²³²⁶ *NYT,* Wednesday, January 17, 1934, 21:7.

Roosevelt asked Congress on January 15 to enact legislation that would give him the power to put the dollar on a modified or gold bullion basis, valued at sixty cents. The House passed a bill embodying the president's request on January 20 after limited debate; the Senate approved it on January 27. Three days later, Roosevelt signed the bill, known as the Gold Reserve Act of 1934.

Rumors that Garbo (see Note 2064) and Rouben Mamoulian, Russian-born American film maker who directed Garbo in *Queen Christina* (1933), planned to marry gained momentum when, shortly after the release of *Queen Christina,* they left Hollywood together for a motor trip to the Grand Canyon. They were spotted before they reached their destination, and, thereafter, were trailed mercilessly by reporters and gossip columnists. Simply close friends, the couple was never married.

2327   *NYT,* Thursday, January 18, 1934, 23:7.

For the "sixty-cent dollar" see Note 2326.

2328   *NYT,* Friday, January 19, 1934, 21:7.

Three different men held the presidency of Cuba during a volatile four-day period in January of 1934. Ramón Grau, provisional president since September of 1933, was forced to resign on January 15, with Carlos Hevia taking his place. Hevia, who assumed office on January 16, resigned two days later in the face of almost unanimous public opposition. General Carlos Mendieta Montetur, a veteran of the Cuban war of independence and a popular old-school politician, was sworn into office on January 18. He served as provisional president until his resignation in December of 1935.

Edward Joseph Flynn, New York City Democratic party leader and longtime supporter of Franklin Roosevelt. Once an ally of Tammany Hall, Flynn and his Bronx organization broke with the once-powerful Democratic machine during the mayoral election of 1932 in which the Tammany candidate suffered a telling defeat. The influence of Tammany had declined greatly during the 1930s, with internal squabbling partially to blame. In one such incident on January 18, 1934, fourteen Tammany leaders bolted the organization and coalesced with Flynn to defeat the Tammany candidate for clerk of the New York City Board of Aldermen.

2329   *NYT,* Saturday, January 20, 1934, 17:7.

For the "sixty-cent dollar" see Note 2326.

Five Japanese tourists in Kearney, New Jersey, were arrested in mid-January for taking photographs of a local bridge. The picture-takers were later released, but not before a Japanese newspaper had commented: "Unfortunately, Japan has no airplane capable of crossing the Pacific and the United States, dropping bombs at Kearney, and returning to Japan."

For unrest in Cuba see Note 2328.

A 726-carat diamond was unearthed at Elansfontein, South Africa, in early January. Named for its original owner, the Jonkr Diamond—at the time the fourth largest ever found—was sold on January 18 to a mogul of the South African gem industry.

2330   *NYT,* Monday, January 22, 1934, 17:7.

For the "sixty-cent dollar" see Note 2326.

The Japanese foreign office issued a tartly worded statement on January 20 in which it assailed the American refusal to recognize Manchukuo, the country Japan had created after its seizure of the Chinese provinces of Manchuria and Jehol. The United States, however, held to a policy of non-recognition of "governments made by the sword." Of the major countries, only Japan, Italy, and Germany extended diplomatic recognition to the puppet state.

Graham McNamee, sports and general announcer for National Broadcasting Company and one of the best known broadcasters in the country. McNamee married the former Ann Lee Sims on January 20, 1934.

2331   *NYT,* Tuesday, January 23, 1934, 21:7.

Hull (see Note 2162) returned to the United States on January 21 from the Pan-American Conference at Montevideo (see Note 2280) and from an extensive tour of Latin America (see Note 2310).

For Philippine independence see Note 2289; for Cuba and the Platt Amendment see Note 2188.

2332   *NYT,* Wednesday, January 24, 1934, 19:7.

Sadao Araki, Japanese minister of war from 1931 until his resignation on January 22, 1934. A supernationalist, General Araki was an ardent advocate of militaristic education and Japanese domination of Asia. He was succeeded as war minister by General Senjuro Hayashi, a militarist whose views closely paralleled those of his predecessor.

Koki Hirota, Japanese foreign minister from 1932 to 1936 and in 1937. A promoter of fascism in Japan, Hirota was hanged as a war criminal in 1948.

2333   *NYT,* Thursday, January 25, 1934, 21:7.

The Civil Works Administration (CWA), an emergency unemployment relief program established in November of 1933 to offset a drop in the business revival of mid-1933 and to cushion economic distress over the winter of 1933-1934. An investigation of alleged graft within the CWA began in January of 1934, with one arrest on January 23 for misapplication of $100,000. The CWA was terminated by law on March 31, 1934.

The United States recognized the new Cuban government of Carlos Mendieta Montefur (see Note 2328) on January 23.

Henry Justin Allen, Republican United States senator from Kansas from 1929 to 1930. Allen, a former governor of Kansas, was chairman of the board of a newspaper publishing company in Wichita.

2334   *NYT,* Friday, January 26, 1934, 19:7.

Carter (see Note 2126) was host at one of more than 5,000 parties held across the country on January 30 to celebrate the birthday of President Roosevelt and to benefit the Georgia Warm Springs Foundation, an institution founded by Roosevelt for sufferers of infantile paralysis. See also DT and Note 2338.

For Alfalfa Bill Murray see Note 2106.

2335   *NYT,* Saturday, January 27, 1934, 15:7. Variant: *LAT* gives "Gypsey" in first sentence.

Gipsy Rodney Smith, British evangelist who began his ministry in 1877 at the age of sixteen. He remained active as an internationally-known revivalist until his death in 1947.

For Alfalfa Bill Murray see Note 2106.

James Edward "Pa" Ferguson, Democratic governor of Texas from 1915 to 1917 who was impeached on several charges including misappropriation of state funds. A colorful populist, Ferguson attempted to run for a second term in 1924, but a court ruled that he could not be a candidate. His wife, Miriam, promptly entered the race and won with the open support of her husband.

2336   *NYT,* Monday, January 29, 1934, 17:7.

Alice Roosevelt Longworth, daughter of President Theodore Roosevelt, widow of Speaker of the House Nicholas Longworth, and prominent Washington hostess.

For the Gold Reserve Act see Note 2326.

2337   *NYT,* Tuesday, January 30, 1934, 21:4.

For Huey Long see Note 2064; for the Gold Reserve Act ("the money stabilization bill") see Note 2326; for Roosevelt's birthday celebration see Note 2334.

2338   *NYT,* Wednesday, January 31, 1934.

Ettie Rheiner Garner, wife of Vice President Jack Garner. The Garners hosted more than 2,500 guests at a benefit ball in Washington, D. C., on January 30 in honor of Roosevelt (see Note 2334). Rogers acted as master of ceremonies at the celebration.

The Vinson Naval Parity Act, signed on March 27, 1934, provided for the enlargement of the United States naval forces to the limits allowed by treaties signed in 1922 and in 1930. The president was authorized to begin construction of a 15,000-ton aircraft carrier, of 99,200 tons of destroyers, and of 35,530 tons of submarines, to replace old vessels.

2339   *NYT,* Thursday, February 1, 1934, 21:7.

Mills, an aspirant for the Republican presidential nomination in 1936 and a leading opponent of the New Deal liberalism of the Roosevelt administration (see also Note 2102), called for the government to modify its tariffs and for the administration to abandon its idea of a planned national economy, which he declared could be achieved only at "a frightful social cost." Mills delivered his message, which was considered the opening thrust of his presidential campaign, at Topeka, Kansas, on January 29.

2340   *NYT,* Friday, February 2, 1934, 19:7.

The Saint Lawrence Development treaty, which provided for joint American-Canadian improvement of the Saint Lawrence River for deep-draft navigation and development of water power, was signed at Washington, D. C., in 1932. The treaty received a favorable vote in the Senate on March 14, 1934, but fell short of the necessary two-thirds for ratification. Approval for joint construction of the Saint Lawrence Seaway finally came in the 1950s. The international waterway, which provides passage to the Great Lakes for large ocean-going vessels, was opened in 1959.

For Alexander Troyanovsky, Soviet ambassador to the United States, see Note 2277.

2341   *NYT,* Saturday, February 3, 1934, 17:7.

Verne Sankey, American crime figure who was an early suspect in the kidnapping and murder in 1932 of the infant son of Charles Lindbergh. Sankey was arrested by federal agents in Chicago on January 31. Although cleared in the Lindbergh case, Sankey hung himself in his jail cell on February 8, 1934, while awaiting trial on other kidnapping charges.

John Herbert Dillinger, American bank-robber and murderer who headed one of the most notorious gangs of criminals in the Middle West during the early 1930s. Dillinger was captured in 1933 after a highly-publicized nationwide manhunt. He escaped from a county jail in Indiana on March 3, 1934, and another intensive manhunt ensued. The end finally came on July 22, 1934, when he was ambushed and killed by federal agents outside a Chicago movie house.

2342 *NYT,* Monday, February 5, 1934, 17:7.

Henry Morgenthau, Jr., United States secretary of the treasury from 1934 to 1945. The Gold Reserve Act of 1934 (see Note 2326) provided for a $2 billion gold fund for the use of the Treasury Department in stabilizing the value of the dollar on foreign exchanges.

2343 *NYT,* Tuesday, February 6, 1934, 23:7.

A manufacturers' sales tax was not included in revenue legislation passed by Congress in 1934.

2344 *NYT,* Wednesday, February 7, 1934, 21:7.

For Henry Morgenthau see Note 2342; for Bernard M. Baruch see Note 2151.

2345 *NYT,* Thursday, February 8, 1934, 21:7. Variant: *NYT* omits fourth and fifth sentences.

For Jesse Jones see Note 2107.

2346 *NYT,* Friday, February 9, 1934, 21:7.

Serious riots erupted in Paris in January and February of 1934 following the disclosure of a financial and political scandal which involved highly placed officials in the French government. The disturbances led to the resignation of the ministry of Edouard Daladier on February 7, following a day of fighting in which eighteen persons were killed and 2,291 injured.

Taxi drivers in New York City staged a disorderly strike in early February to protest a five-cent tax on cab fares.

2347 *NYT,* Saturday, February 10, 1934, 17:7.

For Verne Sankey see Note 2341.

Gaston Dumergue, veteran French statesman and former president of the republic who was called out of retirement in February of 1934 to head a coalition government and to restore order to the country following severe rioting. Although Dumergue's return to government was welcomed at first, his call for extraordinary powers led to the fall of his cabinet in November of 1934.

2348 *NYT,* Monday, February 12, 1934, 17:7.

All air-mail contracts were cancelled by Roosevelt on February 9 after a senatorial investigation indicated possible fraud and collusion on the part of domestic air-mail operators in the securing of government contracts. Carrying of air mail on domestic routes was then made the responsibility of the United States Army. The military, however, began the mail flights during one of the most severe storms of the year and shocked the nation with a series of crashes that caused the deaths of twelve Army fliers. Public sentiment forced the temporary cancellation of all air-mail service. Domestic airlines carried the first mail authorized under new contracts on May 8, 1934.

2349 *NYT,* Tuesday, February 13, 1934, 19:7.

For Alice Roosevelt Longworth see Note 2336; for the air-mail controversy see Note 2348.

2350 *NYT,* Wednesday, February 14, 1934, 21:7. Variant: *LAT* gives "Capt. Harley," in first sentence.

S. S. *Leviathan,* German-built passenger ship which was seized by the American government during World War I and which became one of the premier luxury liners of the 1920s. A consistent money loser, the *Leviathan* made its last voyage as a passenger vessel in September of 1934; it was sold to British salvagers in 1937.

Herbert Hartley, American sea captain. As commander of the *Leviathan* from 1923 to 1928, Hartley met and befriended rulers, business tycoons, adventurers, film stars, and other famous personalities, including Rogers.

For Greta Garbo see Notes 2064 and 2326; for the air-mail controversy see Note 2348.

2351   *NYT,* Thursday, February 15, 1934, 21:7.

The Austrian government's suppression of socialists precipitated a bloody revolt in early 1934 in which more than 1,000 persons died. The socialist resistance was crushed within a few days, and soon thereafter a totalitarian government was established under the dictatorship of Engelbert Dollfuss.

2352   *NYT,* Friday, February 16, 1934, 21:7.

For the Austrian crisis see Note 2351.

2353   *NYT,* Saturday, February 17, 1934, 17:7.

For the air-mail controversy see Note 2348.

2354   *NYT,* Monday, February 19, 1934, 17:7. Variants: *NYT* gives "with 'em." to end fifth sentence omitting next ten words/*LAT* gives "Dollfuss" in sixth sentence.

Albert I, king of the Belgians from 1909 until his death in a mountaineering accident near Namur, Belgium, on February 17, 1934.

For George V see Note 2129.

Victor Emmanuel II, king of Italy from 1900 until his abdication in 1946. Unwilling to prevent the fascist seizure of power in Italy, Victor Emmanuel was reduced to a figurehead under Mussolini's dictatorship.

For Engelbert Dollfuss see Note 2237.

2355   *NYT,* Tuesday, February 20, 1934, 23:7. Variant: *NYT* omits "(and ... heads)" in tenth sentence.

For the air-mail controversy see Note 2348.

Henry Harley "Hap" Arnold, American military officer who served as commanding officer at various military airfields from 1922 to 1936 and who later became general of the United States Air Force.

2356   *NYT,* Wednesday, February 21, 1934, 21:7. Variant: *NYT* omits fourth paragraph.

Donald "Don" Wackwitz, first lieutenant in the United States Army Air Corps. Wackwitz flew from Cleveland to Newark in a converted B-6 bomber on February 20. His landing, made in a blinding snowstorm, marked the start of mail service to Newark by Army pilots.

Maurice Mars, pilot for United Air Lines. Mars was guided through the snowstorm by a radio directional beam.

The New York Stock Exchange delayed its opening by one hour on February 20 because of the blizzard that struck the city overnight. It was only the third time since 1888 that the exchange had opened late.

2357 *NYT*, Thursday, February 22, 1934, 21:7. Variant: *NYT* gives "by the ballot" in first sentence.

The Senate voted on February 21 to amend the Independent Offices Appropriation bill to restore by July 1, 1934, a 15 percent government pay cut. Roosevelt vetoed the measure, but Congress overrode the veto on March 28. This action represented the most conspicuous refusal by the current Congress to follow Roosevelt's lead in a major policy matter.

Hugo La Fayette Black, Democratic United States senator from Alabama from 1927 until his appointment to the United States Supreme Court in 1937. Black chaired the special senatorial committee which investigated domestic air-mail contracts and which brought the charges that led to the cancellation of the contracts (see Note 2348).

Walter Folger Brown, United States postmaster general from 1929 to 1933. Brown was responsible for awarding air-mail contracts during the Hoover administration and thus was the primary target of the Black Committee investigation.

2358 *NYT*, Friday, February 23, 1934, 21:7.

Augusto Cesar Sandino, Nicaraguan revolutionary who opposed the intervention of the United States in Nicaraguan affairs. Sandino was captured and executed by the Nicaraguan National Guard on February 21, 1934.

United States Marines landed in Nicaragua in October of 1925 to restore order during a rebellion against a pro-American ruler. The Marines remained in Nicaragua until 1933, supervising local elections and lending aid during natural catastrophes such as the devastating earthquake that struck the capital city, Managua, in March of 1931. Rogers visited Managua in 1931 to help raise funds for quake victims.

2359 *NYT*, Saturday, February 24, 1934, 15:7.

Byron Patton "Pat" Harrison, Democratic United States senator from Mississippi from 1919 to 1941.

Robert Marion La Follette, Jr., Progressive-Republican United States senator from Wisconsin from 1925 to 1947. The Senate Finance Committee held hearings on a bill to fix quotas on the marketing of domestic sugar. The measure, the Jones-Costigan bill, was signed into law on May 9, 1934.

In the continuing investigation of the New York Stock Exchange (see also Note 2077), the chief counsel for the Senate Banking and Currency Committee revealed on February 23 that twenty major American corporations had extended $20 billion in "call" loans in 1929 to finance trading on the exchanges.

2360 *NYT*, Monday, February 26, 1934, 19:7. Variant: *NYT* gives "women away from him." in third sentence.

Clark Gable, American leading man of the cinema who became known as the "king" of Hollywood actors. *It Happened One Night*, a film for which Gable won an Academy Award, premiered in New York City on February 22.

For the stock market investigation see Notes 2077 and 2359.

2361 *NYT*, Tuesday, February 27, 1934, 21:7.

John Joseph "Little Napoleon" McGraw, manager of the New York Giants baseball team from 1902 to 1932. During McGraw's tenure as manager, the Giants won ten league and three world championships. McGraw died on February 25, 1934, at age sixty.

2362 *NYT*, Wednesday, February 28, 1934, 21:7.

Johnson, who had become by early 1934 one of the most conspicuous figures in the country (see Note 2151), met with hundreds of critics of the NRA in Washington, D. C., on February 27. Johnson vigorously defended the work of the NRA, despite a barrage of protests from the crowd of small businessmen, labor spokesmen, and consumers angry about unfair monopolistic practices by big business and excessive regulation by the government.

Borah (see Note 2282), supported by a vote of forty-five to thirty-nine, amended the Independent Offices Appropriation bill ((see Note 2357) to bar a pay-cut restoration for government employees—including members of Congress—who received $6,000 or more.

2363 *NYT,* Thursday, March 1, 1934, 21:7.

An army of 51,000 CWA workers were to have joined in the snow-removal operations in New York City on February 27, but only 3,322 appeared on the job.

For Hugh Johnson see Notes 2077 and 2362.

2364 *NYT,* Friday, March 2, 1934, 21:7.

The decision of the United States to prohibit the payment of public obligations in gold prompted the Panamanian government in March of 1934 to refuse to accept a $250,000 check for rental of the Canal Zone. Panama insisted that the United States comply with the Treaty of 1904, which specified that the annual payment be made in gold.

Henry Pu-yi, last Manchu emperor of China and Japan's puppet emperor of Manchukuo. Enthroned on March 1, 1934, with the title of Kang Teh, Pu-yi reigned as emperor until the fall of Japan in 1945.

2365 *NYT,* Saturday, March 3, 1934, 15:7. Variant: *NYT* gives "I arrived" to begin second sentence.

Oscar Westover, assistant chief of the United States Army Air Corps from 1932 to 1935 and, later, chief of the Air Corps. Brigadier General Westover directed the air-mail operations of the Army.

Horace M. Hickman, lieutenant colonel in the United States Army Air Corps and a regional commander of air-mail operations of the Army.

2366 *NYT,* Monday, March 5, 1934, 17:7.

For Henry Pu-yi, emperor of Manchukuo, see Note 2364.

2367 *NYT,* Tuesday, March 6, 1934, 23:7. Variant: *NYT* gives "was 8 o'clock" in second sentence.

Roosevelt, at a session of the NRA Code Authority conference in Washington, D. C., on March 5, rebuked the critics of the recovery program who had labeled it fascist and communist and announced that the NRA would continue as a permanent part of the government.

Lillian Holley, sheriff of Lake County, Indiana, from whose jail John Dillinger escaped on March 3. Holley had incarcerated Dillinger in an "escape proof" new section of the jail. A fifty-member force assigned to guard Dillinger included a squad of deputies, several members of the local Farmers' Protective Association, and a detachment of National Guardsmen.

2368 *NYT,* Wednesday, March 7, 1934, 21:7.

For Roosevelt's message on the NRA see Note 2367.

2369 *NYT,* Thursday, March 8, 1934, 21:7.

When Dillinger fled from the Lake County jail (see Note 2367) he took two guards, sixty-four-year-old turnkey Sam Cahoon and Deputy Sheriff Ernest Blunk, as hostages. The two lawmen later were indicted by a grand jury for aiding and abetting Dillinger's escape.

The Fletcher-Rayburn bill provided for federal regulation of the markets dealing in securities and for the establishment of the Securities and Exchange Commission (SEC) to license stock exchanges. Known also as the Securities Exchange Act, it was signed into law on June 6, 1934.

2370 *NYT,* Friday, March 9, 1934, 21:7. Variant: *NYT* gives "it was then." to end fourth sentence, omitting next nine words.

Roosevelt proposed on March 7 that the flying of air mail be returned to private companies in an open and competitive bidding system. Bids were opened on April 20, 1934. Three weeks later, Transcontinental and Western Airways and United Airlines carried the first air-mail authorized under the new contracts.

Zara Agha, 160-year-old "old man of Turkey" known as the "Modern Methuselah," died at Istanbul on June 29, 1934. He spent nine months in the United States in 1930, earning money as a commercial attraction.

2371 *NYT,* Saturday, March 10, 1934, 15:7.

Otto Wienecke, second lieutenant in the United States Army Air Corps who crashed on March 9 during a storm on the Newark-Cleveland air-mail run. Wienecke was the sixth airman to die since the Air Corps had begun its air-mail operation. Rogers confused Wienecke with First Lieutenant Donald Wackwitz (see Note 2356).

For the Dillinger escape see Notes 2367 and 2369; for Baby Le Roy see Note 2249.

2372 *NYT,* Monday, March 12, 1934, 19:7. Variant: *LAT* gives "Army is going" in seventh sentence.

Roosevelt called a temporary halt to the Army air-mail service on March 10. During the suspension a curtailed schedule was worked out which confined flights to the safer routes.

Edward Vernon "Eddie" Rickenbacker, American aviator and airline executive who as a flight commander during World War I personally disabled twenty-six enemy aircraft. Ironically, prior to the start of the Army air-mail operations on February 19, Rickenbacker copiloted the final mail flight from Los Angeles to New York for Transcontinental and Western Airways.

2373 *NYT,* Tuesday, March 13, 1934, 23:7.

The *M-10001,* a new ultra-streamlined, air-conditioned passenger train of the Union Pacific line went on public display in Los Angeles on March 12. The six-car, diesel train left Los Angeles on October 22, 1934, and arrived in New York City on October 25, making the 3,258-mile run in fifty-six hours and fifty-five minutes.

2374 *NYT,* Wednesday, March 14, 1934, 21:7.

The Barrymores—Lionel, John, and Ethel (see Note 2288)—were among the leading actors of the American stage and screen. John was renowned for his electrifying portrayals of Hamlet.

2375 *NYT,* Thursday, March 15, 1934, 23:7. Variant: *NYT* gives "Rome." to end third sentence, omitting next nine words.

Gyula von Gömbös, Hungarian general and Fascist party leader who served as premier of Hungary from 1932 until his death in 1936. In March of 1934 Gömbös, Dollfuss, and Mussolini met in Rome where they forged closer political and economic ties. By the Rome Protocols of March 17, 1934, and the bilateral commercial treaties of May 14, 1934, Italy and Austria agreed to purchase annually 15,400,000 bushels of Hungarian wheat, and allowed Italy important tariff concessions on manufactured goods.

2376 *NYT,* Friday, March 16, 1934, 23:7.

For the Saint Lawrence Development treaty see Note 2340.

2377 *NYT,* Saturday, March 17, 1934, 17:7.

Samuel Insull II, English-born American utilities and transportation magnate. Insull fled the United States in April of 1932, soon after his utility companies went into receivership. After his indictment in an American federal court for mail fraud, a spectacular international legal fiasco ensued with the United States endeavoring to obtain Insull's return. In 1934 he finally was seized in Greece and returned to the United States, where he was tried on mail fraud charges. He was acquitted.

The Silver Purchase Act, a compromise remonetization measure, was enacted in June of 1934 to meet the demands of agricultural and silver interests in Congress for additional inflation.

For William Jennings Bryan see Notes 2079 and 2305.

2378 *NYT,* Monday, March 19, 1934, 19:7.

The Army resumed its air-mail service on March 18 after a one-week halt to work out safer routes and flying procedures.

2379 *NYT,* Tuesday, March 20, 1934, 25:7.

For Huey Long see Note 2064.

2380 *NYT,* Wednesday, March 21, 1934, 23:7.

Roosevelt announced on March 25 that a threatened general strike in the automobile industry had been averted. A settlement was reached that provided for the establishment of a mediation board and the recognition of the workers' organizations.

2381 *NYT,* Thursday, March 22, 1934, 23:7. Variant: *LAT* gives: "P. P. gang," in eighth sentence.

For James A. Farley see Note 2250.

2382 *NYT,* Friday, March 23, 1934, 25:7.

Balzar (see Note 2058) died on March 21 at age fifty-three.

2383 *NYT,* Saturday, March 24, 1934, 17:7.

For the Securities Exchange Act providing for the regulation of the stock exchanges, see Note 2369; for William E. Borah see Note 2282.

2384 *NYT,* Monday, March 26, 1934, 19:7.

2385 *NYT,* Tuesday, March 27, 1934, 23:7.

For the strike by automobile workers see Note 2381.

Roosevelt took a cruise to the Bahamas in late March aboard the yacht of Vincent Astor (see Note 2211).

2386 *NYT,* Wednesday, March 28, 1934, 25:7. Variant: *NYT* gives "They want" in seventh sentence, omitting "are pleading guilty, but".

Philip Knight Wrigley, president of William Wrigley, Jr. Company from 1925 to 1961. Wrigley, whose father was founder of the Chicago-based chewing gum firm, devised a novel employee insurance plan that assured company workers pay during lay-off periods.

For the Securities Exchange Act providing for the regulation of the stock exchanges, see Note 2369.

The "brain trust," a group of academicians who served as advisers and officials in the Roosevelt administration. Dr. William Albert Wirt, an Indiana educator, charged in late March of 1934 that the "brain trust" was engaged in revolutionary activities and Roosevelt himself was to be the "Kerensky" of an American communistic revolution. A congressional investigation was held with Wirt becoming a chief figure in the inquiry. After several hearings, three Democrats on the investigatory committee reported no foundation for the charges, while two Republicans asserted that no thorough probe had been conducted.

2387 *NYT,* Thursday, March 29, 1934, 25:7. Variant: *LAT* gives "to the pools" in fifth sentence.

2388 *NYT,* Friday, March 30, 1934, 23:7.

For John Dillinger see Note 2341.

Walter James Vincent "Rabbit" Maranville, free-spirited shortstop whose major league baseball career began in 1914 and included a stint with the Boston Braves from 1928 to 1935. For all practical purposes Maranville's big league career ended in the spring of 1934 when he broke a leg while sliding into home plate during an exhibition game. He was inducted into the National Baseball Hall of Fame in 1954.

George Herman "Babe" Ruth, extremely popular baseball player who starred for the New York Yankees from 1920 to 1935. Renowned as a home run slugger, Ruth was named to the Hall of Fame in 1936, the second player to be so honored.

2389 *NYT,* Saturday, March 31, 1934, 13:7.

2390 *NYT,* Monday, April 2, 1934, 19:7.

The United States Fleet from April to November of 1934 engaged in a protracted series of maneuvers that took it from the West to the East Coast and back.

2391 *NYT,* Tuesday, April 3, 1934, 23:7.

Louise Eustis Hitchcock, American socialite and horsewoman who trained the champion polo team captained by her son, Thomas "Tommy" Hitchcock, Jr. Mrs. Hitchcock died on April 1 from injuries suffered in a fall from her horse.

2392 *NYT,* Wednesday, April 4, 1934, 23:7.

2393 *NYT,* Thursday, April 5, 1934, 23:7.

For John Dillinger see Note 2341; for Samuel Insull see Note 2377.

²³⁹⁴ *NYT*, Friday, April 6, 1934, 23:7.

James Rowland Angell, president of Yale University from 1924 to 1937; husband of the former Katherine Cramer Woodman.

Edward Stephen Harkness, American financier and heir to a petroleum and railroad fortune. Member of a family noted for its generous philanthropy to educational and welfare agencies, Harkness contributed during his lifetime more than $13 million to his alma mater, Yale University.

²³⁹⁵ *NYT*, Saturday, April 7, 1934, 17:7. Variant: *LAT* gives "BEVERLY HILLS" as place of origin.

For Samuel Insull see Note 2377. Insull's "Memoirs" remain unpublished.

The Senate defeated an amendment to a revenue bill on April 5 that would raise the normal levy on income from 4 to 6 percent and that would impose surtaxes ranging from 6 to 71 percent. The Revenue Act of 1934, signed by Roosevelt on May 10, set a tax schedule of 5 to 59 percent.

²³⁹⁶ *NYT*, Monday, April 9, 1934, 19:7.

For John Dillinger see Note 2341.

²³⁹⁷ *NYT*, Tuesday, April 10, 1934, 23:7.

For the United States Fleet see Note 2390.

²³⁹⁸ *NYT*, Wednesday, April 11, 1934, 23:7.

Harry Chandler, publisher of the *Los Angeles Times* from 1917 until his death in 1944. Rogers spoke at the laying of the cornerstone of the new $3 million Times Building in Los Angeles on April 10.

²³⁹⁹ *NYT*, Thursday, April 12, 1934, 23:7.

²⁴⁰⁰ *NYT*, Friday, April 13, 1934, 21:7. Variant: *NYT* adds the following postscript: "*[Editor's Note—The New York Times believes that 'Honest Taxpayer' is none other than Mr. Will Rogers. Why he has chosen to hide, modestly, his identity could not be learned last night.]*"

²⁴⁰¹ *NYT*, Saturday, April 14, 1934, 17:7. Variant: *NYT* omits "the way they got it" from third sentence.

The Senate adopted a tax bill on April 13 designed to provide the Treasury a net increase in revenue of $481 million. The major feature of the measure, a proposed surtax of 10 percent on each payer's income tax bill, was struck from the bill in conference commitee. The final version of the bill, as it was signed into law in June, was expected to increase federal revenue by only $332 million (see Note 2395).

²⁴⁰² *LAT*, Monday, April 16, 1934, I:1:2. *NYT* did not print the DT.

²⁴⁰³ *NYT*, Tuesday, April 17, 1934, 23:7.

Roosevelt asked congressional leaders on April 15 for an appropriation of $1.5 billion for relief. The Deficiency Appropriation Act, signed on June 20, 1934, provided $1.83 billion for the PWA, for drought relief, and for other relief and emergency purposes.

²⁴⁰⁴ *NYT*, Wednesday, April 18, 1934, 21:7.

2405 *NYT,* Thursday, April 19, 1934, 27:7.

William Wirt (see Note 2386) testified at a congressional hearing on April 10 that he had first heard of a plot by "brain trusters" to overthrow the government while attending a dinner party in a Washington, D. C., suburb. The hostess and all other guests who had attended the dinner largely discredited Wirt when they testified on April 17 that discussion of a communist revolution had not taken place at the famous gathering.

2406 *NYT,* Friday, April 20, 1934, 23:7.

For Frances Perkins see Note 2099.

2407 *NYT,* Saturday, April 21, 1934, 17:7. Variant: *NYT* omits second sentence.

For the Wirt Affair see Notes 2386 and 2405.

Japan, while tightening its grip on Manchuria, boldly proclaimed its overlordship of Eastern Asia in a statement issued by the Foreign Office on April 18. Japan claimed exclusive responsibility for the maintenance of peace in the Far East and announced that it would take forceful action in the event of interference by the League of Nations and the western powers. The Japanese government softened its stance on April 20, but the United States and Great Britain nevertheless issued vigorous protests against the latest Japanese pronouncement.

2408 *NYT,* Monday, April 23, 1934, 19:7.

2409 *NYT,* Tuesday, April 24, 1934, 25:7.

FBI agents, informed of the presence of Dillinger and his gang at Little Bohemia, a Wisconsin resort lodge, surrounded the building on April 22 in an attempt to capture the unsuspecting outlaws. The lawmen, however, mistook five local residents for gang members and prematurely opened fire. In the confusion Dillinger and his compatriots escaped, leaving behind one dead federal agent.

2410 *NYT,* Wednesday, April 25, 1934, 23:7.

Dillinger continued to elude capture. On April 23 he and two companions fought a running gun battle with lawmen in a suburb of Saint Paul, Minnesota, before outdistancing their pursuers and escaping into a nearby wooded area. Meanwhile, three women who had accompanied Dillinger's gang to Little Bohemia were arrested and jailed at Madison, Wisconsin.

It was widely believed at the time that Dillinger had carved a gun and had used it in his brazen escape from the Lake County, Indiana, jail in March. Although Dillinger did flash around a fake firearm at the time, his primary weapon was a quite lethal gun that had been smuggled to him from the outside.

Eleanor Roosevelt (see Note 2089) had been accused by Senator Thomas David Schall, a Republican from Minnesota, of making use of her position as First Lady to "profiteer" in the sale of furniture from a New York factory which she co-owned. Roosevelt, who denied the charges in a public statement issued on April 23, claimed that the factory was not a profit-making enterprise and had been started long before her husband had considered running for president.

2411 *NYT,* Thursday, April 26, 1934, 25:7.

Dillinger reportedly was seen in various locations in the United States on April 24 but actually cornered nowhere, despite a massive five-state manhunt by more than 5,000 federal agents and other lawmen.

Rexford Guy Tugwell, Columbia University economics professor and a leading member of Roosevelt's "brain trust." On April 24 Tugwell was appointed assistant secretary of agriculture, a post that he would hold from 1934 to 1937. The remarks Rogers attributed to Tugwell were made at a meeting of the American Society of Newspaper Editors in Washington, D. C., on April 21.

Albert Einstein, German-born American physicist who received a Nobel Prize in 1921 for his work in theoretical physics, notably on the photoelectric effect.

2412 *NYT*, Friday, April 27, 1934, 23:7. Variant: *NYT* gives "comes through in a day and a half that" in sixth sentence.

The United States Fleet, numbering more than 100 vessels (see Note 2390), took more than forty-seven hours to pass through the Panama Canal on its way to the East Coast in late April.

Criticism of the Dillinger episode was widespread. Republicans accused the FBI and the Roosevelt administration of bungling the whole affair, and many called for the demotion or dismissal of the director of the FBI, John Edgar Hoover.

2413 *NYT*, Saturday, April 28, 1934, 17:7. Variant: *NYT* omits "native" in fourth sentence.

Alfred Lee Bulwinkle, Democratic United States representative from North Carolina from 1921 to 1929 and from 1931 to 1949. Bulwinkle chaired the congressional committee that investigated the Wirt Affair (see Notes 2386 and 2405).

2414 *NYT*, Monday, April 30, 1934, 17:7.

Will S. "Willie" Tevis, Jr., California horseman known as "The Iron Man of the Age" for his horse racing endurance feats.

Ibrahim Ibni Almarhum Abu Bakar, sultan of Johore from 1895 until his death in 1959. Sir Ibrahim, who ruled his rubber-rich state in southern Malaya with the aid of British advisers, was one of the wealthiest men in the Far East.

2415 *NYT*, Tuesday, May 1, 1934, 23:7.

Rogers was in San Francisco to appear in a West Coast stage production of Eugene Gladstone O'Neill's *Ah, Wilderness!* This was the only time that Rogers assumed a character role in a legitimate drama.

Francis Brett "Bret" Harte, American writer of humorous short stories. In 1868 Harte cofounded the *Overland Monthly*, a literary magazine which Harte published in his adopted California and in which appeared the first of his renown stories of local color, "The Luck of Roaring Camp."

Samuel Langhorne Clemens, "Mark Twain," celebrated American author and humorist. Clemens spent five and one-half years in California and Nevada in the 1860s as a prospector, journalist, and writer.

2416 *NYT*, Wednesday, May 2, 1934, 23:7.

The complicated question of Soviet-American debts and claims was discussed by representatives of the two governments early in 1934, first in Moscow and later in Washington, D. C. The amounts involved were not large as compared to other international obligations (Russia owed $337,223,288 in unfunded war debts in 1934), but the matter of setting a precedent for much larger debtors and creditors proved a stumbling block to settlement of the problem in 1934 and 1935.

The Philippine legislature, meeting in special session on May 1, voted to approve the Tydings-McDuffie Act, providing for the eventual independence of the Philippine Islands (see Note 2289).

2417 *NYT,* Thursday, May 3, 1934, 21:7.

For Jesse Jones see Note 2107.

2418 *NYT,* Friday, May 4, 1934, 23:7.

Silas Hardy Strawn, American corporation attorney and virulent critic of Roosevelt's economic policies. A former president of the United States Chamber of Commerce, Strawn addressed that organization's annual convention in Washington, D. C., on May 2.

2419 *NYT,* Saturday, May 5, 1934, 17:7.

2420 NYT, Monday, May 7, 1934, 19:7.

2421 *NYT,* Tuesday, May 8, 1934, 23:7.

Fred Andrew Stone, American vaudeville and musical comedy star and close personal friend of Rogers.

2422 *NYT,* Wednesday, May 9, 1934, 21:7.

Insull returned to the United States on May 7 to face federal mail fraud charges (see Note 2377).

For the silver issue and the Silver Purchase Act see Note 2377.

2423 *NYT,* Thursday, May 10, 1934, 23:7.

Sophie Tucker, lusty songstress of Broadway, vaudeville, and radio fame, known worldwide as "The Last of the Red-Hot Mamas." Tucker was among a large group of American vaudevillians who gave a "command performance" for the British royal family.

2424 *NYT,* Friday, May 11, 1934, 21:7.

Roosevelt announced on May 9 that foreign governments in debt to the United States were free to present their cases and to seek revision of their debt obligations before the next installment came due on June 15, 1934. Despite the willingness of Roosevelt to judge each case on its individual merits, all war-debtor nations, except Finland, defaulted in full on June 15 and again on December 15.

J. P. Morgan & Co. (see Note 2059) held a major portion of the funded indebtedness of the allied nations to the United States. In the post World War I period, the great banking house floated securities of foreign governments and corporations reaching $2 billion.

2425 *NYT,* Saturday, May 12, 1934, 17:7.

A drought, the most destructive that a great part of the agricultural West had known, lasting until midsummer of 1934, destroyed many crops and severely crippled the livestock business. Blinding dust storms afflicted much of the region at the same time, causing the area to become known as the Dust Bowl.

2426 *NYT,* Monday, May 14, 1934, 19:7.

For the Securities Exchange Act providing for the regulation of the stock exchanges, see Note 2369.

2427 *NYT,* Tuesday, May 15, 1934, 23:7.

2428 *NYT,* Wednesday, May 16, 1934, 21:7.

Los Angeles police on May 14 rescued William F. Gettle, a wealthy Beverly Hills oilman, who had been kidnapped a few days earlier. Four men and two women were arrested in connection with the abduction.

2429 *NYT,* Thursday, May 17, 1934, 23:7.

Three men, accused of the kidnapping of William F. Gettle of Beverly Hills (see Note 2428), pleaded guilty and were given life terms in San Quentin Prison on May 15—only twenty-four hours after the oilman had been freed by police.

2430 *NYT,* Friday, May 18, 1934, 23:7. Variant: *NYT* gives "talk with the people" in eighth sentence.

2431 *NYT,* Saturday, May 19, 1934, 15:7.

The three self-confessed abductors of William F. Gettle (see Notes 2428 and 2429) entered San Quentin Prison on May 17 to begin serving life sentences.

The S-42, a giant four-engined flying boat capable of carrying a load of fifty passengers, plus mail and express, for distances up to 3,000 miles, set a world altitude record of 21,800 feet during a test flight on May 17. The Pan American plane, christened the *Brazilian Clipper,* later was used regularly on the New York City-Buenos Aires run.

2432 *NYT,* Monday, May 21, 1934, 19:7. Variant: *NYT* gives "shows how" in first sentence.

2433 *NYT,* Tuesday, May 22, 1934, 23:7.

Clarence Seward Darrow, prominent American defense attorney and civil libertarian whose court cases were almost invariably headline material. On March 7, 1934, Darrow was appointed to head the National Recovery Review Board which was established to investigate the NRA. The first report of the board, published on May 20, almost immediately brought rejoinders by Hugh Johnson, head of the NRA (see Note 2151). The board accused the NRA of allowing large interests to dominate the code authorities, to the damage of smaller firms. Two supplementary reports and a caustic exchange of remarks between Darrow and Johnson ensued. No direct action was taken on the findings of the board.

2434 *NYT,* Wednesday, May 23, 1934, 21:7.

George William Norris, United States senator from Nebraska from 1913 to 1943. An independent Republican, Norris was known as the "Father of the Twentieth Amendment," popularly called the "Lame Duck Act." His attempts to abolish the electoral college failed to win sufficient support in Congress.

2435 *NYT,* Thursday, May 24, 1934, 23:7.

James Watson Gerard, American lawyer and diplomat who served as United States ambassador to Germany from 1913 to 1917. In August of 1930, Gerard named a group of fifty-nine as the "men who rule the United States." He included leading capitalists and financiers on his list but did not name individuals holding public office.

2436 *NYT,* Friday, May 25, 1934, 21:7.

2437 *NYT,* Saturday, May 26, 1934, 19:7. Variant: *NYT* omits fifth and sixth sentences.

A poppy drive is held annually by the American Legion to raise funds for disabled veterans in soldiers' institutions nationwide.

Bonnie Parker and Clyde Barrow, a young Texas couple who terrorized the Midwest in a two-year crime spree of murder and robbery, were ambushed and killed by lawmen near Black Lake, Louisiana, on May 23. The mothers of the quick-shooting duo rejected double funeral services and side-by-side burials.

2438   *NYT,* Monday, May 28, 1934, 21:7.

Two French fliers, Maurice Rossi and Paul Codos, attempted in May of 1934 to fly nonstop from Paris, France, to San Diego, California, a distance of 6,100 miles. Their plane, the *Joseph Le Brix,* which had flown from the United States to Syria a year earlier, developed mechanical problems while over the Atlantic, forcing the fliers to land at New York City. Although they fell short of their goal, Rossi and Codos were the first to fly nonstop both ways between the continents of Europe and North America.

The *Zephyr,* a new streamlined, diesel-powered train of the Chicago, Burlington & Quincy Railway streaked from Denver to Chicago on May 26 at a record-breaking average speed of 77.6 miles per hour. In November of 1934, the *Zephyr* became the first high-speed train to be placed in regularly scheduled service.

2439   *NYT,* Tuesday, May 29, 1934, 21:7.

For Henry A. Wallace see Note 2200.

2440   *NYT,* Wednesday, May 30, 1934, 19:7. Variant: *NYT* gives "murmuring: 'Oh, what have I done that' " in third sentence.

For Henry A. Wallace see Note 2200.

2441   *NYT,* Thursday, May 31, 1934, 21:7. Variant: *LAT* gives "sit right" in ninth sentence.

As part of Roosevelt's Good Neighbor Policy, the United States and Cuba successfully negotiated a treaty on May 29 which abrogated the Platt Amendment (see Note 2188) and which removed other limitations previously imposed on Cuban sovereignty.

Roosevelt transferred jurisdiction of Puerto Rico on May 29 from the Bureau of Insular Affairs in the War Department to the newly-created Division of Territories and Island Possessions in the Interior Department.

For Philippine independence see Notes 2289 and 2416.

2442   *NYT,* Friday, June 1, 1934, 23:7.

Rolph (see Note 2242) died on June 2, 1934, of heart disease. His health problems began in early 1934 in the midst of a stumping tour of California, during which he sought vindication for his outspoken views on a San Jose lynching (see Note 2288).

2443   *NYT,* Saturday, June 2, 1934, 17:7.

2444   *NYT,* Monday, June 4, 1934, 19:7.

2445   *NYT,* Tuesday, June 5, 1934, 23:7.

John Francis O'Hara, American clergyman and educator who served as vice president of Notre Dame University from 1933 to 1934.

Charles Leo O'Donnell, American priest and university official who served as president of Notre Dame University from 1928 until his death on June 4, 1934, at age forty-nine. O'Donnell was succeeded by Father O'Hara, who served as president from 1934 to 1939.

For Knute Rockne see Note 2293.

2446 *NYT,* Wednesday, June 6, 1934, 23:7.

The British decision to default on the June 15 payment was followed by similar action of other debtors who previously had made only token payments.

For Babe Ruth see Note 2388; for the appropriation bill, the Deficiency Appropriation Act of 1934, see Note 2403.

2447 *NYT,* Thursday, June 7, 1934, 23:7.

Henry Prather Fletcher, American diplomat who served as ambassador to Italy from 1924 to 1929. Fletcher was elected chairman of the Republican National Committee on June 6; he served in that office from 1934 to 1936.

2448 *NYT,* Friday, June 8, 1934, 21:7. Variant: *NYT* gives "steel business" in first sentence.

Steel workers, dissatisfied with the repeated refusals of the steel companies to permit employees to bargain collectively through representatives of their own choosing, threatened in 1934 to stage a general strike, the first one in the industry since 1919 and one which would affect 400,000 workers. It was only through the intervention of the chief of the American Federation of Labor that the steel strike, scheduled to begin on June 16, was averted.

The Dionne quintuplets—Cecile, Yvonne, Annette, Emilie, and Marie—were born on May 28, 1934, to Enzire, wife of Oliva Dionne, of Callander, Ontario, Canada. When the babies were only seventy-two hours old, promoter Ivan Spear sued their father for $1 million, the amount of damage he claimed he had suffered when the father reputiated a contract that would have put the babies on exhibition at the Century of Progress Exposition in Chicago.

2449 *NYT,* Saturday, June 9, 1934, 17:7.

The warning by Treasury Secretary Morgenthau (see Note 2342) followed the dismissal of two federal tax collectors who had been discovered soliciting political funds.

For the Dionne quintuplets see Note 2448.

Baer (see Note 2137) was scheduled to fight Primo Carnera of Italy for the world heavyweight title on June 14 in New York City. In an attempt to gain publicity, Baer's manager claimed that his fighter was not in shape to box. The stunt backfired, however, when a New York State Athletic commissioner visited Baer's camp on June 7 and officially declared the fighter unfit. The next day, Baer underwent an examination by the State Athletic Commission and was pronounced well; the bout went on as planned (see Note 2455).

The Wheeler-Howard Act, signed into law on June 18, 1934, attempted to secure new rights for Indians on reservations. Known as the Indian New Deal, it ended land allotments in severalty and provided for the reinvestment or tribal ownership of surplus lands formerly open to sale.

John Collier, American sociologist and educator who served as United States commissioner of Indian affairs from 1933 to 1945.

The old Indian to whom Rogers referred was a ninety-two-year-old millionaire Creek, Jackson "Jack" Barnett, the subject of a bitter custody battle between the federal government who claimed to be his legal guardian and his wife of fourteen years, the former Anna Laura Lowe. Barnett, who had amassed an oil fortune of $4 million but who had been declared legally incompetent, died on May 29, 1934, at his Los Angeles mansion.

2450   *NYT,* Monday, June 11, 1934, 19:7.

For the threatened steel strike see Note 2448.

For John Dillinger see Notes 2341 and 2410.

2451   *NYT,* Tuesday, June 12, 1934, 23:7.

Section 7(a) of the National Industrial Recovery Act (NIRA) of 1933 provided employees with the right to organize and bargain collectively. The Supreme Court in May of 1935 ruled against certain non-labor features of the NIRA, thus invalidating the entire act. The collective bargaining provision, however, was reenacted in the Wagner-Connery Act (National Labor Relations Act) of 1936, the constitutionality of which was upheld by the Supreme Court in March of 1937.

2452   *NYT,* Wednesday, June 13, 1934, 23:7.

The appointment of Tugwell (see Note 2411) to the post of assistant secretary of agriculture was approved by the Senate on June 11.

2453   *NYT,* Thursday, June 14, 1934, 23:7.

2454   *NYT,* Friday, June 15, 1934, 23:7.

The first meetings between Mussolini and Hitler were held at Venice, Italy, on June 14-15. During their closed-door discussion sessions, the two European dictators apparently agreed to respect the independence of troubled Austria and to attain parity of armaments for Germany. The effect of the Venice accords largely was nullified by continuing Nazi terrorism in Austria.

Plutarco Elías Calles, former president of Mexico who was a dominant force in Mexican politics during the early 1930s.

2455   *NYT,* Saturday, June 16, 1934, 17:7.

Max Baer (see Note 2137) knocked out defending heavyweight champion Primo Carnera of Italy in the eleventh round of a scheduled fifteen-round title bout in New York City on June 14 (see also Note 2449).

William Green, president of the American Federation of Labor from 1924 until his death in 1952. Green was instrumental in averting a threatened general strike in the steel industry in the summer of 1934 (see Note 2448). His proposal for an impartial three-member board to arbitrate the steel dispute culminated in the creation by Roosevelt on June 28, 1934, of the National Steel Relations Labor Board.

2456   *NYT,* Monday, June 18, 1934, 19:7.

For the threatened steel strike see Notes 2448 and 2455.

2457   *NYT,* Tuesday, June 19, 1934, 21:7.

2458   *NYT,* Wednesday, June 20, 1934, 23:7.

For Irvin Cobb see Note 2233.

2459   *NYT,* Thursday, June 21, 1934, 23:7.

2460   *NYT,* Friday, June 22, 1934, 21:7.

2461   *NYT,* Saturday, June 23, 1934, 15:7.

Baruch (see Note 2151) indicated on June 22 that he would disassociate himself from his stock market dealings and would begin writing his memoirs. Publication of his autobiography was delayed for several years; the first volume appeared in 1957, and the second in 1960.

The National Collegiate Athletic Association held its annual championship field and track meet at Los Angeles from June 22-23. Stanford University won the team title.

2462 *NYT*, Monday, June 25, 1934, 17:7.

For the Chaco War between Bolivia and Paraguay see Note 2297.

2463 *NYT*, Tuesday, June 26, 1934, 21:7. Variant: *NYT* gives "Roosevelt received some Tammany" in fifth sentence.

For the meeting between Hitler and Mussolini see Note 2454.

William Allen White, owner and editor of the *Emporia* (Kansas) *Gazette* from 1895 until his death in 1943; recipient of a Pulitzer Prize in 1923. White received the annual Roosevelt Award in June of 1934.

2464 *NYT*, Wednesday, June 27, 1934, 21:7.

2465 *NYT*, Thursday, June 28, 1934, 23:7. Variant: *NYT* gives "invested than" in fifth sentence.

Roosevelt broadcasted another of his famed "fireside chats" with the American public on June 28. The radio talk came only a few days before his departure on a forty-one-day vacation trip to Hawaii.

2466 *NYT*, Friday, June 29, 1934, 21:7. Variant: *NYT* gives "Aviation is" to begin second sentence.

James R. "Jimmy" Wedell, designer, builder, and flier of the Wedell-Williams airplanes, the fastest land planes of the era. Wedell was injured fatally on June 24 while giving elementary flight instruction to a student at the air facilities of the Wedell-Williams Air Service Corporation in Louisiana.

2467 *NYT*, Saturday, June 30, 1934, 15:7.

A federal grand jury, investigating the circumstances that preceded the banking crash in Michigan in 1934, indicted on June 28 thirteen prominent Michigan bank executives, including the former heads of the largest bank holding companies in Detroit.

Marie Dressler, American comedienne of silent and early talkie films; winner of an Academy Award in 1931. Dressler, who had been gravely ill for three months, died on July 28, 1934, at age sixty-four.

For Roosevelt's speech of June 28 see Note 2465.

2468 *NYT*, Monday, July 2, 1934, 21:7.

Roosevelt left on July 1 aboard the cruiser U. S. S. *Houston* for a forty-one-day vacation trip to the Hawaiian Islands.

For Jesse Jones see Note 2107.

Hitler's bloody purge of Nazi Storm Troopers in the summer of 1934 effectively crushed opposition among his followers and eliminated a number of potential rivals.

John Jacob Astor III and Ellen Tuck French were married at Newport, Rhode Island, on June 30. Heirs to great landed wealth and social position, young Astor and French had had a highly-publicized on-again, off-again courtship.

2469 *NYT,* Tuesday, July 3, 1934, 21:7.

For the meeting between Hitler and Mussolini see Note 2454; for Hitler's purge of Nazi Storm Troopers see Note 2468.

2470 *NYT,* Wednesday, July 4, 1934, 17:7.

Fletcher (see Note 2447) on July 2 opened the Republican party's radio campaign for the congressional elections of 1934. Labeling the New Deal as undemocratic, Fletcher asserted that the issue in the campaign was "the right of the people to govern themselves."

2471 *NYT,* Thursday, July 5, 1934, 19:7.

For "Amos 'n Andy" see Note 2090.

2472 *NYT,* Friday, July 6, 1934, 19:7. Variant: *LAT* omits "again" in fourth sentence.

Borah (see Note 2282), a maverick Republican, supported most early New Deal legislation, and only on occasion did he openly criticize the Roosevelt administration. One such moment came during a national radio broadcast in early July of 1934. Long an opponent of the NRA, Borah criticized the recovery program for having fastened a bureaucratic stranglehold on the country and for condoning the creation of unmanageable monopolies.

2473 *NYT,* Saturday, July 7, 1934, 15:7.

2474 *NYT,* Monday, July 9, 1934, 17:7 .

For Hitler's purge of Nazi Storm Troopers see Note 2468.

Hull (see Note 2162) thanked Finland on July 7 for having paid its war debt obligation in full. The Scandinavian nation was the only country ever to repay fully its war debt obligation to the United States.

2475 *NYT,* Tuesday, July 10, 1934, 23:7.

Walter Richard Rudolf Hess, German Reich minister and Nazi party official who created a sensation in 1941 by a solo flight to Scotland on a mysterious, undisclosed mission that eventually ended in his imprisonment as a war criminal.

President Hoover remarked, following a visit to the Virgin Islands in March of 1931, that the United States had obtained "an effective poorhouse" by its "unfortunate" acquisition of the islands. His statement provoked considerable protest from local residents.

2476 *NYT,* Wednesday, July 11, 1934, 19:7.

The Mashed O, a 120,000-acre hereford ranch in Lamb and Bailey counties, Texas. Ewing Halsell managed the ranch and was a good friend of the Rogers family. His father, William Electius Halsell, a co-founder of the Mashed O, and Will's father, Clem Vann Rogers, were friends and business associates.

The XIT Ranch, established in the Texas Panhandle in the 1880s, comprised the largest fenced range in the world. Its 3,050,000 acres was patented by the state to a Chicago syndicate in exchange for money to build a capitol at Austin. Pressing obligations during the next twenty years forced the syndicate to sell most of its original holdings.

For Miriam Ferguson see Note 2175; for James "Pa" Ferguson see Note 2335.

²⁴⁷⁷ *NYT*, Thursday, July 12, 1934, 19:7.

For Henry T. Rainey see Note 2105.

²⁴⁷⁸ *NYT*, Friday, July 13, 1934, 19:7.

For Cordell Hull see Notes 2162 and 2310; for the Pan-American Conference of 1933 see Note 2280.

The Federal Housing Administration (FHA) was established in July of 1934 to help home owners finance repairs and to stimulate residential construction through federal mortgages.

James Andrew Moffett, American oilman who headed the FHA from 1934 to 1935.

²⁴⁷⁹ *NYT*, Saturday, July 14, 1934, 15:4.

²⁴⁸⁰ *NYT*, Monday, July 16, 1934, 17:7.

A paralyzing general strike broke out in the San Francisco Bay area on July 16, 1934. The dispute started in May of 1934 as a localized conflict among longshoremen; within a week the longshoremen had enlisted the support of 15,000 members of ten maritime workers' unions in the area. Involving ultimately 75,000 workers and costing millions of dollars, the general strike occasioned considerable violence and widespread radical activity. On July 17 groups of so-called vigilantes raided the strikers' headquarters, effectively crippling their organization. The strike was called off on July 19, and the participants resumed work.

²⁴⁸¹ *NYT*, Tuesday, July 17, 1934, 21:7.

For James A. Farley see Note 2250.

²⁴⁸² *NYT*, Wednesday, July 18, 1934, 19:7.

For Max Baer see Notes 2137 and 2455.

Helen Leslie Kilbourne "Bobbie" Johnson, wife of General Hugh Johnson.

Frank Finley Merriam, Republican governor of California from 1934 to 1939. The presence in San Francisco of the National Guard, ordered by Merriam to protect the state-owned harbor facilities, was resented deeply by striking longshoremen and added to the cause of calling a general strike (see Note 2480).

²⁴⁸³ *NYT*, Thursday, July 19, 1934, 19:7.

For the San Francisco general strike see Note 2480.

²⁴⁸⁴ *NYT*, Friday, July 20, 1934, 17:7.

A general strike of industrial and service laborers in England in 1926 was called to force the government to subsidize the workers' low wages, particularly those of coal miners. The strike collapsed because of successful governmental efforts to continue services and industrial operations.

For the San Francisco general strike see Note 2480.

²⁴⁸⁵ *NYT*, Saturday, July 21, 1934, 13:7.

For the San Francisco general strike see Note 2480; for James A. Farley see Note 2250; for Baby Le Roy see Note 2249.

²⁴⁸⁶ *NYT,* Monday, July 23, 1934, 17:7.

The San Francisco-Oakland Bay Bridge, which was under construction in July of 1934, opened to traffic on November 12, 1936. Construction contracts on the Golden Gate Bridge were let in June of 1931, and the bridge was opened to traffic six years later.

For the San Francisco general strike see Note 2480; for John Dillinger see Note 2341.

²⁴⁸⁷ *NYT,* Tuesday, July 24, 1934, 17:7. Variant: *NYT* omits last sentence.

Dillinger (see Note 2341) was shot and killed by federal agents as he left a Chicago motion picture theater on July 22.

²⁴⁸⁸ *NYT,* Wednesday, July 25, 1934, 19:7.

Melbourne, Australia, held its centenary celebration in October of 1934. A special feature of the festivities was the $50,000 MacRobertson Air Race from England to Melbourne (see Notes 2561 and 2563). Post (see Note 2168) was one of the sixty-four original entrants in the competition, but he had to withdraw when he was unable to arrange financing for the venture.

²⁴⁸⁹ *NYT,* Thursday, July 26, 1934, 21:7. Variant: *NYT* gives "it" in second sentence.

For Roosevelt's cruise to Hawaii see Note 2468.

²⁴⁹⁰ *NYT,* Friday, July 27, 1934, 19:7.

Dollfuss (see Note 2237) was assassinated by Nazi rebels on July 25 during an unsuccessful attempt to overthrow the Austrian government.

²⁴⁹¹ *NYT,* Saturday, July 28, 1934, 15:4. Variants: *NYT* omits "and make 'em bring stocks out of the water for him." and *LAT* gives "sticks" in fifth sentence.

For Roosevelt's cruise to Hawaii see Note 2468; for Hugh Johnson see Note 2151.

²⁴⁹² *NYT,* Monday, July 30, 1934, 15:7. Variant: *NYT* omits "nothing under seven-eighths thoroughbred," in fourth sentence.

The Parker Ranch, a 300,000-acre spread on the island of Hawaii, runs the second largest hereford herd in the world.

²⁴⁹³ *NYT,* Tuesday, July 31, 1934, 19:7.

²⁴⁹⁴ *NYT,* Wednesday, August 1, 1934, 19:7. Variant: *LAT* gives "Weykiki" in eighth sentence.

Frank F. Baldwin, powerful Hawaiian sugar grower, cattleman, and politician. Between 1909 and 1941, Republicans, under the direction of the Baldwin family, completely dominated the local government on the island of Maui.

²⁴⁹⁵ *NYT,* Thursday, August 2, 1934, 19:7. Variant: *LAT* gives "there much signs" in third sentence.

²⁴⁹⁶ *NYT,* Friday, August 3, 1934, 19:7.

For Engelbert Dollfuss see Notes 2237 and 2490.

Paul Ludwig Hans Anton von Beneckendorff und von Hindenburg, German soldier and statesman who served as president from 1925 to 1934, a time of extreme economic distress and political factionalism in Germany. He died on August 2, 1934, at age eighty-six.

2497 *NYT,* Saturday, August 4, 1934, 13:7.

Homer Stille Cummings, United States attorney general from 1933 to 1939.

Long's control of Louisiana politics and his virulent criticism of Roosevelt and the New Deal brought him much publicity during 1934.

2498 *NYT,* Monday, August 6, 1934, 17:7. Variant: *NYT* gives "I miss" in ninth sentence.

Raphael Floyd Phillips Gibbons, American journalist, author, and radio commentator recognized as the "premier war correspondent of his generation." Rogers and Gibbons traveled together on a voyage to China in late 1931.

Roosevelt returned to Washington, D. C., on August 10, following an extensive cruise to Hawaii and other American possessions.

2499 *NYT,* Tuesday, August 7, 1934, 19:7. Variant: *NYT* omits "or is this one going in Tuesday" in fourth sentence.

2500 *NYT,* Wednesday, August 8, 1934, 19:7.

Carlos Martíns Pereira e Sousa, Brazilian ambassador to Japan.

For Ruth Bryan Owen see Note 2079.

Hitler announced on August 5 that the combined office of president and chancellor, which he now held because of the death of Hindenburg, would last only until rejection by national vote. Hitler received an 88% vote of approval in a plebiscite held on August 19, 1934.

2501 *NYT,* Friday, August 10, 1934, 19:7. Variant: *NYT* gives "herself. Fine trip." in third sentence.

No DT is available for Saturday, August 11, 1934.

2502 *NYT,* Monday, August 13, 1934, 15:7.

Dwight Whitney Morrow, United States ambassador to Mexico from 1927 to 1930. Coolidge's decision to appoint his friend Morrow, a New York City attorney and banker, as ambassador proved beneficial in improving Mexican-American relations.

2503 *NYT,* Tuesday, August 14, 1934, 19:7. Variant: *NYT* gives "one race, but swimming on his stomach lost" in sixth sentence.

An American swimmer, Arthur Highland of Chicago, won his first trial heat in the 100-meter free style event at the Japanese National Swimming championships in Tokyo on August 12; however, he lost in the finals the next day.

2504 *NYT,* Wednesday, August 15, 1934, 19:7.

At the Japanese swimming meet in Tokyo on August 13 (see Note 2503), Albert Vande Weghe of New Jersey set a world record in the 200-meter backstroke with a time of 2 minutes and 32.2 seconds. Japanese male swimmers had overwhelmed the American team at the Olympics of 1932 by winning all but one event.

2505 *NYT,* Thursday, August 16, 1934, 19:7.

The Harvard University baseball team ended its tour of Japan on September 11, posting a record of three wins and six losses.

2506 *NYT,* Friday, August 17, 1934, 17:7. *LAT* did not print the DT.

2507 *NYT,* Saturday, August 18, 1934, 11:7.

2508 *NYT,* Monday, August 20, 1934, 15:7.

2509 *NYT,* Tuesday, August 21, 1934, 19:7. Variant: *LAT* gives "get a county" in third sentence.

Paraguay named a captured fort in the war-torn Chaco region (see Note 2296) for Long because of the Louisianan's statements in the Senate that were regarded as favorable to Paraguay. For the "Long Island battle" see Note 2206.

2510 *NYT,* Wednesday, August 22, 1934, 19:7.

Kurt von Schuschnigg, chancellor of Austria from 1934 to 1938. Schuschnigg met with Mussolini in Rome on August 21. The chancellor's efforts to prevent German absorption of Austria failed when he lost Mussolini's support in 1937.

For Rexford G. Tugwell see Note 2411.

2511 *NYT,* Thursday, August 23, 1934, 19:7. Variant: *NYT* gives "American Indian," in second sentence.

2512 *NYT,* Friday, August 24, 1934, 17:7.

2513 *NYT,* Saturday, August 25, 1934, 15:7.

For Wiley Post see Note 2168.

2514 *NYT,* Monday, August 27, 1934, 17:6.

For Henry Pu-yi, emperor of Manchukuo, see Note 2364; for William Allen White see Note 2463.

2515 *NYT,* Tuesday, August 28, 1934, 23:7.

Primo Carnera, Italian boxer known as the "Ambling Alp" who reigned as world heavyweight champion from 1933 to 1934.

Dolly Curtis Gann, American society figure. Gann served as official hostess for her widowed half-brother, Charles Curtis, when he served as vice president under Hoover.

2516 *NYT,* Wednesday, August 29, 1934, 19:7.

Maurice Gerschon Hindus, Russian-born American free-lance writer who annually visited his native country as a correspondent for various American magazines.

Walter Duranty, English journalist who served as *New York Times* correspondent in the Soviet Union from 1921 to 1934; recipient of a Pulitzer Prize in 1932 for a series of articles on the Soviet Union.

Louis Fischer, American foreign correspondent, expert on the Soviet Union, and award-winning biographer.

²⁵¹⁷ *NYT*, Thursday, August 30, 1934, 21:7. Variant: *LAT* gives "down to the" in first sentence.

For William C. Bullitt see Note 2277.

George Charles Hanson, American foreign service officer and Far Eastern specialist who served as consul general at Harbin, Manchuria, from 1931 until his transfer to Moscow in 1933.

Aleksei Maksimovich Peshkov, "Maxim Gorki," Russian novelist, playwright, and revolutionary who through his popular writings rose from bitter poverty to immense riches and renown.

²⁵¹⁸ *NYT*, Friday, August 31, 1934, 19:7.

For *David Harum* see Note 2321.

²⁵¹⁹ *NYT*, Saturday, September 1, 1934, 15:7.

Leon Trotsky, Russian Communist leader and revolutionary who was banished from Russia in 1929 after he fell out of favor with the existing government. In early 1917 Trotsky lived in New York City where he coedited a radical newspaper.

Upton Beall Sinclair, American novelist, socialist, and Pulitzer Prize winner (1942). Running on a platform of "end poverty in California" (EPIC), Sinclair was defeated in 1934 as the Democratic candidate for governor of the state.

²⁵²⁰ *NYT*, Monday, September 3, 1934, 15:7.

The Battleship Potemkin (Bronenosets Potemkin), classic Soviet-made motion picture (1925) commemorating the Revolution of 1905 and based on a mutiny on board the battleship *Potemkin* of the Russian Black Sea Fleet.

²⁵²¹ *NYT*, Tuesday, September 4, 1934, 21:7. Variant: *LAT* gives "Helsingfors." in second sentence.

²⁵²² *NYT*, Wednesday, September 5, 1934, 23:7.

William Edward Albright, United States minister to Finland from 1933 to 1937. Finland was the only country that paid its war debt obligations in full.

For Paavo Nurmi see Note 2322.

²⁵²³ *NYT*, Thursday, September 6, 1934, 21:7.

²⁵²⁴ *NYT*, Friday, September 7, 1934, 23:7.

Gustavus V, king of Sweden from 1907 until his death in 1950. Better known as Gustaf, the aged monarch was a popular sovereign whose astounding vitality enabled him to play tennis until age eighty-seven.

²⁵²⁵ *NYT*, Saturday, September 8, 1934, 17:7.

²⁵²⁶ *NYT*, Monday, September 10, 1934, 19:7.

²⁵²⁷ *NYT*, Tuesday, September 11, 1934, 23:7.

Black Shirts, a colloquial term generally used to refer to Fascists and specifically to Mussolini's Fascist organization in Italy whose members were identified readily by their black shirts.

²⁵²⁸ *NYT,* Wednesday, September 12, 1934, 25:7.

Marie, queen consort of Rumania and queen dowager from 1927 until her death in 1938.

²⁵²⁹ *NYT,* Thursday, September 13, 1934, 25:7. Variant: *LAT* gives "boushwa." in eighth sentence.

For Carol II, king of Rumania, see Note 2260; for Marie see Note 2528; for Joe Robinson see Note 2105.

²⁵³⁰ *NYT,* Friday, September 14, 1934, 29:7.

Hungarian monarchists continued a prolonged, but unsuccessful campaign in 1934 to restore the Hapsburg dynasty which had collapsed after World War I.

²⁵³¹ *NYT,* Saturday, September 15, 1934, 17:7.

Poland declared on September 13 that it would no longer observe its treaty obligations to racial minorities within the country. The treaty, which had been signed by Poland and the Allied powers following World War I, was an essential precondition to the reestablishment of Poland as a nation. The announcement brought such sharp rebukes from the Allied nations that Poland quietly withdrew its declaration a week later.

²⁵³² *NYT,* Monday, September 17, 1934, 19:7.

The American yacht *Rainbow,* skippered by Harold Stirling Vanderbilt, retained the coveted America's Cup against the strong challenge of Britisher Thomas Octave Murdoch Sopwith's *Endeavour,* in a six-race series off Newport, Rhode Island, in September. The British yacht had as crew members amateurs, who had answered Sopwith's call for volunteers when the professional crew struck for higher wages two days before *Endeavour* left England. The inexperience of Sopwith's crew led to a number of unfortunate incidents that caused the races to end amid hard feelings.

²⁵³³ *NYT,* Tuesday, September 18, 1934, 23:7.

For the America's Cup yachting competition see Note 2532.

Blackbirds, an annual song and dance revue by American black performers, opened in London in September of 1934.

²⁵³⁴ *NYT,* Wednesday, September 19, 1934, 21:7.

Mary, queen consort of King George I of Great Britain and queen dowager from 1936 until her death in 1953. The queen presided at the launching of the Great Cunard White Star luxury liner *Queen Mary* at the shipyards at Clydesbank, Scotland, on September 26.

²⁵³⁵ *NYT,* Thursday, September 20, 1934, 25:7.

²⁵³⁶ *NYT,* Friday, September 21, 1934, 25:7. Variants: *NYT* gives "trusting 'em. Hold 'em, cowboys." in fifth and sixth sentences.

For the America's Cup competition see Note 2532.

In a rematch of the East-West polo series of 1933 (see Note 2199), an all-star team from the East defeated its western counterpart two matches to none in competition at Westbury, Long Island, on September 19 and 25.

²⁵³⁷ *NYT,* Saturday, September 22, 1934, 17:7. Variant: *LAT* gives "Saturday, in Russia. If" in seventh and eighth sentences.

For polo see Note 2536.

²⁵³⁸ *NYT,* Monday, September 24, 1934, 19:7. Variant: *NYT* gives "strikers were going back" in fifth sentence.

American textile workers, on strike since September 3, went back to work on September 23, after failing to win their demands for an increased minimum wage, a shorter work week, and recognition of their union.

²⁵³⁹ *NYT,* Tuesday, September 25, 1934, 23:7.

For Jesse Jones see Note 2107; for the America's Cup yachting competition see Note 2532.

²⁵⁴⁰ *NYT,* Wednesday, September 26, 1934, 23:7.

For the East-West polo series see Note 2536. After the matches of 1934, the intersectional competition did not resume until 1947.

²⁵⁴¹ *NYT,* Thursday, September 27, 1934, 25:7.

Johnson resigned as NRA administrator on September 25.

For Bobbie Johnson see Note 2482.

²⁵⁴² *NYT,* Friday, September 28, 1934, 25:7. Variant: *LAT* gives " 'Dew Deal' " in third sentence/*LAT* gives "President by tomorrow is" in sixth sentence.

The Washington Monument was cleaned and repaired in the fall of 1934 as part of a $100,000 beautification project.

For Jesse Jones see Note 2107.

Roosevelt, following the resignation of Hugh Johnson (see Note 2541), recast the organization of the NRA on September 27, creating an administrative National Industrial Recovery Board and a deliberative Industrial Policy Committee, each of five members. The net effect, at least on paper, was to decentralize what had been a highly unified agency.

²⁵⁴³ *NYT,* Saturday, September 29, 1934, 17:7.

Donald Randall Richberg, general counsel for the NRA from 1933 to 1935 and executive director of its Industrial Policy Committee (IPC) from 1934 to 1935. Other members of the IPC included Interior Secretary Harold Ickes, Labor Secretary Frances Perkins, AAA Administrator Chester Davis, and FERA Administrator Harry Lloyd Hopkins.

For Bobbie Johnson see Note 2482.

The National Industrial Recovery Board was composed of Walton Hale Hamilton, a law professor at Yale University; Arthur Dare Whiteside, president of a national stockbrokerage firm; Leon Carroll Marshall, economist and educator; Sidney Hillman, labor leader; and Samuel Clay Williams, tobacco executive.

²⁵⁴⁴ *NYT,* Monday, October 1, 1934, 19:7. Variant: *NYT* gives "classes as 'liberty' another might class as 'poison.' " in third sentence.

²⁵⁴⁵ *NYT,* Tuesday, October 2, 1934, 23:7.

Jay Hanna "Dizzy" Dean, ace pitcher for the Saint Louis Cardinals from 1932 to 1936; an inductee of the Baseball Hall of Fame in 1953. The Cardinals met the Detroit Tigers at Detroit on October 3 in the first game of the World Series of 1934.

²⁵⁴⁶ *NYT,* Wednesday, October 3, 1934, 23:7.

Paul Dee "Daffy" Dean, pitcher who starred for the Saint Louis Cardinals from 1934 to 1939; brother of Dizzy Dean.

²⁵⁴⁷ *NYT,* Thursday, October 4, 1934, 25:7.

Dizzy Dean (see Note 2545) pitched the Cardinals to an 8 to 3 victory in the first game of the World Series on October 3.

For Alfalfa Bill Murray see Note 2106.

Gordon Stanley "Mickey" Cochrane, star major league catcher who as player-manager of the Detroit Tigers in 1934 guided the team to its first pennant in twenty-five years; named to the Baseball Hall of Fame in 1947.

Lynwood Thomas "Schoolboy" Rowe, pitcher for the Detroit Tigers from 1933 to 1942. Rowe posted his best single season record (24-8) in 1934 at age twenty-two.

Paul Dean (see Note 2546) was slated to face Rowe in the second game of the World Series on October 4, but a pitching change was made by the Cardinals at the last moment. The Tigers, bolstered by the seven-hit pitching of Rowe, outlasted the Cardinals, 3 to 2, in twelve innings.

²⁵⁴⁸ *NYT,* Friday, October 5, 1934, 25:7. Variant: *LAT* gives "Hallihan" in third and eleventh sentences.

Frank Francis Frisch, smooth-fielding player-manager for the Saint Louis Cardinals from 1933 to 1937; inducted into the Baseball Hall of Fame in 1947; known as the "Fordham Flash."

William Anthony "Wild Bill" Hallahan, pitcher for the Saint Louis Cardinals from 1925 to 1936.

For Paul Dean see Notes 2546 and 2547; for Schoolboy Rowe see Note 2547.

No DT is available for Saturday, October 6, 1934. The following article appeared in *NYT* and *LAT* on that day: "The daily 'Remarks' of Will Rogers failed to reach *The Times* last night, and efforts to reach the philosopher-humorist proved unavailing. He had intended to witness the World Series game at St. Louis yesterday."

²⁵⁴⁹ *NYT,* Monday, October 8, 1934, 19:7.

Paul Dean (see Note 2546) defeated the Tigers, 4 to 1, in the third game of the World Series in Saint Louis on October 5. The Tigers, however, won the next two games, which were played in Saint Louis, to hold a three games to two edge in the series.

²⁵⁵⁰ *NYT,* Tuesday, October 9, 1934, 21:7. Variants: *LAT* gives "Cochran" in sixth sentence/*LAT* gives "Hallahan" in eleventh sentence.

In the sixth game of the World Series, Paul Dean (see Note 2546) scattered ten hits and contributed a game-deciding single in the seventh inning to lead the Cardinals to their third victory in six games. Rowe (see Note 2546) took the loss for the Tigers.

William Holmes McGuffey, American educator best known for his series of *Eclectic Readers* (1836-1837).

For Dizzy Dean see Note 2545; for Mickey Cochrane see Note 2547; for Henry Ford see Note 2212; for Wild Bill Hallahan see Note 2548.

Alvin Floyd "General" Crowder, pitcher for Washington, Saint Louis, and Detroit of the American League from 1926 to 1936. Crowder, who was traded from Washington to Detroit in mid-season of 1934, started the first game of the World Series.

2551   *NYT,* Wednesday, October 10, 1934, 25:6-7.

Kenesaw Mountain Landis, former federal judge who served as major league baseball commissioner from 1920 until his death in 1944.

Dizzy Dean (see Note 2545) pitched a six-hit shutout as the Cardinals overwhelmed the Tigers, 11 to 0, in the final game of the World Series on October 8.

Joseph Michael "Ducky" Medwick, free-swinging member of the Saint Louis Cardinals in the 1930s; inducted into the Baseball Hall of Fame in 1968. Medwick, around whom controversy constantly swirled, bowled over the Tiger third baseman with a slashing slide in the seventh inning of the last game. When Medwick went to his position in left field, the Detroit fans showered him with food and debris to such an extent that Judge Landis removed him from the game.

Marvin James "Marv" Owen, third baseman for the Detroit Tigers from 1931 to 1937.

For Mickey Cochrane see Note 2547.

John Leonard Roosevelt "Pepper" Martin, aggressive third baseman for the Saint Louis Cardinals from 1928 to 1944.

For Paul Dean see Note 2546.

Joe Evan Brown, American comedian and screen star noted for his extraordinarily-wide mouth.

2552   *NYT,* Thursday, October 11, 1934, 25:7. Variant: *LAT* gives "Johnston" in seventh sentence.

For Dizzy Dean see Note 2545; for Paul Dean see Note 2546.

Walter Perry Johnson, hard-throwing pitcher for the Washington Senators. His career as a player and manager lasted from 1907 to 1935; he was elected to the Baseball Hall of Fame in 1936.

Tristram E. "Tris" Speaker, center fielder for several American League baseball clubs, including the Cleveland Indians from 1916 to 1926; inducted into the Baseball Hall of Fame in 1937.

For Rabbit Maranville see Note 2388.

2553   *NYT,* Friday, October 12, 1934, 27:7. Variants: *NYT* gives "sorority hop" and *LAT* gives "soriety hope" in second sentence/*NYT* gives "Don't tire." for tenth sentence/*NYT* gives "keep on." to end eleventh sentence.

Mary Scott Lord Dimmick Harrison, widow of President Benjamin Harrison.

Edith Kermit Carow Roosevelt, widow of President Theodore Roosevelt.

Helen Herron Taft, widow of President William Howard Taft.

Grace Anna Goodhue Coolidge, widow of President Calvin Coolidge.

Lou Henry Hoover, wife of President Herbert Hoover.

Eleanor Roosevelt celebrated her fiftieth birthday on October 11, 1934.

Edith Bolling Galt Wilson, widow of President Woodrow Wilson.

2554 *NYT,* Saturday, October 13, 1934, 15:7.

Alexander I, king of Yugoslavia from 1921 until his death in 1934. King Alexander was assassinated by a Macedonian terrorist on October 9 while enroute to Paris to discuss with the French his proposal for a reconciliation between Yugoslavia and Italy, whose relations were strained because of the active promotion by Italy of Yugoslav dissident groups, including the Croats and Macedonians.

The American Liberty League, an anti-administration group established in August of 1934 and which drew its following from industrialists, financiers, corporation lawyers, conservative Democrats, and others.

2555 *NYT,* Monday, October 15, 1934, 19:7. Variant: *NYT* omits ninth sentence.

For Alexander I, king of Yugoslavia, see Note 2554.

Poland moved away from its traditional alliance with France in 1934 toward a closer understanding with Germany, particularly following the signing in January of 1934 of a Polish-German ten-year nonaggression pact.

2556 *NYT,* Tuesday, October 16, 1934, 25:7. Variant: *LAT* gives "yesterday on Sundays. Politics" in first and second sentences.

2557 *NYT,* Wednesday, October 17, 1934, 25:7.

Stone (see Note 2421) starred in Sinclair Lewis and Lloyd Lewis' *Jayhawker* in Washington, D. C., on October 15. The play opened on Broadway in early November.

Twelve hundred coal miners at Pecs, Hungary, imprisoned themselves underground without food for five days in October. They threatened to commit mass suicide if their wages were not raised. The strike ended on October 16.

For longshoremen in San Francisco see Note 2480.

2558 *NYT,* Thursday, October 18, 1934, 25:7.

2559 *NYT,* Friday, October 19, 1934, 25:7.

2560 *NYT,* Saturday, October 20, 1934, 17:7.

Hoover Dam, one of the largest dams in the world, is located on the Colorado River between Nevada and Arizona. Built between 1931 and 1936, it was known originally as Boulder Dam.

2561 *NYT,* Monday, October 22, 1934, 17:7.

The MacRobertson Air Race (see Note 2488) from England to Australia began on October 20. Dutch pilots Koene Dirk Parmentier and Jan Johannes Moll, flying a KLM Airlines Douglas DC-2, held the early lead and eventually finished second. American fliers Roscoe Turner (see Note 2175) and Clyde Pangborn placed third in the competition in a Boeing transport.

For Upton Sinclair see Note 2519; for Wiley Post see Notes 2168 and 2488; for Frank Hawks see Note 2234; for Jimmy Doolittle see Note 2234.

Alford Joseph "Al" Williams, Jr., research pilot with the United States Navy from 1917 to 1930 and holder of several air records and aviation awards.

For Charles Lindbergh see Note 2135.

Charles Edward Kingsford-Smith, Australian aviator, war veteran, and pilot of the Southern Cross, the first plane to fly from the United States to Australia (1928). Kingsford-Smith returned over the same course in the fall of 1934, flying from Brisbane, Australia, to Oakland, California, in fifty-two hours elapsed flight time.

2562   *NYT,* Tuesday, October 23, 1934, 21:7. Variant: *LAT* gives "Old New" in second sentence.

For Frank Merriam see Note 2482; for Upton Sinclair see Note 2519.

Raymond LeRoy Haight, California attorney who ran for governor on the Progressive and Commonwealth tickets in 1934.

2563   *NYT,* Wednesday, October 24, 1934, 23:7. Variant: *NYT* gives "Brisbane this very morning." in tenth sentence.

Two English fliers, Charles William Anderson Scott and Thomas Campbell Black, won the MacRobertson Air Race (see Note 2488 and 2561). They landed at Melbourne on October 23 with one engine dead and with only two hours of sleep in three days.

For the Dutch fliers see Note 2561.

Clyde Pangborn, American flier who was the first aviator to fly nonstop across the Pacific Ocean (1931). Although Pangborn and Turner (see Note 2175) briefly became lost over India and one of their engines failed over the Timor Sea, they nevertheless placed third in the MacRobertson Air Race.

For Arthur Brisbane see Note 2060.

2564   *NYT,* Thursday, October 25, 1934, 25:7. Variant: *LAT* gives "Piccards," in third sentence.

Felix Jean Piccard, Swiss chemist and aeronautical engineer who with his wife, Jeannette Ridlon Piccard, reached an altitude of 57,979 feet during a stratospheric balloon flight over Michigan and Ohio. The flight ended in a tree-top on a farm near Cadiz, Ohio, on October 23.

For Dizzy Dean see Note 2545.

Roosevelt addressed the annual convention of the American Bankers' Association in Washington, D. C., on October 24.

2565   *NYT,* Friday, October 26, 1934, 17:7.

Twain (see Note 2415) first heard the legend of the famous jumping frog during a stay at Angel's Camp, California, in 1864. The frog became the subject of Twain's first widely distributed and popular story, "The Celebrated Jumping Frog of Calaveras County."

For Bret Harte see Note 2415; for Roosevelt's speech to the bankers see Note 2564.

2566   *NYT,* Saturday, October 27, 1934, 17:7.

William Averell Harriman, chairman of the board of Union Pacific Railroad from 1932 to 1946. The *M-10001*, a new streamlined and air-conditioned train of the Union Pacific, made the 3,258-mile run from Los Angeles to New York City on October 22-25 at an average speed of 57.2 miles per hour.

2567   *NYT,* Monday, October 29, 1934, 19:7.

Long headed a large delegation of Louisianans who "invaded" Nashville, Tennessee, on October 27 to attend the Louisiana State University-Vanderbilt University football game. LSU, with an early season record of 5-0-0, defeated Vanderbilt, 29-0.

The United States Military Academy, which finished the season with a record of 8-3-0, defeated Yale University (5-3-0), 20 to 12, on October 27. The United States Naval Academy suffered only one loss in nine games in 1934, while Harvard University finished at 3-5-0.

2568   *NYT,* Tuesday, October 30, 1934, 21:7.

2569   *NYT,* Wednesday, October 31, 1934, 21:7.

Patrick Gordon "Bill" Taylor, Australian flier and air navigator. Taylor accompanied Kingsford-Smith (see Note 2561) on several notable flights, including a transpacific flight from Australia to the United States in the fall of 1934.

2570   *NYT,* Thursday, November 1, 1934, 23:7.

2571   *NYT,* Friday, November 2, 1934, 25:7. Variant: *NYT* gives "something." to end eighth sentence, omitting last twelve words.

The Century of Progress Exposition in Chicago (see Note 2087) closed in the early morning hours of November 1 after a two-year run that had attracted nearly 39 million visitors and had boosted the local economy by $700 million.

For Sally Rand see Note 2269.

2572   *LAT,* Saturday, November 3, 1934, I:1:2. *NYT* did not print the DT.

James Francis Thaddeus O'Connor, Los Angeles attorney who served as United States comptroller of the currency from 1933 to 1938.

Dorothy Frooks, American attorney, author, and newspaper columnist. Frooks, candidate of the Law Preservation party for representative-at-large from New York, "crashed" a dinner party given by supporters of her Democratic opponent, Caroline O'Day, in a vain attempt to question the special guest, Eleanor Roosevelt, regarding her efforts to campaign publicly for O'Day.

2573   *NYT,* Monday, November 5, 1934, 21:7.

For Charles Kingsford-Smith see Note 2561.

2574   *NYT,* Tuesday, November 6, 1934, 27:7. Variant: *NYT* gives "awful good" in sixth sentence.

For Arthur Brisbane see Note 2060.

Janet Gaynor, American screen actress who was immensely popular in mostly sentimental films during the 1920s and 1930s. An Academy Award winner in 1927, she appeared with Rogers in *State Fair* in 1933.

Warner Baxter, American leading man of motion pictures who won an Academy Award in 1929 for his performance in *In Old Arizona*.

²⁵⁷⁵ *NYT,* Wednesday, November 7, 1934, 23:7.

²⁵⁷⁶ *NYT,* Thursday, November 8, 1934, 25:7.

Democrats strengthened their hold on Congress as a result of the mid-term elections held on November 6, gaining nine seats in the Senate and thirteen in the House.

²⁵⁷⁷ *NYT,* Friday, November 9, 1934, 23:7.

²⁵⁷⁸ *NYT,* Saturday, November 10, 1934, 17:7.

For Arthur Brisbane see Note 2060; for William E. Borah see Note 2282; For Robert M. La Follette, Jr., see Note 2359.

Hiram Warren Johnson, Republican United States senator from California from 1917 until his death in 1945. A supporter of early New Deal policies, Johnson ran for reelection in 1934 on both the Republican and Democratic tickets.

Upton Sinclair, Democratic candidate for governor of California and originator of the EPIC plan (see Note 2519), was defeated by incumbent Frank Merriam by about 240,000 votes.

²⁵⁷⁹ *NYT,* Monday, November 12, 1934, 21:7.

For the United States Fleet see Note 2390.

Joseph Mason Reeves, American naval officer who served as commander-in-chief of the United States Fleet from 1934 to 1936.

Robert Edward Lee, chief military officer of the Confederate armies during the American Civil War.

²⁵⁸⁰ *NYT,* Tuesday, November 13, 1934, 19:7.

²⁵⁸¹ *NYT,* Wednesday, November 14, 1934, 21:7.

Long adopted the Louisiana State University football team as his special sideshow. After Tiger star Abe Mickal threw the winning pass against George Washington University on November 10, Long offered him a seat in the state senate, even though Mickal was a resident of Mississippi and not of voting age. The Syrian-born Mickal refused to cooperate.

²⁵⁸² *NYT,* Thursday, November 15, 1934, 23:7. Variants: *LAT* gives "Irenne DuPont," in first sentence/*LAT* gives "estimitable" in ninth sentence.

For John J. Raskob see Note 2209.

Irenee Du Pont, American industrialist and former president of the huge, family-owned chemical manufacturing company, E. I. du Pont de Nemours & Company.

Edward Francis Hutton, self-made multimillionaire who founded the stockbrokerage firm of E. F. Hutton & Company in 1904 and who served as chairman of the board of General Foods Corporation from 1923 to 1935. Hutton, Du Pont, and Raskob were leaders of the anti-New Deal American Liberty League (see Note 2554).

²⁵⁸³ *NYT,* Friday, November 16, 1934, 25:7.

The Louisiana legislature enacted forty-four laws during the week of November 12, 1934, effecting the famous "Share the Wealth" scheme advocated by Long. One piece of legislation made it possible for all harrassed debtors to obtain a moratorium of two years in the repayment of their obligations.

For Upton Sinclair see Note 2519.

2584   *NYT,* Saturday, November 17, 1934, 17:7.

For Huey Long see Notes 2064 and 2583.

The University of Minnesota football team went undefeated and untied in 1934; however, a conference rule forbidding participation in post-season games prohibited the Gophers from playing Stanford University in the Rose Bowl. Louisiana State University went 7-2-2 in 1934 but failed to receive a bid to a post-season game.

For Upton Sinclair see Note 2519; for Aimee Semple McPherson see Note 2064.

2585   *NYT,* Monday, November 19, 1934, 19:7.

Federal old-age and survivors' insurance was provided by the Social Security Act of August of 1935.

The 4-H, a national organization to enable rural youth to "learn by doing," was founded in 1902 in Clark County, Ohio.

2586   *NYT,* Tuesday, November 20, 1934, 23:7.

Roosevelt attacked private power companies in a speech on November 18 at Tupelo, Mississippi, the first city to contract for all of its power requirements from the federally-financed Tennessee Valley Authority. Invoking the expression of "rugged community individualism," Roosevelt called on all communities in the country to oust private control of local power resources.

Gloria Laura Morgan Vanderbilt, ten-year-old heiress to a vast American railroad fortune, was the subject of an exhaustive two-year guardianship struggle between her widowed mother, Gloria Morgan Vanderbilt, and her late father's sister, Gertrude Vanderbilt Whitney. The aunt won the court battle, which finally ended in 1935 when Mrs. Vanderbilt was declared an unfit mother.

2587   *NYT,* Wednesday, November 21, 1934, 21:7.

2588   *NYT,* Thursday, November 22, 1934, 23:7.

Smedley Darlington Butler, retired major general of the United States Marine Corps and veteran of fifteen military operations. Butler testified before the House Committee on Un-American Activities on November 20 that during the summer of 1934 a group of Wall Street brokers had urged him to lead a Fascist march on Washington, D. C., and that they had offered to finance the undertaking. None of his allegations could be verified.

Two bodies, later identified to be that of a German adventurer and a Norwegian sailor, were swept ashore on an island in the Galapagos chain in November. The story received wide coverage in the American press because of the mysterious circumstances of the appearance of the bodies and speculation as to their identities.

2589   *NYT,* Friday, November 23, 1934, 21:7.

Tom Bass, nationally recognized horsetrainer and originator in 1894 of the American Royal Horse Show in Kansas City, Missouri. Bass died on November 20 at age seventy-three.

Negro Add, black American cowboy who worked for the LFD Ranch in Texas and was noted for his expertise at roping and riding. He is remembered in the old ballad "Whose Old Cow."

2590   *NYT,* Saturday, November 24, 1934, 17:7.

Prince George, the fourth son of the ruling house of the British empire, married Princess Marina of the exiled royal family of Greece in a lavish ceremony at Westminster Abbey on November 29, 1934. The princess was a grandneice of Prince George's grandmother.

For Marie, queen dowager of Rumania, see Note 2534.

2591   *NYT,* Monday, November 26, 1934, 17:7.

2592   *NYT,* Tuesday, November 27, 1934, 23:7. Variant: *NYT* gives " 'Well, we' " in seventh sentence.

Patrick Jay Hurley, Oklahoma attorney and businessman who served as secretary of war in Hoover's cabinet.

Phineas Taylor Barnum, American showman who cofounded the Barnum & Bailey Circus in 1881 and who remained in the circus business until his death in 1891. When asked to explain his success as a promoter, Barnum often responded, "There's a sucker born every minute."

2593   *NYT,* Wednesday, November 28, 1934, 23:7.

Clinton Lloyd Bardo, American industrialist who served as president of the National Association of Manufacturers from 1934 to 1936.

2594   *NYT,* Thursday, November 29, 1934, 27:7.

2595   *NYT,* Friday, November 30, 1934, 21:7. Variant: *NYT* gives "those old-timers and" in fifth sentence.

For the royal wedding see Note 2590.

Dmitri Pavlovitch, exiled grand duke of Russia, husband of an American heiress, and for a while in the 1930s a champagne salesman in Florida.

Xenia Alexandrovna, Russian grand duchess and exiled sister of the last czar of Russia.

Vladimir Kyrilovich, assumptive grand duke of Russia and latter-day pretender to the Russian throne.

For George V see Note 2129.

Joseph Stalin, Russian Communist leader and virtual dictator of the Soviet Union from 1927 until his death in 1953.

2596   *NYT,* Saturday, December 1, 1934, 15:7.

Nancy Langhorne Astor, American-born English viscountess who was the first woman to sit in the House of Commons, serving from 1919 to 1945; noted for her caustic and irreverent comments on virtually any subject.

2597   *NYT,* Monday, December 3, 1934, 19:7.

2598   *NYT,* Tuesday, December 4, 1934, 21:6. Variants: *LAT* gives "Marianna" in first sentence/*NYT* gives "drifted over Bartlesville," in fifth sentence.

Irish anti-royalists hissed and booed when scenes of the wedding of Prince George and Princess Marina (see Note 2590) were shown in movie theaters in Ireland on December 2, prompting the Irish government to ban showing of similar footage in Ireland.

Post (see Note 2168)) flew his *Winnie Mae* of around-the-world fame to an unofficial altitude of 48,000 feet during a flight over Oklahoma on December 3. He could not claim a world record because his altitude recorder malfunctioned.

2599   *NYT,* Wednesday, December 5, 1934, 25:7.

The United States Supreme Court upheld on December 3 a California state court decision that the University of California, as well as other land grant colleges in the country, may require military training as a part of their curricula (see Note 2320).

Tulane University defeated the Louisiana State University Tigers, 13 to 12, on December 1. The one-point winning margin resulted from Tiger hero Abe Mickal's failure to connect twice on point-after-touchdown attempts. A bill later was introduced into the Louisiana state legislature outlawing extra points. Tulane played Temple University in the first Sugar Bowl game on January 1, 1935.

2600   *NYT,* Thursday, December 6, 1934, 25:7.

For Charles Kingsford-Smith see Note 2561.

Three Australian fliers, pilot Charles T. P. Ulm, copilot George Littlejohn, and navigator J. Leon Skilling, took off from Oakland, California, on December 3 in an attempt to retrace the route of Kingsford-Smith and Ulm's epochal United States-Australia flight of 1928. They advanced to somewhere north of the Hawaiian Islands, where for an unknown reason they ditched their plane in the ocean. An extensive air and surface search for the men proved in vain.

Harold Gatty, noted Australian air navigator who with Post (see Note 2168) set a world record in 1931 for an around-the-world flight.

For Charles Lindbergh see Note 2135.

2601   *NYT*, Friday, December 7, 1934, 25:7.

The American munitions industry was the subject of an intensive Senate inquiry (1934-1936) headed by Senator Gerald Prentiss Nye, an isolationist who was convinced that munitions makers had conspired to drag the United States into World War I. The probe revealed, however, that the munitions industry profited far more from neutrality than from participation in the war.

2602   *NYT,* Saturday, December 8, 1934, 17:7.

In Russia the chairman of the Leningrad Soviet and member of the Politburo was shot and killed by a young Communist on December 1, 1934. The murder usually is regarded as the starting point of a wave of purges that swept the country during the years 1935-1938 and that virtually wiped out the Old Guard of the Russian Communist party.

Yugoslavia accused neighboring Hungary of complicity in the October assassination of King Alexander I. On December 6 Hungary appealed to the League of Nations to prevent a retaliatory expulsion from Yugoslavia of numerous Hungarians under what was described as brutal circumstances. Reports of the character and extent of the expulsions later were proven exaggerated. By December 10 the two countries had agreed to a return to the *status quo.*

Norman Hezekiah Davis, American financier who served as Roosevelt's special ambassador to economic and disarmament conferences. Davis informed Japan on December 6 that the United States would not alter the ship ratio established by the Washington Naval Treaty of 1922. Japan formally renounced the treaty on December 29, 1934.

2603   *NYT*, Monday, December 10, 1934, 23:4.

The Notre Dame University football team defeated the University of Southern California, 14 to 0, on December 8. William V. "Bill" Shakespeare, triple-threat halfback for the Fighting Irish, keyed the victory with a fifty-one-yard touchdown pass in the first quarter of play.

For Knute Rockne, late coach of Notre Dame, see Note 2293; for Charles L. O'Donnell, late president of Notre Dame, see Note 2445; for John F. O'Hara see Note 2445; for Elmer F. Layden see Note 2293.

Both Italy and France formally espoused the cause of their respective allies, Hungary and Yugoslavia, in the controversy between the two Balkan nations (see Note 2602). Nevertheless, the two major powers each exerted its influence for peace, working through the League of Nations to arrange a return to the *status quo*.

2604   *NYT*, Tuesday, December 11, 1934, 25:4.

Winthrop Aldrich, chairman of the board of Chase National Bank of New York City, arrived in Los Angeles in early December to visit with local bankers and to tour the studios of Fox Motion Pictures, an enterprise of Chase National. Aldrich was accompanied by Dr. Benjamin McAlester Anderson, an economist at Chase National from 1920 to 1939.

2605   *LAT*, Wednesday, December 12, 1934, I:1:4. *NYT* did not print the DT.

For Hirosi Saito, Japanese ambassador, see Note 2308; for Max Baer see Note 2137.

Shirley Temple, American child film star who began to appear in leading roles in 1934, enjoying phenomenal popularity in a succession of winsome roles.

2606   *NYT*, Thursday, December 13, 1934, 25:7.

William Thomas Waggoner, Texas cattleman and oilman whose Three D Ranch in west central Texas embraced more than 1,000,000 acres at the height of its operation from 1889 to 1903. Waggoner died on December 11, 1934, at age eighty-two.

2607   *NYT*, Friday, December 14, 1934, 25:7.

A three-power naval disarmament conference between Great Britain, Japan, and the United States, which had convened in London in October of 1934, ended on December 20 with no agreement reached regarding Japanese demands for equality in armaments.

For Norman Davis see Note 2602.

2608   *NYT*, Saturday, December 15, 1934, 25:4. Variant: *NYT* gives "have any, anyway." to end ninth sentence.

For the Wright brothers see Note 2093.

2609   *NYT*, Monday, December 17, 1934, 21:7.

A cold wave swept through the Florida peninsula, carrying freezing temperatures as far south as the Everglades and causing the severest agricultural losses since 1895.

²⁶¹⁰ *NYT*, Tuesday, December 18, 1934, 23:7.

The National Resources Board, a presidential advisory body, released a report on December 16 which recommended a permanent federal public works program that would cost $105 billion in its first few years of operation.

²⁶¹¹ *NYT*, Wednesday, December 19, 1934, 25:7.

For the Yugoslavian-Hungarian conflict see Notes 2602 and 2603.

Italian and Ethiopian troops first clashed at the border of Ethiopia and Italian Libya on December 5, 1934. Italy, whose leader Mussolini was determined to establish an Italian empire in North Africa, refused all offers of conciliation and on October 3, 1935, started war by invading Ethiopia. Italy conquered the North African nation in 1935-1936, easily overcoming the ineffective sanctions imposed by the League of Nations.

²⁶¹² *NYT*, Thursday, December 20, 1934, 25:7.

The gun which Dillinger (see Note 2341) used in his escape was smuggled to the felon by a judge who had been bribed by a friend of Dillinger.

²⁶¹³ *NYT*, Friday, December 21, 1934, 25:7.

²⁶¹⁴ *NYT*, Saturday, December 22, 1934, 17:7.

²⁶¹⁵ *NYT*, Monday, December 24, 1934, 15:7.

Soviet infantry units which invaded Japanese-controlled Manchukuo on December 22 quickly were met and repulsed by Manchukuoan troops. The Soviet Union, however, denied charges that its troops crossed the border, and Japan dismissed the entire incident.

Richberg (see Note 2543) and Johnson (see Note 2151) clashed in December over a proposed series of articles by the former NRA administrator for the *Saturday Evening Post,* with Richberg threatening legal action if the magazine allowed "the publication of character assassinations." By the end of the year the men had resolved their differences, even to the point of exchanging Christmas greetings.

²⁶¹⁶ *LAT*, Tuesday, December 25, 1934, I:1:5. *NYT* did not print the DT.

Rumors of the impending marriage of the Prince of Wales (see Note 2130) and Ingrid Victoria Sophie Louise Marguerite, Swedish princess, circulated widely in December of 1934. The stories proved false, however; Prince Edward remained a bachelor until his marriage to an American divorcee in 1936, a year after Princess Ingrid's marriage to the crown prince of Denmark.

The fourth volume of the memoirs of David Lloyd George (see Note 2214) appeared in the fall of 1934.

²⁶¹⁷ *NYT*, Wednesday, December 26, 1934, 17:7. Variant: *NYT* omits "Madam and" in fifth sentence.

Thoroughbred horse racing returned to Southern California in December of 1934 after an absence of twenty-five years. The racing season opened Christmas Day at the new Santa Anita track near Los Angeles.

For Graham McNamee see Note 2330; for Greta Garbo see Note 2064.

Twenty Grand, champion American race horse which won the Kentucky Derby and the Belmont Stakes in 1931.

2618   *NYT*, Thursday, December 27, 1934, 23:7.

2619   *NYT*, Friday, December 28, 1934, 23:7.

A six-year investigation by the Federal Trade Commission culminated in a series of adverse reports issued in 1935 on the property and methods of public utility companies.

2620   *NYT*, Saturday, December 29, 1934, 17:6.

2621   *NYT*, Monday, December 31, 1934, 15:7. Variant: *NYT* omits last two sentences.

2622   *NYT*, Tuesday, January 1, 1935, 3:5.

2623   *NYT*, Wednesday, January 2, 1935, 10:4. Variant: *LAT* gives "Pennsylvania one" in fifth sentence.

The University of Alabama defeated Stanford University, 29 to 13, in the Rose Bowl of 1935.

Tulane University, which was chosen over Louisiana State University to play in the inaugural Sugar Bowl, defeated Temple University, 20 to 14, in the post-season classic.

2624   *NYT*, Thursday, January 3, 1935, 25:7.

For the Alabama-Stanford football game see Note 2623.

2625   *NYT*, Friday, January 4, 1935, 23:7.

Millard Filmore "Dixie" Howell, football star at the University of Alabama from 1932 to 1934. Known as the "Human Howitzer," Howell completed nine of twelve passes for 160 yards and one touchdown in the Rose Bowl of 1935.

2626   *NYT*, Saturday, January 5, 1935, 19:7.

In his annual "State of the Union" address, Roosevelt urged the abolition of the "evils of holding companies," federal control of which was strengthened by the Public Utilities Companies Act of August of 1935, and the creation of the Works Progress Administration (WPA), a federal agency designed to increase the purchasing power of persons on relief by employing them on useful projects.

2627   *NYT*, Monday, January 7, 1935, 19:7.

Bruno Richard Hauptmann, German-born carpenter who was accused of the kidnapping and murder in 1932 of the infant son of Charles and Anne Morrow Lindbergh. Although captured in September of 1934 with part of the $50,000 ransom in his possession, Hauptmann maintained his innocence through a sensational two-month long trial at Flemington, New Jersey, in early 1935. Found guilty, he was electrocuted on April 3, 1936.

2628   *NYT*, Tuesday, January 8, 1935, 23:7.

Pierre Laval, French minister of foreign affairs from 1931 to 1932 and from 1935 to 1936. Laval and Mussolini signed a series of agreements at Rome on January 7 that included a proposal for a multilateral pact to safeguard the independence of Austria.

Francis Joseph Otto, Austrian archduke, member of the Hapsburg royal family and pretender to the Austro-Hungarian throne; in exile from 1919.

2629 *NYT,* Wednesday, January 9, 1935, 21:7.

Roosevelt presented to Congress on January 7 a proposed federal budget for 1935 totaling $8,520,413,609.

Betty Gow, Scottish-born nurse for the Charles Lindbergh family. Gow testified for the prosecution on January 7 in the trial of Bruno Hauptmann, accused kidnapper-murderer of the Lindbergh's infant son (see Note 2627).

Johnson (see Note 2151) wrote a series of articles for the *Saturday Evening Post* in early 1935. In the first essay, which appeared in the January 12 issue, he called for enlightened government policies toward businessmen.

The Supreme Court declared unconstitutional on January 7 the first important piece of New Deal legislation to come before it—the section of the National Industrial Recovery Act under which the government attempted to control oil production.

2630 *NYT,* Thursday, January 10, 1935, 21:7.

2631 *NYT,* Friday, January 11, 1935, 25:3.

The Supreme Court heard arguments in early 1935 on four cases involving the constitutionality of a congressional resolution of 1933 which nullified the gold clause in private and public contracts. The power of the government to so act in private contracts was affirmed in three cases decided on February 18. In the fourth the congressional resolution was held unconstitutional, but because of a legal technicality in the case the action of the government was upheld.

2632 *NYT,* Saturday, January 12, 1935, 17:7.

For Supreme Court action see Note 2631; for Max Baer see Note 2137.

2633 *NYT,* Monday, January 14, 1935, 17:7. Variant: *LAT* gives "show this week." in first sentence.

2634 *NYT,* Tuesday, January 15, 1935, 21:7.

The Saar, a semi-autonomous territory formerly owned by Germany and which after World War I was administered by France under League of Nations supervision. Ninety percent of the votes cast in a plebiscite on January 13 favored the return of the Saar to Germany. The region was restored in March of 1935.

2635 *NYT,* Wednesday, January 16, 1935, 19:7.

Doolittle (see Note 2234) crossed the United States in eleven hours and fifty-nine minutes on January 15, setting a new transcontinental record for transport planes.

Post (see Note 2168) attempted a transcontinental stratospheric flight on February 22, but mechanical difficulties forced him to end the flight shortly after taking off from Los Angeles. For the flight he built a flying suit which was a forerunner of modern-day space suits.

2636 *NYT,* Thursday, January 17, 1935, 21:7.

Helen Richey, flier for Central Airlines and the first woman copilot for a commercial airline.

The Senate voted on January 29 against American membership in the World Court (see Note 2074).

2637 *NYT,* Friday, January 18, 1935, 25:7.

For the World Court see Notes 2074 and 2636.

2638 *NYT*, Saturday, January 19, 1935, 15:7.

2639 *NYT*, Monday, January 20, 1935, 17:7. Variant: *NYT* gives "Jones, outside . . . tax. (Brother, . . . efficient.) The" in ninth and tenth sentences.

For Jack Garner see Note 2105; for Jesse Jones see Note 2107.

2640 *NYT*, Tuesday, January 22, 1935, 21:7.

Thomas Joseph "Tom" Mooney, American labor agitator who was convicted and sentenced to death for his participation in the bomb killings of nine persons in San Francisco in 1916. His case aroused international interest because of the widely held belief in his innocence. The United States Supreme Court, however, denied a writ for *habeas corpus* on January 20, 1934. He finally was granted an unconditional pardon in 1939 and was released.

For the gold-clause decisions see Note 2631.

2641 *NYT*, Wednesday, January 23, 1935, 19:7.

Roosevelt indicated on January 20 that he wanted Garner (see Note 2105) as his runningmate in 1936.

2642 *NYT*, Thursday, January 24, 1935, 21:3.

Samuel "Sam" Houston, American soldier and statesman who led the revolt of Texas against Mexico in the 1830s.

2643 *NYT*, Friday, January 25, 1935, 23:7.

For the World Court see Notes 2074 and 2636.

2644 *NYT*, Saturday, January 26, 1935, 19:7.

The House passed an administration-sponsored $4.8 billion work relief bill on January 24 and sent it to the Senate. Known as the Emergency Relief Appropriations Act, it was signed into law on April 8, 1935.

2645 *NYT*, Monday, January 28, 1935, 17:7.

2646 *NYT*, Tuesday, January 29, 1935, 23:6.

One hundred armed opponents of Long gathered at the Baton Rouge airport on January 26 but were dispersed by 500 National Guardsmen and state policemen armed with rifles, machine guns, and tear gas. Known as the "battle of the airport," the incident stemmed from the imposition of a state tax on petroleum.

The thirty-four-story Louisiana State Capitol was completed in 1932 at a cost of $5 million.

Smith (see Note 2115) was a cobuilder of the 102-story Empire State Building in New York City. Completed in 1931, it was for many years the tallest building in the world.

2647 *NYT*, Wednesday, January 30, 1935, 21:7.

2648 *NYT*, Thursday, January 31, 1935, 21:7.

For the World Court see Notes 2074 and 2636; for Joe Robinson see Note 2105.

²⁶⁴⁹ *NYT*, Friday, February 1, 1935, 23:7.

For Fiorello H. La Guardia see Note 2265.

²⁶⁵⁰ *NYT*, Saturday, February 2, 1935, 15:7.

For Fiorello H. La Guardia, mayor of New York City, see Note 2265.

²⁶⁵¹ *NYT*, Monday, February 4, 1935, 17:7.

²⁶⁵² *NYT*, Tuesday, February 5, 1935, 21:7.

Donald Wills Douglas, president of Douglas Aircraft Company from 1928 to 1957.

For the gold clause decisions see Note 2631.

²⁶⁵³ *NYT*, Wednesday, February 6, 1935, 21:7.

²⁶⁵⁴ *LAT*, Thursday, February 7, 1935, I:1:5. *NYT* did not print the DT.

For Max Baer see Note 2137; for Roger Babson see Note 2180.

Frank Richardson Kent, American syndicated newspaper columnist from 1924 until his death in 1958.

For Walter Lippmann see Note 2078; for Arthur Brisbane see Note 2060.

John Stuart Martin, managing editor of *Time* magazine from 1929 to 1937.

The March of Time, a series of twenty-minute film "magazines" of current events issued monthly in the United States from 1935 to 1951 and produced by the publishers of *Time* magazine.

²⁶⁵⁵ *NYT*, Friday, February 8, 1935, 23:7. Variant: *NYT* gives "talking about it, and never had any" in third and fourth sentences.

²⁶⁵⁶ *NYT*, Saturday, February 9, 1935, 17:7. Variant: *LAT* gives "to man" in fourth sentence.

Robert Stephenson Smyth Baden-Powell, British military officer and nobleman who founded the Boy Scouts in 1908.

²⁶⁵⁷ *NYT*, Monday, February 11, 1935, 19:7.

²⁶⁵⁸ *NYT*, Tuesday, February 12, 1935, 23:7.

Federal unemployment compensation was provided by the Social Security Act of August of 1935.

For the gold clause decisions see Note 2631; for the Hauptmann trial see Note 2627.

²⁶⁵⁹ *NYT*, Wednesday, February 13, 1935, 21:7. Variant: *NYT* gives "It will soon be in" in third sentence.

David T. Wilentz, attorney general of New Jersey from 1935 to 1943. The chief prosecuting attorney at the Hauptmann trial (see Note 2627), Wilentz delivered an emotional summation speech on February 12, pleading with the jury to show no mercy toward the accused.

Edward J. "Big Ed" Reilly, veteran American criminal attorney who headed the defense counsel at Hauptmann's trial.

2660   *NYT,* Thursday, February 14, 1935, 23:7.

The American dirigible *Macon* crashed on February 12 as a result of structural failure during a comparatively gentle storm off the California coast. The loss of the *Macon* came less than two years after the fatal crash of another United States airship, the *Akron.*

2661   *NYT,* Friday, February 15, 1935, 21:3.

For James O'Connor see Note 2572.

2662   *NYT,* Saturday, February 16, 1935, 15:7. *LAT* did not print the DT.

For Post's stratospheric flight attempt see Note 2635.

2663   *NYT,* Monday, February 18, 1935, 17:7.

Francis Everett Townsend, California physician who conceived and promoted an old-age pension scheme known as the Townsend Plan. Certain aspects of his proposal were embodied in the Social Security Act of August of 1935.

2664   *NYT,* Tuesday, February 19, 1935, 23:7.

2665   *NYT,* Wednesday, February 20, 1935, 21:7.

For the gold clause decisions see Note 2631.

2666   *NYT,* Thursday, February 21, 1935, 21:7.

Frank West Bering, popular executive with the Hotel Sherman in Chicago from 1910 until his retirement in 1960.

2667   *NYT,* Friday, February 22, 1935, 23:7.

Wallace Beery, American motion picture actor noted principally for tough, but easy-going character roles.

Donald "Don" Meade, American jockey who was the leading rider in the country in 1939 and 1941. Meade rode Ted Clark to a fifth place finish in the inaugural running of the $127,000 Santa Anita Handicap on February 23.

2668   *NYT,* Saturday, February 23, 1935, 13:7.

For Post's stratospheric flight attempt see Note 2635.

The Senate approved an amendment to an unemployment relief bill on February 21 that required the payment of "prevailing wages" on various types of relief work; the Senate in a later vote rescinded this action.

2669   *NYT,* Monday, February 25, 1935, 19:7.

Azucar won the rich Santa Anita Handicap on February 23 by two lengths. The converted steeplechaser earned $108,400, at the time the largest purse ever won by a thoroughbred in a single race.

2670   *NYT,* Tuesday, February 26, 1935, 21:7.

²⁶⁷¹ *NYT*, Wednesday, February 27, 1935, 21:7. Variant: *NYT* gives "talk on world" in first sentence.

For Charlie Chaplin see Note 2244.

William James "Will" Durant, American philosopher and writer; winner of a Pulitzer Prize in 1968. Durant taught at the University of California at Los Angeles in 1935.

²⁶⁷² *NYT*, Thursday, February 28, 1935, 21:7.

Abyssinia, former name for Ethiopia. For the Italo-Ethiopian War see Note 2611.

Haile Selassie, emperor of Ethiopia from 1930 to 1936 and from 1941 to 1974.

²⁶⁷³ *NYT*, Friday, March 1, 1935, 21:7. Variant: *NYT* omits second paragraph.

Morgan (see Note 2059), feeling the pinch of the depression, sold six masterpieces in January of 1935 for $1.5 million and disposed of 900 valuable miniatures a month later.

For the Emergency Relief Appropriations Act of 1935 see Note 2644.

²⁶⁷⁴ *NYT*, Saturday, March 2, 1935, 17:7. Variant: *NYT* gives "baby bond now." to end eighth sentence, omitting eleven words.

Prajadhipok, king of Siam (Thailand) from 1925 until his abdication on February 28, 1935.

For the Saar see Note 2634.

²⁶⁷⁵ *NYT*, Monday, March 4, 1935, 19:7.

Eleutherios Venizelos, Greek statesman who served as premier five times, including in 1933. Leader of opposition to the existing Greek government, Venizelos instigated an unsuccessful military and naval revolt in March of 1935. He died in exile in 1936 at age seventy-one.

For David Lloyd George see Note 2214.

²⁶⁷⁶ *NYT*, Tuesday, March 5, 1935, 21:7.

For Greece see Note 2675; for the Italo-Ethiopian War see Note 2611; for the Emergency Relief Appropriations Act see Note 2644.

²⁶⁷⁷ *NYT*, Wednesday, March 6, 1935, 21:3.

Sixty-nine-year-old Governor Merriam of California (see Note 2482) endorsed the Townsend old-age pension plan (see Note 2663) on March 4.

²⁶⁷⁸ *NYT*, Thursday, March 7, 1935, 25:3.

Robinson (see Note 2105) denounced the "ravings" of Long in a speech in the Senate on March 5. The Arkansan's bitter remarks followed an attack by Long on Roosevelt and his administration.

For Jack Dempsey see Note 2169.

²⁶⁷⁹ *NYT*, Friday, March 8, 1935, 23:3.

²⁶⁸⁰ *NYT*, Saturday, March 9, 1935, 17:5. Variant: *NYT* gives "have made that." in first sentence.

Malcolm Campbell, English businessman and automobile racer who set several world automobile records for speed, including a mark of 276.816 miles per hour at Daytona Beach, Florida, on March 7, 1935.

For the Emergency Relief Appropriations Act see Note 2644.

²⁶⁸¹ *NYT*, Monday, March 11, 1935, 19:7.

Oliver Wendell Holmes, associate justice of the United States Supreme Court from 1902 to 1932. Holmes, who died on March 5, 1935, at age ninety-three, bequeathed more than one-half of his $568,000 estate to the United States government.

²⁶⁸² *NYT*, Tuesday, March 12, 1935, 23:7.

²⁶⁸³ *NYT*, Wednesday, March 13, 1935, 21:7. Variant: *LAT* gives "between nations, if you just . . . out. All the" in third and fourth sentences.

²⁶⁸⁴ *NYT*, Thursday, March 14, 1935, 23:7.

Roosevelt on March 12 called for an end to the monopolistic public utility holding company device for controlling gas and electric operating companies. The Public Utility Holding Companies Act, signed on August 28, 1935, outlawed such practices and gave various federal commissions the power to regulate the rates and financial practices of these companies.

Charles Edward Coughlin, American priest who attracted a wide following with his frequent radio broadcasts in the 1930s assailing American financial leaders for having caused the depression.

For Hugh Johnson see Note 2151.

²⁶⁸⁵ *NYT*, Friday, March 15, 1935, 23:7.

²⁶⁸⁶ *LAT*, Saturday, March 16, 1935, I:1:5. *NYT* did not print the DT.

John Steven McGroarty, Democratic United States representative from California from 1935 to 1939. Known primarily for his historical writings, McGroarty penned *The Mission Play* in 1911; it was performed annually at San Gabriel, California.

²⁶⁸⁷ *NYT*, Monday, March 18, 1935, 19:7.

For the Italo-Ethiopian War see Note 2631.

Hitler abrogated the military clauses of the Versailles Peace Treaty on March 16 when he announced that Germany would return to the old pre-World War I policy of the conscription of all young men. The French and British were appalled, but they did nothing except to protest and to start negotiations with Germany on nonaggression pacts.

²⁶⁸⁸ *NYT*, Tuesday, March 19, 1935, 23:7.

²⁶⁸⁹ *NYT*, Wednesday, March 20, 1935, 23:7.

For Germany see Note 2687.

²⁶⁹⁰ *NYT*, Thursday, March 21, 1935, 25:7.

For Germany see Note 2687.

2691 *NYT,* Friday, March 22, 1935, 25:7.

2692 *NYT,* Saturday, March 23, 1935, 17:7.

For public utility holding companies see Note 2684.

2693 *NYT,* Monday, March 25, 1935, 17:7.

Hoover, in his first public statement since leaving office, labeled the policies of the Roosevelt administration as "un-American regimentation and bureaucratic domination." The remarks were made in a letter from Hoover read before a convention of young California Republicans on March 23.

2694 *NYT,* Tuesday, March 26, 1935, 21:7.

2695 *NYT,* Wednesday, March 27, 1935, 23:7.

2696 *NYT,* Thursday, March 28, 1935, 23:7.

Perkins (see Note 2099) spoke on March 23 at the sixty-seventh anniversary of the chartering of the University of California. Her appearance at Berkeley was protested by Martha Ijams, an alumna who objected to the selection of a "mere politician" as the first woman Charter Day speaker. Eleanor Roosevelt publicly criticized Ijams for "snubbing" Perkins.

Mae West, platinum-wigged American leading lady of the screen who combined sexuality, suggestiveness, and humor in a successful film career that began in 1932.

Jane Addams, American humanitarian, social reformer, and cofounder of the Hull House settlement project in Chicago in 1889; corecipient of the Nobel Peace Prize of 1931.

2697 *NYT,* Friday, March 29, 1935, 23:7.

2698 *NYT,* Saturday, March 30, 1935, 17:7. Variant: *LAT* gives "Thorman the II." in sixth sentence.

Mary Amelia Rogers, only daughter of Will and Betty Rogers. Mary Rogers made her debut as a stage actress in 1934.

Three Men on a Horse, a three-act comedy by John Cecil Holm and George Abbot, opened in New York City on January 30, 1935.

Alfred "Alfie" Byrne, lord mayor of Dublin, Ireland, from 1930 to 1939.

2699 *NYT,* Monday, April 1, 1935, 21:7.

2700 *NYT,* Tuesday, April 2, 1935, 23:7. Variant: *LAT* gives "Cattle had a good price." for fourth sentence.

Ernest Whitworth Marland, Democratic governor of Oklahoma from 1935 to 1939.

Alfred Mossman "Alf" Landon, Republican governor of Kansas from 1933 to 1937; unsuccessful Republican presidential nominee in 1936.

2701 *NYT,* Wednesday, April 3, 1935, 25:7.

2702 *NYT*, Thursday, April 4, 1935, 25:5.

2703 *NYT*, Friday, April 5, 1935, 25:7.

Austria announced on April 3 that it would introduce two-year compulsory military service and would increase the size of its army from 30,000 to 60,000 men. The Austrian move followed closely similar action by Germany (see Note 2687).

2704 *NYT*, Saturday, April 6, 1935, 17:7. Variant: *NYT* omits first paragraph.

2705 *NYT*, Monday, April 8, 1935, 21:7.

For the Emergency Relief Appropriations Act see Note 2644.

2706 *LAT*, Tuesday, April 9, 1935, I:1:5. *NYT* did not print the DT.

For Arthur Brisbane see Note 2060.

2707 *NYT*, Wednesday, April 10, 1935, 33:7.

Adolph Simon Ochs, publisher of the *New York Times* from 1896 until his death on April 8, 1935, at age seventy-seven. The *Times* was the first newspaper to publish Rogers' Daily Telegrams.

Warren Delano Robbins, American career diplomat who served as minister to Canada from 1933 until his death on April 7, 1935, at age forty-nine. Robbins served as counselor at the American embassy at Rome from 1925 to 1928 and minister to San Salvador from 1928 to 1930.

For Rogers' interview with Mussolini in 1926 see Rogers' *Letters of a Self-Made Diplomat to His President*.

2708 *NYT*, Thursday, April 11, 1935, 23:3. Variants: *NYT* omits first paragraph/*NYT* gives "of boys" in sixth sentence.

Hitler gave the bride away at the wedding of General Hermann Goering, president of the *Reichstag,* and Emmy Sonnemann, German actress.

Fielding Harris Yost, head football coach at the University of Michigan from 1901 to 1925 and athletic director at Michigan from 1921 to 1941.

Amos Alonzo Stagg, head football coach for fifty-seven years including at the University of Chicago from 1892 to 1932 and at College of the Pacific from 1933 to 1946. His victory total, 314 games, surpasses that of any other college coach.

Glenn Scobey "Pop" Warner, head football coach at Temple University from 1933 to 1938. Warner, who began his coaching career at the University of Georgia in 1895, was one of the greatest innovators in the history of the sport.

2709 *NYT*, Friday, April 12, 1935, 25:7.

At a conference at Stresa, Italy, in April of 1935, representatives of Great Britain, France, and Italy made (but never implemented) a decision to maintain a common posture toward Germany, following the latter's decision to rearm in violation of the Treaty of Versailles.

2710 *NYT*, Saturday, April 13, 1935, 17:3.

2711 *NYT*, Monday, April 15, 1935, 21:7. Variant: *NYT* omits " 'at Stresa, Italy.' " in first sentence.

For the Stresa Conference see Note 2709.

2712   *NYT,* Tuesday, April 16, 1935, 23:7.

For the rearming of Germany see Note 2687.

2713   *NYT,* Wednesday, April 17, 1935, 25:7.

2714   *NYT,* Thursday, April 18, 1935, 25:6.

Harold Le Clair Ickes, United States secretary of the interior from 1933 to 1939 and administrator of public works from 1933 to 1939. Ickes and Long clashed repeatedly in April of 1935 after Ickes threatened to cancel all federal projects in Louisiana if Long did not cease his attempts to put federal spending in Louisiana under state control.

Ruth (see Note 2388) hit a home run and a single to power the Boston Braves to a 4 to 2 opening day victory over the New York Giants on April 16. Ruth, in the twilight of his career, had been traded to the Braves in 1935 following fifteen brilliant seasons with the New York Yankees.

Dean (see Note 2545) was injured by a line drive during the Saint Louis Cardinals' opening day game with the Chicago Cubs on April 16.

2715   *NYT,* Friday, April 19, 1935, 23:7.

A Pan-American Airways Clipper flew from California to Hawaii on April 16-17 in a record time of eighteen hours and thirty-seven minutes.

Earhart (see Note 2135) flew from Honolulu to San Francisco in January of 1935, the first solo Pacific flight by a woman.

Huey Long attempted in April of 1935 to gain control of federal spending in Louisiana (see also Note 2714).

2716   *NYT,* Saturday, April 20, 1935, 15:7.

Eugene Talmadge, Democratic governor of Georgia from 1933 to 1937 and from 1941 to 1942. Because Talmadge had attempted to control the use of federal road funds in Georgia, Ickes (see Note 2714) cancelled four federal public works loans for Georgia on April 18.

Germany, Great Britain, Italy, and other European powers continued to clash over the decision by Germany to rearm (see Note 2687).

Johnson (see Note 2151) appeared at a Senate hearing on April 18 to plea for the continuance of the NRA. Admitting that mistakes had been made under his administration, Johnson nevertheless warned that abolition of the NRA would mean "chaos" for the American economy.

2717   *NYT,* Monday, April 22, 1935, 19:7. Variant: *LAT* gives "directly to blame" in fifth sentence.

2718   *NYT,* Tuesday, April 23, 1935, 23:7. Variant: *NYT* gives "learn. Children's crossword puzzles" in fourth, fifth, and sixth sentences.

"Gunga Din," poem by Rudyard Kipling, English poet and writer of short stories and novels; from his *Barrack-Room Ballads* (1892).

2719   *NYT,* Wednesday, April 24, 1935, 23:7.

2720   *NYT,* Thursday, April 25, 1935, 23:7.

432

For Frank Kent see Note 2654; for Walter Lippmann see Note 2078.

Old marriage records uncovered in Wisconsin in April revealed that a Mae West had married a Frank Wallace in Milwaukee in 1911. Mae West the actress (see Note 2696) denied ever having been married, however. Later, after a stage actor named Frank Wallace appeared and confirmed the marriage, West retracted her statement. The marriage was dissolved legally in 1943.

2721 *NYT,* Friday, April 26, 1935, 21:7.

Tugwell (see Note 2411) was appointed on April 24 to direct rural rehabilitation under a $4 billion work relief program established in 1935.

2722 *NYT,* Saturday, April 27, 1935, 19:6.

A veterans' bonus bill, requiring immediate payment of twenty-year certificates issued in 1925, failed by a narrow margin in May of 1935 to become law over Roosevelt's veto.

For John J. "Black Jack" Pershing see Note 2072.

2723 *NYT,* Monday, April 29, 1935, 17:7. Variant: *NYT* omits "he can speak . . . editorials against it." in third sentence.

Roosevelt delivered another fireside chat on April 28, advocating the measures then pending for extending the life of the NRA (not yet invalidated by the Supreme Court), for social security, and for federal regulation of public utilities.

2724 *NYT,* Tuesday, April 30, 1935, 19:3.

For Roosevelt's speech see Note 2723.

2725 *NYT,* Wednesday, May 1, 1935, 23:7.

2726 *NYT,* Thursday, May 2, 1935, 23:3. Variant: *LAT* gives "was in favor" in first sentence.

Richard Bedford Bennett, prime minister of Canada from 1930 to 1935.

James Aloysius Lyons, prime minister and treasurer of Australia from 1932 to 1939.

James Barry Munnik Hertzog, prime minister of South Africa from 1924 to 1939.

George William Forbes, prime minister of New Zealand from 1930 to 1935.

2727 *NYT,* Friday, May 3, 1935, 21:7. Variant: *NYT* gives "never perfected." to end fourth sentence.

2728 *NYT,* Saturday, May 4, 1935, 15:7. Variants: *NYT* gives "In this U. S." to begin first sentence/*NYT* gives "in a tie." to end second sentence, omitting next seven words.

Ruby Laffoon, Democratic governor of Kentucky from 1931 to 1935.

"Send-a-Dime" chain letters poured into post offices throughout the country in the spring of 1935.

Edward Riley Bradley, professional gambler and horseman from Kentucky. Owner of four previous Kentucky Derby winners, Bradley sent Boxthorn into the derby running of 1935 as a favorite with many bettors. Bradley's entry finished out of the money, however.

2729   *NYT,* Monday, May 6, 1935, 21:3.

Omaha won the sixty-first running of the Kentucky Derby on May 4. In 1935 he went on to become the third horse ever to win the Triple Crown—the Kentucky Derby, Preakness, and Belmont Stakes.

The United States Fleet, including 400 naval airplanes, engaged in an extensive series of maneuvers in the Pacific Ocean in the spring of 1935. During the exercises, virtually the entire fleet entered Pearl Harbor to test its usefulness as a base of operations.

2730   *NYT,* Tuesday, May 7, 1935, 25:7.

Rogers was at Santa Anita to film race scenes for the motion picture *In Old Kentucky.*

2731   *NYT,* Wednesday, May 8, 1935, 21:7.

For Frank Hawks see Note 2234.

Fog was blamed for the crash of a passenger plane in Missouri on May 6 in which Senator Bronson Murray Cutting of New Mexico and five other persons died.

2732   *NYT,* Thursday, May 9, 1935, 23:7.

Amelia Earhart (see Note 2135) on May 8 became the first aviator to fly nonstop from Mexico City to New York City.

For Eleanor Roosevelt see Note 2089.

2733   *NYT,* Friday, May 10, 1935, 23:7. Variants: *LAT* gives "forty-eight" in first and third sentences.

Forty-three United States naval planes flew in a massed flight from Pearl Harbor to Midway as part of naval maneuvers in the Pacific.

2734   *NYT,* Saturday, May 11, 1935, 19:7. Variant: *NYT* gives "Maybe someone hid" in second sentence.

For Frank Hawks see Note 2234 and DT 2731.

2735   *NYT,* Monday, May 13, 1935, 17:7.

Barbara Hutton, often-married American heiress to the vast Woolworth dime store fortune. She married Count Kurt von Haugwitz-Reventlow on May 14, the second time in less than three years that she had taken a titled European as her husband.

2736   *NYT,* Tuesday, May 14, 1935, 23:7.

For Eugene Talmadge see Note 2716.

2737   *NYT,* Wednesday, May 15, 1935, 23:7.

William A. Van Brunt, eighty-eight-year-old retired manufacturer living in Los Angeles, gave $280,000 to veteran employees of his Wisconsin firm.

2738   *NYT,* Thursday, May 16, 1935, 25:7.

The Patman bonus bill, providing for a $2.2 billion payment in cash on **the adjusted compensation** certificates held by World War I veterans, was passed by Congress in early May. Roosevelt vetoed the bill, however, chiefly on grounds that the measure would spur inflation. The House overrode the veto on May 22, but the Senate sustained it one day later.

2739 *NYT*, Friday, May 17, 1935, 23:7.

Edward Fitz Randolph "Eddie" Vail, California cattleman and philanthropist.

For Jack Garner see Note 2105.

2740 *NYT*, Saturday, May 18, 1935, 19:7.

2741 *NYT*, Monday, May 20, 1935, 19:7.

The *Maxim Gorki*, the largest airplane in the world at the time, collided with a stunt plane near Moscow on May 18. All forty-eight persons aboard the huge Russian passenger liner perished in the accident.

2742 *NYT*, Tuesday, May 21, 1935, 21:3.

For the Patman bonus bill see Note 2738.

2743 *NYT*, Wednesday, May 22, 1935, 21:7.

For Eleanor Roosevelt see Note 2089.

President Roosevelt established a precedent by appearing on May 22 before a joint session of Congress to deliver a veto message in person. For the Patman bonus bill see Note 2738.

2744 *NYT*, Thursday, May 23, 1935, 25:6. Variant: *LAT* gives " 'wouldn't care to' " in second sentence.

Hitler delivered a major speech before the Reichstag on May 21, promising to respect all clauses of the Versailles Treaty and proposing that the German army be made a bulwark against communism.

2745 *NYT*, Friday, May 24, 1935, 23:7. Variant: *NYT* gives "something about the work of Jane Addams since they were celebrating the anniversary of a women's league she had founded." in first sentence.

Kathleen Norris, American writer and feminist who authored more than eighty romantic novels between 1911 and 1959.

Addams (see Note 2696) died on May 21, 1935, at age seventy-five.

For Irvin S. Cobb see Note 2233.

2746 *NYT*, Saturday, May 25, 1935, 17:7.

Roberta Campbell Lawson, an Oklahoman whose ancestry was one-eighth American Indian, was elected president of the General Federation of Women's Clubs in a hotly-contested election on June 10. She served as president from 1935 to 1938.

2747 *NYT*, Monday, May 27, 1935, 19:6. Variant: *LAT* gives "Ohio University" in fourth sentence.

For Babe Ruth see Note 2388.

William Lawson Little, Jr., American golfer who was the only player to win the United States and British amateur championships in the same year twice in a row—1934 and 1935.

James Cleveland "Jesse" Owens, American track star and member of the United States Olympic team of 1936. At the Big Ten Conference championships in May of 1935, Owens set or equaled four world records over a period of seventy minutes.

²⁷⁴⁸ *NYT,* Tuesday, May 28, 1935, 27:7.

For the Frazier-Lemke Farm Bankruptcy Act see Note 2228.

The National Industrial Recovery Act, of which the NRA was a part, was invalidated by the Supreme Court in the case of *Schechter Poultry Corporation v. U. S.*

William Ewart Humphrey, United States federal trade commissioner from 1925 to 1933. Humphrey, who had refused to step down from the commission at the request of Roosevelt, was summarily removed by the president in October of 1933. As a result he instituted federal court action to test the president's power of removal without cause. On May 27, 1935, the Supreme Court invalidated Roosevelt's action on grounds that he had exceeded his powers.

For Jesse Owens see Note 2747.

²⁷⁴⁹ *NYT,* Wednesday, May 29, 1935, 23:7.

²⁷⁵⁰ *NYT,* Thursday, May 30, 1935, 19:7.

²⁷⁵¹ *NYT,* Friday, May 31, 1935, 17:7.

For EPIC and Upton B. Sinclair see Note 2519.

²⁷⁵² *NYT,* Saturday, June 1, 1935, 17:7. Variant: *NYT* gives "Now the popular" in fourth sentence.

For Jack Garner see Note 2105.

Nicholas Longworth, Republican United States representative from Ohio from 1903 to 1913 and from 1915 until his death in 1931. Longworth was a close personal friend of Garner, his successor as Speaker of the House.

²⁷⁵³ *NYT,* Monday, June 3, 1935, 19:7.

Daniel Calhoun Roper, United States secretary of commerce from 1933 to 1938.

²⁷⁵⁴ *NYT,* Tuesday, June 4, 1935, 25:7.

A new French luxury liner, the S. S. *Normandie,* broke the existing record for an Atlantic crossing during its maiden voyage in late May and early June of 1935.

²⁷⁵⁵ *NYT,* Wednesday, June 5, 1935, 21:7.

²⁷⁵⁶ *NYT,* Thursday, June 6, 1935, 23:7.

²⁷⁵⁷ *NYT,* Friday, June 7, 1935, 23:7.

The Wagner Act, also known as the National Labor Relations Act, guaranteed employees the right to self-organization and to bargain collectively through representatives of their own choosing. Enacted on July 15, 1935, the Wagner Act retained many of the labor relation features of the invalidated National Industrial Recovery Act.

The Guffey-Snyder Coal Act was enacted on August 30, 1935, and sought to stabilize the bituminous coal-mining industry. It created the National Bituminous Coal Commission to administer production quotas and labor regulations based on the NRA soft coal code. Invalidated by the Supreme Court in 1936, the act was succeeded by the Guffey-Vinson Act of 1937.

Alice Ames Winter, California clubwoman and author. A former national president of the General Federation of Women's Clubs, she served with the Motion Picture Producers and Distributors of America from 1929 to 1942.

2758 *NYT*, Saturday, June 8, 1935, 17:7.

Maurice Auguste Chevalier, debonair French entertainer who gained an international reputation in the Paris music halls of the 1920s. He also achieved fame as a star of American films, beginning with his appearance in *The Love Parade* in 1930.

2759 *NYT*, Monday, June 10, 1935, 19:3.

Murray (see Note 2106) presided at the Oklahoma Constitutional Convention of 1907 and was a noted authority on constitutional law. Murray supported Roosevelt's Republican opponents in 1936 and 1940.

Clem Vann Rogers, prominent rancher and banker of early-day Oklahoma and father of Will Rogers.

2760 *NYT*, Tuesday, June 11, 1935, 23:7.

Two of three suspected kidnappers of nine-year-old George Philip Weyerhaeuser were apprehended by federal agents on June 9. They later were convicted and sentenced to long prison terms. A third alleged participant never was captured.

2761 *NYT*, Wednesday, June 12, 1935, 23:3.

A "Grass Roots" convention of conservative Midwestern Republicans was held at Springfield, Illinois, on June 10-11, 1935.

2762 *NYT*, Thursday, June 13, 1935, 25:3.

Stepin Fetchit, American black comedian who appeared in several motion pictures with Rogers, including one of the Oklahoman's last films, *Steamboat 'Round the Bend* (1935).

Owens (see Note 2747) won four events at a dual meet at Los Angeles between Ohio State University and the University of Southern California.

James Francis "Jim" Thorpe, widely-hailed athlete of American Indian descent. A native of Oklahoma, Thorpe earned all-American honors in 1911 and 1912 as a running back at Carlisle Institute and won gold medals in the pentathlon and decathlon at the Olympics of 1912.

2763 *NYT*, Friday, June 14, 1935, 25:7.

Long was filibustering against a proposed renewal of the NRA.

2764 *NYT*, Saturday, June 15, 1935, 17:7.

Baer (see Note 2137) lost his world heavyweight title to James J. "Jim" Braddock in an upset nine-round bout in New York City on June 14. Known as the "Cinderella Man," Braddock reigned as world champion from 1935 to 1937.

Kathryn Elizabeth "Kate" Smith, American singer and entertainer who achieved immense popularity during the 1930s and 1940s. A show business legend,

Smith became renowned as the "Moon Over the Mountain" girl because of her theme song.

For Dizzy Dean see Note 2545.

2765 *NYT,* Monday, June 17, 1935, 19:7.

2766 *NYT,* Tuesday, June 18, 1935, 23:7.

2767 *NYT,* Wednesday, June 19, 1935, 21:3.

Bolivia and Paraguay signed a truce on June 12 that effectively ended three years of fighting between the two countries over possession of the Gran Chaco region (see Note 2296).

Landis (see Note 2551) took an unprecedented step on June 18 in ruling that a former athletic star at Sing Sing Prison was eligible to play professional baseball despite his criminal past. In 1907 Landis presided at the Standard Oil of Indiana rebate cases trial; he found the defendents guilty and fined them $29,240,000.

2768 *NYT,* Thursday, June 20, 1935, 21:7.

The California Pacific International Exposition was held at San Diego in 1935-1936.

2769 *NYT,* Friday, June 21, 1935, 21:7.

Roosevelt declared on June 19 that the tax laws had "done little to prevent an unjust concentration of wealth and economic power." His recommendations for higher taxes on large incomes and estates were embodied in the Wealth Tax Act, enacted in August of 1935 and which served to blunt the force of Long's "Share-the-Wealth" movement.

2770 *NYT,* Saturday, June 22, 1935, 17:7.

The University of California won the Intercollegiate Rowing Association varsity championship at Poughkeepsie, New York, with a split-second victory over Cornell University on June 18.

Rush Dew Holt, Democratic United States senator from West Virginia from 1935 to 1941. Holt was unable to take his seat on the beginning day of his term, January 3, because he had not reached the minimum age required by the Constitution. He finally took office on June 21, 1935, two days after his thirtieth birthday.

2771 *NYT,* Monday, June 24, 1935, 19:7.

For the Wealth Tax Act see Note 2769; for Joe Robinson see Note 2105.

2772 *NYT,* Tuesday, June 25, 1935, 21:3.

2773 *NYT,* Wednesday, June 26, 1935, 23:7.

For chain letters see Note 2728; for technocracy see Note 2070.

2774 *NYT,* Thursday, June 27, 1935, 23:3.

Joe "Brown Bomber" Louis, American prize fighter who held the world heavyweight title from 1937 to 1949. On June 25 Louis recorded his twenty-third consecutive professional win with a sixth-round knock-out of Primo Carnera (see Note 2515).

For Jim Braddock see Note 2764; for Max Baer see Note 2137; for Bugs Baer see Note 2137; for Max Schmeling see Note 2137.

2775   *NYT*, Friday, June 28, 1935, 23:3.

The National Youth Administration (NYA) was established by executive order on June 26 to administer a $50,000,000 work relief and employment program for persons between the age of sixteen and twenty-five. By 1936 some 600,000 young persons were engaged in NYA activities.

2776   *NYT*, Saturday, June 29, 1935, 17:6.

The Gold Clause Act of August of 1935 allowed the government to withdraw its consent to be sued on its gold obligations.

2777   *NYT*, Monday, July 1, 1935, 21:7.

2778   *NYT*, Tuesday, July 2, 1935, 23:7.

For Italy and Ethiopia (Abyssinia) see Note 2611.

2779   *NYT*, Wednesday, July 3, 1935, 19:7.

For the Public Utility Holding Companies Act see Note 2684.

2780   *NYT*, Thursday, July 4, 1935, 17:7.

For Arthur Brisbane see Note 2060.

2781   *NYT*, Friday, July 5, 1935, 15:7.

2782   *NYT*, Saturday, July 6, 1935, 15:7.

2783   *NYT*, Monday, July 8, 1935, 17:7.

Helen Wills Moody, in a dramatic comeback from a painful loss to Helen Jacobs in 1933 (see Note 2204), defeated Jacobs in three sets on July 6 to win her seventh Wimbledon title.

Helen Hull Jacobs, American tennis star of the 1920s and 1930s and winner, at least once each, of most major women's titles.

2784   *NYT*, Tuesday, July 9, 1935, 23:7. Variant: *NYT* omits third sentence.

For John D. Rockefeller, Sr., see Note 2059.

2785   *NYT*, Wednesday, July 10, 1935, 23:7.

Tutankhamen, ancient Egyptian monarch whose tomb was discovered in 1922 in the Valley of the Kings along the Nile River.

2786   *NYT*, Thursday, July 11, 1935, 23:7.

For Italy and Ethiopia (Abyssinia) see Note 2611; for Haile Selassie, emperor of Ethiopia, see Note 2672.

2787   *NYT*, Friday, July 12, 1935, 21:7. Variant: *LAT* gives "the U. S. or chairman of the committee. 'Mr. Jones' " in first and second sentences.

2788   *NYT*, Saturday, July 13, 1935, 15:7.

For Italy and Ethiopia (Abyssinia) see Note 2611.

²⁷⁸⁹ *LAT*, Monday, July 15, 1935, I:1:3. *NYT* did not print the DT.

²⁷⁹⁰ *NYT*, Tuesday, July 16, 1935, 21:3.

For Pat Hurley see Note 2592.

²⁷⁹¹ *NYT*, Wednesday, July 17, 1935, 21:7. Variants: *NYT* gives "much of a remark I had made about" in fourth sentence/*NYT* gives "Hays, who served under" in seventh sentence.

For Pat Hurley see Note 2592.

Curtis Dwight Wilbur, United States secretary of the navy from 1924 to 1929.

For Will Hays see Note 2169.

Warren Gamaliel Harding, United States president from 1921 until his death in 1923.

Harry Whinna Nice, Republican governor of Maryland from 1935 to 1939.

Man o' War, American-bred race horse which won twenty of twenty-one races from 1919 to 1920 and set five American track records during a brief racing career.

Albert Cabell Ritchie, Democratic governor of Maryland from 1920 to 1935 and president aspirant in 1932.

²⁷⁹² *NYT*, Thursday, July 18, 1935, 21:7.

A New York judge on July 17 annulled the marriage of an American heir and an Austrian countess on grounds that the young man had been a victim of a plot by the "so-called nobility" of Europe to obtain wealth.

²⁷⁹³ *NYT*, Friday, July 19, 1935, 19:7. Variant: *NYT* omits tenth and eleventh sentences.

The processing taxes of the AAA were ruled unconstitutional by the Federal Court of Appeals at Boston on July 16. The Supreme Court invalidated the AAA in January of 1936.

The British Labor ministry moved on July 17 to bolster home talent by banning American chorus girls from performing in Great Britain.

²⁷⁹⁴ *NYT*, Saturday, July 20, 1935, 15:7. Variant: *NYT* gives "lawyers and judges" in eighth sentence.

²⁷⁹⁵ *NYT*, Monday, July 22, 1935, 17:7.

Lázaro Cárdena, president of Mexico from 1934 to 1940. As part of a national campaign against gambling, Cárdenas banned gambling at the border resorts of Tijuana and Agua Caliente on July 20. The new policy forced 600 jockeys, horse trainers, and casino employees out of work.

For Ettie Rheiner Garner see Note 2338; for Albert Einstein see Note 2411.

Thomas Alva Edison, American inventor responsible for numerous practical applications of electricity, including the first commercially successful incandescent lamp.

Robert Fulton, American engineer and inventor who developed and operated the first successful steamboat in 1807.

2796 *NYT*, Tuesday, July 23, 1935, 21:7.

The Soviet Union planned an Arctic flight in July of 1935, but mechanical difficulties forced a postponement of the attempt. Two years later, three Russian fliers made the first nonstop flight across the North Pole, flying from Moscow to Vancouver, Canada, in less than sixty-four hours.

2797 *NYT*, Wednesday, July 24, 1935, 19:7.

For Wiley Post see Note 2168.

Great Britain served notice on July 22 that it had abandoned its effort to secure naval limitation by the ratio principle established at the Washington Conference of 1921-1922 (see Note 2247), claiming that the ratios injured the pride of some countries.

2798 *NYT*, Thursday, July 25, 1935, 21:3.

Bertrand Hollis Snell, Republican United States representative from New York from 1915 to 1939. Snell, the minority leader in Congress, created a stir in Congress when he remarked on July 22 that Roosevelt had trod "perilously close" to impeachable grounds.

Fish (see Note 2191), in a speech on the floor of Congress on July 23, fell short of calling for the impeachment of Roosevelt, but did remark that "the president has usurped the powers of Congress and it is time we called a halt."

Mutt and Jeff, successful daily newspaper cartoon feature; created by Harry Conway "Bud" Fisher in 1907.

2799 *NYT*, Friday, July 26, 1935, 17:7.

2800 *NYT*, Saturday, July 27, 1935, 15:7.

For Wiley Post see Note 2168.

Waite Phillips, American oilman and industrialist who cofounded the Phillips Petroleum Company in 1917. He owned and operated large livestock ranches in the Southwest, including the Philmont, which embraced 325,000 acres near Cimarron, New Mexico.

2801 *NYT*, Monday, July 29, 1935, 17:7.

For Wiley Post see Note 2168.

2802 *NYT*, Tuesday, July 30, 1935, 21:7.

Geronimo, American Apache chieftain who led a sensational campaign from 1885 to 1886 against whites in the Southwest.

The Boer War, a conflict between Great Britain and the two Boer, or Afrikaner, republics, the Orange Free State and the South African Republic (Transvaal), from 1899 to 1902.

Hernando Cortes, Spanish conqueror of Mexico (1521).

The Yanquis of Sonora, Mexico, repeatedly rose in revolt against civil authority in Mexico. Three thousand Yaqui warriors held off nearly 5,000 Mexican troops between 1885 and the turn of the century, and other uprisings occurred periodically.

2803 *NYT*, Wednesday, July 31, 1935, 19:7.

Roberta Star Semple Smythe, evangelist daughter of Aimee Semple McPherson (see Note 2064).

For Joe Robinson see Note 2105.

2804 *NYT*, Thursday, August 1, 1935, 25:4. Variant: *NYT* omits "Dr. Jasbo, . . . of office." in second sentence.

Roy Orchard Woodruff, Republican United States representative from Michigan from 1913 to 1915 and from 1921 to 1953.

2805 *NYT*, Friday, August 2, 1935, 19:7.

2806 *NYT*, Saturday, August 3, 1935, 15:7. Variant: *NYT* gives "ranch life." to end DT.

The World Championship Rodeo contest was held near Los Angeles from August 3 to 11.

Robert Anderson "Wild Horse Bob" Crosby, colorful and controversial New Mexico rodeo performer of the 1920s and 1930s known as the "King of the Steer Ropers."

2807 *NYT*, Monday, August 5, 1935, 17:7. Variant: *NYT* gives "his Spring in '35" in third sentence.

Farley (see Note 2250) was on a six-week vacation trip to Hawaii.

2808 *NYT*, Tuesday, August 6, 1935, 19:3.

For San Francisco bridges see Note 2486; for the California Pacific International Exposition at San Diego see Note 2768.

2809 *NYT*, Wednesday, August 7, 1935, 21:7. Variants: *NYT* gives "Los Angeles and a few hours by plane to Spokane, . . . Chicago." in first sentence/ *NYT* gives "Today I saw" in third sentence.

The Boeing 299 bomber, the largest land plane in the United States at the time, had its first test flight on June 28, 1935, at the Boeing Field in Seattle. Later redesignated the B-17, it became known as the Flying Fortress.

Roosevelt proposed in July of 1935 new doughnut-shaped half-cent and one-mill coins that would be used to pay taxes. Congressmen concerned about the constitutionality of the plan killed it in committee.

Victor A. "Vic" Meyers, orchestra leader and musician who served as Democratic lieutenant governor of Washington from 1933 to 1953.

2810 *NYT*, Thursday, August 8, 1935, 19:7. Variants: *NYT* gives "rain came up and we just" in third sentence/*NYT* gives "old boy Wiley Post" in fifth sentence.

Rogers was accompanying Wiley Post (see Note 2168).

2811 *NYT*, Friday, August 9, 1935, 19:7. Variant: *LAT* omits fourth sentence.

John Weir Troy, Democratic governor of Alaska from 1933 to 1939.

2812 *NYT*, Saturday, August 10, 1935, 15:7.

Rex Ellingwood Beach, American novelist and miscellaneous writer noted for his rough-hewn portrayals of life in Alaska.

²⁸¹³ *NYT,* Monday, August 12, 1935, 17:7. Variant: *LAT* gives "With no night, it's" in seventh and eighth sentences.

For Wiley Post see Note 2168.

²⁸¹⁴ *NYT,* Tuesday, August 13, 1935, 19:4. *LAT* did not print the DT.

For Wiley Post see Note 2168.

²⁸¹⁵ *NYT,* Wednesday, August 14, 1935, 21:7. Variants: *LAT* gives "country if they . . . U. S. They . . . future." in first and second sentences/*NYT* gives "country. They run clear" in fifth sentence.

By the Louisiana Purchase of 1803 the United States acquired from France the former Spanish region of Louisiana, comprising much of the present-day United States lying north of Texas between the Mississippi River and the Great Basin.

William Henry Seward, United States secretary of state from 1861 to 1869; negotiated the purchase of Alaska from Russia in 1867.

²⁸¹⁶ *NYT,* Thursday, August 15, 1935, 21:4. Variants: *LAT* gives "fine pilot in the Lockheed Electra. We scaled" in first and second sentences/*NYT* gives "bear. Down . . . valley now, out" in fifth and sixth sentences.

Joe Crosson, well-known Alaskan pilot who flew the bodies of Rogers and Post to Seattle from Point Barrow, Alaska, following the crash of their plane on August 15.

For Wiley Post see Note 2168.

Joe Barrows, Alaskan "bush pilot."

²⁸¹⁷ *NYT,* Friday, August 16, 1935, 17:3. Variant: *LAT* gives "workmen. Paid regular wages but it's" in seventh and eighth sentences.

The Matamuska Valley colony was established in May of 1935 as a New Deal project to settle and develop Alaska and to give a new start to scores of destitute farm families. In June of 1935 several discontented colonists made public their complaints about the operation of the settlement. Federal and state officials quickly remedied the situation, however. The Matamuska colony continued to thrive into the 1970s.

LeRoy Philip Hunt, Sr., United States Marine Corps officer who served as first director of the Matamuska Valley project.

INDEX

Abyssinia: *see* Ethiopia
Actors and actresses: 240, 256, 238; in motion pictures, 5, 39, 69, 75; divorce among, 238
Addams, Jane: 292, 313
Africa: 325; diamonds in, 130
Agricultural Adjustment Administration (AAA): 82, 134
Agriculture: 172; crop prices, 36, 47, 294-95; crop production control, 69-70, 73; livestock production control, 69-70
Agriculture, Department of: 154
Airmail: 137, 138, 139-40, 142, 145, 148, 150, 151-52, 156
Alabama, prohibition repeal in: 56
Alaska: 344, 347; territorial governor of, 344; territorial legislature of, 344
Albert I, king of Belgium: 140
Albright, William E.: 214
Albuquerque, N. M.: 280; newspapers in, 20
Aldrich, Winthrop W.: 3
Alexandrovna, Xenia: 247
Allahabad, India: 232
Allen, Henry J.: 131
Amarillo (Tex.) *Daily News:* 268
American Bar Association: 332-34, 336
American Legion, national convention of: 86, 88
American Liberty League: 229, 241
American Mercury (magazine): 118
"Amos 'n Andy" (radio program): 191
Anderson, Heartley W. ("Hunk"): 113
Angell, James R.: 158-59
Angels Camp, Calif.: 234
Arbuckle, Roscoe C. ("Fatty"): 47
Arctic: 346, 347
Argentina: 121; president of, 88
Arizona: 9, 20, 49, 128, 131, 232, 260; legislature of, 9
Arizona Republic: 49
Arkansas: 13, 132, 259, 260, 339-40; prohibition repeal in, 56
Armistice Day: 71, 186, 199, 322
Arnold, Henry M. ("Hap"): 141
Astor, John J. III: wedding of, 190
Astor, Nancy L.: 247
Astor, W. Vincent: 75; yacht of, 155, 157
Athens, Greece: 232, 283
Atterbury, William W.: 120
Austin, Tex.: 195, 267
Australia: 20, 50, 232, 234, 249, 264; aviator from, 232; prime minister of, 304

Austria: 87, 140, 150, 201, 217, 261, 295; political turmoil in, 139; chancellor of, 209
Autographs: 140
Automobiles: 126; industry, 71, 262, 278; Ford models, 138; racing, 285
Aviation: 13, 16, 18, 20, 23, 28, 34, 38, 54, 56, 57, 67, 83, 86, 94, 131-32, 134, 175, 177-78, 189-90, 220, 236, 237, 248, 249, 252-53, 264, 265, 267, 169, 272, 277-78, 280, 285, 296, 300, 307-309, 328, 344; national air races, 45, 48; Italian air armada, 53; in Japan, 86; in Russia, 86, 213, 311-12, 336-37; in Italy, 102; MacRobertson Air Race, 200, 232-33, 234, 236; in Hawaii, 202, 203; navigation, 249; polar flights, 337; military, 342; in Alaska, 347; in Canada, 347

Babson, Roger W.: 60, 274
Baby Le Roy: *see* Winnebrenner
Bacculaureate addresses: 317
Baden-Powell, Robert S. S.: 275
Baer, Arthur ("Bugs"): 39, 325
Baer, Maximilian A. ("Max"): 39, 182, 197, 251, 264, 274, 321, 325
Baghdad, Iraq: 232
Balancing the budget: 25, 32, 40, 320
Balbo, Italo: 56, 66, 102
Baldwin, Frank F.: 202
Ballet: 214
Ballooning and balloonists: 107, 234
Balzar, Fred B.: 2-3, 58, 153-54
Bankers and banking: 1, 3, 4, 5, 17, 31, 59, 63, 83, 108, 114, 117, 130, 136, 145, 234, 235, 251, 256, 266, 274, 279; international, 2, 23; relief for, 37; convention of, 136; in Detroit, 190
Bank holiday, national: 1, 2-3, 12, 52
Bardo, Clinton L.: 246
Barnum, Phineas T.: 246
Barrie, James M.: 9
Barrows, Joe: 347
Barrymore, Ethel: 111
Barrymores (theatrical family): 150
Bartlesville, Okla.: 248
Baruch, Bernard M.: 46, 92, 96, 136, 187; magazine article by, 107
Baseball: 79, 86-87, 143, 163, 206, 208, 223-26, 228, 299, 314, 332, 341
Bass, Tom: 244

445

Baton Rouge, La.: 269, 270
Battleship Potemkin, The (motion picture): 213
Baxter, Warner: 238
Beach, Rex E.: 344-45
Beer: 11, 13, 14-15, 16, 17, 35; in Oklahoma, 29; retail licenses, 34; on Indian reservations, 38
Beery, Wallace: 280
Belgium: 76, 217, 268
Bering, Frank W.: 279
Beverly Hills, Calif.: 10, 15, 138, 145, 197, 242
Big business: 36, 260, 317; relief for, 37
Black, Hugo L.: 142
Blue Boy (champion hog): 70
Blue Prince (race horse): 293
Boer War: 339
Bolivia: 209, 286, 322
Bonanza, Alaska: 346
Bonds, government: 61; *see also* Stocks and bonds
Bonus armies: 31; *see also* Veterans' bonus
Boone, Daniel: 157
Bootleggers and bootlegging: 13, 16, 70, 132
Borah, William E.: 108-109, 144, 154, 192, 239
Boris III, king of Bulgaria: 99
Boulder Dam: *see* Hoover Dam
Boston, Mass.: 197, 272, 311
Boxing: 39, 184, 197, 262, 264, 320, 321, 325, 341
Boy Scouts of America: 275
Braddock, James J. ("Jim"): 325
Bradley, Edward R.: 306
"Brain trusts": 72, 155, 156, 159, 164, 166, 187, 212, 219, 258, 337, 341
Brazil: 88, 329; ambassador from, 205; military aviation in, 309
Bridge (card game): 69, 73, 126, 279
Brisbane, Arthur: 3, 21, 28, 35, 233, 238, 239, 274, 296, 328
Brown, Joe E.: 228
Brown, Walter F.: 142
Brownsville, Tex.: 328
Bryan, William Jennings: 13, 118-19, 151
Bryce Canyon: 339
Bucharest, Rumania: 216
Buckingham Palace: 125
Budapest, Hungary: 217
Buenos Aires, Argentina: 307, 309
Buffalo Bayou, Tex.: 100
Bullitt, William C.: 106, 212
Bulwinkle, Alfred L.: 167
Burke, Mary ("Billie"): *see* Ziegfeld
Business and businessmen: 315; and government, 168, 169, 310, 319
Butler, Nicholas Murray: 114, 123
Butler, Smedley D.: 244

Cairo, Egypt: 232
Calcutta, India: 232
California: 5, 17, 49, 56, 77, 90, 109, 123, 128, 132, 134, 141, 177, 178, 223, 242, 288, 291, 295, 300, 314, 316, 328; earthquakes in, 3, 8, 13, 45; prohibition repeal in, 47; newspapers in, 62, 75, 200; state income tax, 62, 63; murder trial in, 71; senatorial investigation in, 106; liquor laws of, 118; state supreme court of, 126; ranches in, 170, 174; crime in, 173; governor of, 197, 284; election in, 237, 238, 240; college students in, 248; state legislature of, 290, 316, 322;
California, University of (Berkeley): 292
California Bar Association: 258
Calles, Plutarco E.: 184
Campaign promises: 20-21
Campbell, Malcolm: 285
Canada: 151, 182, 264, 287, 297; prime minister of, 304; aviation in, 347
Capone, Alphonse ("Scarface Al"): 16
Carnera, Primo: 211, 325
Carol II, king of Rumania: 99, 216
Carr, Harry: 115
Carter, Amon G.: 35, 93, 132
Cattlemen: 174, 195, 252, 268, 295
Cermak, Anthony: 2
Chaco War: 115, 188, 209, 322
Chain letters: 139, 325
Chambers of commerce: 6, 90, 103, 160, 197, 259, 275, 330, 344; *see also* United States Chamber of Commerce
Chandler, Harry: 160
Chaplin, Charles S. ("Charlie"): 90, 281-82
Cherokee Indians: 80
Chevalier, Maurice A.: 318
Cheyenne, Wy.: 58, 67
Chicago, Ill.: 16, 35, 66-67, 69, 88, 103, 134, 145, 147, 169, 178, 270, 279, 342
Chicago Century of Progress Exposition: 28, 34-35, 102, 182, 236-37
Chicago (Ill.) *Tribune*: 70-71
Chile: 121; nitrate sales by, 146
China: 5, 33, 91, 164, 170, 185, 233, 251, 286, 319, 321, 342; brokerage business in, 135; foreign affairs expert from, 210, 212
Chinese Eastern Railway: 210
Chita, Siberia: 210
Christmas: 117, 119, 254, 256
Cincinnati, Ohio: 31, 267
Civic clubs: 6-7
Civilian Conservation Corps (CCC): 82, 159, 348
Civil Works Administration (CWA): 132

446

Claremore, Okla.: 87, 211, 238, 248, 294, 295, 328
Claremore (Okla.) *Progress:* 195, 294
Clark, Bennett Champ: 5
Clemens, Samuel L. ("Mark Twain"): 168, 234
Cleopatra: 282
Cleveland, Ohio: 141, 265, 320
Cobb, Irvin S.: 84, 186, 313
Cochrane, Gordon S. ("Mickey"): 224, 225, 226
Collective bargaining: 183
Collier, John: 182
Colorado: 292-93
Columbia University, football team of: 113-14, 123
Columbus, Christopher: 90
Columbus, Ohio: 58
Comedians: 31, 68, 282; salaries of, 5
Communism and communists: 57, 72, 168, 198, 216; in France, 127
Conferences, international: 49, 50, 52, 59-60, 92, 113, 115, 121, 150, 252, 300-301, 327
Confidence: 81, 119
Confucius: 136
Congressional Record: 140
Connally, Thomas T. ("Tom"): 25, 105
Connelly, "One-Eyed" (boxer): 39
"Conscience Fund": 307
Conscientious objectors: 126
Conventions: 22, 336
Coolidge, Calvin: 42, 205, 334
Coolidge, Grace A. G. (Mrs. Calvin): 228
Cooper, Jackie: 93
Copeland, Royal S.: 105
Cornell University: 51
Cortes, Hernando: 339
Coughlin, Charles E.: 287
Couzens, James: 36
Crawford, John H. ("Jack"): 50
Credit, buying on: 327
Crime and criminals: 78-79, 135, 177, 185-86, 319; suicides, 137; jail escapes, 148, 165, 166; government campaign against, 173; pardons, 231, 319; prevention, 258
Crippled children: 18
Crockett, Davey: 157
Cronin, Joseph E. ("Joe"): 89
Crosby, Robert A. ("Wild Horse Bob"): 341
Cross, Wilbur L.: 58
Crosson, Joe: 347
Crossword puzzles: 8, 301
Crowder, Alvin F. ("General"): 226
Croy, Homer: 110
Cuba: 64-65, 67, 76-77, 79, 82-83, 86, 107; president of, 66, 82, 129, 131; U.S. intervention in, 78, 80, 82, 122; U.S. relations with, 130, 179

Cummings, Homer S.: 204
Curtis, Charles: 314
Czechoslovakia: 217

Darling, Jay N. ("J. N. Ding"): 99
Darrow, Clarence S.: 175
David Harum (motion picture): 126, 213
Davis, Norman H.: 250, 252
Dawson City, Alaska: 346
Dean, Jay Hanna ("Dizzy"): 223, 224, 225-26, 228, 234, 299, 321
Dean, Paul Dee ("Daffy"): 223, 224, 225-26, 228
Death Valley, Calif.: 127
Deficit spending: 271, 282, 284, 300, 302, 317
Democratic party and Democrats: 3, 8, 10, 12, 14, 15, 20, 23, 26-27, 30, 44, 53, 58, 64, 74, 81, 90, 93, 105, 115, 138, 156, 159, 161, 165, 167, 171, 192, 194, 202, 217, 231, 237, 238, 239, 241, 262, 264, 267, 279, 288, 291, 292, 294, 298, 309, 317, 344
Dempsey, William H. ("Jack"): 54, 56, 284
Denmark: 12-13, 305, 215
Denver, Colo.: 178
Depression, economic: 10, 31, 59, 87-88, 102, 122, 211, 268, 271, 341
Des Moines, Ia.: 99
Detroit, Mich.: 190, 223, 225, 226, 228, 234, 318
Dictators: 101, 118, 191, 209, 229, 228
Dillinger, John H.: 135, 147, 156, 158, 166, 167, 169, 175, 183, 199-200, 254
Diplomacy and diplomats: 49-50, 76, 80, 89, 181, 304, 307
Dirigibles: 277
Disarmament: 5, 13, 30, 40, 92, 104, 252, 304
Divorce: 54, 59, 75, 253
Dogs: 111
Dollar: 115, 116; exchange rate of, 44, 48, 49, 51, 98, 103; value of, 74, 114, 128, 129, 130, 144-45, 262
Dolfuss, Engelbert: 87, 140, 150, 201, 203
Doolittle, James H. ("Jimmy"): 86, 232, 264
Douglas, Ariz.: 94
Douglas, Donald W.: 272
Douglas, Lewis W.: 25, 32
Dressler, Marie: 190
Drought: 18, 205, 229, 268, 332; in Oklahoma, 195
Dublin, Ireland: lord mayor of, 293

447

Dude ranching: 17
Du Pont, Irénée: 241
Durango, Colo.: 339
Durant, William J. ("Will"): 281
Duranty, Walter: 212
Dust storms: 18, 292-93

Earhart, Amelia: 38, 300, 308
Earthquakes: 3, 8, 13; in Calif., 45; in Nicaragua, 142
Economists: 99, 107, 251, 281
Economy: condition of, 1, 2, 5, 7, 12, 14, 37-38, 54, 87-88, 146, 170-71, 220, 293; recovery of, 255, 322
Edge, Walter E.: 90
Edinborough, Scotland: 218
Edison, Thomas A.: 336
Edmonton, Canada: 347
Edward Albert, prince of Wales: 36, 52, 256, 286
Einstein, Albert: 166, 336
Eldorado, Alaska: 346
Elections: 109-10, 228, 230, 236; congressional, 167, 184, 189, 191, 238-40; in Calif., 171, 199, 237, 238, 240; presidential, 309, 333, 340
Electoral college, abolition of: 176
El Paso, Tex.: 94, 269
Empire State Building: 269
End Poverty in California plan (EPIC): 241, 316
England: 9, 23, 45, 76, 89, 99, 101, 117, 138, 139, 140, 157, 181, 186, 203, 217, 251, 256, 268, 275, 285, 286, 295, 300, 301, 304, 309, 318, 319, 321, 325, 332, 334, 337, 338; U.S. ambassador to, 36; golf tournament in, 50; royalty of, 99; economic condition of, 115; criminals in, 137; postal system in, 152-53; royal wedding in, 244-45, 247, 248; House of Lords, 247; national debt of, 262
Eric the Red (Nordic explorer): 90
Eskimos: 346
Estonia: 214
Ethiopia: 342; relations with Italy, 254, 282, 288, 321, 325, 327, 330, 332, 334, 337, 338, 339; king of, 282, 284, 330
Europe: 9, 22, 30, 39, 48, 49, 96, 103, 131, 146, 168, 184, 211, 214, 216, 219, 221, 245, 261, 262, 268, 274, 289, 298, 300, 304, 309, 318, 327; war in, 229-30
Evolution: 180

Fairbanks, Alaska: 347
Falconi, Tito: 46, 48

Farley, James A.: 93, 94, 105, 153, 197, 199, 306, 341-42
Farmers: 24, 28, 29, 94, 181, 183, 195, 294; relief for, 8, 88, 98; strikes by, 82; mortgages for, 93; convention of 99, 101; leaders of, 99-100; efficiency of, 178
Fascism: 216
Fatherhood: 43
Father's Day: 43
Fear: 119
Federal Emergency Relief Administration (FERA): 82
Federal employees: 141
Federal Reserve Board: 25, 37
Federal Trade Commission: 257, 315
Federation of Women's Clubs: 314, 318
Ferdinand, Louis: 111
Ferguson, James E. ("Pa"): 132, 195
Ferguson, Miriam A. ("Ma"): 58, 61, 79, 93, 195
Fetchit, Stepin: 320
Financiers: 104, 107, 114, 116, 169
Finland: 43, 126, 194, 214-15, 270
Fischer, Louis: 212
Fish, Hamilton, Jr.: 65, 337-38
Flagpole sitting: 314
Fletcher, Henry P.: 181, 191
Fletcher-Rayburn Act: see Securities Exchange Act
Florida: 28, 156, 166, 238, 296; hurricane in, 75; weather in, 253
Flynn, Edward J.: 129
Football: 89, 98, 109, 113-14, 123, 126, 159, 228, 235, 241, 242, 247, 248-49, 259, 260; professional, 128, 259
Ford, Henry: 75, 96, 100, 223, 224, 225, 234, 247, 278, 321
Fort Worth, Tex.: 31, 35, 93, 94, 131-32, 252, 269, 328
4-H Clubs: 242-43
Fourth of July: 328-29
France: 23, 26, 45, 48, 50, 80, 90, 99, 105, 111, 116, 127, 129, 138, 139, 155, 177, 184, 186, 191, 194, 217, 229, 230, 250, 261, 268, 282, 285, 289, 292, 295, 309, 317, 318; U.S. relations with, 12, 17, 21, 53; president of, 66; relations with Germany, 105, 125; espionage in, 118; train wreck in, 119-20; House of Deputies, 137; politics in, 137
Franklin, Benjamin: 107, 243
Frazier-Lemke Farm Bankruptcy Act of 1934: 82, 315
Fresno, Calif.: 167
Frisch, Frank F.: 224
Frooks, Dorothy: 237
Fulton, Robert: 336

448

Gable, Clark: 143
Gambling: 281; on horse racing, 47; in Mexico, 336
Gann, Dolly C.: 211
Garbo, Greta: 5, 13, 128, 138, 256
Garner, Ettie R. (Mrs. Jack): 133, 336
Garner, John N. ("Jack"): 25, 93, 94, 133, 134, 266, 267, 311, 316
Gatty, Harold: 249
Gaynor, Janet: 238
Geers, Edward F. ("Pop"): 126
George, prince of England: 248
George V, king of England: 36, 40, 50, 77, 100, 140, 171, 247
Georgia: 277, 309; governor of, 300
Geneva, Switzerland: 115
Gerard, James W.: 176
Germany: 5, 18, 46, 70-71, 72, 76, 91, 104, 105, 138, 139, 155, 186, 194, 268, 283, 286, 289, 295, 297, 299, 304; relations with France, 105, 125; political disruptions in, 106; purges in, 190, 191; ex-royalty of, 247
Geronimo: 339
Gibbons, R. Floyd P.: 204
Gilroy, Calif.: 311
Glasgow, Scotland: 218
Glass, Carter: 31, 125
Glass-Steagall Act of 1933: 31
Gold: 108, 110, 114, 119, 128, 168, 171, 177, 285, 326, 348; U.S. purchases of, 96-97, 98, 100, 102, 116; price of, 97, 102, 104; control of, 99; mining of, 234; court decisions concerning, 262, 267, 272, 276, 279
Gold Reserve Act of 1934: 133
Gold standard: 12, 20, 21, 23, 37, 40, 48, 50, 80, 111, 113, 317
Gold Star Mothers: 32
Golf: 50, 126, 163, 168, 174, 279, 314; in Japan, 208
Gömbös, Gyula von: 150
Gorki, Maxim: see Peskov
Goshen, N.Y.: 126
Governors: national conference of, 57-59, 60; midwestern, 99
Gow, Betty: 261
Grand Canyon: 339
Grayson, Cary T.: 125
Great Britain: see England
Greece: 151; revolution in, 283, 286
Green, Theodore F.: 58
Green, William: 184-85
Greenway, Isabella S.: 9
Grey, Edward: 76
Guffey-Snyder Coal Act of 1935: 318
"Gunga Din" (poem): 301

Haight, Raymond L.: 233
Hallahan, William A. ("Wild Bill"): 224, 225
Halsell, Ewing: 194
Hamilton, Alexander: 136, 243
Hanson, George C.: 212
Hapsburg royal family: 261
Harbin, Manchuria: 211, 212
Harding, Warren G.: 334
Harkness, Edward S.: 158
Harlem, N.Y.: entertainers from, 218
Harness racing: 126; in Russia, 213
Harriman, W. Averell: 234
Harrison, Bryon P. ("Pat"): 142
Harrison, Mary S. L. D. (Mrs. Benjamin): 228
Hart, William S.: 110
Harte, F. Brett ("Bret"): 168, 234
Hartley, Herbert: 138
Harvard University: 45, 51, 165, 235, 311, 323; professor from, 135; baseball team from, 208
Hauptmann, Bruno R.: 261, 276
Hawaiian Islands: 201, 202, 203-204, 222, 249
Hawks, Francis M. ("Frank"): 86, 232, 307, 309
Hays, William H. ("Will"): 54, 334
Helsingfjord, Finland: 214
Heroes: 38, 322
Herriot, Édouard: 22, 53
Herschel Island: 346
Hess, W. R. Rudolf: 194
Hickman, Horace M.: 145
Hindenburg, Paul von: 203
Hindus, Maurice G.: 212
Hirota, Koki: 131
Hitchcock, Louise E. (Mrs. Thomas): 157
Hitler, Adolf: 10, 30, 32, 36, 45, 105, 139, 184, 194, 204, 221, 223, 247, 288, 289, 291, 297, 300, 313, 314, 332; purges by, 190, 191; speech by, 205
Hoarding: 14-15
Hog-calling: 299
Holdenville, Okla.: 224
Hollywood, Calif.: 31, 59, 147, 197, 256, 275, 318; women from, 96
Holmes, Oliver Wendell: 285-86
Hong Kong: 168
Honolulu, Ha.: 159, 189, 197, 199, 201, 203, 205, 296, 308
Hoover, Herbert C.: 59, 80, 156, 194, 291, 311, 320, 322, 334
Hoover, Lou H. (Mrs. Herbert): 228
Hoover Dam: 67, 69, 231-32, 339
Horicon, Wis.: 310
Horsemanship: 16-17, 157
Horse racing: 5, 93, 256, 289-81, 285, 293, 306, 318; in Russia, 212-13; see also Harness racing
Horses: 126, 170
Horseshoe pitching: 314
House, Edward M.: memoirs of, 76
Housing, federal support for: 195-96

449

Houston, Samuel ("Sam"): 268
Houston, U.S.S.: 190
Howell, Millard F. ("Dixie"): 260
Hull, Cordell: 51, 53, 63, 71, 121, 130, 194, 195
Humphrey, William E.: 315
Hungary: 150, 217, 230, 261; relations with Yugoslavia, 250
Hunt, LeRoy P.: 348
Hurley, Patrick J.: 245-46, 333, 334
Hutchinson (film executive): 117
Hutton, Barbara: 309
Hutton, Edward F.: 241

Ickes, Harold L.: 299, 300
Idaho: 108
Ijams, Martha: 292
India: 233, 264, 283, 286
Indiana: 132, 165; woman sheriff from, 146; politics in, 266
Indianapolis, Ind.: 266
Indians, American: 264, 314, 347
Industrialists: 104, 255, 306
Infantile paralysis (polio): 269, 340
Inflation: 20, 21, 24-25, 29, 40, 73-74, 81, 92, 107, 108, 171, 223, 251, 257
Insull, Samuel II: 151, 158, 159, 171
Interior, Department of: 179
Internal Revenue Service: 11
International dateline: 204
Iowa Farmers Holiday Association: 82
Ireland: 162, 248, 250, 256
Italy: 25-26, 102, 140, 150, 181, 261, 289, 295; war with Ethiopia, 254, 282, 288, 319, 321, 325, 327, 330, 332, 338, 339

Jacobs, Helen H.: 329
James, Jesse: 142
Japan: 33, 45, 91, 115, 120, 131, 139, 150, 155, 157, 160, 164, 166, 200, 201, 205, 210, 213, 221, 233, 248, 255, 261, 274, 286, 308, 319, 321, 322, 332, 342; relations with U.S., 17, 127, 129, 170; aviation in, 86; relations with Russia, 125; naval admiral from, 127; minister of war, 131; navy of, 206; baseball in, 208; golf in, 208; ambassador from, 251
Jask, Iran: 232
Jefferson, Thomas: 309
Jews: 32
Johannesburg, South Africa: 20
Johnson, Helen L. K. ("Bobbie"): 197, 221, 222
Johnson, Hiram W.: 239

Johnson, Hugh S.: 46, 64, 68, 70, 71, 100, 144, 175, 197, 201, 222, 255, 261, 287, 300; retirement of, 221
Johnson, Walter P.: 228
Johore, Sultan of: 167, 168
Jones, Jesse H.: 26, 96-97, 100, 116, 117, 125, 136, 169, 190, 220, 221, 266-67
Juneau, Alaska: 344
Jung, Guido: 26

Kansas: 3-4, 18, 131, 188, 211, 292-93, 94; governor of, 294
Kansas, University of: football team of, 89
Kansas City, Mo.: 35, 243, 295
Karachi, Pakistan: 232
Kelly Field, Tex.: 94
Kent, Frank R.: 274, 302
Kentucky: 306; honorary colonels of, 84; elections in, 102-103
Kentucky Derby: 306
Ketchikan, Alaska: 344
Kidnappers and kidnapping: 35, 64, 66, 84, 86, 319-20; Missouri law against, 60; in Calif., 173-74
Kindergarten: 301

LFD Ranch (Tex.): 244
Labor: 22, 91
Labor Day: 74
Lafayette, marquis de: 90
Laffoon, Ruby: 306
La Follette, Robert M., Jr.: 109, 142, 239
La Guardia, Fiorello H.: 102, 271
Lake Tahoe, Calif.: 58
"Lame ducks": 176
Landis, Kenesaw M.: 226, 322
Lardner, Ringgold W. ("Ring"): 83
Laughing Bill Hyde (novel): 346
Lawler, Oscar: 77
Lawyers: 68-69, 258, 272, 332-33; as judges, 336
Layden, Elmer F.: 113, 250
Leaders: 99-100
League of Nations: 91, 104, 105, 217, 218, 264, 330
Lee, Robert E.: 240
Lehman, Herbert H.: 105
Leningrad, Russia: 214
Leviathan, S.S.: 138
Lexington, Ky.: 126
Lexington, Mass.: citizens of, 164
Liberty: 328-29; definition of, 222-23
Liberty party: 171

Library of Congress: 44
Lincoln, Abraham: 138
Lindbergh, Charles A.: 38, 86, 232, 249, 277
Lippmann, Walter: 12, 274, 302
Little, W. Lawson, Jr.: 314
Little Rock, Ark.: 31
Lloyd George, David: 256, 283; memoirs of, 76
Lobbyists: 4, 142, 144, 167, 264, 332, 336; in Calif., 295
Lompoc, Calif.: 310-11
London, England: 103, 167, 171, 200, 217, 218, 232, 247; Hyde Park in, 216
London Naval Conference of 1930: 252
Long, Huey P.: 5, 17, 69, 72, 152, 153, 204, 205, 209, 217, 235, 241, 248, 259, 265, 269, 270, 284, 285, 287, 299, 300, 308, 309, 313, 321, 323; debt cancellation plan of, 242
Longevity: 162
Long Island, N.Y.: 7 2
Longshoremen: 230
Longworth, Alice Roosevelt: 132-33, 138
Longworth, Nicholas: 316
Lorimer, George H.: 107
Los Angeles, Calif.: 58, 78-79, 94, 97, 103, 134, 197, 231, 242, 254, 269, 281, 288, 298, 307, 309, 342; policemen in, 173
Los Angeles Bar Association: 243
Los Angeles Times Building: 160
Louis, Joe ("Brown Bomber"): 325
Louisiana: 17, 69, 72, 152, 177, 209, 235, 242, 264, 270; state legislature of, 249; state capitol of, 269, 270
Louisiana State University: 248-49
Ludwig, Emil: 90

McCormic, Mary: 52
McCormick, Robert R.: 70-71
McCroarty, John Steven: 288
MacDonald, J. Ramsay: 22, 26, 40, 42
McGraw, John J.: 143
McGuffey, William H.: 225
Machado, Gerardo: 77
McIntyre, Oscar O.: 111
McKee, Joseph V.: 83
McNamee, Graham: 130, 256
McPherson, Aimee Semple: 5, 45-46, 56, 60, 242; daughter of, 339-40
Madison, James: 243
Maine: 196
Managua, Nicaragua: earthquake in, 142
Manchukuo: *see* Manchuria

Manchuria: 91, 115, 130, 150, 208, 210, 211, 255; 264; emperor of, 144; relations with Russia, 208-209
Manhattan Island, N.Y.: 347
Man o' War (race horse): 334
Maranville, Walter J. V. ("Rabbit"): 156, 228
March of Time, The (news serial): 274
Marie, queen consort of Rumania: 216, 245
Marina, princess of Greece: 248
Mars, Maurice: 141
Martin, John L. R. ("Pepper"): 226
Martin, John S.: 274
Mary, queen consort of England: 218
Mashed O Ranch (Tex.): 194-95
Massachusetts: 49
Mass production: 282, 332; in Russia, 212
Matamuska Valley, Alaska: 347-48
Mattern, James J. ("Jimmy"): 38, 50, 86
Mayo, Charles H.: 125
Mayo brothers (physicians): 125
Mdivani, Alexis Z.: 42
Mdivani, Serge: 52
Meade, Donald ("Don"): 280
Medwick, Joseph M. ("Ducky"): 226
Melbourne, Australia: centennial, 200
Memoirs: 255
Merriam, Frank F.: 233
Mesa Verde: 339
Mexican War: 97
Mexico: 10, 97, 205, 287, 325, 328, 339; president of, 336
Mexico, Mo.: 244
Mexico City, Mexico: 308
Michigan: 340
Michigan, University of: 397
Michigan City, Ind.: 165
Middle West (as a region): 200, 293
Midgets: 37
Midway Islands: 308
Miller, Leslie A.: 58
Millionaires: 62, 74, 75
Mills, Ogden L.: 24, 134
Miners, in Hungary: 230
Minneapolis, Minn.: 342
Minnesota: 215
Minnesota, University of: football team of, 242
Missionaries, in Hawaii: 203-204
Mission Play, The: 288
Mississippi: 13, 142
Mississippi, U.S S.: 77
Missouri: 29, 35, 132; kidnapping in, 60, 64
Moeur, Benjamin B.: 9
Moffett, James A.: 196
Moffett, William A.: 13
Moley, Raymond C.: 64, 72
Money: 1, 285, 290; value of, 303; *see also* Dollar

Monterey, Calif.: 197
Montevideo, Uruguay: 107
Moody, Helen Willis: 71, 329
Mooney, Thomas J. ("Tom"): 267
Morgan, John Pierpont, Jr.: 3, 4, 12, 33-34, 40, 42, 67, 106, 172, 282; investigation of, 35-36, 37
Morgenthau, Henry, Jr.: 135, 136, 310
Morrow, Dwight W.: 205
Moscow, Russia: 54, 155, 212, 214, 247, 269, 308, 311, 340
Moses, George H.: 16
Mothers' Day: 172
Motion pictures: 161, 200, 318; industry, NRA code for, 54; theater owners' convention, 161
Munitions industry, investigation of: 249-50
Murray, William H. ("Alfalfa Bill"): 26, 52, 58, 61, 79, 132, 224, 319
Muskogee, Okla.: 248
Mussolini, Benito: 10, 26, 36, 45, 46, 48, 53, 66, 72, 102, 118, 139, 140, 150, 152, 180, 184, 188, 191, 209, 229, 247, 254, 261, 269, 282, 284, 288, 289, 297, 300, 303-304, 214, 321, 325, 327, 330, 332, 339
Mutt and Jeff (cartoon series): 338

Napoleon I, emperor of France: 90
National Association of Manufacturers: 246
National Guard: 197, 269
National Recovery Administration (NRA): 46, 64, 67, 70, 74, 77-78, 82, 88, 98, 109, 124, 144, 146, 175-76, 183, 197, 221, 222, 230, 287, 311, 317, 318; industrial codes of, 60, 67-68, 71, 89, 144; invalidation of, 315
National Resources Board: 253
Navajo Indians: 51
Nebraska, legislative plan in: 277
Negro Add (horseman): 244
Nevada: 54, 97-98, 153-54
Newark, N. J.: 141, 144, 148
New Deal: 192, 196, 221, 232, 238, 241, 260, 262, 314-15, 317; public works programs of, 114
New Jersey: 81
New Mexico: 20, 131, 337
New Orleans, Lou.: 308; senatorial investigation in, 105-106; airport in, 270
Newspapers: 140, 166, 185, 198, 272, 274, 287, 291, 303, 323; in Calif., 3, 62, 75, 200; columnists for, 5, 179, advertising in, 15; partisanship of, 15; freedom of, 17-18; in Washington, D. C., 23-24; local, 35; in U. S., 44; Republican, 285

New Year's predictions: 257
New York (state): 4, 49, 105
New York City, N. Y.: 11, 22, 24, 34, 48, 83, 89, 107, 113-14, 121, 135, 136, 145, 168, 178, 186, 213, 240, 251, 262, 267, 269, 271, 272, 273, 276-77, 293, 325, 342; harbor of, 77; mayoral election in, 101; violence in, 103; taxicab riots in, 136; weather in, 143, 144
New York Giants (baseball): 79, 87, 89, 143
New York Stock Exchange: 63, 81, 84, 141, 159, 235, 279
New York (N. Y.) Times: 222-23, 296
New Zealand, prime minister of, 304
Nicaragua, U. S. intervention in: 142
Nice, Harry W.: 334
"Noble experiment": 112
Nogales, Ariz.: 9
Norris, George W.: 176
Norris, Kathleen: 313
North Carolina, prohibition repeal in: 102
Northwest Mounted Police: 346
Norway: 12-13, 215
Notre Dame University: 79, 147, 180, 250, 264; football team of, 89, 113, 181
Nurmi, Paavo: 126, 214

Oakland, Calif.: 58
Ochs, Adolph S.: 296-97
O'Connor, James F. T.: 237, 277
Odessa, Russia: 212, 213
O'Donnell, Charles L.: 180, 250
O'Hara, John F.: 180, 250
Ohio: 132
Ohio State University: 314, 320
Oklahoma: 3, 25-26, 28-29, 35, 80, 132, 200, 223, 225, 226, 232, 233, 238, 294, 300, 319, 341; prohibition repeal in, 52; Texas bridge controversy, 61; bank robbery in, 186-87
Oklahoma, University of: football team of, 259
Oklahoma Military Academy: 294
Old-age pensions: 278, 288
Omaha, Nebr.: 67
Oolagah, Okla.: 163, 238
Opera: 120-21, 216, 217
Oregon, University of: football team of, 98
Orlando, Fla.: 6-7
Osage Indians: 80
Otto, Francis Joseph: 261
Owen, Marvin J. ("Marv"): 226
Owen, Ruth Bryan: 12-13, 205
Owens, James C. ("Jesse"): 314, 315, 320

Paducah, Ky.: 84
Panama: 144-45
Panama Canal: 145, 166, 168
Pan-American Conference, Sixth (1933): 107, 115, 121
Pangborn, Clyde: 233
Parachutes: 45-46
Paraguay: 209, 286, 322
Parenthood: 60-61
Paris, France: 51, 183, 308; riots in, 136-37
Park, Guy B.: 58
Parker, Bonnie: 177
Parker Ranch (Hawaii): 201-202
Parsons, Kans.: 299
Patriotism: 10, 67, 77
Patronage: 74
Pavlovitch, Dmitri: 247
Pearl Harbor, Ha.: 203
Pecora, Ferdinand: 36, 38, 106
Pedley, Eric: 67
Pennsylvania: 259
Perkins, Frances: 22, 70, 71, 164, 292
Pershing, John J. ("Black Jack"): 9, 90, 303
Peru: 121
Peskov, Aleksei M. ("Maxim Gorki"): 212
Petroleum industry: 75, 80, 261, 268, 327; "czar" for 28, 29-30; NRA code for, 52, 68-69; in Calif., 79; in Russia, 213
Philadelphia, Pa.: 107, 240, 266
Philippine Islands: 65, 203, 222, 264, 321; independence for, 112, 130, 168, 179, 205
Phillips, Frank: 52
Phillips, Waite: 338
Phoenix, Ariz.: 94, 116-17, 269, 294
Physical Culture (magazine): 118
Piccard family (balloonists): 234
Point Barrow, Alaska: 346
Poland: 217, 230, 297
Polar exploration: 107
Police chiefs: 221
Polio: *see* Infantile paralysis
Politicians: 4, 13, 72, 86, 87, 94, 97, 160, 178, 192, 240, 283, 288, 313, 342; from the South, 81
Politics: 22, 320, 322
Polo: 15, 66-67, 69, 157, 163, 219, 220-21, 238
Portugal: 170
Post, Wiley H.: 54, 56, 57, 59, 86, 200, 201, 232, 233, 248, 249, 264, 277-78, 280, 337, 338, 339, 344, 346, 347
Postal system: in U. S., 152, 197, 306; in England, 152-53
Postmasters: 298; literacy tests for, 52-53
Potemkin: see *Battleship Potemkin*
Poughkeepsie, N. Y.: 323

Preachers: 103, 175
Preparedness, military: 30, 64, 133, 233, 307
Prescott, Ariz.: 49
Priests: 103
Prince of Wales: *see* Edward Albert
Princeton University, professor from: 135
Professors: 72, 73, 99, 107, 154, 180, 222, 302, 326, 337
Progressive party: 171
Prohibition: 34, 146; repeal of, 5, 6, 11, 13, 14-15, 16, 29, 47, 56-57, 71, 101, 102, 103, 112-13, 114, 126
Prohibition party: 171
Propaganda: 29
Public utility holding companies: 260, 287, 327, 332
Public Works Administration (PWA): 82
Puerto Rico: 179
Putnam, Amelia Earhart: *see* Earhart
Pu-yi, Henry: 145

Quezon y Molina, Manuel L.: 112
Quien Sabe Ranch (Calif.): 174
Quintuplets: birth of, in Canada, 182

Radio: 7-8, 126, 237; announcers on, 4; popularity of, 38; industry, 83; sports broadcasters on, 86-87; sports events on, 321
Railroads: 23, 35, 83, 86, 119-20, 134, 148, 150, 178, 197, 234-35, 266
Rainey, Henry T.: 25, 195
Rand, Sally: 103, 236
Randolph Field, Tex.: 94
Raskob, John J.: 74, 105, 241
Reconstruction Finance Corporation (RFC): 26, 31, 67, 82, 98, 100, 117, 125, 136, 169, 266-67
Reeves, Joseph M.: 240
Reforestation: 11, 58, 87
Reilly, Edward J. ("Big Ed"): 276
Religion: 27
Repatriation: 281
Republican National Committee: 125, 181
Republican party and Republicans: 3, 8, 12, 14, 15, 16, 20, 26-27, 36, 47, 58, 64, 65, 74, 76, 90, 100, 115, 123, 124, 125, 129, 138, 153, 159, 161, 167, 171, 181, 191-92, 195, 200, 204, 228, 231, 232, 237, 238, 239, 245, 260, 261, 264, 268, 291, 293, 294, 298, 301, 314, 315, 317, 319, 333, 337, 340

Revere, Paul: 241
Revolutions: 79; in Latin America, 75-76
Reynoldstown (race horse): 293
Richberg, Donald R.: 222, 255
Rickenbacker, Edward V. ("Eddie"): 148
Ritchie, Albert C.: 334
Rivera, Diego: 29
Robbins, Warren D.: 297
Robinson, Joseph T. ("Joe"): 25, 217, 270, 284, 324, 340
Rochester, Minn.: 125
Rockefeller, John D.: 3, 28, 51, 329
Rockefeller, John D., Jr.: 3, 29
Rockne, Knute K.: 113, 181, 250
Rodeo: 327-28, 341
Rogers, Betty Blake (wife): 48, 167, 231, 293, 313
Rogers, Clement Vann (father): 319
Rogers, Mary Amelia (daughter): 293
Rogers, William Penn Adair ("Will"): as an air traveler, 18, 20, 23, 28, 31, 34, 35, 54, 57, 58, 67, 93, 94, 115, 131, 132, 134, 138, 141, 142, 143, 145, 197, 213, 214, 215, 217, 265, 266, 267, 269, 270, 272, 280, 292, 294, 328, 337, 338, 339, 343, 344, 347; Chicago world's fair, 28; in motion pictures, 80, 126, 158, 260, 307, 320, 344, 346; as Kentucky Colonel, 84; pet dog of, 111; as "college student," 123; Nicaragua, 142; in Far East, 167-68; in Virgin Islands, 194; in England, 198; around-the-world trip, 199-220, 229, 232, 261, 262, 272, 283, 297; in vaudeville, 218; birthday, 238; in Alaska, 344, 346-48
Rolph, James, Jr.: 89, 111, 179
Rome, Italy: 150, 232, 269
Roosevelt, Edith K. C. (Mrs. Theodore): 228
Roosevelt, Eleanor (Mrs. Franklin D.): 16, 17, 38-39, 166, 292, 308, 312; birthday of, 228
Roosevelt, Franklin D.: 1, 2, 6, 12, 13, 14, 15, 22, 23, 24, 25, 26-27, 28, 29, 30, 31, 32, 35, 36, 38, 39, 42, 43, 46, 49, 50, 52, 54, 57, 59, 60, 61, 63, 64, 65, 70, 71, 75, 79, 82, 86, 87, 88, 89, 91, 96, 101, 106, 107, 108, 114, 116, 123-24, 125, 127, 130, 131, 133, 138, 139, 141, 143, 147, 148, 150, 153, 155, 156, 157, 158, 159, 161, 162, 165, 166, 169-70, 172, 175, 176, 179, 181, 182, 184, 185, 187, 188, 189, 190, 192, 194, 196, 197, 200, 201, 202, 204, 205, 210, 218, 221, 223, 229, 233, 234, 235, 237, 239, 240, 243, 245, 246, 247, 248, 252, 254, 257, 261, 262, 264, 266, 267, 268, 271, 276, 280, 287, 288, 289, 290, 294, 301, 303, 306, 309, 312-13, 316, 318, 320, 322, 326, 327, 337, 340, 342, 344; radio speech by, 4, 5, 27, 38, 113, 121, 146, 189, 190, 222-23, 260, 303, 313; Latin American policy of, 121, 130; birthday, 132, 133, 269; health of 254-55
Roosevelt, Theodore: 53
Roper, Daniel C.: 316-17
Rose Bowl football game: 109, 113-14, 121, 235, 242
Rough Riders: 65
Rowe, Lynwood T. ("Schoolboy"): 224, 225
Rowing: 51, 323
Royalty: 43, 283
Rumania: 216
Russia: 45, 139, 152, 160, 168, 208, 210, 212, 213, 219, 221, 251, 255, 272, 274, 286, 291-92, 297, 319; aviation in, 86, 311-12, 336-37; ambassador from, 106; Japanese relations with, 125, 131, 134, 150; writers in, 212; czar of, 213; executions in, 250; U. S. recognition of, 253, 275
Ruth, George H. ("Babe"): 156, 181, 299, 314

Saar Territory: 264, 283
Saint Lawrence Development Treaty: 134, 151
Saint Louis, Mo.: 267
Saint Louis Cardinals (baseball): 224, 226
Saint Patrick: 288
Saito, Hirosi: 120
Salinas, Calif.: 57, 170
Salt Lake City, Utah: 67, 134, 141, 145
Salvation Army: 253
San Antonio, Tex.: 94
San Diego, Calif.: 178; world's fair at, 322, 342
Sandino, Augusto C.: 142
San Francisco, Calif.: 58, 167, 168, 174, 197, 199, 202, 342; general strike in, 196; longshoremen from, 230
San Juan Capistrano, Mission: 178
Sankey, Verne: 135, 137
San Salvador, president of: 297
Santa Anita, Calif.: race track at, 307
Santa Barbara, Calif.: 158; fiesta in, 62
Santa Maria, Calif.: 310
Saturday Evening Post (magazine): 255
Savannah, Ga.: 162
Schmeling, Max S.: 39, 325

Schofield Barracks, Ha.: 203
Schumann-Heink, Ernestine R.: 72
Scientists: medical, 104; aeronautical, 107
Scotland: 126, 218-19
"Scrip": 1, 2
Seattle, Wash.: 342, 344, 347
Securities Exchange Act of 1934: 147, 155, 172-73
Seligman, Ariz.: 272
"September Morn": 286
Seward, William H.: 347
Shakespeare, William: 150, 250
Shaw, George Bernard: 8-9, 16
Siam: *see* Thailand
Siberia: 210-11, 337
Silver: 177, 208; price of, 297
Silver Purchase Act of 1934: 151
Sinclair, Upton B.: 213, 232, 233, 242, 316
Singapore: 167, 168, 200, 232
Skagway, Alaska: 344
Skiatook, Okla.: 256
Slot machine operators: 279
Smackover, Ark.: 224
Smith, Alfred E. ("Al"): 30, 45, 70, 101, 105, 108, 109, 269
Smith, Gipsy R.: 132
Smith, Kathryn E. ("Kate"): 321
Smithsonian Institution: 180
Snell, Bertrand H.: 337-38
"Soak the rich": 323, 324, 341
Socialist party: 171
Sonora, Calif.: 233
South Africa, prime minister of: 304
South America: 195, 309; war in, 115; trade with, 175
South Carolina: 240
South Dakota: 147
South Pole: 16
Soviet Union: *see* Russia
Spain: 170
Spanish-American War: 64
Speaker, Tristram E. ("Tris"): 228
Speeches and oratory: 34, 168
Spokane, Wash.: 342
Sprague, Oliver M. W.: 108
Stagg, A. Alonzo: 297
Stalin, Joseph: 247, 269, 288, 332
Stamford, Tex.: 327
Stamps, rare postage: 108
Stanford University: 314; football team of, 109, 123, 242, 259
Statesmen: 53, 104, 192, 243, 326
States' rights: 319, 332
Statues: 157
Stock market: 24, 59, 96; investigation of, 33-34, 35-36, 37; *see also* Wall Street *and related topics*
Stocks and bonds: swindles involving, 103-104, 106; buying and selling of, 108, 117, 135, 220, 223, 297, 315, 334

Stone, Fred A.: 170, 230
Stotesbury, Edward T.: 120
Straus, Jesse I.: 105
Strawn, Silas H.: 169
Stresa Conference: 297, 298
Strikes, labor: 82, 91, 153, 155, 177, 182-83, 194-85, 220, 245; prohibition of, 63; in San Francisco, 196, 198, 199; in England, 198
Submarines: 304
Sugar Bowl football game: 249
Sulphur Springs, Md.: 255
Swanson, Claude A.: 76
Sweden: 12-13, 215; king of, 215; princess of, 256
Swimming: 206
Switzerland: 51, 66, 104, 253, 268
Swope, Gerald: 101

Taft, Helen H. (Mrs. William Howard): 228
Talmadge, Eugene: 309
Tammany Hall: 11, 22, 81, 84, 96, 102, 129, 188
Tariffs: 177
Tasmania: 79
Taxation: 17, 97, 134, 162, 247, 256, 262, 289, 310, 334; on income, 7, 11, 62, 135, 159, 267, 293, 341; on sales, 32, 34, 56, 57; on wheat, 51; on gasoline, 56; on alcohol, 56-57, 112, 127; on property, 62; stock exchange, 81, 84; on manufacturers' sales, 135; in England, 247, 301; on inheritance, 323
Tax-exempt bonds: 7, 324
Taxicabs, in New York City: 136
Taxpayers: 32, 84, 117, 161-62, 164, 172, 260, 290
Taylor, Patrick G. ("Bill"): 236
Teachers: 103; in Chicago, 16, 28
Technocrats and technocracy: 8, 25, 325
Telephones: 291
Temple, Shirley: 251
Tennessee: 235; prohibition repeal in, 57
Tennis: 50, 71, 215, 329
Terry, William H. ("Bill"): 89
Tevis, Will S. ("Willie"), Jr.: 167
Texas: 5, 61, 93, 131, 132, 213, 252, 260, 266, 267, 268, 277, 328; prohibition repeal in, 71; hurricane in, 75
Thailand, king of: 283
Thanksgiving Day: 110, 246
Theories: 72
They Had to See Paris (novel): 110
Thomond II (race horse): 293
Thorpe, James F. ("Jim"): 320

455

Three D Ranch (Tex.): 252
Three Men on a Horse (play): 293
Tijuana, Mexico: 336
Time (magazine): 274, 316
Tokyo, Japan: 164, 205, 211, 308
Tourists, in Japan: 206
Townsend, Francis E.: 278; pension plan of, 284
Track and field: 187, 214, 314, 320
Transcient camps, federal: 116-17
Treasury, Department of the: 6, 61, 182, 317
Trinidad, Colo.: 339
Trotsky, Leon: 213
Troyanovsky, Alexander A.: 106, 134
Tuberculosis, cure for: 104
Tucker, Sophie: 171
Tucson, Ariz.: 94, 156, 269
Tugwell, Rexford G.: 165, 183, 209, 302
Tulane University, football team of: 248, 259
Tulsa, Okla.: 28, 132, 328
Tupelo, Miss.: 243
Turkey: 158, 213
Turner, Roscoe: 58, 83, 86, 115, 232, 233
Tuscaloosa, Ala.: 260
Tutankhamen, tomb of: 330
Twain, Mark: *see* Clemens
Twenty Grand (race horse): 256

Udet, Ernst: 46, 48
Unemployment and the unemployed: 1, 57, 82, 188, 119, 164, 250, 316, 320; relief for, 8, 11, 271, 276, 277, 280, 281, 284, 285, 287, 296; in England, 115; insurance for, 155
Unions, labor: 63, 71, 310
United States: 151, 251; intervention by, 64-65, 76-77; national debt of, 75, 262; foreign intervention in, 77; foreign image of, 113; Japanese relations with, 170; sightseeing in, 339
United States Army: 52, 179, 300, 308, 339; and air-mail, 137, 140-41, 145, 147-48, 150, 152, 203; in Ha., 203
United States Chamber of Commerce: 26, 37, 106, 107, 169-70, 245, 306
United States Congress and congressmen: 1, 4, 5-6, 13, 14, 16, 17, 25, 25, 27, 30, 32, 38, 39, 40, 42, 44, 48, 63, 68, 72, 82, 93, 94, 100, 101, 123-24, 127, 129, 133, 134, 144, 145, 156, 158, 160, 162-63, 164, 166, 169, 172, 175, 181, 185, 186, 187, 188-89, 194, 196, 201, 202, 223, 235, 238, 242, 247-48, 254, 260, 261, 264, 266, 268, 274, 284, 288, 302-303, 306, 314, 315, 324, 326, 327, 328, 330, 334, 336, 46; investigations by, 158, 161, 167, 249-50, 257, 330, 332
United States Constitution: 96, 241, 243, 284, 315, 319, 321, 332, 333, 338, 346; revision of, 317
United States Fleet: 76, 160, 166, 197, 240, 307
United States House of Representatives: 8, 24, 130, 142, 152, 195, 316; *see also* United States Congress
United States Marine Corps, in Nicaragua: 142
United States Military Academy, football team of: 109, 235
United States Naval Academy, football team of: 235
United States Navy: 150, 160, 300, 308; in Ha., 203
United States Senate and senators: 5, 6, 12, 14, 15, 17, 27, 31, 32, 33, 38, 68, 70, 72, 73, 93, 105, 109, 126, 127, 130, 132-33, 134, 141, 142, 144, 151, 158, 159, 161-62, 172, 176, 196, 241, 265, 266, 268, 270, 276, 278, 279, 280, 284, 303, 312, 321, 323-24, 326, 340; investigation by, 23, 103, 105-106, 142-43; *see also* United States Congress
United States Supreme Court: 183, 245, 248, 261, 262, 266, 267, 275, 276, 279, 302, 314-15, 316, 317, 319
United States Tenth Cavalry: 284
Uruguay: 121
Uvalde, Tex.: 94, 336

Vail, Edward F. R. ("Eddie"): 310
Van Brunt, William A.: 310
Vancouver, Canada: 344
Vanderbilt, Gloria L. M.: 243
Venizelos, Eleutherios: 283
Vermejo Ranch (N. M.): 338
Vermont, election in: 129
Versailles Peace Conference: 92
Versailles Peace Treaty of 1919: 289
Veterans' bonus: 156, 302-303, 310, 312, 313
Vice presidency: 94
Victor Emmanuel II, king of Italy: 140
Vienna, Austria: 216, 217, 261
Vines, Henry E., Jr.: 50
Vinson Naval Parity Act of 1934: 133
Virginia: 68
Virgin Islands: 194
Voters: 236; registration of, 231

Wackwitz, Donald ("Don"): 141
Waggoner, William T.: 257
Wagner Act of 1935: 318
Waikiki Beach, Ha.: 202
Wallace, Henry A.: 70, 71, 73, 178-79
Wall Street: 4, 54, 56, 62, 75, 101, 143, 154, 156, 177, 187, 244, 260; *see also* Stock market *and related topics*
Walsh, Thomas J.: 2
War: 30-31, 40, 71, 76, 77, 91, 104, 154, 188, 218, 219, 244, 253, 286-87, 289, 291, 330; in Europe, 229-30, 327
War debts and reparations: 5, 27, 39, 42, 43, 44, 89, 100, 116, 119, 126-27, 168, 172, 181, 184, 213, 214, 272, 274, 314
Warner, Glenn S. ("Pop"): 297
Washington (state): prohibition repeal in, 73; lieutenant governor of, 342
Washington, D. C.: 4, 23-24, 25, 31, 32, 52, 67-68, 74, 89, 93, 106, 107, 113, 125, 132, 134, 143, 144, 148, 156, 162, 167, 169, 181, 184, 188, 196, 221, 224, 230, 265, 266, 267, 269, 270, 272, 275, 280, 282, 286, 317, 322, 326; prohibition repeal in, 145
Washington, George: 142, 221, 243, 328
Washington, University of: football team of, 98
Washington Conference of 1921-1922: 92, 337
Washington Monument: 221
Washington Senators (baseball): 79, 87, 163
Watson, James E.: 16, 90
Wedell, James R. ("Jimmy"): 189-90
West, Mae: 292, 302
Westover, Oscar: 145
West Virginia: 323; prohibition repeal in, 47
Wheeler-Howard Act of 1934: 182
White, George: 58
White, William Allen: 188, 211
White House: 106, 165, 192, 228, 326
Wichita, Kans.: 18
Wienecke, Otto: 147-48
Wilbur, Curtis D.: 334
Wilentz, David T.: 276
Williams (aviation promoter): 189
Williams, Alford J. ("Al"), Jr.: 232

Williams, Hubert W. ("Rube"): 67
Wills, Helen: *see* Moody
Wilson, Edith B. S. (Mrs. Woodrow): 229
Wilson, Woodrow: 125, 283
Winchell, Walter: 35, 90
Winnebrenner, Le Roy ("Baby Le Roy"): 93, 148, 199
Winter, Alice A. (Mrs. Thomas G.): 318
Wirt, William A.: 163, 164, 167
Wise, Stephen S.: 32
Women: 73, 75, 157, 228, 285; and babies, 23; and war, 71; in Russia, 212; in aviation, 265, 296
Woodin, William H.: 25, 105
Woodruff, Roy O.: 340
World Court: 10, 265-66, 268, 270
World Monetary and Economic Conference, London: 36, 40, 42, 44, 45, 47, 48-50, 51, 52, 53, 54, 56, 59, 63
World Series (baseball): 223-26, 228; radio announcers of, 86-87
World War I: 46-47, 64, 76, 92, 139, 286
Wrestling: 338, 341
Wright, Orville: 20, 252-53
Wright, Wilbur: 20, 252-53
Wrigley, Philip K.: 155

XIT Ranch (Tex.): 195

Yachting: 75, 217-18, 219, 220
Yale University: 51, 158-59, 187, 235, 323
Yaqui Indians: 339
Yokohama, Japan: 66, 204, 205
Yost, Fielding, H.: 297
Young, Clarence M.: 20
Yugoslavia: 254; king of, 229, 230; relations with Hungary, 250

Zara Agha: 147
Zion Canyon: 339
Ziegfeld, Billie Burke: 110
Ziegfeld, Florenz, Jr. ("Flo"): 83
Ziegfeld Follies: 83